A Truer Liberty

Critical Social Thought

Series editor: Michael W. Apple
Professor of Curriculum and Instruction and Educational Policy
Studies, University of Wisconsin-Madison

Already published

A Truer Liberty

Simone Weil and Marxism

LAWRENCE A. BLUM &
VICTOR J. SEIDLER

Routledge

New York   London

To Anna and Judy, and Ben, Sarah, Daniel, Lily and Laura

First published in 1989 by
Routledge
An imprint of Routledge, Chapman and Hall, Inc.
29 West 35 Street
New York, NY 10001

Published in Great Britain by
Routledge
11 New Fetter Lane
London EC4P 4EE

Copyright © 1989 by Routledge, Chapman and Hall, Inc.

Printed in the United States of America

Library of Congress Cataloging in Publication Data
Blum, Lawrence A.
    A truer liberty : Simone Weil and Marxism / Lawrence A. Blum and
Victor J. Seidler.
        p.   cm. — (Critical social thought)
    Bibliography: p.
    Includes index.
    ISBN 0–415–90046–8; ISBN 0–415–90195–2 (pb)
    1. Weil, Simone, 1909–1943—Political and social views. 2. Weil,
Simone, 1909–1943—Views on communism. I. Seidler, Victor J.,
1945– . II. Title. III. Series.
B2430.W474B56 1989
320.5′092′4—dc19   88–39081
                                                                                     CIP

British Library Cataloguing in Publication Data
Blum, Lawrence A.
    A truer liberty: Simone Weil and Marxism.—
(Critical Social thought)
    1. French philosophy. Weil, Simone, 1909–1943
I. Title II. Seidler, Victor J. (Victor
Jeleniewski,) 1945–
III. Series
194

ISBN 0–415–90046–8
ISBN 0–415–90195–2 (pb)

Contents

Series Editor's Introduction

There is now a major rebirth of interest in Simone Weil. This is to be welcomed since she stands as one of the most intriguing and provocative figures in twentieth-century leftist theory. Her work and her life—though all too brief—provide crucial insights into important silences within some aspects of the Marxist tradition and into the roots of many of the debates and conflicts that have become even more powerful today.

There are a number of reasons Weil, and especially Blum and Seidler's book, will appeal to a wide and growing audience. Weil's focus on dignity as a constitutive part of the human condition, the place of religious values in her analysis, her criticisms of orthodox Marxism while at the same time engaging in significant political activity, the insistent focus on the labor process in her work, the political importance she gives to education, and her anticipation of certain aspects of feminist philosophy, all make *A Truer Liberty* important reading for a wide range of individuals.

What stands at the center of so much of Weil's writing is a *moral* vision. For her, even when we think about one of the most economically grounded activities in modern capitalism—that of waged labor—we need to evaluate it not only in distributive terms but in what are profoundly ethical terms. This is grounded not only in her points about how the rationalization of labor under capitalism is exploitative in the technical sense of owners taking the surplus value of a worker's labor, but in other aspects of her critique. Such rationalization deprives workers of their dignity. In asserting the irreducible human dignity of the less powerful, Weil supplies a number of necessary ingredients for an alternative moral vision.

Weil's central concern was with "the conditions of oppression, the lot of the oppressed, and with sustaining human dignity." For her, struggle against such conditions was essential. However, even given her close connections with workers, unions, and Marxist groups, these struggles could not be guided only by a vision of political action involving the taking of state power. Politics of this sort "becomes dangerous and corrupt when it loses its grounding in morality." Morality and politics must be joined. Traditional proposals for reform and revolution are found wanting. Radical change—and the changes she envisioned *were* radical—was to be "animated by a spirit capable of promoting and sustaining dignity."

Thus, Weil roots her critique of capitalism not only in an economic understanding of oppression—though she experienced, and was influenced by, such economic oppression—but in a distinctly moral way. At the same time, though, she is not an apologist for the ideologies of, say, the unattached individualism that have so markedly influenced the liberal tradition. Her search, one that was contradictory and filled with both tension and insight, was for a "third way."

Weil's work takes on even more importance today given the emerging reconstruction of Marxist and neo-Marxist theory and practice. The growth of an anti-reductionist and anti-economistic tradition, the increased attention given to cultural analysis, the reassertion of genuinely democratic political elements and processes, these and more provide a context in which Simone Weil needs to be placed.[1]

Linkages are also clear between much of what Weil said and the arguments advanced by liberation theology. As Blum and Seidler demonstrate, the relevance of Weil to Solidarity, to the struggles of the Nicaraguan people for the right of self-determination, and to other movements to democratize the economy, polity and culture are clearly visible. At the same time, on a more theoretical level, Blum and Seidler also see in Weil the beginnings of a possible critique of some of the recent defenses of the theory of the primary of productive forces in which the development of productive forces and human well-being go hand in hand.[2]

Many of these concerns find their resonance in a number of recent commentaries. In their own attempt to rethink the Marxist and liberal traditions, Bowles and Gintis point to the poverty of nearly all strands of economic theory as a basis for thinking about democracy. In the process, they demonstrate some of the unfortunate consequences of the dominance of economic metaphors in our political and moral thought.[3] Theirs is a dual critique—the first of liberal theory and practice under capitalism since "no capitalist society today may be reasonably called democratic in the straight-forward sense of securing personal liberty and rendering the exercise of power socially accountable, and the second of traditional Marxist approaches since their "discursive structure lacks the fundamental theoretical vocabulary to represent the conditions of choice, individual liberty, and dignity."[4] This has the effect of hiding those areas of domination and exploitation that are nonclass and noneconomic—"whether of the state, of white over black, of nation over nation, or of men over women—as surely as liberal discourse serves as protective cover for the power of capital."[5]

Yet it is not just at the level of theory that changes are occurring. The Christian radicalism of the "base communities" in Latin America, the more democratic socialist positions being advanced by, say, workers within state bureaucratic socialist countries, movements by women and people of color, all of these, too, signify the political ferment now having such an impact throughout the world. None of this can be fully captured by orthodox Marxist categories.[6] Readers involved in these movements will find much to ponder in Blum and Seidler's discussion of Weil's work.

With this said, however, we need to be very careful not to overstate the criticisms of Marxist theory. The debates within the Marxist and neo-Marxist traditions, and the self-renewal that is going on there, have led to some remarkable gains. Furthermore, as Andrew Levine has shown in his exceptional comparison of the capitalist and socialist theoretical positions, the theories that have evolved around the socialist tradition show clear superiority when applied to such issues as equality, freedom, welfare, rights, and so on.[7]

What is important in all of this is the ferment itself. The sense of vitality, the question for new approaches to understand and act upon domination, and the extension and rebuilding of our ways of dealing with these issues are as significant today as they were when Simone Weil graced us with her presence. All of these concerns can be found in her writing.

By focusing on both her life and her thought, and on the continuities and changes found in each, *A Truer Liberty* gives us a remarkably clear and detailed analysis of a corpus of work that prefigured and influenced a series of radical movements throughout the world. The reader will leave the book with an enhanced sense of why this was and still is the case.

Michael W. Apple
The University of Wisconsin, Madison

Acknowledgments

We were introduced to the ideas of Simone Weil in a seminar of Peter Winch's in the late 1960s. It was not uncommon for students of Ludwig Wittgenstein, as we were, to be drawn also to Weil. Both of those thinkers' work is informed by a striking intensity and moral seriousness. Both are suspicious of a form of philosophy abstracted from the ways that people live their lives, though in Weil philosophy is much more directly concerned with politics and political engagement. Weil is also a difficult and uncomfortable thinker, with striking blindnesses. Yet she refuses to forsake truths that she has made her own, and she ties an extraordinary depth of thought and an integrity in facing up to difficult realities to her blind spots.

We came to the idea of writing a book on Simone Weil in the very different world of the 1980s. Weil's writings and her own struggles to find a form of political thought and activity appropriate to a time of political pessimism and decline seem particularly relevant to current realities. Weil provides an important voice lacking in the widespread discussion of the crisis of Marxism and the need for renewal of our political language. In bringing morality and politics in closer relationship to a central concern with human dignity, Weil could help rework our fundamental political ideals. If her own vision became increasingly pessimistic toward the end of her short life, this too is something from which we can and need to learn in facing up to realities of our own world.

A Truer Liberty is a product of many years of friendship and collaborative effort. All the ideas in the book have been discussed by the authors many times over. We have each read and commented on the other's portions. We recognize that the book reflects our different disciplinary backgrounds, histories, and relationships with Marxism as well as our divergent styles. We hope that these differences have helped us to produce a more textured understanding of the possibilities that exist within Simone Weil's writings.

The general division of responsibilities is as follows: The Introduction, Chapters 1 through 3, and the final section of chapter 5 were written by Blum. Chapters 4 through 9 were written by Seidler.

Each of us has been aided in completing this work by many persons besides each other. Larry Blum would like to thank Joshua Cohen and Paul Breines for useful conversations concerning Marxism and Marxist theory at an early stage of the project; Maria Tillmanns for painstaking research into Weil's early notebook entries on the subject of work; Russell Keat and Andreas Teuber for acute suggestions on large portions of Blum's segment of the manuscript; Wilhelmina Van Ness for some excellent suggestions and probing questions on the penultimate draft; and, especially, Mary Dietz and Dorothy McFarland for marvelously detailed and extraordinarily helpful comments on the penultimate draft. Blum would also like to thank the University of Massachusetts/Boston students in his infrequently-offered course on Simone Weil for their tremendous enthusiasm for and stimulating response to a thinker not yet given her deserved place in the corpus of twentieth century philosophy. Finally, Larry Blum would like to thank his wife Judy Smith, from whom he has learned the importance of history for philosophical thought. Larry would also like to thank Judy and their children, Ben, Sarah, and Laura, for all their love and support during the long and sometimes disruptive course of this project.

Vic Seidler would like to thank Steve Burns and Peter Winch for helpful comments made at his presentation to the American Weil Society Colloquium in 1983; Isaiah Berlin for his skepticism about the value of Weil's work; Peggy Scherer for introducing him to the ideas of Dorothy Day and *The Catholic Worker*;

Harold Klug, Clive and Kerstin Lindsey-Jones, Steven Schenk, Carol and Hilmar Schonalier for stimulation and insightful conversations; Annie and Bob Moore for their wisdom, support, and understanding while on sabbatical leave in Denmark in the summer of 1986; Asta and Hans Fink for simulating conversations on themes that were eventually developed in the concluding chapter; Sidney Williamson for conversations about work, politics, and spirituality; David Boadella, Lucy Goodison, and Anna Ickowitz for helpful insights into the relationship of spirituality to politics; Paul Morrison, Anthony Goldstone, Tony Seidler and Rob Senior for their continuing encouragement and support; students taking the sociology of knowledge at Goldsmiths' College, University of London for their continuing patience and enthusiasm. He wants also to thank Janet Ransom for detailed comments and suggestions that helped to shape the final draft and without whose assistance at a crucial stage the project may never have been completed.

Vic Seidler wishes also to thank Anna Ickowitz who has helped him believe that this project would end and has extended her love and support in hard times. Daniel, now six, has lived with it patiently since soon after his birth and lent Vic his rubber eraser at a crucial stage. Anna and Vic's daughter, Lily—just born when the writing was over—brought with her new energy that made its completion imperative. We have all learned from the experience.

Together, we would like to thank George Abbott White for his encouragement for the project; Norman Franklin and Stratford Caldecott for their support for it; Tatiana Holway for her exceptionally meticulous copy-editing; and Leonnie Caldecott for suggesting its title. We also wish to thank Maureen MacGrogan for seeing the project through to completion.

Introduction

In her short life (1909–1943) Simone Weil was a philosophy teacher, a trade union militant, a political activist, a factory worker, and an unflinching seeker after truth. This quest led her through intensive studies of science and technology, Greek and Roman civilization, Asian religious thought, and in the final years of her life, to a form of Christian spirituality. Because the daunting range of her learning has defied disciplinary divisions, Weil's thought in general has (in the English-speaking world) been given little of the scrutiny it deserves. Weil's entirely negative assessment of Judaism as a historical religion and culture, her lack of sensitivity to the plight of Jews in Europe, and (until 1939) her historical misjudgment of nazism's threat to Europe and the world have blinded many to the power and originality of her political thought (including, ironically, her penetrating insights into the political and moral culture of fascism). Finally, for many people Simone Weil's extraordinary life, about which much has been written, has overshadowed her thought.[1]

One aspect of Simone Weil's life and thought that has been given little attention is the complex and original critique she developed of Marxism in the 1930s. There are many reasons for the neglect of Weil's relationship to Marxism and of her political thought more generally. She is most commonly thought of as a religious thinker. The great bulk of her writings translated into English were, until quite recently, from the last four years of her life; in those years, partly as a result of several personal religious experiences, her thought turned in a Christian direction. Her endeavors and writings from the early and mid-1930s, when she was engaged in left-wing political activity whose forms of organization she eventually almost entirely rejected, have generally been viewed from the vantage point of the light they throw on Weil's personality; they are seen as having little significance in their own right.[2] And Weil herself is often thought to have forsaken her earlier political concerns as a result of her religious experiences.

This picture of Simone Weil's life and thought is seriously misleading. Her life cannot be neatly divided up into "political" and "religious" periods. She never abandoned a concern for political and social questions; they remained at the heart of her thinking through her turn to Christianity. She never wavered from her central preoccupations: the problem of the dignity and spiritual condition of the most vulnerable and powerless in society, particularly the manual worker; the question of work and its place in society; and the role of science and technology in shaping the moral character of a civilization. In fact, Simone Weil's turn toward Christianity must be understood at least partly in terms of her search for answers to precisely these concerns. Although she came to feel that these answers could not be found in the secular realm alone, she never ceased considering their political dimension.

We do not mean to deny the traditional picture's emphasis on the substantial changes that Weil's views underwent in the course of her life. But there were also some important continuities. In particular, her assessment of Karl Marx and orthodox Marxism remained strikingly constant throughout her life and writings, at least from 1934 on. Both earlier and later in her life, she saw Marxism as making some contributions of permanent value: Marx's affirmation of the dignity of labor; his analysis of how capitalism can degrade the worker; and his taking of society as the basic unit of inquiry and studying it in terms of relationships of power. At the same time, at every period in her life Weil was deeply critical of Marx's theory of history and of the primacy given, especially within orthodox Marxist social analysis, to purely economic forces in society. Finally, Weil was also critical of Marxism as a guide to political activity in the service of the oppressed, charging it with fostering both passivity and an illusory sense of power in the proletariat as well as undermining the necessary moral foundations of political activity.

The continuities in Weil's life pertain not only to her concerns and her views but to her activism as well. The form of her political activity and its philosophical underpinning changed. But to believe without acting, to sit back while others suffered and struggled—for Weil those were as impossible in the "secular-political" as in the "religious-political" periods of her life. Increasingly dissatisfied with the French political organizations and movements in the early 1930s, from 1934 on Simone Weil periodically proclaimed her withdrawal from political action, only to be pulled back into it by the compelling events of her time—by peace demonstrations in the mid-1930s, the sit-down strikes of 1936, the Spanish Civil War in 1938, and finally World War II and the nazi occupation of France.

Most important, as we hope to indicate, the early, secular period of Simone Weil's life and her involvements in the political movements of her time led her to strikingly original and important perspectives on Marxism and on political thought more generally. Her essays on Marxism and on modern capitalist and Communist societies, written when she was only in her mid-twenties, reveal an insight into these phenomena that far surpassed that of observers and theorists of her time and from which there is still a great deal to learn.

Finally, while Simone Weil was very much a political thinker at every stage in her life—religious as well as secular—she challenged received notions of what "politics" is. She struggled toward new conceptions of political thought and activity that could address her central concern with the conditions of oppression and the lot of the oppressed and with the sustaining of human dignity. She rejected all forms of parliamentary politics—associated with social democracy and reformist socialism—and, more broadly, she rejected the liberal notion of the political arena as one of compromise among competing interests.

At the same time, despite her close ties to worker, trade union, and Marxist groups (ties that are underplayed by focusing only on her written criticisms of Marxism) Weil was never satisfied with the traditional Leninist conception of politics as a struggle for state power. While for her politics must always be a matter of struggle rather than accommodation—and a struggle for quite radical changes in society—she came early on to be suspicious of the notion of revolution as providing the context and goal of that struggle. Rejecting both reform and revolution, she sought radical change animated by a moral spirit capable of promoting and sustaining dignity, and the sustaining of individual dignity became the standard by which Weil assessed political movements, societies, and institutions. For her, politics becomes dangerous and corrupt when it loses its grounding in morality. Thus, Weil's philosophy brings morality and politics into a much closer relationship with each other than does either traditional Marxism or liberalism. This relationship is an important part of what is still to be learned from Weil.

For Anglo-American philosophers liberalism in some form (including its right- and left-wing versions) provides the set of background assumptions for theorizing about politics. But Simone Weil was in many important respects non-liberal in her thinking throughout her changes from a secular to a religious outlook. In contrast to her attitude toward Marxism, she never regarded liberalism as a live political or philosophical option. She entirely rejected its picture of society as a collection of individuals, its conception of justice as a fair distribution of goods, its faith (shared, she believed, with Marxism) in the inevitability of progress, its implicit belief (seen, for example, in Immanuel Kant) that an individual's sense of dignity is generated solely from inside herself or himself and is essentially independent of society, and its counterposing of a universal, minimal standard of "right" to a purely personal and morally arbitrary "good." Thus, while harshly critical of many aspects of Marxism, Weil remained in many ways further from the liberalism that is seen by many today as Marxism's only alternative.

Simone Weil's critique of the Marxism of the European Communist parties in the 1920s and 1930s—what we will call "orthodox Marxism"—is particularly significant in our current context. Marxism as a living political philosophy is in a state of crisis. Countries governed officially by Marxist ideology hardly seem to exemplify the ideals for which Marx struggled and hoped. Nor has Marxism offered convincing and illuminating analyses of the failures of these societies. Marxism as a political movement seems to be losing ground in the West as well. Marxist parties, once large and influential in France and Italy, have clearly entered a period of diminished allegiance and significance.

Simone Weil's criticisms of the tradition of orthodox Marxism can help us understand these failures—the failure of Marxist societies adequately to move beyond capitalist structures of labor organization, the new forms of oppression that have emerged in these societies, and their one-sided emphasis on productive advance.

In addition, the power of Marxism to set an agenda for change has been challenged from many directions—feminist, ecological, democratic, ethnic. These new social movements point to forms of oppression, injustice, and abuse in society and nature marginalized or ignored in traditional Marxism. Weil's rejection of a purely economic understanding of oppression and her emphasis on the oppressive dynamic of power in many areas of social life provide a framework in which many of these challenges to Marxism can be placed.

Finally, in the Third World, while orthodox Marxism is still quite influential, it has had to coexist with new sources of radical thought, emerging from indigenous African and Asian philosophies and from Christianity. Especially in Latin America, a radical form of Christianity—liberation theology—has taken hold both to challenge and to enrich Marxist thought. And this Latin American radicalism has both influenced and been influenced by currents of Catholic radicalism in the United States and Europe. Simone Weil's later turn to Christianity and her concern with a moral and spiritual dimension of life that is rejected by Marxism involve the beginnings of the fruitful interaction between Christianity and Marxism that has issued in these contemporary forms of Christian radicalism.

Yet, at the same time that Marxism has weakened or proven deficient as a political and historical force, in the Anglo-American academic world Marxism has established a respectability unthinkable twenty years ago. Particularly noteworthy is the appearance within academic philosophy of a revival of interest in orthodox (economic or technologically based) versions of Marxism.[3] This revival gives an added significance to Weil's criticisms of orthodox Marxism.

Western Marxism (as represented by Georg Lukács, Karl Korsch, Antonio Gramsci, Theodor Adorno, Herbert Marcuse, Jürgen Habermas, and others)—grounded largely in a rethinking of Marx's relationship to Hegel—has been a powerful intellectual influence and source of criticism of orthodox Marxism during and since Simone Weil's time. This tradition has often struggled with the crisis of Marxism as an inability to resolve the tension between its sense of the objective conditions of existence and human subjective experience of those conditions. Weil's writings can be seen as a contribution to this same concern. However, Weil's criticisms and outlook remain substantially distinct from those now familiar in the tradition of Western Marxism. While she sheds light on issues of the undermining of the human subject in capitalist culture, the ways that science is not a neutral area of enquiry but is deeply implicated in the machinery of oppression in contemporary society, and the consolidation of new modes of power and oppression in advanced capitalist society, she approaches these issues in a manner quite distinct from that of Western Marxism. Weil's analysis is much more deeply grounded in a concern with the moral foundation of social criticism and with the organization of and social evaluation of labor than one finds in Lukács and the Frankfurt School.

Thus, Simone Weil's pre-religious political writings point the way toward a form of thinking that is neither Marxist nor liberal and that rejects both communism and capitalism. Weil's writings can help us to understand the deficiencies of orthodox Marxism as well as some critical shortcomings of our own liberal inheritance, and they can help us to assess the possibilities for new directions in radical thought. It is this task that we undertake in this book.

Although many traditional discussions of Simone Weil have overemphasized her life at the expense of her thought, it remains true that she was someone whose thought and life deeply informed one another. Her thought and her action were very much a response to her particular times—to the hopes and illusions fostered by the Russian Revolution, to the horror and despair of European fascism, to the coming of World War II. We will give a brief account of what seems essential in Simone Weil's biography, emphasizing what has often been omitted or insufficiently credited in traditional accounts, namely her political engagement on behalf of the subordinated and oppressed.

Chapters 1, 2, and 3 situate Weil's life and thought in its

historical context and look analytically at the main strands in her criticism of orthodox Marxism. Chapters 4 through 7 articulate the positive political theory or philosophy that emerges from Weil's critique of Marxism and how it provides the terms for a renewed critical engagement with Marxism and liberalism.

More specifically, in Chapter 1 we discuss Simone Weil's youth and early involvement in the workers' and trade union movements. We give an account of her relationship to some of the important political and intellectual influences on her and on the political terrain within which she operated—the tradition of French syndicalism, the Second and Third Internationals, the French Communist party, and Trotskyism.

Chapters 2 and 3 present Weil's critique of orthodox Marxism, as found primarily in the major work of the secular period of his life, *Reflections Concerning the Causes of Liberty and Social Oppression* (hereafter referred to as *Reflections*). We also look at some of the continuities and discontinuities between that work's view of Marx and Marxism and the view taken in later essays, including ones from the explicitly Christian period of Weil's life.

Chapter 4, "Liberty," focuses on Weil's understanding of the nature of liberty in *Reflections* and shows how she draws on a Kantian formulation that shifts in her later work. Although she sees mind as a realm of liberty she connects liberty with the quality of our activity in the world. This provides a challenge to both Marxian and liberal conceptions of liberty.

Chapter 5, "Oppression," shows how Weil's thinking on oppression—the second dominant theme of *Reflections*—is developed in relation to Kant's injunction that people should never be treated merely as means. Weil develops a critique of the form of science and technology and the organization of the labor process in terms of rationalization, as well as pointing to Marxism and liberalism's silence on the conception of oppression.

Chapter 6, "Work," looks specifically at the centrality of work in Weil's thinking and the part it plays in her understanding of the relationship between freedom and necessity. She sees work as a condition of servitude in contemporary life and argues that the historical development of science has contributed to this. Weil's experience of factory work had sensitized her to dimensions of oppression in the workplace that had been unacknowledged in other theoretical traditions. This contributed to her own shift towards Christianity.

Chapter 7, "Power," examines how power becomes central to Weil's later writing and considers how her understanding of power becomes all-pervasive to her understanding of society. Power is seen by her as the pivot of a process whereby the proper relationship of means to ends is reversed. Yet if Weil is driven to a deepened pessimism, we argue also that her notion of power allowed her to identify a range of crucial weaknesses in other understandings of power.

The concluding chapter, "Morality, Truth, and Politics," draws some political lessons from the direction of Weil's thought in both her secular and religious periods and shows briefly how her work has been taken up in the writings of Solidarity in Poland, has influenced the development of liberation theology in Europe and Latin America, and has been a source of Catholic radicalism in the United States and France as well as how Weil helps to redefine a relationship between spirituality and politics.

1

Simone Weil's early life and politics

1 Youth

Simone Weil was born in 1909 in Paris. Her parents were cultured, freethinking, well-to-do Jews.[1] The Weils were a close family to whom Simone remained completely devoted throughout her very unconventional, rebellious, and nonbourgeois life.[2] Her outlook was political and radical from an early age. She said later in life that at age ten she was a Bolshevik. At school she would draw hammer-and-sickle insignias on her school reports and papers, and she read the Communist party newspaper, *L'Humanité*.

An important early intellectual and moral influence was Alain (Emile-Auguste Chartier), an inspiring and influential teacher of Weil's generation of students, with whom Weil studied from 1925 to 1928 at the Lycée Henri IV. Although deeply engaged with political events of his time, Alain was suspicious of organized political parties. He emphasized the importance of freedom of individual thought, was skeptical of political ideologies, and criticized socialism for insufficiently protecting the individual against abuses of power. Alain was animated by a deep moral concern conveyed forcefully to his students, which helped to inform the moral perspective from which Weil always assessed social and political questions.

During her years at the lycée Weil began an involvement with workers' education, which in one form or another continued to be a personal and political concern throughout her life. With some other students of Alain's, Weil taught in a school for

railroad workers, set up through the (Communist-led) railroad union by a friend of Alain's. This project was an outgrowth of the "people's universities" and workers' education movement begun early in the century, itself an outgrowth of French syndicalism.
French syndicalism, and its later variant, anarcho-syndicalism, deeply influenced Weil's political thinking. Syndicalism was an important force in the French labor movement (much more so than the British or German) up until World War I. Its roots went back to Pierre-Joseph Proudhon and the French trade union movement of the mid-1800s. Syndicalism emphasized worker self-activity, hostility to the state, and suspicion of political parties and organizations. Around the turn of the century, anarchism brought to syndicalism an emphasis on direct revolutionary action, a vision of small-scale, decentralized economic organiza-tion, and a spirit of individualistic anti-authoritarianism. The founding in 1895 of the first confederation of French trade unions, Confédération Générale du Travail (Confederation of French Labor), spread syndicalist influence to the national level in the early twentieth century. This syndicalist influence con-tributed to the French trade union movement's greater inde-pendence from national political parties (such as the Socialist party) than trade unions in Germany, Britain, or Italy were able to achieve.[3]

An especially important element of syndicalist thought for Weil was its emphasis on workers' education. Local federations of trade unions, called *bourses du travail* sponsored classes for workers. The *bourse du travail* movement, led by Fernand Pelloutier, an important syndicalist figure within the labor movement, was a forerunner of the worker education projects with which Weil became involved in her years at the Ecole Normale Supérieure and afterwards. Weil expressed this con-tinuing commitment to workers' education in a letter to a former student in 1934, in which she wrote, "The most important [positive work for the foundation of a new and more humane order than our present one] is the *popularization of knowledge*, and especially of scientific knowledge. Culture is a privilege which, in these days, gives power to the class which possesses it" (*Seventy Letters*, 8).

From early on Simone Weil showed an exceptional and striking concern for the oppressed and victimized, a concern that,

2

in her teens, focused especially on the working class. Her sympathy for the plight of the working class was shared by many of her contemporaries at the lycée and university; but Weil was unusual among them in valuing manual work in its own right and desiring to engage in it herself. While at the lycée she worked on the farm of a fellow student. In 1928 she volunteered to be part of an international brigade engaging in manual work as civilian service, an alternative to military service. Her application was, however, turned down, presumably because she wished to work in the fields, a kind of work reserved for men only. The following year she made use of a visit to relatives to work ten-hour days picking potatoes. In 1931, as she prepared to assume her first teaching position, she visited a Breton fishing town with her parents, where, as Simone Pétrement, Weil's lifelong friend and biographer, reports, Simone prevailed on the fishermen to let her share their work. This experience had a particularly profound influence on her, providing a model for how human work and effort is able to operate against and to direct the much greater power of nature: "At every moment the helmsman—by the weak, but *directed*, power of his muscles on tiller and oar—maintains an equilibrium with that enormous mass of air and water. There is *nothing* more beautiful than a boat" ["Pre-War Notebook," 20).

Weil's sense of the human importance of work was reflected in some writing she did in 1929 that lead up to her dissertation, "Science and Perception in Descartes." There she accords work or activity in the world a kind of philosophical significance, as a way of connecting sense impressions to an extended world. Work provides a model, which Weil thought could be found in René Descartes, for a kind of science importantly distinct from the current understanding of it, which in her view had become excessively specialized and abstracted from the world. (For more on this topic, see chapter 6, section 4.)

Although apparently not as a member of any specific political group, Weil was intensely politically active in her years at the Ecole Normale Supérieure (1928–1931), where she studied to be a philosophy professor. She worked to raise money for the unemployed and attended pacifist demonstrations; she regarded herself as a revolutionary. Pétrement describes what Simone Weil seemed like to some of her contemporaries:

Simone did not have many friends at the Ecole Normale, even among the students. Many of them feared or were in awe of her. "They tried to avoid her in the corridors because of the blunt, thoughtless way she had of confronting you with your responsibilities by asking for your signature on a petition . . . or a contribution for some trade union strike fund."[4]

In 1931 Weil passed her *agregation*, an exam conferring the status of professor. She applied to teach in a port or industrial city, where she would be near work that she valued and could participate in workers' struggles. However, through her outspoken expression of revolutionary political views while at the Ecole Normale, she had offended an important administrator who apparently saw to it that she instead was posted to a girls' lycée in Le Puy, a small city in southeastern France.

2 Political activity in the workers' movement

From 1931 to 1934 Simone Weil taught in girls' lycées[5] in Le Puy, Auxerre, and Roanne. This was a period of intense political activity for her but, significantly, by all accounts she was a devoted and generous teacher, and inspired great loyalty among her students, though she often offended the schools' administrations. The importance of education continued to play a central role in her outlook, and exchanges of letters with her students and notes taken by students on Weil's lectures testify to her deep respect for her students as learners. A statement from one of her students conveys her impression of Simone Weil as a teacher:

The clumsiness of her gestures, above all of her hands, the special expression on her face when she would concentrate on her thought, her piercing look through thick glasses, her smile—everything about her emanated a feeling of total frankness and forgetfulness of self, revealing a nobility of soul that was certainly at the root of the emotions she inspired in us, but that at first we were not aware of.[6]

Although Weil had been sent to Le Puy to deprive her of an appropriate setting for her revolutionary commitments, in fact she became deeply involved in political struggles in the area and continued this activity in Auxerre (in 1932–1933) and Roanne (1933–1934). Le Puy was three hours by train from St.-Etienne, an industrial city; Simone Weil traveled there at least once a week for several months to meet with workers and trade union militants and leaders. She taught courses for miners through the St.-Etienne Labor Exchange, a creation of the union movement in that area and a remnant of the syndicalist *bourse du travail* movement.[7] Later she taught a course on Marx at the request of workers at Le Puy. In January, 1933, Simone Weil wrote:

> We should never forget that our task is the preparation of a society "in which the degrading division of work into manual work and intellectual work will be abolished" (Marx). Among the particular tasks implied by this general task, one of the most important is to create, in the different branches of culture, the basis for a true diffusion of knowledge.[8]

Simone Weil also sought out contacts with revolutionary syndicalists, some of whom had once been in the French Communist party and thus were considered "dissident communists." She discovered such a group connected with the journal *La Revolution proletarienne*, which rejected both reformism and affiliation with a political party and advocated militant class struggle. Weil regarded this journal as the only independent revolutionary review; she wrote occasionally for it, and her important article "Prospects: Are We Heading for the Proletarian Revolution:" was published in it. She remained in close contact and sympathy with revolutionary syndicalism throughout this period, much closer than she was to the Marxism of the Communist party.

While at Le Puy, Simone Weil also plunged immediately into trade union activity in both St.-Etienne and her own Haute Loire region. She managed to join the local teachers union that encompassed not only her own stratum of professor but the much larger group of secondary school teachers. At the time two national federations dominated the union movement in France—

the Confédération Générale du Travail (CGT) and the Confédération Générale du Travail Unitaire (CGTU—United General Confederation of Labor). The CGT had lost much of the syndicalist-inspired revolutionary spirit of its pre-war days; but it adhered to a principle in which Weil believed deeply—the independence of trade unions from political parties. The CGTU, formed in 1921 by revolutionary syndicalists who had opposed the CGT leadership's support for French entry into World War I, rejected the principle of trade union independence and became affiliated with the newly-formed Communist party; but Weil regarded the CGTU as the more militant of the two unions, more effective in waging class struggle than the more reformist CGT. Seeing strengths and weaknesses in both confederations, she felt that the competition and division between the two unions weakened the cause of the working class. She devoted much energy to a movement for unity between the two unions and in service to this goal managed to join both the CGT and CGTU locals of the teachers' unions.

Weil was also occasionally politically active in a publicly visible manner. In December of 1931 she participated in a series of demonstrations, organized by the local Communist party, in which the unemployed of Le Puy marched to the mayor's city council's offices. To see a professor of philosophy—and a woman no less—leading a group of unemployed men shocked the town establishment, who briefly threatened Weil's dismissal from the lycée. But students at the lycée and their parents rallied to her defense, and nothing came of the threat.

3 Simone Weil's political outlook

Although Simone Weil participated in many kinds of activities within the labor and left movements of her time and had friends and comrades of many different political sympathies, her political outlook during this period could not be identified fully with any extant political formation on the left—revolutionary syndicalism, communism, trade union militancy. Nevertheless, certain general tendencies in her views regarding political activity and organization can be discerned.

She continued to share with the syndicalists a distrust of political organizations and a relatively greater faith in workers' organizations such as trade unions. She saw political parties as based on the insubstantial tie of shared political beliefs rather than on the deeper bonds created by shared experience of work and working conditions, and she saw the former as having no power to bring about real change in society—that is, change that would truly alleviate the oppression of the worker. She wrote in an article in early 1932:

Experience has shown that a revolutionary party can effectively, according to Marx's formula, take possession of the bureaucratic and military machinery, but not in order to smash it. For power really to pass into the hands of the workers they would have to unite, not through the imaginary ties created by the community of opinion but through the real ties created by the community of their productive function.[9]

Weil was also entirely nonsectarian in her outlook. Despite her suspicion of parties, she was willing to join with any group that seemed to her to be taking steps to mitigate the workers' plight, however differently those groups conceived of that activity and however alien other aspects of their beliefs were to her. This principled participation in political activity, especially with regard to the French Communist Party, is evident in her participation, in December of 1931, in the demonstration of unemployed workers organized by the Communist party in Le Puy. She later wrote of this incident:

The Communists at Le Puy had decided to demand a city welfare fund for unemployment. For my part, since I thought it right that an unemployed person should have something to eat and believed it my duty to help unfortunates unable to defend themselves, I accompanied the unemployed several times to the city council and the mayor . . .[10]

Weil also believed that any organization capable of genuinely helping the working class had to reflect within its own structure control by the workers themselves. She was concerned about the bureaucratic structure of both trade unions and political organizations, in which a small group, often (though not necessarily) of bourgeois origins, ran the organization, with the members being entirely passive. This structure seemed to her to replicate the very powerlessness of the worker that it was the professed goal of radical organizations to overcome. She thought that this problem plagued the revolutionary syndicalists as well: "The 'revolutionary syndicalists' are against bureaucracy I know. But syndicalism is itself bureaucratic!"[11]

Her criticisms of these political organizations had not yet led Simone Weil to abandon, as she did later (see below, chapter 2, section 8), the Marxist belief that the working class was to be the *agent* of any radical transformation of society. At this point she still sought a form of organization of the working class that was capable of bringing about radical change and yet would reflect the values of worker dignity and empowerment that the workers' movement's ultimate goal of a society based on liberty and equality embodied.

For Weil the problem of restoring to the worker his or her rightful place in the work process was not a question of formal organization only but continued to be one of cultural and educational efforts as well:

the important thing is to distinguish, among the attempts at working-class culture, those that are conducted in such a way as to strengthen the ascendency of the intellectuals over the workers, and those conducted in such a way as to free the workers from domination. . . . This domination of those who know how to handle words over those who know how to handle things is rediscovered at every stage of human history.[12]

Finally, Weil was intensely concerned with the moral basis of political activity and in particular with her own moral relationship to that activity. This moral concern presaged the moral perspective that lay at the heart of her political thought throughout her life. Her fundamental moral commitment was to be on the side of the oppressed—that is, (as she saw it at the time) on the side of the working class. But she was sensitive to the moral differences between her own role in the workers' movement as a member of a relatively privileged intellectual stratum and the situation of the workers engaged in the same struggle. She did not want to be in a position of "leading" workers toward a goal they did not themselves actively aspire to nor of pushing them to take risks she herself was not called upon to take (e.g., of losing one's job and having little prospect of another). Moreover, she felt that she herself had much to learn from the workers and could not pretend to have answers to the problems they themselves confronted without sharing their life in some way.

Simone Weil's moral concern was consistent with her critique of bureaucratism in workers' organization, and it involved a rejection of the Leninist view (shared by Trotsky also) of the "vanguard party": Lenin argued that the proletariat would never spontaneously develop a revolutionary consciousness but only a "trade union consciousness" aimed at securing merely economic gains. The working class movement had to be led by a party of professional revolutionaries and politically conscious workers who understood the direction of history and the tasks of the revolution. (These issues are discussed from another perspective in chapter 3, section 8.)

Weil saw the dangers that Lenin's view contained for justifying and encouraging a sharp division between leaders and ordinary workers in the workers' movement; this division could readily come to constitute an oppressive force similar to what workers experienced in capitalist society. In this regard Weil's view is akin to that of Rosa Luxembourg, for whom Weil had great admiration. Luxembourg feared that the vanguard party would inhibit the spontaneous self-activity of the workers (to be expressed in its most revolutionary form in the "mass strike"), and she was critical of Lenin on these grounds. But Weil lacked Luxembourg's revolutionary optimism that the working class would be or is likely ultimately to attain a revolutionary consciousness on its own. At this point in her life Weil had no particular confidence that such a revolutionary consciousness could be attained. She only *hoped* that it could be and believed that if it were not, it was not her or other intellectuals' role to try to create it in the working class. It should also be said that in contrast to Luxembourg Weil was not in general drawn to mass spontaneous action as a form of political activity; she was moving toward a more methodical approach that lent itself to the more individualistic perspective on political action that came to inform her important political writings of 1933 and 1934. For herself Weil was determined not to be a leader but a foot soldier in the workers' cause. She wrote in a letter in 1933:

> If the proletarians are satisfied with the reforms, they are welcome to them. They are the ones who bear the risks and above all the responsibilities of a revolution; it is up to them whether to make the revolution or not. I wish to help them with it if I can, not to push them into it.[13]

Weil took seriously the possibility that the working class movement would not make a revolution at all, but would suffer significant defeats. And, consistent with her fundamental commitment to the oppressed, she was concerned to work out her own relationship to this possibility:

> For my part, I have decided for some time now that the "above-the-fray" position being in fact practically impossible, I would always choose, even in the eventuality of certain defeat, to share the defeat of the workers rather than the victory of their oppressors; but as for shutting one's eyes because of the fear of weakening one's belief in victory, I do not want to do this at any price.[14]

Simone Weil's previous work experiences as well as her contact with miners at St.-Etienne and other workers in the various courses she taught over the years gave her a perspective unusual among socialist intellectuals of the time. For most of them adherence to socialism and radicalism stemmed substantially from a hatred of bourgeois society or an attraction to the explanation of history that Marxism seemed to promise; it involved at best a distanced and disembodied solidarity with the proletariat. For Weil the cause of the oppressed was at the center of her commitment, and it was strengthened by her attraction to and increasing knowledge of the world of manual labor.

Weil's close contact with work and working class life during

1931 and 1932 began to give clearer shape to her fundamental political concerns. A particularly important experience in the development of Weil's focus on workplace oppression was a visit to a mine in March of 1932 (not ordinarily allowed to women, but arranged through Urbain Thévenon [see above, note 7]), where she used a pickax and compressed air drill. In a subsequent article she wrote:

> This machine [the air drill] is not modeled on human nature but on the nature of coal and compressed air, and its movements follow a rhythm profoundly alien to the rhythm of life's movements, violently bending the human body to its service. . . . It will not be enough for a miner to expropriate the companies in order to become master of the mine. The political and economic revolutions will become real only if they are extended into a technical revolution that will re-establish, within the mine and the factory, the domination that it is the worker's function to exercise over the conditions of work.[15]

Because the work process itself was the fundamental locus of oppression and of potential freedom and dignity, for Weil the reorganization of work had to be the standard by which the efforts of political groups were to be measured. She distinguished between two types of machines: the "instrumental" machine, "adaptable to all sorts of tasks, to which the workman's relationship is analogous to that of the sailor with his ship"; and the "automatic" machine, which leaves nothing for the worker to do but tend it ("Pre-War Notebook," 38). The latter type of machine undermines the dignity of the worker by depriving him of intellectual control over the process of his work, whereas the former type of machine extends the workers' conscious control over the process and materials of work.

Simone Weil's outlook regarding political organization and the goals of political activity implied for her that no extant form of political movement would be able to compel her loyalty. Nevertheless, her reluctance to abandon the workers' struggle in the organized forms it then took led her to complex relations with the influential forces on the left at that time, especially with the French Communist Party and with Trotsky.

4 Simone Weil and the French Communist Party

The Parti communiste français (PCF—the French Communist Party) was the most significant force on the French left during the period in which Simone Weil was coming to maturity as a political thinker and activist, and her complex and changing relationship with the PCF is an important part of her development. More generally, in order to grasp the significance of Simone Weil's developing critical stance toward Marxism, it is necessary to understand some of the political and historical background of the Marxism of the French Communist Party.

Between 1889 and 1914 the Second International, a largely Marxist federation of national parties and organizations, saw itself as coordinating an international revolutionary working-class movement. The most important Marxist thinkers of this era— Karl Kautsky, Lenin, Luxembourg—worked within the Second International, to which virtually all Marxist revolutionaries looked to advance the goals articulated by Marx. Kautsky, the leader of the Second International's largest affiliate, the Sozialdemokratische Partei Deutschlands (SPD—the German Social Democratic Party), developed what came to be the "orthodox" view of Marxism, a view that was contested from the right and the left but that came to represent the dominant position within the Second International.

But World War I brought about a collapse of the Second International as the leaders of the major European affiliates supported their own national governments in the war rather than resisting war in the name of proletarian internationalism. Drawing on antiwar sentiments as well as support for the successful Bolshevik Revolution of 1917, the Third International (the Communist International, or Comintern) was formed in 1919, seeing itself as making a decisive break with the Second International, especially with what it saw as the Second International's leaders' betrayal of the international working class. Kautsky, in particular, was greatly vilified by Lenin, the leading theorist and political leader of the early years of the Third International.

A majority group within the Section française de l'Internationale ouvrière (SFIO—the French socialist coalition), the

French affiliate of the Second International, broke with that group to form the French Communist Party (PCF) in 1920, which affiliated with the Third International. The PCF was able to turn the strong French tradition of revolution—stemming back to the revolution of 1789 and drawing on the uprising of 1848 and the Paris Commune of 1871—in the direction of a favorable attitude to the Soviet Union and the recent Soviet revolution. In this way the PCF was able to attract many former revolutionary syndicalists whose ideology was in many ways quite different from Marxian communism. And because of Lenin's opposition to the war, anti-war sentiment before and after the war (which was felt by many syndicalists who believed themselves betrayed by the CGT leadership's capitulation to the war effort) was able to find a home in the PCF. Thus, at its inception the PCF brought together an ideologically quite diverse body of followers.

In spite of its diversity, from very early on—though this process intensified much more strongly in the late 1920s and 1930s—the Third International became dominated by the highly centralized, bolshevik model for its affiliated parties.[16] The range of acceptable political views became increasingly narrow, comprising only the official version of Marxism grounded in Lenin's thought, especially as interpreted by his successors in the Soviet Union. The narrowing of Marxist and revolutionary thought was even more pronounced in the French Communist party than in other prominent European parties, several of which produced theorists who in some way challenged the Soviet-defined orthodoxy (Lukács in Hungary, Korsch in Germany, Gramsci in Italy). By the mid-1920s most former syndicalists and other "dissident Communists" had left the PCF; however, many of them still saw themselves as the true Communists or Marxists and hoped to reshape or regain the influence within the revolutionary left that then belonged, partly by virtue of the influence of the Bolshevik Revolution, to the PCF. The syndicalist group connected to *La Revolution proletarienne* to whom Simone Weil was closest in the early 1930s consisted of several former members of the PCF.

Chapters 2 and 3 concern the specific doctrines of the Marxism of the Second and Third Internationals and Weil's criticisms of them. Suffice it to say at this point that the Marxism of the PCF with which Weil was concerned relied primarily on certain key

Marxist texts (*Capital*, *German Ideology*, *Communist Manifesto*),[17] on Engels, and on Lenin. And while the theories of the Second International were officially discredited by its "reformism" and capitulation to nationalism in the face of World War I, its intellectual positions, as represented primarily by Kautsky, drew on essentially these same canonical texts and continued to inform the PCF's understanding of Marxism.

What was Simone Weil's relationship with communism and the PCF? She worked closely with many Communists—teachers in the teachers' union (especially at Roanne in 1933–34) and miners in St.-Etienne—and found honorable and dedicated men in the Communist ranks, as she did in every group with which she had some ties (unions, syndicalist groups, etc.) She apparently attended some Communist cell meetings in St.-Etienne. Because of her close association with many Communists, she herself was often considered a Communist and until the early 1940s did little to disabuse people of this view of her.

Something of the flavor of Weil's willingness to work with the Communist party, yet her ambiguous relationship to it is captured in another part of the description she gives of the unemployed demonstration at Le Puy in 1931:

> During all this [the flap over the demonstrations] the local Communists kept telling me that they considered me to be on the other side of the barricades in relation to them and treated me on occasion as such; at the same time, they were very happy to see me exposed to repression instead of them, since I was suspected of being one of their followers.[18]

In the early 1930s Weil seemed to have contemplated joining the PCF. Despite her suspicion of political parties and her differences with the PCF in particular, for a time she believed it to be in the forefront of militant class struggle. Her dissident Communist friend Boris Souvarine claimed that had the party been run differently she would have joined it, even in 1932. And Simone Canguilhem, a fellow teacher at Le Puy with whom Weil shared a room while living at Le Puy, said that Weil still wondered in 1932 whether she should join the Party. Finally, her brother, André, reports that he once saw in their parents' house a draft of a letter by Weil apparently intended for the PCF, asking for membership; but this letter seems never to have been sent.

On the other hand, much later in her life (in the same letter describing the unemployed demonstration), Simone Weil wrote this about her relation to the Party:

> I have always wanted a social transformation to the advantage of the less fortunate, but I was never favorably inclined toward the Communist party, even during my adolescence. When I was eighteen, only the trade union movement attracted me. Since then I have never stopped going farther and farther away from the Communists, even to the point of regarding them as the principal enemy at a period when they still deceived many politicians who today hold high positions. When I attended the Ecole Normale from 1928 to 1931 I readily manifested my non-conformist feelings, and perhaps with some exaggeration, as often happens when one is 20 years old.[19]

This seems an overstatement, and Pétrement suggests that Weil undoubtedly wrote it in the early days of the war, at a time when, desiring to participate in the defense of the country and meeting with distrust on the part of the organizers to whom she offered her services, she tried to make them understand that she had never had ties with the Communist party.[20]

What does seem true is that in this early period of her life Weil could never have become a wholehearted party member; she was too distrustful of parties and too much dedicated to following out her own thought to adhere to a party line. And even from the beginning she was closer politically to other groups (especially the syndicalists) than to the Communist party. Nevertheless, we can make sense of her working with the PCF and contemplating joining it by remembering that she saw her primary commitment as alleviating the plight of the working class. If she perceived a group as effective in this endeavor even for a time, the possibility of joining could not have been entirely unthinkable for her.[21]

However, the summer of 1932 marked a turning point in Weil's view of the Communist party and of the Communist International. The notion that in contrast to the CGT unions the

Party was militant in waging class struggle was shattered for her by a visit to Germany in summer 1932. Hitler's Nazi party had scored spectacular electoral success in the previous year's elections, and the horrifying face of nazism was becoming evident. Yet rather than uniting with the Social Democrats (the other large workers' party) to attempt to stem the Nazi tide, the German Communist Party followed the "class against class" position enunciated by the Comintern in 1928 and followed by all affiliated Communist parties. According to this doctrine, social democratic parties were seen as fostering bourgeois illusions in the working class, thus dulling revolutionary consciousness. Hence the German Communist party did not do what was then needed to organize the proletariat against the Nazi threat, which would have involved combining with the Social Democrats; rather they saw fascism as the last dying gasp of capitalism, to be followed by a Communist revolution. ("Nach Hitler, uns!")

Observing this situation, Weil was appalled at the passivity of the Party in face of the Nazi threat and at the conjunction of revolutionary phrases and total inaction. On returning, she wrote her impressions to Albertine and Urbain Thévenon:

> As a kind of reward, in Germany I lost all the respect that in spite of myself I still felt for the Communist Party. . . . Actually it seems to me as culpable as the Social Democracy. I think that at the present moment all compromise with the Communist party or any reticence in criticizing it is criminal.[22]

According to orthodox Marxist theory, a crisis in capitalism should provoke revolutionary activity in the proletariat; and yet, for the second time in twenty years (the first being World War I), the German working class's Marxist organizations had capitulated to reaction in the face of political and economic crisis.

In March 1933, when Hitler finally triumphed, stamping out all forms of opposition, Weil continued to blame the party and the Comintern.[23] From then on her criticisms of the Communist party and the Third International became increasingly harsh, though she continued to work politically with Communists and Party members on specific issues.

Throughout the 1930s Simone Weil continued to decry a

situation of which she had become increasingly aware—the subordination of the PCF as an affiliate of the Third International to the foreign policy interests of the Soviet Union. She particularly separated herself from the Trotskyists who in the spring of 1933 were still calling for reform of the Comintern, seeing it as essentially revolutionary though having made important mistakes (e.g., in Germany). She called on Trotsky (to whose views hers were more akin than to mainstream Communists') to take an unequivocal stance of rejection of the Third International; on behalf of a group of like-minded dissident Communist comrades, she defined her position thus:

> [T]he Third International, despite the proletarian character and confusedly revolutionary orientation of its rank and file, has ceased to represent communism according to Marx's definition. . . . [T]he present duty of alert militants is to break morally with the bureaucratic Third International as they have broken with the bourgeoisified Second International. . . . [F]rom now on one must work for a reorganization of alert revolutionaries, which should be done without any ties to the bureaucracy of the Russian state.[24]

5 Simone Weil and Trotsky

Simone Weil never seems to have shared the PCF's enthusiasm for the Soviet Union as a beacon of socialism, though the early ideological diversity in the Party may have mitigated the extent to which her critical stance translated immediately into hostility to the PCF itself. In any case, long before entirely giving up on the PCF as a progressive force in the French workers' movement, Simone Weil had maintained a critical distance on the Soviet Union typical of the syndicalist and Trostkyist dissident Communists with whom she associated.

Simone Weil's critique of the Soviet Union was developed most fully in an important article written for the syndicalist journal *La Revolution proletarienne* in August 1933, called "Prospects: Are We Heading for the Proletarian Revolution?"

This critique can best be understood by relating it to another theme in the article, Weil's relationship with Trotskyism. The article involves some important Trotskyist ideas, and indeed within Communist circles Weil was often taken for a Trotskyist. At the same time her increasing distance from orthodox Marxism involved some important differences with Trotsky as well.

Trotsky had been a leader of the Bolshevik Revolution and an enthusiastic supporter of Lenin, but in 1922 Trotsky and his allies (later called the "Left Opposition") were edged from power by Josef Stalin. Trotsky's power and influence were progressively eroded in the 1920s and he was finally exiled from the Soviet Union in 1929. Living for a time in France during the 1920s (and also in the first years of World War I), Trotsky had an important impact on the French dissident Communists with whom Weil associated in these years. His developing criticisms of the Soviet Union echoed certain syndicalist themes. In the mid-1920s the French Communist Party had followed the directives of the by-then entirely Stalinist-dominated International to expunge Trotskyists and left oppositionists (including former syndicalists and Simone Weil's later friend Boris Souvarine[25]). This split in the Communist movement left the door open for Trotskyist influence among dissident and syndicalist-influenced Communists who had already left the party in the early 1920s.

For many on the left, include Simone Weil, Trotsky remained an important revolutionary figure and an individual of great strength of character and mental lucidity; hounded for years by Stalin's agents and driven from country to country, Trotsky maintained his revolutionary spirit and dedication to the cause of the international proletariat.

Trotsky believed, and Lenin came to concur with him, that the Soviet Revolution could not ultimately succeed without support from revolutions in Western countries; there could not be "socialism in one country." As the prospects of support for the Soviet Revolution from the Western proletariat became dimmer and dimmer in the early 1920s, Trotsky became increasingly concerned about the growing centralization of economic power. The burgeoning stratum of bureaucrats, factory managers, technical intelligentsia, military officers, and party functionaries were becoming increasingly remote from the masses of Soviet citizens. This centralization and bureaucratization seemed a deviation from the true tasks and spirit of the Bolshevik Revolution. Such a critique echoed worries Lenin himself had voiced in his last years (he died in 1924) that the state administration had swollen out of proportion to its usefulness and had become increasingly divorced from the people whom it was meant to serve. By the mid-1920s Trotsky had mounted a full-scale critique of "bureaucratism" as a feature of Soviet political life, a critique he developed and intensified throughout the 1930s.

Trotsky came to see the bureaucratic-administrative stratum of Soviet society, which in Lenin's thought was supposed to be transitional only, as a self-perpetuating caste exercising power over the proletariat. He regarded this bureaucratic formation as a distortion and an "excrescence" on the Soviet society, which would have to be removed through political reform. By the 1930s Trotsky came to feel that this restoration of the original direction of the Bolshevik Revolution could be accomplished only by a second proletarian revolution, though a revolution which would alter only the *political* structure and not the more fundamental *socio-economic* character of the society.

Yet while Trotsky was one of the harshest critics of the Soviet Union in the 1930s on the left, he continued to support the Soviet Union in the international arena and to maintain that the Soviet Union was a "worker's state," although one with "bureaucratic deformations." That is, according to Trotsky, since private property had been abolished, Soviet society had transcended capitalism and was therefore on the road to socialism. The growth of bureaucracy represented a backward tendency but one that did not affect the socio-economic foundations of Soviet society. Trotsky saw himself as defending Lenin's true vision of Soviet communism against Stalin's perversions of it. He remained an adherent of Lenin's view of the role of the vanguard party and, while calling for somewhat more democratic participation within the party, did not challenge the need for the party to have full control over political life.

In "Prospects: Are We Heading for the Proletarian Revolution?" Weil agrees with Trotsky that the existing Soviet regime had betrayed the goals of the Revolution; that a bureaucratic caste had emerged in Russia that oppressed the working class; and that the attempt to build socialism in one country was a source of oppressive features of the Soviet social order. But she rejects any notion of the Soviet Union as fundamentally socialist, as having taken any significant steps toward or removed any obstacles to a non-oppressive social order. There is no evidence, Weil says, for Trotsky's view that the state bureaucracy has a provisional character. Rather the bureaucracy shows every sign of entrenching itself further and extending its power. Weil rejects Trotsky's assumption, shared with orthodox Marxism, that "capitalism" and "socialism" are the only alternatives. The Soviet Union, she believes, is *neither* capitalist *nor* socialist; it is an entirely different form of social order altogether, one not anticipated in the Marxist scheme and operating according to a "different social mechanism" (5). Marxism had also failed to anticipate fascism, which, according to Weil, is also essentially a new kind of society, like the social-political system of the Soviet Union; to call fascism "the last gasp of a dying capitalism" is mere rhetoric, not analysis (6–7).

In "Prospects" Weil sees the Soviet Union not merely as a workers' state with deformations but not a workers' state in any sense at all. She writes that "to call a state a 'workers' state' when you go on to explain that each worker in it is put economically and politically at the complete disposal of a bureaucratic caste, sounds like a bad joke" (4). Weil agreed that the Soviet system contains "deformations." But she saw these deformations as part of the inner character of that social form itself, not, as Trotsky claimed, external "excrescences" added to something of a fundamentally socialist character. While Trotsky's criticism of Stalin were harsh, Weil thought that he did not see that the foundations of Stalinism were laid within the Leninism to which Trotsky remained committed.

Weil suggests that Marxists (including Trotsky) had over-estimated the importance of private property in the mechanism by which the proletariat is oppressed:

> To the conflict set up by money between buyers and sellers of labour has been added another conflict, set up by the very means of production, between those who have the machine at their disposal and those who are at the disposal of the machine. The Russian experiment has shown that, contrary to what Marx too readily assumed, the first of these conflicts can be eliminated without entailing the

disappearance of the second. (10)

For Weil the bureaucratic mechanism, which Trotsky saw as antithetical to the true social character of Soviet communism, in fact characterises the heart of that system. She even suggests that "oppression exercised in the name of management" (9) constitutes a new species of oppression, historically succeeding—though also interacting with—oppression based on ownership of capital.

Weil's sense of the character of Soviet society and its dismal departure from the ideals and values of Marx and even of Lenin can be seen in the following passage:

> Instead of genuine freedom of the press, there is the impossibility of expressing a free opinion . . . without running the risk of being deported; instead of the free play between parties within the framework of the soviet system, there is the cry of "one party in power, all the rest in prison"; instead of a communist party destined to rally together, for the purposes of free co-operation, men possessing the highest degree of devotion, conscientiousness, culture, and critical aptitude, there is a mere administrative machine, a passive instrument in the hands of the Secretariat . . . ; instead of soviets, unions, and co-operatives functioning democratically and directing the economic and political life of the country, there are organizations bearing, it is true, the same names, but reduced to mere administrative mechanisms; . . . lastly, and above all, instead of public officials, permanently subject to control and dismissal, who were to ensure the functioning of government until such time as "every cook would learn how to rule the State," there is a professional bureaucracy, freed from responsibility, recruited by co-option and possessing, through the concentration in its hands of all economic and political power, a strength hitherto unknown in the annals of history. (3–4)

Weil's critique is here still expressed in the name of the ideals of communism and socialism—of participation, cooperation, democracy, direct accountability to the people, and true liberty.

At this point she still seemed to accept, if more tentatively, much of the traditional Marxist critique of capitalism. It is in part those same charges that she here levels against the Soviet system—that in it the worker is not the master but the subject of the machines with which he or she works; that the mental and spiritual powers of labor are appropriated by a class set over and above the workers, controlling them for their own ends; that the degrading division between manual and mental labor and laborers permeates the organization of work and of society itself. Despite her commitment to Marxist ideals and her rejection of capitalism, it is significant that Weil seems to feel that these processes of bureaucratic oppression had progressed further in the Soviet Union than in the capitalist countries. She speaks of them as threatening "the very existence of everything which still remains precious for us in the bourgeois regime (16) such as freedom of thought and cultural life. So, even if the specific form of work oppression she so decries was most developed in the capitalist countries (specifically in the United States), she nevertheless considers that this *general* form of bureaucratic or administrative domination had more deeply permeated the general social system in the Soviet Union.

6 Moral underpinnings of political struggle

The "Prospects" essay is an important benchmark in Simone Weil's developing skepticism about traditional political forms and organizations. In it she speaks the truth about the Soviet Union as she saw it and in the process casts doubt on a clear vision of a socialist future, in which resided the hope of many activists on the left. Searching for a continuing foundation of political activism in the face of diminishing hope, she writes:

> The only question that arises is whether we should or
> should not continue the struggle; if the former then we shall
> struggle with as much enthusiasm as if victory were assured.
> There is no difficulty whatever, once one has decided to act,
> in maintaining intact, on the level of action, those very
> hopes which a critical examination has shown to be well-

nigh unfounded; in that lies the very essence of courage.
(22)

Few indeed were those of Weil's comrades who were able to continue engaging in demanding political struggle in the total absence of any assurances or even hopes that progress toward their goals was grounded in the forces of history. Yet Weil's stance here is consistent with the fundamental moral spirit that continually informed her political commitments: One continues to work toward justice or the mitigation of oppression even if one has no historical evidence that such justice is to be achieved. It is not the sense of history that should or needs to ground such struggle but only a moral commitment to the lessening of oppression in the specific conditions of one's own time and place.

Moreover, there is one area of activity in which the overwhelming forces ranged against revolutionary hopes are powerless, and that is "working toward a clear comprehension of the object of our efforts, so that, if we cannot accomplish that which we will, we may at least have willed it, and not just have blindly wished for it" ("Prospects," 23). Elsewhere, in a letter to Urbain Thevénon, Weil comments, "The revolution is a *job*, a methodical task that the blind or people with blindfolded eyes cannot perform. And this is what we are at this moment. . . . We must open our eyes."[26] We must open our eyes, that is, both to the illusory claims made in the name of Soviet communism and to the real tasks of seeking out and combating the true causes of oppression.

Appearing in a revolutionary journal, "Prospects" distressed many of Weil's comrades. It provoked this reply from Trotsky himself: "Despairing over the unfortunate experience of the 'dictatorship of the proletariat,' Simone Weil has found consolation in a new mission: to defend her personality against society. A formula of the old liberalism, refurbished by a cheaply bought anarchist exaltation."[27] This observation is an insightful one and brings out an important and deepening divergence between Weil and Trotsky. Weil was in fact very much concerned with her own relationship to the workers' movement—with ensuring, at least in her own mind, that she be engaging in activities that truly promoted their interests and that did not involve her in betraying them, in contributing to illusory hopes, or in reproducing the domination of intellectuals over workers. Trotsky's confidence that Marxism presented a scientific body of historical truths and certainties that allowed one to dispense with such personal and moral concerns and doubts was for Weil symptomatic of deep inadequacies in Marxism, which she came to explore in her later work.

Trotsky accuses Weil of a kind of individualism here, but it is an accusation that in an important sense Weil accepts. She *is* in fact concerned about her own moral integrity as a political actor and, more generally, with the integrity of individuals acting as political agents. For her political activity is to be firmly rooted in the moral understanding and principles of the individual political actor. The individual's concern with relieving oppression is to be the ultimate motivational foundation of his or her political involvement.

Moreover, this individualism (itself hearkening back to Weil's teacher Alain) is reflected in Weil's understanding of socialism, in a formulation close to traditional anarchism: "In the subordination of society to the individual lies the definition of true democracy and that of socialism as well" ("Prospects," 20). It is the dignity of the individual that is to be the goal of political activity. Individuals as individuals are thus to be both the subject and the object of political action. Morality comes into politics for Weil both as a moral concern for the integrity of the individual political agent and as a moral concern for the dignity of those to be served by political action.

Around the time "Prospects" was published, Trotsky himself had moved closer to Simone Weil's view of the Third International and had begun to talk of forming a Fourth International, a task implied by what Weil and her comrades had been proposing. And Weil met Trotsky in December of 1933, at a time when he was persona non grata in France. Partly because of her principle of helping the persecuted and partly because of her admiration for and interest in him (despite their increasing differences), Weil arranged for Trotsky and some of his comrades to use her parents' home for a clandestine meeting. (As a condition of his stay, the French government had forbidden Trotsky to take part in political meetings.) Weil and Trotsky had an enormous argument, apparently concerning the nature of Soviet society. According to her brother, André, at the end of this evening Trotsky said to her, "I see you disagree with me in almost everything. Why do you put me up in your house? Do you belong to the Salvation Army?"[28] Trotsky's failure to grasp an act of personal political principle and comradeship that cut across serious ideological differences is revealing of his own moral stance; but no doubt Simone Weil was herself pleased at the chance to put her own criticisms to Trotsky himself and to see if he had a satisfactory response to them.

Events of 1933 and early 1934—the triumph of fascism in Germany and Italy, the organizational and political deficiencies of working class organizations in France and Germany, the armaments race, and the general rise of intense nationalism in Europe—eventually discouraged Weil about any ongoing forms of political activity. Increasingly she turned toward the one useful political task she felt was available—namely, analyzing the causes of oppression. In March, 1934, she wrote to her friend Simone Pétrement:

> I have decided to withdraw entirely from any kind of political activity, except for theoretical work, that does not absolutely exclude possible participation in a great spontaneous movement of the masses (in the ranks, as a solider), but I don't want any responsibility, no matter how slight, or even indirect, because I am certain that all the blood that will be shed will be shed in vain, and that we are beaten in advance.[29]

The theoretical work she mentions issued in the major work of her early life, *Reflections Concerning the Causes of Liberty and Social Oppression*. This work is the most complete expression of Weil's reflections on the state of civilization in her time, on the sources of oppression and unfreedom within it and on the failures of contemporary ideologies (and especially Marxism) to point a way out.

2
Simone Weil on Marxism: work relations, production, and progress

The year 1934 marked an important point in Simone Weil's intellectual development in relationship to politics. Reflecting on her own political experience and on the society in which she lived, Weil attempted to come to grips with the failure of the political movements of her time, especially the Marxian Communist movement, to mitigate the oppression of the worker. Her inquiries led her to trenchant criticisms of Marxism, to a deepening understanding of social oppression, and to original speculations about Western civilization.

In discussing Simone Weil's criticisms of Marxism (in this and the next chapter), we will draw primarily from the major work of this period—*Reflections Concerning the Causes of Liberty and Social Oppression*. But we will look also at some essays and fragments written in 1936–1937 that express similar concerns regarding Marxism and at one of Weil's final essays, "Is There a Marxist Doctrine?" in which these earlier concerns are gathered up into the Christian framework that came to permeate her thought in the last several years of her life. In all this we will be paying attention to the continuities as well as the changes in Weil's view of Marxism.

1 Work: oppressive and nonoppressive

As in all of her work of this period, Weil's own starting point for political analysis and philosophy is the oppression of the workers, especially under capitalism. A good introduction to Weil's developing understanding of oppression is found in notes from her lectures at the lycée at Roanne, transcribed by one of her students and published as *Lectures on Philosophy*. Weil was concerned to present the tradition of Western thought to her students, and the pedagogically serious but respectful tone of these lecture notes contrasts with the deeply politically engaged, passionate, sometimes biting and sarcastic tone of the political writings. Nevertheless, Weil is struggling here too with the problem of social oppression. She defines oppression by saying that it involved people being treated as a means, in violation of Kant's principle (*Lectures on Philosophy*, 136), and this formulation corresponds to the way she has understood Marx's analysis also—as a reversal of subject and object, of means and ends. In addition to this formal definition, much of her discussion of oppression invokes a picture of oppression as a kind of weight, a social force crushing a group of persons, insulting their dignity or depriving them of it. Weil puts forth the idea that the point of a science of society is to enable us to discern how to minimize oppression in a given set of social conditions. Although the minimization of oppression is the goal, Weil seems unsure how it is to be accomplished and indeed whether such a minimization is to any appreciable extent possible. This ambivalence about oppression is continued and deepened in *Reflections*.

Reflections measures oppression against a standard of dignified work, or work embodying liberty. Such work ideally involves a harmonious interaction of manual and intellectual capacities, transforming and subduing nature in according with the necessities presented by the task at hand. Ideally, the worker is given a general task—for example, the erection of the foundation for a building—the point of which he understands.[1] He uses his own judgment and initiative to figure out, given the available materials, how to carry out this task in accordance with the skills and knowledge at his command, and he then guides the movement of his body by this understanding. When this happens, the worker is the "subject" in the work process; he is in control of it, not in the sense that he (alone or in concert with other workers) necessarily sets the overall initial task—this is seen by Weil as presented by some "necessity" (the need for a house, for example)—but in the sense that the execution of the task is guided by his own judgment. He is himself the master of the process, not merely a "factor" to be used by the owner in order to produce something.

In *Reflections* the role of thought and judgment is central to Weil's understanding of the humanly ideal form of work and of the way in which work can, but can also fail to, embody and support the dignity of the worker; for Weil, "the only mode of production absolutely free would be that in which methodical thought was in operation throughout the course of the work" (95). "Thought is certainly man's supreme dignity" (105), Weil says, and she devotes a good deal of space in the essay to showing how in the process of work this dignity can be stripped away as thought is severed from the movements of the worker's body. The understanding of how to build a car, for example, can be embodied in a machine, so that an auto worker can come to do no more than put one piece of metal on another as it comes by her on the assembly line; and she can do this without herself understanding how the car gets built and even without under-standing very much about how her particular task fits into the whole operation of manufacturing a car. Or the understanding of the larger process can be given to the manager who commands the worker while the worker merely passively executes her orders, again without necessarily understanding what role her movements play in the larger task and certainly without making use of her own intellectual capacities. "Hence," says Weil, "one is brought face to face with a paradoxical situation; namely that there is method in the motions of work, but none in the mind of the worker" (92).

In *Reflections* this division of labor—the specialization of task that separates those who design and conceive of the work from those who directly execute it manually—is precisely what constitutes oppression: The intellectual understanding of the process of work is contained in the minds of the scientists, engineers, and managers and is built into the operations of the machines, but is denied to the worker. The worker executes but does not conceive, and his motions can be carried out an indefinite number of times without his understanding. This inability to guide one's movements by one's thoughts violates the worker's dignity; and it is in this way that capitalism, or modern industrial organization in general, oppresses the worker. (Issues of thought and action will be further discussed in chapter 4, section 2.)

So *understanding* becomes, for Weil, central to a human form of work. Workers need to understand the nature of the technical processes underlying their own work in order that they be executing their work according to their own intelligence and knowledge—that is, so that their own knowledge will be adequate to the tasks of skilled work in a complex technological setting. If they have to decide how to place certain materials together in a structure, they must understand the physical processes underlying the various alternative ways of doing so. Such understanding should not be the province of management, scientists, and technocrats alone but must be re-appropriated by the workers.

This emphasis on education is not meant to imply that Weil thought that workers would be freed from oppression merely by studying. Rather, the requisite knowledge can be fully gained only by challenging the power that management and capital now exert over the worker, since that power partly consists in their monopoly on the understanding of the processes of work. The gaining of knowledge must go hand in hand with this challenge to managerial power.

2   Orthodox Marxism and Weil's criticisms

Weil's central interest in and criterion for assessing all political action is the mitigation of oppression and the promotion of a humane and dignified form of work organization. It is in this light that in *Reflections* Weil scrutinizes particularly closely the philosophical basis that Marxism provides for its claim to be a philosophy of workers' liberation. The Marxism with which *Reflections* is concerned is the Marxist tradition as it had come to be appropriated and developed in the international Communist movement and especially in the French Communist Party. We have referred to this view as "orthodox Marxism," a historical appellation usually denoting specifically the orthodox position within the Second International (generally identified with Kautsky); orthodox Marxism as Weil is concerned with it is also referred to as "historical materialism," though this term is of somewhat broader compass.

Weil's critique of Marxism in *Reflections* and in the later essays sometimes, though not always clearly, distinguishes what is directed at orthodox Marxism from what is directed as well, or only, at Marx himself. Although Weil became aware of Marx's early writings sometime in the mid-1930s and favorably mentions Marx's "philosophy of labor" in her later writings, she never seems to have rethought her view of the Marxist corpus in light of them. Thus her overall sense of what Marxism is remains very much filtered through the canonical texts of orthodox Marxism (*Capital*, *German Ideology*, *Communist Manifesto*, and the like).

Yet at some points Weil focuses very explicitly on Marx himself, in distinction from later developments in Marxism, and her overall assessment of Marx is worth noting preliminary to a detailed examination of her criticisms of orthodox Marxism. Materialism, understood as a method for studying society in terms of power relationships, is for Weil an idea of permanent value in Marx. (Materialism will be discussed below, in chapter 3, sections 4 and 5). Another is

> that which has been almost forgotten by what is called
> Marxism: the glorification of productive labor, considered
> as man's highest activity; the assertion that only a society
> wherein the act of work brought all of man's faculties into
> play, wherein the man who works occupied the front rank,
> would realize human greatness to the full. ("On the
> Contradictions of Marxism," 154)

At the same time, central to Simone Weil's assessment of Marx and permeating her more detailed criticisms of historical materialism is what she called "certain contradictions of the first importance," which she claims to have noted when first reading *Capital* in her youth (147). The foremost of these contradictions is that between the noble idealism of Marx's conception of communist society—of a society of liberty and equality in which labor would be accorded its true value—and Marx's materialist method for studying society. According to Weil, "Marx became a revolutionary in his youth, under the influence of noble sentiments; his ideal at this period was, indeed, humane, clear, conscious, reasoned, quite as much as—and indeed considerably more than—during the subsequent years of his life" (147). But Marx convinced himself, Weil says, that his method for studying history and societies also indicated that his ideals would actually be realized in society. In all her writings on Marx, Weil claims that Marx had no basis whatever for this belief, and she continually tries to understand how he could have held on to it. She suggests that his generous spirit could not stand the thought that the just society of his dreams could fail to be realized, and so he distorted the true insights of his method of social analysis to imply that it guaranteed the future existence of such a world.[2]

While Weil takes the intellectual context constituted by orthodox Marxism for granted in her discussion of Marxism, at the same time studies of Weil have generally failed to attend closely to this context. Hence it may be useful to give a brief and necessarily somewhat oversimplified account of the tenets of historical materialism as it characterized the central doctrine of orthodox Marxism.

According to historical materialism, capitalism is developing in a direction that will lead to its own destruction and with it to the end of the capitalist form of oppression. In this regard capitalism is only the latest of a historical succession of social and economic systems that have dug their own graves. Each of these systems (e.g., ancient, feudal) generates a form of oppression specific to itself (slave labor, serfdom) that serves the function of developing the forces of production existing within that society. But history has shown that having done so, each system prior to capitalism thereby outlived its own usefulness and made its own form of oppression obsolete. Once the forces of production within a social system are able to develop no further, the stage is set for a new system to be brought about by the motion of these economic forces and by the political action of oppressed and restricted groups of the previous social order. Each system has thus generated its own gravediggers and created the forces of its own undoing. The seed of the new society grows within the old.

But with capitalism there is an important change: No longer is the antiquated system of oppression (capitalism) replaced by a new system of oppression. For the first time in history the day can be envisioned when oppression will no longer be necessary and will disappear. Oppression under capitalism—the severe effort and hardship demanded of the worker, the subjection of the worker to manager and owner that robs the worker of the value of her work, and the increasing division of labor—has been necessary to reach the extraordinary level of material production capitalism has generated; but having done so it has rendered itself unnecessary. For oppression in all its forms depended on material scarcity; and it has been the historical mission of capitalism continually to revolutionize the forces of production —to develop mass production, scientific and technical knowledge, automation, and the like to such an extent that the day is not far off when scarcity will have been abolished and nature will have been finally tamed. More precisely, the only obstacle still in the way of the abolition of oppression is the property relations (the relations of production) of the capitalist form of society; for the institution of private property means that the capitalist class's ownership of the means of production causes gross disparities between the classes regarding access to the fruits of this technological advancement.

The conquest of state power by the proletariat will right this imbalance in the enjoyment of the bounty of capitalist society, and its activity will bring about a new society of socialism or communism, in which oppression will disappear. In previous historical periods the most oppressed groups have fought to overthrow the social order only to find themselves victims of new forms of oppression. In the French Revolution artisans and workers fought on the side of the group who later became their oppressors—the bourgeoisie. Now, for the first time in history, the most oppressed, having under capitalism become the mass of humanity, will themselves become masters of the new order of society.

The movement of historical forces described here is conceived to be a matter for scientific discovery and can be established objectively. "Scientific socialism" is the name of the doctrine and the method that shows how these historical forces are leading to the establishment of socialism.

Thus, while recognizing the terrible suffering of the working class, the orthodox Marxist picture gives reason to hope for its abolition and even to see the intensification of oppression as a factor in this abolition. In doing so, it gives a direction to the political efforts of those desiring an end to oppression—namely, organizing the working class to press its economic and political demands, with the final goal of assuming the reins of power in the new non-oppressive order. The viability of those efforts is guaranteed ultimately by the assurance that history is on the side of the proletariat, the most oppressed group. As capitalism sinks deeper and deeper into crisis, the political organization of the working class will become increasingly stronger, taking a revolutionary direction ultimately conscious of its historically ordained role as creators of a new order, based for the first time in history on a true liberty and equality. So, while capitalism is an inherently and unalterably oppressive system, it simultaneously creates the forces that will bring an end to that oppression.

Although the term "orthodox Marxism" is meant to apply primarily to the position of the Second International, in fact much of the conception just sketched applies as well to the conception of Marxism dominant in the Third International as well, despite the great political differences between the two Internationals. The philosophical differences are primarily ones of emphasis. The most important of these (for understanding Weil) is that Kautsky's emphasis on the laws of capitalist development and their virtually inevitable tendency toward socialism deemphasizes the political struggle of the working class. Kautsky's view sometimes tends to imply that history—including the triumph of socialism—operates "behind the backs" of historical agents so that the revolution becomes as much something that one could confidently await as something to be *created* by working class self-activity. (Hence Kautsky's view is seen as economic determinism.) In contrast, Lenin, articulating the dominant view within the Third International, saw Marxism primarily as a theory of revolutionary struggle—of how the working class is to be guided by a revolutionary consciousness and how it is to take power and build socialism. Without denying the scheme of historical development stated above, Lenin's view tends to downplay its role in setting constraints on what could be accomplished by the revolutionary movement.[3]

In her political writings in and after 1934, especially *Reflections*, Simone Weil almost totally rejects the ultimately quite optimistic picture of the course of proletarian struggle embedded in orthodox Marxism. The remainder of this chapter and the next will be devoted to distinguishing the various interrelated criticisms of Marxism that Weil puts forth primarily in *Reflections*. In this chapter we will consider the following points of criticism: (1) Weil's critique of Lenin's philosophy of work organization, as implemented in the Soviet Union; (2) her critique of the roles of private property and work organization in determining oppression; (3) her rejection of the view of the movement of history implied by the theory of the expansion of productive forces; (4) her rejection of the assumption of progress contained within the orthodox Marxist theory of history; (5) her disputing whether the conquest of scarcity is central to ending oppression; (6) her rejection of the implication that true liberty involves the absence of necessity; (7) her questioning of the relationship between "class struggle" and "the development of productive forces" within Marxism; and (8) her contention that the theory undercuts its own claim that the proletariat can become a revolutionary agent.

In chapter 3 we will go on to consider two other central elements within orthodox Marxism—revolution and materialism —concerning which Weil was critical but aspects or reframed conceptions of which she wanted to preserve in an acceptable political outlook.

Despite her sometimes sarcastic and biting tone, it is with no delight that Weil makes her trenchant criticisms of orthodox Marxism. There is no polemical scoring of points, nor an attempt to undermine a rival political tendency with a view to gaining ascendancy for one's own. For with Weil's rejection of orthodox Marxism was jettisoned any assurance of the form that political action should take; any reason to think that the current workers' and political organizations were heading in an appropriate direction; and, most profoundly, any reason to hope that organized political efforts of any sort would result in the abolition or even the significant mitigation of oppression. Weil was interested only in the plain truth of the current situation in the hopes that at least the removal of illusion would clear the air for a new form of political thinking—and ultimately of acting—that could genuinely address the problem of social oppression.

3   Work relations in the Soviet Union

Weil saw Marx, primarily in volume 1 of *Capital*, as having powerfully and accurately articulated the nature of workers' oppression. She quotes approvingly:

> In the factory there exists a mechanism independent of the workers which incorporates them as living cogs . . . the separation of the spiritual forces that play a part in production from manual labor, and the transformation of the former into power exercised by capital over labor, attain their fulfilment in big industry founded on mechanization. The detail of the individual destiny of the machine-worker fades into insignificance before the science, the tremendous natural forces and the collective labor which are incorporated into the machines as a whole and constitute with them the employer's power. (*Reflections*, 41)

However, while the oppression of the industrial worker remained a fundamental tenet of all forms of Marxism, the subsequent development of Marxism almost entirely abandoned a focus on the labor process itself. Marx's insights in *Capital* were neither developed nor even significantly incorporated into the major theories produced by the Second or Third Internationals, including those prominent Marxists such as Trotsky and Luxembourg who in other ways departed significantly from the "orthodoxy." As we have seen, emphasis in the theories of both Internationals was placed almost entirely on grasping the laws of capitalist development and working out a philosophy of political struggle with the ultimate aim of assuming state power.

Lenin's (and, in this regard, Trotsky's) lack of concern with the nature of factory organization was reflected in the experience of the Soviet Union, where, it seemed to Weil, the organization and experience of work itself was little different from that of capitalist societies. In fact, Lenin had praised the then most advanced form of oppressive capitalist factory organization—that is, the American—based on the idea of "rationalization" as developed by Frederick Taylor in the early part of the century. As Weil describes it in the later essay "La Rationalisation"

(1937),[4] Taylor studied how the motions necessary to engage in certain work operations could be broken down into distinguishable movements and then timed to see exactly how much time it took one of the quicker workers to carry them out. According to Weil, "His goal was to take away from the workers the possibility of determining for themselves the procedures and the rhythms of their work, and to place back into the hands of management the choice of movement to be carried out in the course of production" (94). Work was then organized in terms of these specific movements and their (supposedly) scientifically determined times, and these were made the standard for all workers in a factory. Weil points out that the assembly line developed by Henry Ford is a perfecting of this method, "where, instead of accomplishing a piece of skilled work, all that needs to be carried out is a certain number of mechanical gestures which are repeated constantly" (97).

Lenin wanted to distinguish between the positive aspects of Taylorism—increased productivity through rationalized labor organization—and its negative effects.[5] Negative were the ill effects on the workers' health and well-being caused by the speed-up involved in increased productivity and the fact that the worker's pay was not increased in proportion to his increase in productivity.[6] Communism would reverse exploitation and oppression of the workers under capitalism by making the economic achievements of rationalization benefit the workers themselves, rather than, as in capitalism, only the owners of capital.

But for Weil the ill effects of labor rationalization are integral to what Lenin thought of as its positive effects. She claimed that the rationalizaton of labor is itself what deprives work of dignity—the worker carries out an entirely repetitive task according to a specification that she had no role in creating, nor even in understanding, and the execution of which draws on no powers of her own judgment. For Weil the ill effects of speed-up on the worker are only one part of this picture. The true well-being of the worker cannot be brought about merely or even primarily through gaining a greater share in the product of her work; it must rather be directly supported by the form of work organization itself.

So, even though Weil's analysis of oppression was developed

principally in application to capitalism, the same organization of work characterized Soviet society as well, as the Bolshevik leaders implicitly acknowledged, and Weil's criticisms apply to Soviet society also. There the workers are still treated as objects in the productive process, subject to the power of machines and of the managers rather than controlling the process themselves. That the managers are part of a bureaucratic ruling stratum rather than extractors of profit for the benefit of the capitalist class—that the state is in that sense "proletarian" rather than "capitalist"—is immaterial from the point of view of the organization of the labor process. Concerning this matter, Weil wrote to her friend Albertine Thévenon,

> Only when I think that the great Bolshevik leaders proposed to create a *free* working class and that doubtless none of them—certainly not Trotsky, and I don't think Lenin either—had ever set foot inside a factory, so that they hadn't the faintest idea of the real conditions which make servitude or freedom for the workers—well, politics seems to me a sinister farce. (*Seventy Letters*, 15)[7]

4 Oppression and the system of production

Weil claims that the replication of capitalist modes of factory organization in the Soviet Union and the absence of concern with workplace oppression within the Third International are connected with the assumption within orthodox Marxism and its Leninist variant of the ultimate primacy of private property in determining the subjection of the worker. Orthodox Marxism focuses on exploitation—the appropriation by the capitalist of some of the real value of the product created by the worker—as the fundamental expression of the workers' subjugation. Exploitation concerns the *products* of labor—the worker is deprived by the capitalist of her fair share of the value yielded by the product. Weil emphasizes a notion of oppression that she finds in Marx's writings but that is overshadowed by exploitation. This notion of oppression encompasses at least potentially a deeper element of human well-being than that involved merely in gaining one's rightful reward for what one has produced. Oppression implies not just that the worker is deprived of a fair share of goods but that his dignity is insulted or crushed, inasmuch as he is treated at an object by the capitalist. Weil's focus on oppression allows her to give a central role in social analysis to the human damage caused by a degrading work environment. The notion of exploitation could not, she thought, encompass this notion of human damage. (The themes of oppression and damage are elaborated in chapter 5.)

At the same time, Weil's emphasis on the oppressive structures of work is not merely (though it is partly) a resurrection of an original Marxist view against its later corruptions in orthodox Marxism. In fact, Weil makes clear that she presses Marx's insights about the implications of the labor process for social analysis and political practice further than Marx himself did. For, while Marx did distinguish bureaucratic or administrative domination in the workplace from ownership of the means of production and while he did give a separate analysis of the former, he nevertheless assumed (though, Weil says, his own insights should have kept him from doing so) a much stronger link between the two than Weil sees; and this link gives the orthodox Marxist position a claim to be genuinely (if incompletely) "Marxist." Marx assumed that private property was somehow at the root of work-process oppression, so that if the former were abolished, the latter would disappear with it. For Weil a clear-headed look at the nature of work organization makes it evident that an oppressive form of work organization is entirely compatible with quite different legal forms of property relations, private as well as collective.

So, if "social relations of production" is taken to refer, as it often does in traditional Marxism, to property and ownership relations with respect to the means of production, then in Weil's view the *organization of work*—specifically, power relations within the workplace—is significantly distinct from the social relations of production and is a *more* important factor than the latter in determining the liberty or oppression of the worker.

A different interpretation of Marx places power relations *within* the workplace in the category of social relations of production. The point of this reading is to encompass the Weil-like insight that it is not only the legal structure of ownership of the means of production but also direct relations of power within the workplace that determine the political and cultural character of a society.[8] But Weil would not find the resulting view illuminating of the fundamental character of a society for it groups together as if they were on the same level of explanatory significance a genuinely fundamental determinant of the character of life in society (i.e., power relations in the workplace) and a much less fundamental factor (ownership relations).

In any case, even this broader notion of social relations of production does not encompass all of what Weil thinks of as necessary to understand social oppression since it fails to include the way in which machines themselves can be forces oppressing the worker, independent (to some extent at least) of the direct ownership relations and power relations in the workplace. If a machine is designed in such a way that operating it deprives the worker of real intellectual control of his own motions, then this situation is oppressive, whether that machine has been instituted by management, owners, or workers themselves.

Moreover, while including work relations within the social relations of production has the effect of bringing relations in the workplace more strongly into the center of social analysis as Weil recommends, nevertheless this approach can also shade into the view that technology itself is neutral with regard to human oppression—that it is only the human power relations, within which technology is employed, that can really oppress. Weil would certainly reject such a view; for her the source of oppression lies in the deprivation of the use of intelligence in the operation of work, and this deprivation can be built into machines themselves, no matter what the power relations.

Weil's emphasis on the causal effect of technology on oppression does not make Weil a technological determinist. She does not see the development of technology as an autonomous process but rather one that is itself (at least partly, though *only* partly) determined by power relations in the society.

Thus Weil says that in a sense Marxists and even to some extent Marx himself have failed to inquire into the precise relation between social oppression and the system of production. While Marxists have been right to see that the economic organization of social life is at the root of social oppression, they have failed to inquire into exactly *which* aspects of economic organization are central to this connection and which are not. In *Reflections* Weil begins such an inquiry herself and forcefully hammers home her view that unless one knows the root causes of oppression, it is impossible to engage in responsible political action.

For Weil the humanly debilitating division of labor in the factory permeates the entire culture of her time. Not only the workers but the technicians, engineers, and even the scientists have as their purview only a small element of the overall endeavor in which they are engaged. No more than the workers do they understand the total process that gives meaning to their work; nor do they possess the knowledge that would allow them to guide their own efforts in accord with the dignity potentially inherent in the human process of work. We live in a culture of specialists, Weil says, and unless the tendency toward greater and greater specialization and social ignorance is halted, the possibilities for a society in which oppression will be mitigated will be dim: "The whole of our civilization is founded on specialization, which implies the enslavement of those who execute to those who co-ordinate; and on such a basis one can only organize and perfect oppression, not lighten it" (*Reflections*, 42).

For Weil a human form of work and of civilization would involve all workers understanding the nature of the technical processes underlying their own work in order that their execution of their work be guided by their own knowledge and intelligence. Thus *Reflections* helps to develop the philosophical underpinning for the view Weil had always held of the importance of workers' education and for her own personal involvement in workers' education projects. But she also thought that not only manual workers but all members of society should have an acquaintance with the basic concepts of modern science so that their understanding of the processes of their work will not be limited to one specialized area.

5 Productive forces

Weil rejects a pillar of historical materialism that we can call the "theory of productive forces." According to this doctrine, the level of technical or productive development of a society is the ultimate determinant of its character, for each form of economic organization or social relations of production (e.g., slavery, feudal property relations, private ownership of the means of production) is suited to and (up to a point) suited to developing its particular level of productive forces. There is an ever-present tendency of productive capacity to increase (to the point where scarcity will have been conquered), and this tendency provides the motor of change from one type of society to another. For when the form of economic organization begins to hinder the productive development of society, a transformation to a new and more productive form of society is imminent. In this scheme capitalism has the historical role of developing and revolutionizing the forces of production to the point where for the first time in history abundance for all is possible and is prevented only by the property relations of capitalism (i.e., private ownership of the means of production).

In criticism of the theory of productive forces, Weil claims first that we can have no assurances that the forces of production are steadily increasing, nor can we foresee the day when scarcity will be conquered. A look at our natural resources (coal, for example) suggests that some may be depleting, others not.

> If the present state of technique is insufficient to liberate the workers, is there at any rate a reasonable hope that an unlimited development lies before it, which would imply an unlimited increase in productivity? This is what everybody assumes both among capitalists and socialists, without the smallest preliminary study of the question; it is enough that the productivity of human effort should have increased in an unheard-of manner for the last three centuries for it to be expected that this increase will continue at the same rate. (*Reflections*, 46)

Weil acknowledges that there may be some general historical tendency for societies to attempt to develop their productive capacity; but this is true only for the most part, and many societies have been content to live within their productive resources for many generations. So whatever tendency there might be is by no means the most fundamental force in history; in particular, there is no assurance that the existing forces of oppression at any given time are not stronger than the impetus behind the productive development. A ruling class can hold onto its power even at the expense of productive stagnation or even decline and has often done so throughout history.[9]

Simone Weil's criticism of historical materialism here must be distinguished from both sides in the debate about whether Marx was a technological determinist. One side says that Marx claimed that the technological level of a society completely determines the nature of the social relations of production (which in turn determine the superstructure consisting of social, cultural, and legal forms in the society), whereas the technology itself is a product in the last analysis of an internal developmental logic. The opposing view says that Marx claimed only that there is a *tendency* of technology to determine social relations, a tendency that allows for some autonomy of the social relations of production (and the superstructure) with respect to the forces of production.[10]

Weil does not directly address this particular question, but she implicitly rejects both alternatives—not only the view that the direction of history and the forms of society are entirely *determined* by technological development but even that a nondetermining *tendency* of this sort exists. For Weil productive development is one thing, and the character of a society, especially in terms of its structures of oppression, is quite another; while these are intertwined, they do not stand in a direct causal relationship with one another. It is true, Weil says, that technology can be a significant source of oppression; but the development of technology is not responsive primarily to its own developmental imperatives but to the values of those who develop and employ it. These values are in turn in good part a product of the power relations in society.

6 Progress

Finding no empirical support for the theory of productive forces, Weil speculates how Marx could have come to hold this view. (On this particular matter her criticisms are aimed not only at orthodox Marxism but specifically at Marx himself as well.) It is partly, she thinks, because Marx assumed that an increase in productive forces automatically brings with it a higher level of human liberty or well-being and that class divisions—and thus class oppression—necessarily reemerge in a situation of scarcity. Contrary to his pretensions to a purely "scientific" view of history, Marx seems to assume that it is *because* productive increase is conducive to human well-being that productive advance constitutes such a strong historical tendency.

> Before even examining the Marxist conception of productive forces, one is struck by the mythological character it presents in all socialist literature, where it is assumed as a postulate. Marx never explains why productive forces should tend to increase; by accepting without proof this mysterious tendency, he allies himself not with Darwin as he liked to think, but with Lamarck. . . . why is it that, when social institutions are in opposition to the development of productive forces, victory should necessarily belong beforehand to the latter rather than the former? Marx evidently does not assume that men consciously transform their social conditions in order to improve their economic conditions. . . . he . . . implicitly assumes that productive forces possess a secret virtue enabling them to overcome obstacles. (*Reflections*, 44)

Weil tries to understand how Marx could have held to a theory so devoid of foundation, and finds an important source in an unacknowledged faith in *progress*. This assumption of progress in history is drawn by Marx from Hegel and is shared by nineteenth century thinkers generally, but is rooted ultimately in the Enlightenment. In contrast to the Enlightenment thinkers, however, Marx did not see the progress of history as a linear development. For him every productive advance carried with it its dark underside, its human cost; while capital revolutionized the instruments of production, it also involves the most intense form of exploitation and oppression in history. Progress has thus always involved an ambiguity. Nevertheless, says Weil, Marx's (and Hegel's) less linear, more dialectical understanding of the process of history still involves a kind of faith that ultimately historical development is going in a humanly positive direction. This is what allows Marx to think both that productive advance will continue and, more importantly that productive advance conduces ultimately to human well-being. Weil suggests that "we must remember the Hegelian origins of Marxist thought. Hegel believed in a hidden mind at work in the universe, and that the history of the world is simply the history of this world mind, which, as in the case of everything spiritual, tends indefinitely toward perfection" (*Reflections* 44).

Marx claimed to have adopted the Hegelian idea of a historical dialectic but to have shunned the notion of a mental or spiritual agency in favor of a purely "material" explanation of historical movement. However, Simone Weil claims, Marx did not succeed in dispensing with "spiritual" explanations or with the attribution a kind of spiritual agency to history:

> Marx claimed to "put back on its feet" the Hegelian dialectic, which he accused of being "upside down," by substituting matter for mind as the motive power of history; but by an extraordinary paradox he conceived history, starting from this rectification, as though he attributed to matter what is of the very essence of mind—an unceasing aspiration toward the best. (44)[11]

It is not only a failure to break with a Hegelian-Enlightenment belief in progress that Weil sees in Marx, but a particularly nineteenth century or bourgeois form of this belief. It was the nineteenth century capitalists in particular who identified human progress with productive progress. For them production became a kind of religion "in whose name generations of industrial employers have ground down the laboring masses without the slightest qualm" (45). According to Weil, this religion of productive forces, which has developed so strongly in the United States, is ironically present as well in the (then) current Soviet regime, for whom the increase in productivity has become a mania for which many lives have been sacrificed. Thus, in Weil's view, for all Marx's hatred of capitalism and his eloquent testimony to its vicious stultification of humanity, his theory of productive forces is partly in thrall to capitalist modes of thought. "That is why," she says, "whatever may be the insult inflicted on

Marx's memory by the cult which the Russian oppressors of our time entertain for him, it is not altogether undeserved" (45).

In contrast to what she sees in Marx, for Weil there is no historical tendency whatever toward human progress and thus no assurance that the cause of the mass of oppressed persons will be advanced or even tends to be supported by historical forces. Tendencies of the masses, even when inspired by a genuine assertion of their own humanity, often fail to support genuinely humane change.[12] "The idea of progress is indispensable for whoever seeks to design the future in advance," Weil notes, "but it can only lead the mind astray when it is the past that is being studied" (100). Thus for Weil the notion of progress ought to play a *moral* but not a *historical* role in political action.

7 Scarcity

In orthodox Marxism the conquest of scarcity plays a crucial role in the ending of oppression. It is only in a context of relative abundance that a nonoppressive, or classless, society can exist. In a condition of scarcity an attempt at a classless society would bring about stagnation and decline in material production, and class distinctions would in any case reemerge.[13]

For Weil scarcity has little to do with oppression. Oppressive class divisions can come about in a situation of relative abundance as well as one of relative scarcity. The bourgeoisie does not retain power only or even primarily as a way of ensuring its own disproportionate (in comparison to the proletariat) share of scarce goods. To think it does is to assume that capitalists are moved primarily by material self-interest; but this is not so. As Weil says, "The common run of moralists complain that man is moved by his private interest: would to heaven it were so! Private interest is a self-centered principle of action, but at the same time restricted, reasonable, and incapable of giving rise to unlimited evil" (*Reflections*, 68–69). Rather there is a drive to seek and retain power for its own sake. This drive can make use of the struggle over scarce goods, but it occurs in all social contexts that allow for it—the power of the military officer over the soldier, the manager over the worker, the official over the underling, the ruler over the ruled.[14] And in Weil's view, "Once society is divided up into men who command and men who execute, the whole of social life is governed by the struggle for power, and the struggle for subsistence only enters in as one factor, indispensable to be sure, of the former" (71). Thus Marxists are wrong to hope that once nature is tamed and scarcity conquered, class divisions will disappear or even to hope that their foundations will have become significantly weakened. It is power itself—not scarcity—that lies at the foundation of class oppression, in the Soviet Union as well as under capitalism. (The issue of power in Simone Weil's thought is explored in chapter 7.)

At the same time, Weil's view that scarcity is not determinative of oppression holds out the possibility of creating a less oppressive society *prior* to the conquest of scarcity. Just as the forces of oppression may be stronger than any tendency toward productive advance, so the impulse to liberty may be also. And a society of scarcity can have more freedom than a society of abundance. Drawing on her experience with the Breton fishermen, Weil even says explicitly that a fisherman battling the natural elements with primitive resources is more free than the worker on the assembly line, provided only that he understand the forces ranged against him and guide his action by his understanding.

This demotion of the importance of the conquest of scarcity does not mean, however, that Weil takes as a political goal a pre-industrial primitive utopia. She understands clearly that such an era can not be recovered; and she is concerned throughout this early period of her life not to jettison the level of productivity, nor the material benefits of scale, coordination, and (some degree of) specialization attendant on the factory system.[15] In this way Weil agrees with Marx that socialized production is an accomplishment of capitalism not to be given up. The Breton fisherman does not exemplify the *ideal* of liberty; this role is played, for Weil, by the skilled factory worker of the early capitalist era, before the rationalization of labor had taken hold of capitalism.

Nevertheless, much more than Marx does, Weil sees in pre-industrial forms of work organization some lessons for the present. She advocates a strongly decentralized economy, which, while making use of factories, would keep their size to a level compatible with the individual worker's ability to comprehend the entire process of which his task is a part and to guide his work by this understanding. (Here the influence of anarcho-syndicalism on Weil is evident.) Moreover, while she would not give up the greater productivity achieved by capitalism, neither does Weil see any value in its *maximization*. Productivity must always be contained and limited by the value of dignity in work.

Weil sees in Marxism a generally only implicit but nevertheless definite view of the nature of freedom, one reflected in the historical significance given to the struggle to overcome material scarcity. Somewhat sarcastically, she expresses the view this way:

> the further development of [modern] technique [once freed from capitalist forms of economy] must lighten more and more, day by day, the burden of material necessity, and as an immediate consequence that of social constraint, until humanity reaches at last a paradisal state in which the most abundant production would be at the cost of a trifling expenditure of effort and the ancient curse of work would be lifted. (43)

The implied notion of freedom is that freedom consists in the absence of obstacles to the satisfaction of desire. It consists in being bounded by "necessity" as little as possible.

In response to this view of freedom, Weil says first that it is an illusion to think that scarcity could ever be conquered—that the press of necessity could ever be done away with—to the extent that she sees implied in the Marxist view. For her, "No technique will ever relieve men of the necessity of continually adapting, by the sweat of their brow, the mechanical equipment they use" (52); "It is solely the frenzy produced by the speed of technical progress that has brought about the mad idea that work might one day become unnecessary" (54). More important, not only is it not possible for scarcity to be overcome, it is also not at all desirable. The noblest activity of humanity is precisely labor— that is, coming to grips by means of one's intelligence and body with the necessities of social existence. The image of the truly free person is more the machine tool operator figuring out how to form a particular piece of metal necessary for the construction of a building than the person unconstrained by work who can spend his every moment pursuing whatever desires happen to come upon him. Weil asserts:

> True liberty is not defined by a relationship between desire and its satisfaction but by a relationship between thought and action; the absolutely free man would be he whose every action proceeded from a preliminary judgment concerning the end which he set himself and the sequence of means suitable for attaining that end. (85)

She adds further that "There is no self-mastery without discipline, and there is no other source of discipline for man than the effort demanded in overcoming external obstacles" (84).[16]

(Simone Weil's own view of liberty is discussed in much greater detail in chapter 4.)

It might be thought that in light of Marx's *1844 Manuscripts* (which Weil appears not to have read at the time of writing *Reflections*) these criticisms of Marx are entirely misplaced, since in Marx's early writings there is no suggestion of a paradise in which people have been freed from work. Rather, Marx sees free and creative work as the proper expression of humans' species-being.

The existence of these early writings of Marx would not in any event obviate Weil's criticism of streams of thought within *Capital* on which orthodox Marxists drew, for they also essentially ignored Marx's early writings. There is certainly some kinship between Weil's views of work and Marx's early views, a kinship seemingly acknowledged by Weil in her late essay "Is There a Marxist Doctrine?" (1943). Both Weil and Marx saw labor as the central activity of human life and a source of humanity's dignity.

Yet even in these early writings Marx conceived of the kind of work capable of providing a means of self-expression as taking place outside the realm of necessity. Work in service of producing mere necessities of physical existence (e.g., food, clothing, shelter) is work that is unfree and cannot involve this creative self-expression. In this way the view of free work in *1844 Manuscripts* and that in *Capital*, though differing in what is emphasized, are not really at odds with one another; and both are quite distinct from Weil's views. For the point at issue here is not whether the realm of necessity could ever actually be abolished but Marx's view that truly "free" labor can take place only *outside* that realm. It is this view of freedom, expressed in both his early and late works, that Weil decisively rejects. It is work that in the appropriate way comes to grips with the necessities of life that, for Weil, is truly free.

In rejecting Marx's and orthodox Marxism's view of the relation between work and necessity, Weil also rejects the view, developed in Marx's early writings but arguably presupposed in *Capital*, that work is fundamentally (or ought to be) a means of human or individual self-expression. For Weil the realm of work is not one of realizing a diversity of individual or human capacities but of facing the necessities of production through coordinating body and mind in a way consonant with human dignity. (Weil's view of work is more fully explored in chapter 6.)

8   The proletariat as revolutionary agent

For orthodox Marxism the proletariat is the agent of social change and indeed of revolutionary change. It has, in a Marxian phrase often used by Trotsky, a "world-historical mission" to bring about a socialist society. Capitalism produces the circumstances that enable the proletariat to be formed into a revolutionary agent. In contrast to the more individualized mode of cottage industry or peasantry, the social nature of production makes the interdependence of persons more visible and lays to rest any fantasy of the self-contained individual. Socialized production accustoms the proletariat to collective forms of organization and discipline, readying it for the political organization needed for revolutionary activity. In depriving workers of their traditional, distinctive skills through the rationalization of labor, capitalism breaks down distinctions among workers, distinctions that have been a hindrance to different types of workers making common cause. Capitalism thus creates a proletariat sharing an increasingly manifest common condition, thereby facilitating a greater sense of proletarian solidarity. Finally, the gap between the life conditions of the proletariat and of the bourgeoisie continues to increase, providing a greater motivation for the proletariat to redress this inequality.[17]

Lenin supplements this general picture with an account of how factory organization specifically contributes to this revolutionary development of the proletariat.

> For the factory, which seems only a bogey to some, represents that highest form of capitalist co-operation which has united and disciplined the proletariat, taught it to organize, and placed it at the head of all other sections of the toiling and exploited population. And Marxism . . . is teaching unstable intellectuals to distinguish between the factory as a means of exploitation . . . and the factory as a means of organization (discipline based on collective work).[18]

For Lenin capitalism produces only trade union consciousness— that is, a sense of shared interests in opposition to the bourgeoisie and a need to organize to defend those interests. But it does not produce a revolutionary consciousness—a consciousness of an entirely new form of society based not on private property but on collective ownership. That revolutionary consciousness has to be brought to the workers from outside by a Marxist workers' organization (such as a Communist party is meant to be). But the conditions of their lives will make the workers receptive to this revolutionary outlook.

In "Prospects" Weil had reluctantly moved toward abandoning the notion that the proletariat as a class could be seen as a revolutionary agent. While she had come to think that skilled workmen were "the only ones capable of of feeling themselves ready to take over one day the responsibility for the whole of social and economic life" (21), she saw such skilled workers becoming a decreasing proportion of the working class as capitalism progressively deprived workers of traditional skills. Moreover, she had voiced her continuing worries about workers' organizations in general. Perhaps drawing on the anarcho-syndicalist suspicion of authority and of political organization generally, Weil had come to feel that there is a dynamic inherent in groups struggling against capitalism that seems "almost automatically" to lead to the "secreting" of an "administrative apparatus which, sooner or later, becomes oppressive" (22). The requirements of effective action in a complex society seem to carry "into the very heart of the working class movement 'the degrading division of labor into manual and intellectual' " (22). In "Prospects" this problem is posed without any clear sense of a solution, though not without hope that one could be found. But that essay heralds a shift in her thinking about the agents of social change—toward individuals and away from organizations.

> The working class still contains, scattered here and there, to a large extent outside organized labor, an elite of workers, inspired by that force of mind and spirit that is found only among the proletariat, ready, if need be, to devote themselves wholeheartedly, with the conscientiousness that a good workman puts into his work, to the building of a rational society. (23)

By the time Simone Weil came to write *Reflections*, her rejection of the proletariat as a revolutionary agent and of the notion of a revolutionary worker's organization had become firmer. She probes deeper into the Marxist view of revolutionary agency, and there finds a contradiction that seems to her to undermine the Marxist claim to a coherent view of revolutionary agency. Marx, she says, analyzed acutely the degradation and fragmentation of the worker under capitalism—how workers have been deprived of the use of their own intelligence and initiative in work, how they have become passive instruments in the hands of management and owner, and even machine. Yet the agents of revolution are supposed to be persons who will usher in and be the masters or citizens of a social order based on liberty, equality, cooperation, and self-direction in workplace and society. To do so, they will need to have qualities of mind and character capable of sustaining such an order, qualities of which the workers whom Marx describes have been dispossessed. It seems then that on Marx's own view capitalism has made of the workers a group deprived of the qualities necessary to function as revolutionary agents bringing about the sort of society that Marx envisions.[19]

Weil's argument here depends on taking seriously a psychological dimension of political and social organization that Marx merely suggests and that is all but lost in orthodox Marxism. Oppression causes a certain kind of psychological damage to the worker. (This theme is further explored in chapters 5 and 6.) It undermines the worker's sense of dignity and ability and confidence to direct his or her own actions and even to cooperate with others. At the same time the social organization of communism is a form of social life that requires a certain kind or range of psychological qualities in its members in order to maintain itself. Weil implies that communism cannot be merely an external structure or institutional form that by itself ensures liberty and equality for all participants. When Weil speaks of the skilled worker as manifesting in his work qualities of judgment, autonomy, and cooperation, she is pointing toward the psychological qualities essential to a nonoppressive social order. Workers morally and psychologically damaged by oppressive work do not possess these sorts of qualities.

Attention to this moral and psychological dimension can help us to see why Weil rejects the Marxist picture of how capitalism helps to develop the proletariat into a revolutionary class. (Weil does not address this argument directly; in fact, she says that aside from the theory of productive forces and the increasing monopolization and centralization of economic life, Marx gives no account of how capitalism's development leads toward socialism. ["On the Contradictions of Marxism," 151] But she does provide the material for a response to the more detailed Leninist and Marxist picture of revolutionary development.)

Regarding Lenin's comments about the factory being a school of discipline, Simone Weil would surely agree with Rosa Luxembourg when she replied to Lenin:

> It is nothing but an incorrect use of the word when at one time one designates as "discipline" two so opposed concepts as the absence of thought and will in a mass of flesh with many arms and legs moving mechanically, and the voluntary coordination of conscious political acts by a social stratum.[20]

While Weil agrees with Lenin that the workers do not "naturally" develop a revolutionary consciousness, she would not agree that such a consciousness is the kind of thing that could be given to workers from the outside by providing them with an intellectual understanding of their condition and of the necessity for socialism. For one thing, Weil rejects the particular intellectual understanding of the historical role of the proletariat given in Lenin's and Marx's revolutionary theory. But the more relevant point here is that certain qualities of character and intellect are needed to bring about and sustain a radical transformation of society; these qualities cannot be provided through intellectual knowledge alone to persons whose work situation systematically undermines the psychic basis of those qualities.[21]

9 Simone Weil and the sit-ins of 1936

Thus, while a common work site and common conditions might make some kinds of worker organizing easier, these are far from sufficient, Weil thought, for the sort of revolutionary organization necessary for a genuine social transformation,[22] as her response to the factory sit-in strikes of 1936 illustrates. These occupations of factories by workers were a spontaneous reaction to hopes raised by the election in France of a leftist Popular Front government, headed by Léon Blum in the spring of 1936. The occupations had a revolutionary as well as festive atmosphere, with workers bringing their families into the factories and for the moment appropriating their workplaces as belonging to themselves. These strikes, which at their height involved millions of workers, resulted in negotiations with employers that gave the workers a forty-hour week, the right to collective bargaining, wage increases, and two weeks paid vacation.

Simone Weil journeyed to Paris during this period to visit several factories, especially the Renault factory where she had worked in 1935. She was elated by the sit-ins and expressed "feelings of unspeakable joy and relief this splendid campaign has given me" (*Seventy Letters*, 52, letter to Monsieur Bernard, a factory manager). For her,

> June 1936 provided a moving example of the spontaneity which one imagined had been wiped out, in France, in the blood of the Commune. A tremendous, ungovernable outburst, springing from the very bowels of the masses,

suddenly loosened the vise of social constraint, made the
atmosphere at last breathable, changed opinions in all
minds, and caused things that six months earlier had been
looked upon as scandalous to be accepted as self-evident.
Thanks to the incomparable power of persuasion possessed
by force, millions of men made it clear—and in the first
place to themselves—that they had a share in the sacred
rights of humanity. ("Critical Examination of the Ideas of
Revolution and Progress," 137)

Yet while Weil lauded this spontaneous and self-generated
assertion of dignity and the forcing of reforms that were a
product of this self-assertion, she thought that such political
activity had no chance of truly transforming society in the
direction of giving workers control of the economic institutions of
society. There could be no dispensing with the authority relation
between managers and workers, for "[on] the one hand the
managers should give orders; but on the other hand the
subordinates ought not to feel themselves delivered body and
soul to an arbitrary domination" (*Seventy Letters*, 60, letter to
Detoeuf, manager of several electrical companies). In this letter,
Weil details further what she would see as reforms that would
truly support the dignity of the workers, while rejecting what she
regarded as the impossible dream of workers under capitalism
coming to be the masters of a new social order. She encouraged
Detoeuf to institute and provide accommodation for study groups
on technical, social, and economic issues and to provide for these
groups to call in the factory's technicians and the technicians and
economists of trade unions. Elsewhere she proposes that the
workers' representatives have access to the factory's account
books. All these suggested reforms are directed by Weil's ideal of
dignified labor—that workers come to understand the nature of
their work and the reasons for performing their particular tasks;
that workers are assured that these tasks are not arbitrary but
correspond to necessities of production; and that they be able to
use their knowledge to guide the execution of their work tasks.
While Weil did not see such reforms as revolutionary—or as
involving or even working toward organs of workers' power—for
her they did present a radical challenge to management's

prerogative to disregard the workers' dignity in the design and organization of work.[23]

Taken together with her rejection of history as fundamentally progressive, Weil's rejection of the proletariat as a revolutionary agent is part of her rejection, first articulated in "Prospects," of the notion that any particular social group can be regarded as having an inherent tendency toward progressive change. There is no "historical mission of the proletariat." But the absence of historical guarantees should not, she thinks, affect one's political commitments to the plight of the oppressed. It is right that political activity should be focused on the condition of the proletariat; but this is because it is the most oppressed group in society and because the dignity of labor must be affirmed in order for civilization to embody its own highest values. It is not because the proletariat has any world-historical mission. The commitment to the cause of the oppressed must be a firmly moral, rather than historical, one. "The enlightened goodwill of men acting in an individual capacity is the only possible principle of social progress" (*Reflections*, 60).

While Simone Weil's criticism of the Marxian notion of revolutionary agency depends on taking seriously the psychological dimension of oppression and while she saw Marx's own analysis of the separation of mental and manual labor as providing the framework for understanding that moral psychology, nevertheless in *Reflections* Weil explores the nature of this moral and psychological dimension only very minimally. She does not much examine how the different elements of oppression in the workplace affect the mind and spirit (or character) of the worker. She does not bring the notion of liberty as individually generated thought that guides action into a clear relationship with the more social connotation of the notion of oppression; nor does she examine the nature of the human damage wrought by oppression.

A deeper understanding of the moral psychology of work and oppression was one of the important contributions that Simone Weil's factory work experience in 1934 and 1935 made to her outlook on the world. This contribution will be discussed below, in Chapters 5 and 6. We will see that that later understanding enriched, without actually contradicting, the ideas of *Reflections*. We will also see that the factory work ultimately led Weil away from the rationalist and Kantian emphasis on individual, self-determined thought as the highest expression of human dignity.

10 Class struggle

The idea of the proletariat as revolutionary agent is connected with the more general idea in Marx that class struggle is a fundamental driving force in history. Slaves against masters, serfs against lords, bourgeoisie against aristocracy, proletariat against bourgeoisie, and, more generally, the dominated against their dominators—these struggles, according to Marxism, pervade human history and provide the mode of change from one form of society to another.

In *Reflections* there is very little discussion of the notion of class or class struggle. Weil does not devote the attention to criticizing the Marxist view of class struggle that she gives to the issues of scarcity, progress, and revolution in the Marxian scheme. But some remarks in a later essay help fill out the picture of Weil's relationship to Marxism; and the notion of class struggle—in the way that Weil herself comes to understand it—is in fact an important part of her own view of politics.

In her final essay on Marxism, "Is There a Marxist Doctrine?" written in the last year of her life, Weil queries the relationship between class struggle and the development of productive forces. Each, she says, is seen by Marx as "the sole principle of historical development" (188), so that the struggle of subordinate against dominant classes is supposed somehow to come to the same thing as the struggle of the forces of production to expand against resistance from the relations of producton; yet, Weil says, Marx does not show how one of these can be reduced to the other.[24] It might be thought that for Marxism the link could be seen in the following way: Classes are defined by position in the productive process, giving members of classes common material interests opposed to those of other classes; in struggling against the dominant class to advance their own interests, the subordinate class (say, the proletariat) will also be combating those productive relations that serve to restrain the development of the productive forces and that keep the dominant class in their position of power.

But even if a struggle for greater material benefit were a driving force behind class struggle, this argument would not work, for the oppressed group's striving for greater material benefit would not by itself lead to an expansion of productive forces; it might simply lead to that group's acquiring or striving to acquire a greater share of a fixed output. In addition, even if one supposed that the oppressed group did develop the forces of production, whether consciously or not, we have seen that Weil rejects the supposition that the impetus behind the development of the forces of production is fundamental and necessarily capable of undermining or even counteracting power relations in the productive process.

But most important, Weil does not see proletarian "interest" as primarily a material one but a moral one: the need for dignity. Weil shares with Marx the view that in engaging in a struggle to advance one's fundamental interests (i.e., for Weil, dignity; for Marxism, a rightful share of the value of the product), the proletariat is not necessarily consciously aware of what it is doing. But this means that for Weil the struggle, whether conscious or unwitting, to assert and advance class interests would not necessarily have any particular impact on the development of productive forces; and the converse is true as well.

Yet, severed from any suggestion that such a struggle primarily concerns the disposition of the fruits of production, Weil does agree with Marx that the struggle of dominated groups for dignity is a permanent feature of social life. She says that "Marx was right in regarding the love of liberty and the love of domination as the two motive-springs which keep social life in a permanent state of unrest" ("Is There a Marxist Doctrine?" 189).

Yet, despite the shared emphasis on class struggle, Weil recasts that concept so that it plays a very different role in Marxist thought and in her own. For Weil the notion is not a historically dynamic one; although a permanent feature of social life and one making for social instability, class struggle is not a source of historical change, of movement from one form of society to another. For Weil, what makes the need for this struggle a permanent one is precisely what she came to see (especially after *Reflections*) as the necessity for command and authority in society, coupled with the permanent tendency of the authorities to oppress those under their command. Taken together, it follows that liberty and dignity can never be protected in a stable and permanent way by the institutions of society. Rather, the oppressed must continually struggle to reassert this dignity and liberty. This is the upshot of Weil's analysis of the 1936 sit-ins: that it was good and necessary for the workers to assert and to compel recognition of their dignity, but that the concessions won by them were only a temporary and fragile protection of that dignity.

Significantly, though Weil strongly emphasized the workplace as the central area of workers' lives and the need for redesign of machines and technology and restructuring of relations in the workplace to support dignity and though she saw the need for constant struggle by the oppressed, nevertheless she did not link these two ideas. She did not see changes in the workplace coming about *by way of* workers' initiative. (This may be partly because she saw the workers' organizations of the time as too bankrupt in their political focus to be realistic sources of such initiatives.) While workers asserted their dignity, it was as if it was nevertheless up to management to figure out how to make changes in the structure of work which would support this dignity.[25] This perspective is in fact consistent with the moral psychology of the proletariat implicit in Weil's critique of the Marxist view of revolutionary agency. For if the proletariat has been morally damaged by its oppression under capitalism while yet retaining a permanent desire for liberty and dignity, its assertions of that desire—such as in the sit-ins—will be less likely to take the direction of focused and planned action toward concrete changes in social structures.

3
Simone Weil on Marxism: revolution and materialism

On two issues central to Marxian theory and practice—revolution and materialism—Simone Weil's views underwent important changes in the course of her life. In considering them, it is necessary to look at the later Christian essays on Marxism as well as at *Reflections*.

1 Critique of "Revolution"

Marxism is a theory of revolution. Its view of history aims to support the belief that only under an entirely different social order can the oppression found under capitalism be eliminated and that such an order is itself on history's agenda. Revolution is understood to consist on the economic level in the expanding forces of production breaking the fetters of the previous form of social or property relations that had come to hold back their development and on the social level in the coming to power of a social group subordinated in the previous form of society. Thus, in the one case—the French Revolution—that provided the model through which the general Marxian schema of revolution was understood, especially in France, the bourgeoisie, representing the ascending interests and power of capital, led a revolution against the nobility. By analogy, in the coming socialist revolution, the proletariat would overthrow the bourgeoisie. But the world-historical difference between the socialist revolution and all previous revolutions would be that the social systems resulting from the latter were all based on some form of oppression or exploitation, which was necessary for developing the forces of production. According to Marx, such oppression would no longer be necessary after capitalism, and so a proletarian revolution and its resultant social order would have no need for a division of society into classes—that is, into oppressor and oppressed.

Belief in revolution was contrasted with "reformism." During the period of both the Second and Third Internationals, the workers' movement struggled with the issue of "reform versus revolution." How should Marxists regard the struggle for reforms such as universal suffrage, secret ballot, free public education, shorter work day, improved working conditions, and the like, which seemed to benefit the working class, at least in the short run?

Within the Second International, Karl Kautsky defined what became the orthodox position: Rejecting the view of the "revisionists," such as Eduard Bernstein, who believed that socialism can come about gradually through the introduction of reforms secured by means of cooperation between the working class and (sectors of) the bourgeoisie, Kautsky argued that socialism can come about only as a result of class struggle and an overthrow of the bourgeois form of government that would require some degree of violent class struggle. At the same time Kautsky rejected the "left" view, which came to be identified with Lenin and bolshevism, that the role of the Marxist working class party was solely to prepare for violent revolution and that it should not participate in bourgeois political institutions at all. Kautsky argued that the struggle for reforms was itself an integral part of working class struggle, helping to develop working class consciousness and giving the proletariat experience of participating in political life and economic administration. (In effect, in the context of the nonrevolutionary situation in which the German SPD and most of the major Second International affiliates functioned, the practical implications of Kautsky's position placed it much closer to Bernstein's than to Lenin's and, in the last years of the Second International Kautsky was branded a "reformist" and a "renegade" by Lenin.)

In the French political context of the 1930s the Socialist Party (SFIO), an outgrowth of one tendency (led by Jean Jaurès) of the

French branch of the Second International, was essentially a "reformist" party. By contrast, the Communist Party (PCF) was, or regarded itself as, revolutionary.

Throughout the period 1931–1934, while Simone Weil showed no inclination whatever toward the socialists,[1] she became increasingly uneasy about the notion of revolution. In *Reflections* Weil abandons once and for all the Marxist notion of revolution as providing a meaningful role in the practical guidance or theoretical understanding of political activity and sees its continued use in political discourse on the left as having a corrupting and damaging effect on the workers' movement. Her rich and complex criticisms of the notion of revolution as she perceives it operating in the political outlook of the Communists, the syndicalists, and other "revolutionary" parties—as well as in Marx himself—are contained also in the unpublished fragments "Critical Examination of the Ideas of Revolution and Progress," which Weil might have conceived of as a new version of the beginning of *Reflections*, "On the Contradictions of Marxism," written in 1937 or 1938, as well as the later, unfinished essay, "Is There a Marxist Doctrine?".

No doubt Weil has herself in mind—as well as most of the then existing Marxist and non-Marxist workers' groups—when she says:

> Ever since 1789, there has been one magic word which contains within itself all imaginable futures, and is never so full of hope as in desperate situations—that word is "revolution.". . . That is why the first duty the present period imposes on us is to have enough intellectual courage to ask ourselves if the term "revolution" is anything else but a name, if it has any precise content. . . . This question seems impious, in view of all the pure and noble human beings who have sacrificed everything, their lives included, in the service of this word. But only priests can claim to measure the value of an idea by the amount of blood it has caused to shed. (*Reflections*, 38–39)

She adds, "The word 'revolution' is a word for which you kill, for which you die, for which you send the laboring masses to their death, but which does not possess any content" (*Reflections*,

55); and, she comments, "One magic word today seems capable of compensating for all sufferings, resolving all anxieties, avenging the past, curing present ills, summing up all future possibilities: that word is 'revolution'" ("Critical Examination of the Ideas of Revolution and Progress," 134).[2]

In claiming that the notion of revolution is meaningless or lacks content Weil is, in part, noting that different people mean quite different things by it and envision quite different sorts of changes when they think in terms of it. The worker harried by a superior or unable to afford some desired item, the unfortunate shopkeeper, the ruined rentier, the bourgeois adolescent in rebellion against home and school, the engineer offended by the priority given to financial over technological considerations—all may dream of "revolution" but mean very different and even incompatible things by it. Moreover, there is little connection between what people wish for in the name of revolution "and the realities to which it is likely to correspond if the future should actually have a social upheaval in store" ("Critical Examination of the Ideas of Revolution and Progress," 137).

More substantially, however, Weil regards as illusory and meaningless even the more clearly-defined Marxian notion of a wholesale social transformation ushering in a regime of liberty and equality in which the previously oppressed and dominated masses come to hold power. To understand her view, we have at the outset to distinguish two strands within the Marxian notion of revolution. One (which we will call "social revolution") is that of a radical social transformation that constitutes a clean break with the previous social order. The other (which we will call "revolutionary insurrection") is that of a violent social upheaval in which the reins of government are transferred from the current rulers to a previously suppressed group. The Russian Revolution illustrates how in the Marxian scheme both strands are present in that the violent insurrection of 1917 was thought by its supporters to have brought in its wake radical social transformation.

Weil criticizes the presumed link between these two notions of revolution. As suggested in her critique of the Soviet Union, she believes that revolutionary insurrection has nothing to do with genuine radical change (social revolution) and is not properly seen as its precursor. The kinds of changes that can be brought about by a successful revolutionary insurrection leading to a change in the wielders of state power—changes in legal form, property relations, and the like—do not touch the real sources of oppression and dignity, which concern the structure of work and work relationships. The Bolshevik Revolution showed that a violent transfer of state power can preserve oppressive relationships virtually intact, and, conversely, though without developing this point Weil suggests that genuinely radical change can come about without a violent insurrection.

Weil's underlying conviction here is that genuine social change can only come about slowly; regarding the fundamental social character of a society, there can be no "clean break" with the past. Weil criticizes those who cite the French Revolution of 1789 in support of the notion that a revolutionary insurrection can bring about radical transformation. The power of the French nobility had already been almost entirely eroded by time of the revolutionary insurrection of 1789. Their privileges under the old order had ceased to correspond to any genuine social function. If a bloody struggle does appear to replace one system by another, as in the French Revolution, this is because, Weil says, that "struggle is in reality the crowning point of a transformation that is already more than half accomplished, and brings to power a category of men who already more than half possessed that power" (139).

Nor, Weil claims, has the Russian Revolution brought about anything genuinely new. "All it did was to reinforce those powers which were already the real ones under the Tsars—the bureaucracy, the police, the army." Instead, according to her, "What history offers us is the slow transformation of regimes, in which the bloody events to which we give the name "revolutions" play a very secondary role" (*Reflections*, 78). Moreover, Weil cites Marx himself in support of her view:

> Marx's ideas about revolutions can be expressed thus: a revolution takes place at the moment when it is already nearly accomplished; it is when the structure of a society has ceased to correspond to its institutions that these change and are replaced by others which reflect the new structure. In particular, the section of society which the revolution places in power is the same as that which already, before the revolution, although victimized by the prevailing

institutions, in fact played the most active role. ("On the Contradictions of Marxism," 148)[3]

Perhaps she gives a particularly Weilian reading of Marx in this passage, but Weil does pick up on a tension between two strands of thought in Marx. One, exemplified particularly by Lenin, is that it is violent revolution that brings about radical social transformation. The other is that real change takes place through the development within one society of the forces that will characterize the social order that will replace it; overt change toward this new form of society never takes place until those forces are themselves virtually fully developed. This second line of thought is linked to elements of Kautsky's evolutionism, which partially accounts for his opposition to the Bolshevik Revolution; he asserted that Russian bourgeois capitalist society had not fully developed its own potentialities so as to provide the required foundation for a socialist transformation (see chapter 2, note 14) —a point he makes not only about the development of the forces of production but about the social and political institutions of capitalist society as well. The use Weil makes of this second Marxian strand of thought differs from Kautsky's in one very substantial respect; Weil rejects the orthodox Marxist assumption that this gradual change or evolution is necessarily or even tends to be for the better. Her point is that even when that change happens to go in the direction of diminished oppression, this effect has to have been a result of a very long and slow process.

For Weil, then, in a sense there can never really be a "social revolution." What there can perhaps be is genuine radical change but not change representing a clean and sudden break with the current form of a society. Yet Weil makes it clear that there is one kind of radical change, seemingly promised within Marxist thought, that is entirely impossible, whether brought about suddenly or slowly: that is the kind of revolution in which a mass of people who have been oppressed by a social order come to hold power. Such a social order is inconceivable, "for it would be a victory of weakness over force" (*Reflections*, 78). In Weil's view, "It is impossible for the weak to take possession of social power; those who take possession of social power by force always form—even before this operation—a group to which the human masses are subjected" ("Is There a Marxist Doctrine?" 193).

Weil's pessimism about such a "social revolution" is not meant to deny the possibility of a spontaneous mass movement—such as the 1936 sit-ins discussed earlier (Chapter 2)—capable of having some real impact on society. In the fragment "Meditation on Obedience and Liberty" (1937) Weil sees the sit-ins as having constituted a force at least for a time that the powerful could not contain, and she cites Tacitus (describing a military mutiny) in explanation of its nature:

> The principal sign that it was a deep-seated movement,
> impossible to quell, was that they were not scattered about
> or controlled by a few individuals, but flared up as one man,
> fell silent as one man, with such unanimity and constancy
> that one would have thought they were acting upon a word
> of command. (144)

Yet what this movement was not and could not possibly be was *revolutionary* in the Marxian sense of bringing about a radical transformation in power relationships.

> that unanimity which is produced in the heat of a
> quickening and general emotion is incompatible with any
> form of methodical action. Its effect is always to suspend all
> action and arrest the daily course of life. This temporary
> stoppage cannot be prolonged; the course of daily life has to
> be taken up again, the daily tasks have to be performed.
> The mass dissolves once again into individuals, the memory
> of its victory fades, the erstwhile situation, or its equivalent,
> is gradually re-established; and although it may be that in
> the interval there has been a change of masters, it is always
> the same ones who have to obey. (144)

Why radical transformation is not possible, why daily tasks could not be performed within a very different set of power relationships, Weil never fully explains, though the reason is no doubt connected with her view of necessity and her understanding of the inevitability, for example, of some division between those who command and those who obey. Certainly Weil's view also reflects in part her own observations of the failed radical movements of her time, in which she saw reproduced within the internal structure of those movements themselves the same oppressive relationships it was their avowed goal to combat.

In any case, Weil continued to struggle in her own thought to reconcile this pessimistic assessment of social possibilities with her intense concern for the spiritual well-being of the lowliest social strata. This concern is given a specifically Christian understanding in "Is There a Marxist Doctrine?".

> The idea that weakness as such, while remaining weak, can constitute a force, is not a new one. It is the Christian idea itself, and the Cross is the illustration of it. But it has to do with a force of quite a different kind from that wielded by the strong; it is a force that is not of this world, that is supernatural. . . . Marx accepted this contradiction of strength in weakness, without accepting the supernatural which alone renders the contradiction valid. (194–195)

Marx was right, Weil says, to think that a concern for justice can coexist with a social world in which power, not justice, is the determining factor; but he was wrong to think that justice can *itself* be a material force, that the copresence of justice and power consists in a historical development that leads force to undermine itself in favor of justice. For Weil, the coexistence of power and justice is possible only if one sees justice, and the desire for good more generally, as having a purely supernatural source that has no real place in the social world and yet that can have a local and always precarious but nevertheless real effect.

While Weil criticizes Marx for postulating too close a relationship between "the good" (or "justice") and the course of the world, it is nevertheless striking that Weil herself does not allow for the possibility that there is simply no relationship at all between them—that is, that the desire for justice has a completely arbitrary relation to justice's actually coming about in our world. For her, "The very being of man is nothing else but a perpetual straining after an unknown good" ("Is There a Marxist Doctrine?" 173), and this straining after good is a reflection of God's presence in the world.

In this way Weil's later turn to religion can be seen to have an element of reaction to and to be an outgrowth of the failure of the radical political activity in which she had been engaged earlier: The world and one's comrades may have turned out not to provide the link between the desire for justice and its realization, but God does provide that link. "Man cannot bear for more than a moment to be alone in willing the good. He needs an all-powerful ally. If you do not believe in the remote, silent, secret omnipotence of a spirit, there remains only the manifest impotence of matter" ("Is There a Marxist Doctrine?" 173). In this way, though she takes Marx to task for doing the same thing, Weil avoids the total despair of thinking that there is no hope or leverage for justice in this world at all.

2   "Revolution" and the moral character of workers' struggle

Simone Weil's most serious criticism of the notion of revolution, carried through from *Reflections* to all her subsequent writings, is its deleterious moral effect on the workers' political struggle. For orthodox Marxism the historical materialist grounding of revolution in (supposedly) scientifically demonstrable historical tendencies means a dispensing with moral notions in the revolutionary struggle. The workers' cause is on history's agenda; it is not necessary, not useful, and, arguably, not correct, to speak of it as being "right" or "good." Moral ideas will only confuse the struggle, since they are either contaminated by the ideology of the ruling class against whom the workers are struggling, or they remain entirely abstract and not grounded in the material forces that alone can bring about change. Capitalism is not to be condemned *morally* but only *historically*: it is slated for the historical dustbin.

Weil believes almost the reverse of this orthodox Marxist picture of the role of morality in political struggle. For her the true motivational source of political struggle must be the moral ideals that the struggle takes as its goal—justice, liberty, socialism, dignity. Inspiration by moral ideals confers a nobility to the struggle. The idea that workers have a world-historical mission to be the midwives of a new order, to liberate the forces of production, to bring about the beginning of real human history—these notions involve a pernicious grandiosity that diverts from a focus on mitigating the oppression of actually existing workers in their current reality.

For Weil the historical materialist concept of revolution degrades and debases this struggle. The notion that the revolution is being carried on the tide of history encourages a kind of passivity in the worker; this is especially true of the Kautskian strand in orthodox Marxism. According to Weil, the illusions of historical materialism "lead [the workers] to believe that things are going to be easy, that they have a modern god called Progress to push them from behind and a modern providence called History to do the donkey work for them" ("On the Contradictions of Marxism," 155). These beliefs relieve the workers of taking full responsibility for the ideals at which they aim and for determining the path necessary to achieve them. The revolution comes to be thought of "not as a solution to the problems raised at the present time, but as a miracle dispensing one from solving problems" ("Critical Examination of the Ideas of Revolution and Progress," 136).

At the same time that it encourages passivity and irresponsibility, the belief that the larger movement of history supports and ensures the success of the working class struggle imbues the working class movement with a false sense of power. The claims of historical materialism to be "scientific" contribute to this sentiment by infusing into the workers' struggle the prestige of modern science. Weil sees modern science itself as having come to be abstract and mystified, a kind of secular mystery with its own priest/experts, remote from ordinary people and from the ordinary experience it is meant to illuminate. (See chapter 7, section 4.)

> Nothing entitles one to assure the workers that science is on their side. Science is for them, as indeed for everyone today, that mysterious power which has, in a single century, transformed the face of the world through industrial technique; when they are told that science is on their side, they immediately think they possess an unlimited source of power. Nothing of the kind! ("On the Contradictions of Marxism," 154)

(For an account of Weil's view of science, see chapter 6.)

Thus the historical materialist understanding of revolution has morally corrupted the working class movement. That movement must rather seek its inspiration, Weil believes, in "that spirit of revolt which, in the last century, shone with so pure a light in our country" (154), "in what Marx and Marxists have fought against and very foolishly despised: in Proudhon, in the workers' groups of 1848, in the trade-union tradition, in the anarchist spirit" (148).

Yet at the same time that Weil says that the notion of revolution is devoid of meaning and has become a morally and politically pernicious influence, she does not abandon it altogether and sees a political use for a new understanding of it. "Perhaps one can give a meaning to the revolutionary ideal, if not as a possible prospect in view, at any rate as a theoretical limit of feasible social transformations" (*Reflections*, 55). That limit would be the end of social oppression, and Weil, especially in *Reflections* but to some extent later as well, envisions us as being able to inquire rationally into "what is the least oppressive form of social organization for a body of specific objective conditions" (60). We can then go on to determine what specific steps persons can take to bring this about. "Only on this condition," she says, "could political action become something analogous to a form of work, instead of being, as has been the case hitherto, either a game or a branch of magic" (60).

In "On the Contraditions of Marxism," an essay written in the wake of the sit-ins which is on the whole less politically pessimistic than *Reflections*, Weil also articulates a positive conception of the revolutionary, in contrast to the historical materialist conception. This conception is a specifically moral one, grounded in the fundamental concern for the dignity of the oppressed:

> does being a revolutionary mean calling forth by one's
> wishes and helping by one's acts everything which can,
> directly or indirectly, alleviate or lift the weight that presses
> upon the mass of men, break the chains that degrade labor,
> reject the lies by which it is sought to disguise or excuse the
> systematic humiliation of the majority? In that event it is a
> case of an ideal, a judgment of value, something willed, and
> not of an interpretation of human history and of the social
> mechanism. Taken in this sense, the revolutionary spirit is
> as old as oppression itself and will go on for as long, even

longer; for if oppression should disappear, it will have to continue in order to prevent its reappearance. ("On the Contradictions of Marxism," 153)[4]

There is an important difference in emphasis in these two positive conceptions of the revolutionary, though both retain a fundamentally moral character. The one in *Reflections* emphasizes political activity as a rational and methodical endeavor—what work itself should ideally be—directed toward a definite end, one of creating structures that support the dignity of the worker more than do current institutions. This conception depends on a faith that such structures can be found; and while Weil tended to lose confidence in that possibility, especially after her time in the factory, that same faith is never extinguished and continually reappears in her writings.

The second conception of revolution, in "On the Contradictions of Marxism" involves the idea that the struggle against oppression is a never-ending process of asserting, as the workers did in the sit-ins, the human dignity of the powerless. One must, as it were, continually start from scratch precisely because there are no institutional forms in work organization or society that can truly and finally protect dignity and prevent oppression and because those in power have an inherent tendency to trample the human dignity of those below them.

3 Reform and revolution

We saw that political thinking in the Second and Third Internationals and on the left generally was centered on the choice between "reform" and "revolution." Weil's rejection of the current meanings and political uses of "revolution" did not, however, place her in the camp of the "reformists." In this regard her stance toward reformism changed very little from her earlier more "revolutionary" phase, and she was never attracted to the straightforwardly reformist stance of the SFIO.

Essentially, Weil rejects the "reform versus revolution" framework altogether. In her view, reformists are too accepting of the structure and modes of thought of the capitalist society of which they are a part. They fail to see that radical social changes and radically different ways of thinking about social issues are necessary in order to lessen oppression. This remains true even when reformists believe that an evolutionary process will ultimately usher in socialism. For either that goal remains so distant that it has no effect on the reformists' political thinking in their current situation (as was true of Bernstein and to some extent of Kautsky) or the conception of socialism thought to be the outcome of the evolutionary changes is itself too bound up (as the SFIO's was) with capitalist thinking—as, for example, when socialism is conceived primarily in terms of public ownership of the means of production.

On one point, however, Weil agrees with the reformists, and that is what she calls the "principle of the lesser evil" (*Reflections*, 60). That principle says that, if among one's actual political options all are bad but one is less bad than the others, then one should choose the latter. This view contrasts with the anti-reformist thinking of revolutionary Marxism and syndicalism, which, to put it perhaps over-simply, rejects "less evil" political options because they remain too distant from genuinely revolutionary goals and may contribute to dampening the motivation to achieve them. Since Weil rejects as an unrealistic political goal the traditional revolutionary vision of a world free from oppression and since she believes that in many circumstances a small mitigation of oppression might be the most one can hope for, she therefore rejects this revolutionary criticism of the principle of lesser evil.

On the other hand, Weil says that reformists have never made genuine use of "the principle of the lesser evil" themselves. For "as long as the worst and the best have not been defined in terms of a clearly and concretely conceived ideal, and then the precise margin of possibilities determined, we do not know which is the lesser evil" (61). Until we possess a true understanding of oppression, which Marxism has up to now failed to provide, we cannot inquire into the possibilities that any given set of economic and political circumstances provides for its mitigation. Without this the principle of lesser evil merely serves and has served "as a pretext for capitulation" though "this is due not to the cowardice of a few leaders, but to an ignorance unfortunately common to all" (61).

Weil, then, is neither a revolutionary nor a reformist in the traditional senses. But she retains a sense of the moral commitment of the revolutionary and wavers between, or encompasses both, a conception of such commitment as directed to a methodical but ultimately radical transformation of institutions and a never-ending struggle of the subordinate class against those who command them.

4 Materialism

While Simone Weil is deeply critical of *historical* materialism, her evaluation of what she sees as "materialism" itself is much more complex and changes significantly over the course of her life. Throughout all her writings on Marx, from the earliest to the last, she speaks approvingly of materialism as one of the ideas of permanent value in Marx. At the same time she is often highly critical of ideas that she takes to be aspects of materialism.

In her brief 1933 article "On Lenin's Book *Materialism and Empiriocriticism*," Weil draws a contrast, familiar in the history of Marxist thought, between the "vulgar materialism" of Engels and Lenin and a different kind of materialism in Marx. (This vulgar materialism had always been a more influential view in France than, for example, in Germany.) Engels and Lenin's materialism sees mind and humanity generally as being merely a part or product of nature and as knowing nature through passively "reflecting" it. By contrast, Marx "never regards man as being a mere part of nature, but always as being at the same time, owing to the fact that he exercises a free activity, an antagonistic term vis-a-vis nature" (32). In this essay Weil sees Lenin's emphasis on the passivity of mind as connected with the passive and powerless condition into which the Soviet Union has placed workers. According to Weil, Marx's materialism (but not Lenin's) both involves the worker's necessarily active role in knowing and appropriating the world and provides the conception of the proletarian revolution as returning the worker to his active role as subject rather than object in work. (This line of thought continues Weil's linking of work with traditional epistemological concerns. See Chapter 1.)

Weil's concern with the ontological and epistemological aspects of materialism disappears in *Reflections*, where materialism's more directly social aspect is brought to the fore. Materialism in the sense in which Weil continues to approve of it and to regard it as Marxist becomes the view that "social existence is determined by the relations between man and nature established by production" (*Reflections*, 71). The fundamental character of social life in any given society is a product of the forms of production in that society, geared toward the mastery of nature in order to serve humanity's needs.

The significance of this abstractly stated doctrine for Weil lies in the approach it provides to understanding social change—in particular, change leading to the ending or lessening or oppression. For Weil as for Marx, this notion of materialism was meant to contrast with an "idealist" or purely "moral" understanding of oppression and change. According to Weil, prior to Marx oppression and exploitation tended to be seen as the illegitimate usurpation of power or privilege by one group to dominate or exploit another group. Understanding oppression solely in these moral terms leads to thinking that oppression can be eliminated merely through the force of (moral) ideas or by its direct suppression: "either by simply expressing a radical disapproval of it, or else by armed force placed at the service of justice" (57).[5]

But Weil agrees with Marx that such an understanding of oppression is inadequate, as has been shown repeatedly throughout history and strikingly in the French Revolution. There, in the name of the moral ideals of justice, equality, and liberty the proletariat helped the bourgeoisie to wrest power from the aristocracy, only to find that one set of oppressors (the aristocracy) had merely been replaced by another (the bourgeoisie). The mere replacement of one set of oppressors by another is bound to happen as long as society and oppression are not understood in a materialist fashion—that is, until oppression is seen not as a mere usurpation but as embedded in the very fabric of social existence constituting a particular form of society.

Marx saw oppression in this way by viewing it, in Weil's words, as the "organ of a social function" (57); that social function was, for Marx, the development of the means of production. So, to simplify a bit, for Marx the great productivity characteristic of capitalism is the "function," the "organ" of which is the oppression of workers from whom that productivity is exacted by managers and owners of capital.

In *Reflections* Weil agrees with Marx that oppression cannot be ended until the conditions that ground it in social existence are changed. The oppression of boss over worker is not a matter of evil bosses mistreating workers but lies in the very structure of the relationship of boss and worker in a capitalist system, and the function that relationship plays in the development of the productive forces. Oppression can only be ended if that structure is changed. The fact that a social system is evil or oppressive gives us by itself no reason to think that it will disappear. Real change can come about only through a material transformation of the structure which underlies it.

Weil's attack here on a moralistic understanding of social change (see note 5) and her agreement with what she understands to be Marx's views on this point does not contradict her fundamental sense that political action must be animated by moral concerns rather than by a sense of historical mission or inevitable success. For her conception in *Reflections* is that a moral concern for the dignity and well-being of the worker should lead the workers' movement and its allies to inquire into the actual material structures and conditions (that is, the true source) of oppression in the society. Such an inquiry can then guide the movement to direct its energies against the real conditions making for oppression rather than relying on the illusion that what is morally right will triumph simply by providing the inspiration for action (and perhaps supported by armed might or state power). The political activity emerging from this materialistic understanding is still, for Weil, to be motivated by the moral ideals of justice and dignity; for only then can the results of that activity hope to embody the affirmation of dignity that is its ultimate goal. But its proximate goal is to undermine the material conditions making for oppression.

Thus Weil's view avoids the moralistic conception that morality *by itself* constitutes a force for change, but it also eschews the orthodox Marxist view that the workers' movement can dispense with morality as an animating force by looking to history to underwrite its cause. Thus Weil's view of politics in

Reflections fuses a direct moral concern with a materialistic understanding of social change.

Yet while Weil accepts a materialistic approach to oppression and social change, she disagrees with the Marxist view of the specific ultimate material causes of oppression. For Marx and even more so for orthodox Marxism the root of oppression lies in the property relations of society, which themselves are grounded in the more fundamental fact of the productive forces of a society; this belief is central to historical materialism, and Weil decisively rejects it. She does not herself offer a rival theory of the ultimate institutional or structural sources of oppression except to suppose that its domain is work relationships; it is the inquiry into precisely those sources that *Reflections* takes as a central political task of the present. (At the same time, in *Reflections* Weil begins to suggest the view she develops later that power or force is fundamentally at the root of oppression; but this citation of power is precisely *not* a structural or institutional explanation of oppression.)

5 "Materialism" in the Christian essays

Thus in *Reflections* Weil thinks materialism true and profound if it means an understanding of society and of oppression in terms of power relations embodied in the actual institutions of society but false if it means that these power relations are seen as *deriving* from the forces of production in society and connected with the struggle to overcome scarcity. But this materialist conception of oppression and of action to combat it begins progressively to disappear after *Reflections* though there are signs of this change within that work itself.

Before detailing the changes in Weil's thought from *Reflections* to the late Christian essays, it is necessary to say something of Weil's turn toward Christianity in the late 1930s. In 1935, while physically exhausted and profoundly demoralized from her seven months of factory work (described below, in chapters 5 and 6), Weil visited a small village in Portugal. Viewing a religious procession of fishermen's wives, she had what she later called the first of "three contacts with Christianity that have really counted" ("Spiritual Autobiography," 15). In 1937, in a chapel in Assisi where St. Francis used to pray, Weil says, "something stronger than I was compelled me for the first time in my life to go down on my knees" (15). A year later, during Holy Week services at a Benedictine Abbey famous for its Gregorian chant, Weil says, "the thought of the Passion of Christ entered into my being once and for all" (15).

In the late 1930s Weil continued to move in a more spiritual and religious direction, and she studied Hindu as well as Christian religious texts. Until the end of her life she struggled with the issue of receiving baptism and joining the Catholic Church. Her writings and thinking became distinctly Christian, and her political concerns were viewed through her particular version of Christianity. The important writings on Marxism in the 1940s—"Is There a Marxist Doctrine?" and several passages on Marxism in *The Need For Roots*—are grounded in her Christianity, signs of which begin to appear in the fragmentary political essays of 1937 and 1938, such as "Meditation on Obedience and Liberty".

Weil's Christian outlook shaped her increasing belief in the importance of power to an understanding of society and its relation to Weil's understanding of materialism. In *Reflections* she had already begun to lose the sense that *institutions* of power are in any significant sense changeable. Weil came increasingly to see power as such a deep and primary force in social life that the particular institutions in which it is embedded become almost incidental.

For Weil, understanding social relationships of force is what comes to consitute "materialism," a perspective that Weil sees Marx as having articulated. "Marx was the first . . . to have the twin idea of taking society as the fundamental human fact and of studying therein, as the physicist does in matter, the relationships of force" ("Is There a Marxist Doctrine?" 171). This articulation still preserves the earlier idea of materialism as a method for studying society, though the specific focus of that study has somewhat shifted, and that is the idea to which Weil refers when she says of certain Marxist ideas that "they are not only compatible with Christianity but of infinite value to it" (170).

Yet this later turn to Christianity marks a significant shift in what materialism comes to mean to Weil. The praising of a notion of materialism understood as the conception of and study of society in terms of force is combined with an entire absence of any systematic notion of social change, such as Weil begins to articulate in *Reflections*. For in the later writings the operations of force come so to dominate social existence that there is no room for any concrete organized human efforts to exempt anyone from it. So, while Weil retains from Marx the materialist notion that oppression is embedded in real social relationships whose nature can be understood in a quasi-scientific way, she loses the application of this understanding to political action—that once we understand the real structural causes of oppression, we can work toward changing them.

In the Christian essays Weil counterposes the natural world to the supernatural world. She sees the natural, social world as entirely governed by force. Only by means of the supernatural can humans draw on a source of goodness capable of raising them above the operations of force. Earlier Weil had cautioned that there is no guarantee that the course of the world supports strivings toward the good; now she takes this further to imply that social reality by its very nature is actively hostile to the good: "The social order, though necessary, is essentially evil, whatever it may be" ("Meditation on Obedience and Liberty," 146). From the vantage point solely of the world here below we cannot find anything within ourselves to counter the operations of force; that in us which is capable of doing so is of an entirely supernatural origin. In this way people are passive objects for the operation of force; and this passivity is a strong theme in Weil's later writings, "The *Iliad*, Poem of Might," for example, discussed below in Chapter 7, though hints of this view of power can be found in *Reflections* as well.

Yet, ironically, this notion of human passivity in the face of social forces is quite similar to what Weil criticizes in Lenin and Engels' materialism. Gone from Weil's later conception is the sense that through their free activity persons can work systematically toward structural changes that can place them in control of the ways in which they interact with nature. At the same time, though in one sense Weil returns to a "vulgar" or "mechanical" notion of materialism (as applied to the natural world), she is certainly not in these Christian essays, anything like a "materialist" in the full sense. For, while accepting philosophical materialism as correct about the operations of the human and natural world, Weil continues to reject its claim to be a theory of all of reality. There remains for her an impetus lying outside the operation of force and radically distinct from it, namely the supernatural, which provides a source able to counter it.

> Materialism accounts for everything, with the exception of the supernatural. . . . The universe, minus the supernatural, is only matter. In describing it solely as matter one seizes upon a particle of truth. In describing it as a combination of matter and of specifically moral forces belonging to this world, that are on a level with nature, one falsifies everything. . . . That is why, for a Christian, Marx's writings are of much greater value than those, for example, of Voltaire and the Encyclopedists, who found a way of being atheists without being materialists. ("Is There a Marxist Doctrine?" 177)[6]

This criticism—that material and moral forces cannot both be of this world—is really a version of the critique that Weil continues to level against historical materialism, that it illegitimately attributes to the operations of production (i.e., matter) an inherent tendency toward the good. For her, "materialism, in so far as it attributes to matter the automatic manufacture of the good, is to be classed among the inferior forms of the religious life" (174). Marx was wrong to think that the operations of social life and social power could be made to harmonize with humans' aspiration to justice. Nevertheless these two elements are both essential in human existence.

The fundamental contradiction in human life is that man, with a "straining after the good constituting his very being, is at the same time subject in his entire being, both in mind and in flesh, to a blind force, to a necessity completely indifferent to the good" (173).[7]

We find thus in the course of Weil's life a complex and not always consistent assessment of the notion of materialism. While in one way the progressive jettisoning of a clear sense of political activity aimed at undermining the structures of oppression is a turning away from a materialist understanding of oppression toward a kind of reification of the notion of power, nevertheless, this same direction can be seen as a movement toward a more comprehensively materialist notion of social reality, seeing humanity itself as a kind of "matter." And yet at no time does Weil adopt either the specific form of materialism (i.e., historical materialism) that gives primacy in an understanding of society or social oppression to the forces of production; nor does she adopt a notion of materialism that implies that moral force is entirely illusory or a mere epiphenomenon of material forces. Even in the last essays, where moral force is relegated to a supernatural source, it still remains a deep element in human life: "The very being of man is nothing else but a perpetual straining after an unknown good" (173). This moral force is "infinitely small," yet is capable of having an important effect in the world here below: "The operation of that something infinitely small is decisive" (175). Like a mustard seed, a fermenting agent, or the center of gravity of an object that small, silent, presence is miraculously capable of achieving (though it does so rarely) a semblance of justice in the face of the overwhelming presence of force.

We have, then, shown how Simone Weil's critique of Marxism emerged from her deep involvement with the social and political movements of her time. Although Weil was only twenty-five when she wrote *Reflections Concerning the Causes of Liberty and Oppression*, this work contains the mature expression of her intellectual and political engagement with the Marxism of her time and of what she saw as its failure to provide an adequate underpinning for radical political action. We have looked analytically at the elements of Weil's trenchant criticisms of orthodox Marxism as developed both in *Reflections* and in later essays that continually return to the same concerns. Rejecting Marxism's faith in history, she sought to ground an understanding of society and action taken to change it on a firmly moral foundation.

In the following two chapters we will examine Weil's reconstructed understanding of the two central concepts of *Reflections*—liberty and oppression—in light of this morally grounded perspective and of her rejection of the orthodox Marxist world view. We will see the development of a strikingly original social and political philosophy substantially distinct from both orthodox Marxism and liberalism.

4
Liberty

And yet nothing on earth can stop man feeling himself born
for liberty.
—Simone Weil, *Reflections*

Simone Weil's thinking on liberty underwent a profound
development over the course of her life, yet throughout this
development she was fundamentally concerned to identify the
weaknesses of our inherited traditions to generate an adequate
grasp or a meaningful conception of liberty. For Weil this task
was crucial because if we have an unreal sense of liberty, our
efforts to attain it will be misdirected or, worse, will themselves
undermine our aspirations to freedom by generating different and
deeper structures of subordination. This chapter focuses on the
terms in which Weil's early formulations are set. It is important
that, while she never lost her conviction that the possibilities of
or limits on freedom had to be grappled with in moral and
political terms, in her later writings her doubts that freedom is in
any sense attainable intensify. The contribution that her experience of factory work and the development in her conceptions of
power made to this process will be discussed in Chapters 6 and 7,
respectively.

When she wrote *Reflections Concerning the Causes of Liberty
and Social Oppression*, Weil's conception of liberty was fundamentally tied to a Kantian framework characterized by its
identification of freedom, morality, and reason, with freedom

conceived as an essentially inner quality and the aspiration to freedom inviolable. Weil took from Kant the notion that we must *exercise* our freedom in our thoughts and our actions and employed this idea to challenge both the liberal traditions that encourage us to think of freedom as something that can be given to us from an external source and the utilitarian tradition in which freedom is identified as the absence of pain or the presence of pleasure. And further she brought Kant's sense of moral capacity as the source of dignity in human existence to her thinking on the inadequacies of the conception of freedom she believed implicit in orthodox Marxism.

Yet in these early writings Weil already moves towards a critique of the Kantian inheritance that sees freedom as radically a matter for the individual. In *Reflections* Weil develops a conception of liberty as something that we can exercise only in our relations with the world. Freedom can only be meaningfully thought about in relation to necessity and to our orientation to necessity. This makes work and our relation to our work integral to our potential to actualize our liberty. Freedom thereby gains substance.

1 Dreaming of liberty

For Simone Weil, "Nothing on earth can stop people feeling themselves born for liberty." It is because people are "thinking creatures" that they can never accept servitude. In *Oppression and Liberty* Weil often sets herself up as the enemy of illusions, even if they have brought consolation to people. We have seen (Chapter 3, section 7) that Weil regards Marx's view of liberty as grounded in such illusions: For her Marx's vision of communism is the most recent form of a dream of boundless liberty that haunts the individual either "as a past state of happiness of which a punishment has deprived him, or as a future state of happiness that is due to him by reason of a sort of pact with some mysterious providence" (83); but there can be no such boundless liberty, she believes, and even if there could be, it would not be worth having. As far as she is concerned, "the time has come to give up dreaming of liberty, and to make up one's mind to conceive it" (84). Even if the ideal of liberty that we conceive is just as unattainable as the dream, it "differs from the dream in that it concerns reality" (84).

If we struggle to represent to ourselves a clear notion of perfect liberty, we do not necessarily do so in the hope of attaining it "but in the hope of attaining a less imperfect liberty than is our present condition; for the better can only be conceived by reference to the perfect" (84). We must therefore engage in a systematic investigation of conceptons of "perfect liberty" presented to us in our dominant traditions of social and political thought and examine the false expectations they set up for us. For Weil these traditional conceptions draw us away from a sense of reality, making it harder, not easier, to face reality directly. Since coming to terms with reality means being ready to question existing polarities of political and moral theory, so Weil was as concerned at different points in her writings to challenge assumptions of Marxist theory, even though these are broadly critical of existing social reality, as she was to question assumptions about freedom that are part of the "common sense" of liberal democratic society.[1]

Possibly echoing Kant, Marx's vision of freedom tends to assume, often implicitly, a deep contrast between a realm of necessity that is capitalist society and a realm of freedom that is to come with socialism. He thought that the freedom liberal society presents as a reality is a fiction hiding the reality of determination and necessity that hold both proletarian and capitalist lives firmly in their grip. Only through a socialist revolution can people have the freedom to determine their own lives rather than being controlled by forces beyond them. So it is only with socialism that people can be said truthfully to make history.

In sharp contrast liberal theory says that freedom is guaranteed to people in the freedom of choice they enjoy within a liberal democratic society. The political and legal rights people enjoy as equal citizens stand as proof of their liberty. Since they have the freedom to choose their rulers as well as to replace them and to make their own lives and determine their own futures, they are responsible for the lives they make for themselves. It is not pretended that liberty is perfect but that the fundamental conditions for it already exist.

Weil believed that at some deeper level Marxism avoids facing up to the necessities of social life and, like liberalism implies a notion of "perfect liberty," even if the two traditions disagreed fundamentally about the conditions that can bring it into existence. Weil was firmly against the view that perfect liberty can be "conceived as consisting merely in the disappearance of that necessity whose pressure weighs continually upon us" (84) She thought that as long as people exist as "an infinitesimal fraction of this pitiless universe, the pressure exerted by necessity will never be relaxed for one single moment" (84).

Facing reality for Weil means recognizing that "A state of things in which men had as much enjoyment and as little fatigue as he liked can, except in fiction, find no place in the world in which we live" (84). An existence without the necessities that come with the very notion of work would deliver us to "the play of the passions and perhaps to madness" (84). Weil is clear that "there is no self-mastery without discipline, and there is no other source of discipline for man than the effort demanded in overcoming external obstacles" (84). This is the importance of work—a view fundamentally at odds with Marx's sense of work as self-expression. Although she does not really explain this difficult notion of "self-mastery," it at least involves being able to control our own emotions and whims: "It is the obstacles we encounter and that have to be overcome which give us the opportunity for self-conquest" (84). Weil thus confirms a rationalist view of identity in terms of an individual's control of emotions and desires.[2]

Sometimes Weil echoes a rationalist vision that sees work as a way of giving people control over emotions that might otherwise determine their behavior. Work provides people with goals and purposes that guide their rational behavior and so help people control their feelings and desires. It provides people with a necessary protection. It is as if emotions are in themselves a threat to rational activity, to coming to terms with reality. Weil saw people as "thinking" creatures in the Cartesian tradition; the fact that we are also emotional creatures was only of secondary importance for her. Although she understood that relations of power and subordination work on an emotional level too, so that people often identify with those who have power over them, she never developed this understanding in her early writings.

When we are deprived of liberty, our lives lose their value. Thus we cannot understand liberty simply in terms of negative freedom as "the mere absence of all necessity" (85), since for Weil it is the struggle against necessities that gives our lives to much of their form and meaning. Because we only establish our qualities and so define our individualities through having had to assert them against the necessities that life presents, it is not enough to think of freedom as the absence of obstacles to our pursuing our individual ends. We therefore have to challenge liberal and Marxist traditions that encourage us to think of liberty as the "possibility of obtaining without effort what is pleasurable" (85) and to challenge in particular the moral psychology of individual desire and satisfaction that informs so much utilitarian social and moral theory. To do so, however, upsets our very sense of identity and the ways we see our lives since they are very much formed within a utilitarian culture. We are encouraged to think that it is effort that gets in the way of our happiness and that if we were only left on a desert island with nothing to do we would find "true happiness." This is a vision that has haunted Western culture.[3]

2 Thought and action

The relationship between thought and action is a central focus for Weil's conception of liberty. Her view differs markedly from utilitarian conceptions that focus on the relationship between desire and its satisfaction which we take very much for granted within a liberal moral culture and which underpin a capitalist consumer culture. Assuming that we are free because we have choices that are not available in authoritarian regimes, we easily see our liberty guaranteed in the choices we can make to maximize our satisfactions. As consumers we are free to buy whatever goods we can afford; as citizens we are free to choose the political party that will best represent our interests. So, we argue, a worker is free to choose and so freely chooses the conditions of labor. In all these decisions we can express our desires and so work toward maximizing our satisfactions, thereby guaranteeing our freedom and happiness within a liberal moral tradition.

Within a Marxist tradition these market freedoms are castigated as "bourgeois" because they work to legitimate a fundamental situation of unfreedom within conditions of capitalist labor. Marx showed the formal equality that workers and capitalists are supposed to establish in the wage contract as being in reality a relationship of class power and subordination. Marx refers to the freedom of the worker in his exchange relationship with the capitalist as being merely "formal," masking his or her dependence on capital as a whole. The "legal relation" of contract, in which the parties meet each other as individuals, is "a mere semblance, and a deceptive semblance": in fact, the worker

> sells the particular expenditure of forces to a particular capitalist, whom he confronts as an independent *individual*. It is clear that this is not his relation to the existence of capital as capital, i.e. to the capitalist class. Nevertheless, in this way everything touching on the individual real person leaves him with a wide field of choice, of arbitrary will, and hence of formal freedom.[4]

Workers are obliged to accept very similar conditions of work within capitalist firms since they remain dependent on the sale of their labor to secure means of support. Although Weil was generally in agreement with this aspect of Marx's argument, she also thought that, along with his theory of productive forces guaranteeing emancipation, it helped to explain why so many in the Marxist tradition have treated "democratic ideas with supreme disdain" (*Oppression and Liberty*, 43). While it is a short step from disparaging as merely "formal" the typical bourgeois freedoms to denying them the status of genuine freedoms at all, Steven Lukes's *Marxism and Morality* reminds us that "Marx's own considered view was more complex."[5] Marx acknowledges "a wide field of choice" left to the individual, both as worker choosing whom to work for and as consumer converting money "into whatever use values he desires": "he acts as a free agent; he must pay his own way; he is responsible to himself for the way he spends his wages. He learns to control himself, in contrast to the slave, who needs a master."[6] But the complexities of this view have rarely been faced, and Weil felt the need to investigate the issues of freedom in quite different terms.

Weil thought that, while Marx rejects a liberal, market-based conception of freedom, he does not sufficiently challenge the conception of liberty as the ability to satisfy desire. For her, a free person is a person who *acts freely*, which means that his or her actions flow from an exercise of judgment concerning the ends of action and the sequence of means suitable for attaining this end. From her philosophy classes with Alain until the end of her life, Weil was concerned with the relationship between thought and action. Alain's teacher, Jules Lagneau, following Maine de Biran, taught that the self "knows itself only in the action which it exercises on the exterior world"[7]—a view in the French tradition that broke with a narrow Cartesianism in its attempt to bridge the mind-body split by positing that knowledge is not dependent on the mind alone but on the mind's relation to the body, on willed bodily movements, and hence on action in the world. Alain had been taught by Lagneau, and, as Simone Pétrement explains, Alain taught that the "will does not exist except in action."[8]

The significance to Weil of this view shows itself early in her relationship with Pierre Letellier, a fellow student at the Lycée Henri IV. His father, Leon Letellier, embodied her ideal of a person who was both a manual worker and a thinker: The son of a Norman peasant family, he ran away to sea at sixteen and then returned to study under Lagneau and later published his notes of Lagneau's lectures. Weil did not yet think of work as a way of fusing thought and action but rather as a means of training in moral courage. Her image of the freedom of sailors struggling against the necessities of the sea remained illuminating for her throughout her writings. She invokes it early in a brief essay she wrote on Letellier:

> Having learned, on the Newfoundland boats, that human beings are capable of overcoming apparently insurmountable fatigue and suffering every day, he could hardly allow himself to be seduced by brilliant arguments which demonstrated that man is not free, that there is no human spirit or that truth is only a word.[9]

This account of purposive action is later given a particular emphasis in work and proved significant to the sensitivities Weil developed in her experience of factory work. What crucially mattered to Weil is whether someone can dispose of his or her own capacity for action: "It matters little whether the actions in themselves are easy or painful, or even whether they are crowned with success; pain and failure can make a man unhappy, but cannot humiliate him as long as it is he himself who disposes of his own capacity for action" (*Reflections*, 85).

Within a utilitarian moral culture we automatically focus on whether our actions bring pleasure or pain. Our actions often become means for proving ourselves individually, which means asserting ourselves over others since this is how our sense of self is formed within a competitive culture. Weil seemed well aware of how a false or illusory sense of self might develop in this situation and she struggled to articulate a truer sense of the way people can develop their individuality through the problems and necessities of work. We cannot "cease to be hemmed in on all sides by an absolutely inflexible necessity" (86), but it is in asserting ourselves individually against these necessities that our sense of self and identity form.

The perception of necessity was of moral as well as epistemological significance for Weil. She learned that there is a sense in which people of power are dispossessed of knowledge when their wishes are automatically carried out. Since there is no check on their desires, they enjoy the illusion of a greater freedom, but in reality they are the victims of their own capricious passions: They are "prey to desires to which the clear perception of necessity never comes to assign any limit" (96). For people to become what they should be, the encounter with necessity—as Letellier knew—is

> the source of any kind of virtue [which] lies in the shock produced by the human intelligence being brought up against a matter devoid of lenience and of falsity. It is not possible to conceive of a nobler destiny for man than that which brings him directly to grips with naked necessity, without his being able to expect anything except through his own exertions, and such that his life is a continual creation of himself by himself. (87).

Liberty, then, involves the freedom to bring the mind to grips with necessity; and this is nothing other than to work. For Weil this becomes the way that we can achieve "self-mastery" and a greater sense of reality and truth. It is through the "effort demanded in overcoming external obstacles" (*Reflections*, 84) that work and the conception of necessity that is inseparable from it can provide the structure within which liberty can be defined. Liberty understood as freedom from any restriction—the core of the liberal conception of freedom—is a fantasy, for it has no connection with the real conditions of human existence and therefore, Weil insists, can have no value or meaning. This realization influences the terms in which Weil contrasts servitude and liberty:

> since he is a thinking creature, he can choose between
> either blindly submitting to the spur which necessity pricks
> him on from the outside, or else adapting himself to the
> inner representation of it that he forms in his own mind;
> and it is in this that the contrast between servitude and
> liberty lies. (86)

Weil's contrast between a determination that comes from "outside" as essentially a source of unfreedom and the "inner representation" as a guarantee of freedom shows the deep influence of Kant. The notion of freedom as essentially "inner" and so connected to a sense of individual worth and dignity that can always be sustained is what Weil was forced to challenge in her experience of factory work. It proved an inadequate underpinning for a conception of liberty. At some level we can read her early political writings as an attempt to combine elements of Marx's analysis of oppression in capitalist society with an ethical theory drawn from Kant. This is partly because Weil never appreciated the full weight of the dialectic in Marx's writings or its dependence on Hegel's critique of Kant's ethical theory. It is as if Weil went along with a common assumption in Marxist writing that Marx's analysis had to be supplemented with an ethical theory that it lacked.[10]

Kant helped Weil deepen her sense of oppression since he made issues of dignity and human worth central to his ethical theory. Weil had been haunted by the idea that oppression is an

insult to human dignity, though it was only after her experience
of factory work that she learned to make use of the idea of
dignity. If Kant's emphasis on dignity as an inner quality helped
her direct her early analysis, it also reinforced the tension
between mind and body: she assumed the mind to be the source
of freedom and purposive action, while she saw the body in
essentially instrumental terms. What is striking, though, are the
moments when Weil reaches a deeper appreciation of human
freedom through a historical analogy that upsets our visions of
historical progress and thus throws into sharp relief what we have
learned to take for granted as freedom and progress.

> A man would be completely a slave if all his movements
> proceeded from a source other than his mind, namely either
> the irrational reactions of the body, or else the mind of
> other people . . . the Roman slave perpetually keyed up to
> execute the orders of an overseer armed with a whip, the
> manual worker of our own day engaged in a production
> line, all these approach that wretched condition. (86)

The need for us constantly to assert ourselves against a
resisting necessity is the best way to free ourselves "from the
blind grip of the passions" (87) that would otherwise determine
our behavior and compromise our ability for free action. Weil
never fully escaped from this Kantian vision of our emotions and
feelings. She never gave them a place in her search for ever
greater contact with reality, but at least she does raise our
awareness of the difficulties of acting freely and independently of
the influence of others. Since liberalism fosters the idea that we
are free to make our own choices, we often remain unaware of
influences on our behavior, as long as we are not constrained by
others. Freedom remains fundamentally a matter of the options
that are available to us. But what is critical is the way Weil shifts
our attention away from the initial moments of decision, say, to
get married or to take a factory job, toward the manner of
control that we can exercise over our actions. Our freedom is not
something that we exercise at a single moment when we enter
into contracts and thereby obligate ourselves to others. This is
the way Kant has often been used to serve as a legitimation for
liberal social relations. Weil instead drew a different emphasis to

criticize the *nature of the control* people have over their everyday activities.

Weil invoked Kant to challenge the notion that freedom only exists at the moment of contract so that, for instance, once a person enters a factory her time is no longer her own but is at the disposal of the factory management to use in any way that suits its purpose. For Weil this contract can never be a form of freedom since control over our capacity for action can only be delivered into the hands of others at the price of freedom. This is why Weil thought Marx fundamentally right to see the conditions of modern factory work as a form of wage-slavery. She was not convinced of the capitalist argument that workers are free if they can choose to work or not or to exercise their freedom in the choice of firm. Weil was concerned to show that freedom is not simply an issue of options within an initial choice but that it concerns the very conditions of work. This means that, for instance, factory workers must gain control over the actual processes of work if they are to be thought of as free. Freedom is not simply a matter of counting options people have but also crucially of the nature of the control individual workers exercise over the processes of work. Freedom is no longer an issue simply of maintaining the options available, but concerns the very organization of the control within production.[11]

Weil saw freedom as an individual quest—another sense in which Weil was deeply influenced by Kant. For each person the existence of other people is a factor making for servitude: "man alone can enslave man" (96). If we did not people nature with divine or human wills, then we would be clear that "nature could break man, but she could not humiliate him" (96); it is only in our relations with other people that we can be humiliated. Weil's view seems contradictory since she sometimes allowed that nature can exercise genuine constraint, analogous to other people's constraint. Although she never resolved this problem, for the most part Weil was concerned with the ways people can be degraded through dependence. She did not think, as Kant did, that this dependence can always be avoided or that individuals voluntarily enter these relations of subordination and could always have chosen to live as free and equal individuals.[12] Conditions had changed since Kant's time, and Weil was aware of what she calls "the modern forms of social oppression" (56).

She thought it critical at least to distinguish necessities presented to people in their relationship to nature or matter and people's vulnerability in relations of power and subordination:

> Matter can give the lie to expectations and ruin efforts, it remains none the less inert, made to be understood and handled from the outside; but the human mind can never be understood or handled from the outside. To the extent to which a man's fate is dependent on other men, his own life escapes not only out of his own hands, but also out of the control of his intelligence; judgment and resolution no longer have anything to which to apply themselves; instead of contriving and acting one has to stoop to pleading or threatening; and the soul is plunged into bottomless abysses of desire and fear, for there are no bounds to the satisfactions and sufferings that a man can receive at the hands of other men. (96)

The realization that the human mind can never "be understood or handled from the outside" without compromising human freedom offers a challenge to both a liberal notion that says people have exercised their freedom in their initial choice of workplace and a Marxist notion that, when it thinks of the issues of control, focuses exclusively on the issue of ownership. When a foreman says to a worker, "you are not paid to think, but to do what you are told," he enforces nothing less than a condition of servitude. There is no room for human action when "judgment and resolution no longer have anything to which to apply themselves" and when people are forced to submit without thought to the commands of others. In doing so, people are threatened with being reduced to material objects.

This degrading dependence also affects the powerful since, according to Weil, "as the man of power lives only by his slaves, the existence of an inexorable world escapes him almost entirely" (96). He loses the chance of forming himself against the necessities presented in the real world. This is bound to affect his sense of identity and also the control he learns to exercise over his emotional life. If the oppressed are brought into more direct contact with material necessity, they have constantly to obey the whims of their master, just as the factory worker has to respond to the commands of the foreman even if he is engrossed in a piece of work. Rather than merely being a matter of consciousness and intentionality, freedom involves activities and practices in the material world. It is something that we exercise in our relationship with material necessities; it is not simply something we can be given to enjoy or dispose of in our relations with others. Freedom is something we have to learn to exercise individually—a critical idea for Weil that strengthened her individualism in the different periods of her writing.

The contrast that Weil points to between the powerful and the powerless illuminates the truer liberty that eludes them in quite different ways. The powerful delude themselves in thinking possessions and power can bring individual enrichment. They can bring the satisfaction of desires, but this is different from the freedom Weil wanted to make central to moral and political discussion:

> the man of power's orders seem to him to contain within themselves some mysterious efficacy: he is never capable, strictly speaking, of willing, but is a prey to desires to which the clear perception of necessity never comes to assign any limit. Since he cannot conceive of any other mode of action than that of commanding, when he happens, as he inevitably does, to issue commands in vain, he passes all of a sudden from the feeling of absolute power to that of utter impotence, as often happens in dreams; and his fears are then all the more overwhelming in that he feels himself continually threatened by his rivals. As for the slaves, they are continually striving with material elements; only their lot does not depend on these material elements which they handle, but on masters whose whims are unaccountable and insatiable. (96–97)

Weil's challenge to a liberal conception of freedom, then, extends beyond her grasp of the inadequacy of a conception of freedom defined in terms of the relation between desire and its satisfaction to see the ways in which freedom is compromised through relations of power and dependency. She shows us how these relationships work in a way that subverts both the apparent freedom of the powerful, who "cannot conceive of any other mode of action than that of commanding," and of the oppressed, who depend on them. Her analysis is not causal but rather an inquiry into the ways in which people are deluded about the conditions of their liberty and so fail to grasp the kinds of changes they need to make if a fuller vision of freedom is to be realized. Since we cannot separate our sense of individuals and what they are capable of from our understanding of relations they are in, we require a more *internal* understanding of social relations, which already involves our grasping, for instance, how a person's fate is dependent on others. Nor is it an accidental matter, as liberalism presents it, that people are individually free to choose how to behave within, say, a relationship of subordination and dependency. Liberalism stresses that individuals can behave quite differently in these relations and that their behavior depends on the individuals concerned. Thus liberalism resists Weil's contention that in a relationship where a person's fate is dependent "judgment and resolution no longer have anything to which to apply themselves" (96). Weil does not want to deny that important differences exist in the resistance individuals put up to having their freedom undermined; but nor does she want to place all the responsibility on the shoulders of individuals, as liberalism does.

The particular forms of impoverishment in relations of subordination and dependency Weil draws our attention to are not given public recognition within a liberal moral culture, nor are they clarified within Marxist theory. We tend to think that if someone is rich and powerful then he or she can have everything he or she could possibly want. We rarely learn that people need boundaries within which to develop themselves and forge a sense of individual self. Otherwise we are "prey to desires" that have no limit. This happens in our dreams, but inevitably indicates a lack of control over our waking lives.[13]

Weil seems to hint that it is in gaining "the clear perception of necessity" that some kind of limit is set to our desires. By invoking this conception of necessity, Weil develops her critique of a notion of freedom as defined in a relation between desire and its satisfaction to show that desires are not merely "given" or brute as a utilitarian conception assumes. Our perception of necessity is part of what gives us both the capacity to will and act in our lives and liberty in our emotional lives and our relations with others. She makes the significant point that true freedom is not simply an issue of "striving with material elements" unless our lot somehow depends on these strivings. This freedom is not true of slaves, who depend on "masters whose whims are unaccountable and insatiable," or factory workers, who depend on the disciplines of production and the whims of foremen, as Weil discovered for herself. She learned that instead of "contriving and acting," she had to "stoop to pleading," and it became clearer still that her ability to do so was not a matter of her inner strength but had to do with the workings of the relations of power and subordination. She sums up this realization a few years later in her "Meditation on Obedience and Liberty":

> It is impossible for the most heroically staunch mind to preserve the consciousness for an inward value when there is no external fact on which this consciousness can be based. Christ himself, when he found himself abandoned by everybody, mocked, despised, his life counted for naught, lost for a moment the feeling of his mission. What other meaning can be attached to the cry: "My God, my God, why hast thou forsaken me?" It seems to those who obey that some mysterious inferiority has predestined them to obey from all eternity, and every mark of scorn—even the tiniest—which they suffer at the hands of their superiors or their equals, every order they receive, and especially every act of submission they themselves perform confirms them in this feeling. (145)

Weil's experience of factory work encouraged lasting shifts in her thinking about the possibilities of human freedom. She could no longer believe that individuals could be expected to sustain a sense of "inward value" within relationships of subordination. For her the idea of "inward value" in such a context was not simply an unfair expectation but rather grew from a deeply misleading conception. She needed to challenge the very basis of a Kantian tradition that sees freedom as essentially "inner" while seeing the "external" as a realm of determination and unfreedom, a realm that includes emotions, feelings, and desires that distract people from ends chosen through the inner light of reason.

To say that "every mark of scorn" works to confirm people in their sense of inferiority is to refuse a distinction between the "inner" and the "outer" as independent realms of experience. It also challenges a liberal conception that sees individuals freely exercising a choice to enter relationships and somehow keeping their sense of individual integrity intact. Weil could no longer accept the liberal conception of the autonomous individual that is a firm foundation of bourgeois social theory. She did, however, recognize the vulnerability of individuality, which is subject to the processes of social life, especially in relationships of subordination and dependency. Rather, individuality can be hurt, damaged, undermined, and compromised. Nor is the individual's involvement in social relations a purely contingent matter that will not profoundly affect the quality and form of individual experience.[14]

In *Reflections* Weil consciously develops a new method of social analysis. The analysis starts, as Marx's did, from the relationships of production, but whereas Marx "seems to have wanted to classify the modes of production in terms of output, these would be analysed in terms of the relationships between thought and action" (100). This in no way implies that humanity has progressed from the least conscious to the most conscious forms of production, for when we consider the relation between thought and action our vision of progress is disturbed. Even though the idea of progress "is indispensable for whoever seeks to design the future in advance." (100) it leads us astray when we are studying the past. Thus Weil wants to "replace it by the idea of a scale of values conceived outside time," though it isn't possible or even desirable "to arrange the various social patterns in serial order according to such a scale" (100). All she wants to do is to refer a particular historically specific aspect of social life to this scale. While she believes that certain units of measurements "are given and have hitherto remained invariable, such as the human body, human life, the year, the day, the average quickness of human thought" (109), she realizes that "present-day life is not organized on the scale of all these things" (109). She never really develops the ways a sense of absolute values can be grounded in these brute facts of human experience, but the idea does seem to gain a growing influence especially in the ways she discusses human needs in *The Need for Roots*.

In *Reflections* Weil searches for a method that will enable her to analyze the various modes of social organization "in terms of the ideas of servitude and liberty" (101), which means specifically examining the relation between thought and action. We have to learn the areas of social life where thought is genuinely exercised so we can be aware of "the individual's zones of influence over society" (101). We cannot content ourselves with the negative idea of lessening oppression since it is "indispensable to form at any rate a vague mental picture of the sort of civilization one wishes humanity to reach" (103). According to Weil, Marx underestimated the critical significance of this form of thinking, ridiculing it as utopian because it is not grounded in real historical forces that can bring it into existence. This criticism, part of his political struggle to gain hegemony of the socialist movement, involved Marx's often seeming to misrepresent what he had himself learned from the utopian socialists like Pierre Joseph Proudhon.[15] Weil was more ready to appreciate the strengths of this tradition as she stressed the difference between the fiction of a golden age and a theoretical picture of a free society that is "able to serve, by way of an ideal, as a standard for the analysis and evaluation of actual social patterns" (100). Creating this theoretical picture means discovering "a certain optimum balance" (103) among the different elements of society. Weil summarizes her sense of "the least evil society" as "that in which the general run of men are most often obliged to think while acting, have the most opportunities for exercising control over collective life as a whole, and enjoy the greatest amount of independence" (103).

Before we explore the ways she reaches this conception, it is important to draw attention to the ways she subsumes the experience of women. She rarely talks about the particular oppression of women or the ways women could assume ore control over their lives. She seemed to have identified closely with the values of family life, though she also seems to have deeply resented being treated differently as a young girl from her brother. Her relationship to her femininity was difficult and complicated. Still, she does provide insights and ways of thinking that could be crucial to the development of feminist theory, though she never seemed to appreciate the significance of these connections for herself.

For Weil, life has to be organized according to the human scale if it is to be meaningful. Such a reorganization involves restoring a proper relation between thought and action, which is connected in her thoughts about freedom with the relation between means and ends. For Weil, "an inversion [of means and ends] which is to a certain extent the law of every oppressive society" (111) "becomes total or nearly so, and extends to nearly everything" (111) in modern society. The inversion of means and ends connects Weil's discussion of freedom with her analysis of oppression. It also connects her with an important strand in Western Marxism represented by what George Lukács expresses in his recognition of the centrality of reification in capitalist society in which the relations between people are increasingly replaced by relations between things.[16] In the closing section of *Reflections*, "Sketch of Contemporary Social Life," Weil touches similar themes in showing the extent of this inversion not only in capitalist but also in socialist societies. Thus she had to look beyond the organization of the capitalist economy to understand what she thinks of as "the dispossession of the individual in favour of the collectivity" (111).

3   The image of a free community

Simone Weil was convinced that in modern civilization people had never been "less capable, not only of subordinating their actions to their thoughts, but even of thinking" (*Reflections*, 108). For her accepted traditions of moral and political thought were near to losing all meaning and seemed incapable of identifying and illuminating "the impotence and distress of all men in face of the social machine, which has become a machine for breaking hearts and crushing spirits, a machine for manufacturing irresponsibility, stupidity, corruption, slackness and, above all, dizziness" (108). These features are by no means exclusive to the workings of a capitalist economy. It was partly because of the historical experience of the Soviet Union and the consequent crisis of Marxism that Weil felt a new beginning was needed. She thought that the reason for this painful state of affairs was perfectly clear: "We are living in a world in which nothing is made to man's measure; there exists a monstrous discrepancy between [sic] man's body, man's mind and the things which at the present time constitute the elements of human existence; everything is disequilibrium" (108).

This view hints at a kind of "ecological" form of awareness that had been strengthened for Weil by the Soviet Union's experiments with centralized planning. She thought this destructive disequilibrium was most clearly evident in the young in different countries who were growing up in it and who inwardly reflected the chaos surrounding them. In her view a "happy balance" between thought and action is destroyed, the society that distorts or destroys it is unsound in the most fundamental way. When Weil thinks in terms of "equilibrium"—which became central in *The Need for Roots*—she is not thinking as a systems theorist. She refers to the disruption of the relation between thought and its proper object as both a social and an individual experience. She stresses that this "disequilibrium is essentially a matter of quantity" (108) and draws on Hegel to establish her point that quantity is changed into quality so that a "mere difference in quantity is sufficient to change what is human into what is inhuman" (108).

Weil realized that in the practical affairs of life, we are bound to carry out actions that we don't understand because we either rely on ready-made rules or follow routines. Her vision of a free community, on the other hand, involves the constant widening of the "sphere of conscious work" (95). She does not simply look forward to a different mode of production but compares the activities we already know. She draws a distinction between assembly-line workers working under the discipline of the machine and building workers working out a problem on a site, where, she thinks, "the image of a free community appears almost in its purity" (101):

> [A] team of workers on a production-line under the eye of a
> foreman is a sorry spectacle, whereas it is a fine sight to see
> a handful of workmen in the building trade, checked by
> some difficulty, ponder the problem each for himself, make
> various suggestions for dealing with it, and then apply

unanimously the method conceived by one of them, who
may or may not have any official authority over the
remainder (101).

Those who have the opportunity to think for themselves when
discharging their social function preserve their freedom. But the
division of intellectual and manual labor has made the balance
between thought and action more difficult to sustain since it is no
longer the same people who think and act. Therefore, even if
people have power in society, they can still only exercise a partial
and, as it were, maimed form of thought. Against this the
building workers sustain a cooperative vision of freedom and so
provide a significant example that, if properly considered, could
be extended to other forms of work. In a society founded on
relationships of power and subordination, according to Weil, "it
is not only the weak but also the most powerful who are
bondslaves to the blind demands of collective life, and in each
case heart and mind suffer a diminution, though in different
ways" (102). Weil stresses that in all oppressive societies people
are dependent not only on individuals above or below them but
"above all on the very play of collective life—a blind play which
alone determines the social hierarchies" (97). Being completely
"inaccessible to the senses and to the mind" (97), the collectivity
can make an individual feel "infinitely small" (97). So it is that
"between man and this universe . . . the relation oppression-
servitude permanently sets the impenetrable screen of human
arbitrariness" (97).

With the development of big industry and the exchange
economy, the majority of people are forced into this framework
of relations "in order that their hands may come into contact with
the material of work, to go through a collectivity which swallows
them up and pins them down to a more or less servile state; when
it rejects them, the strength and skill of their hands remain
useless" (112). Even the peasants who had initially escaped this
fate have been forced to submit in many parts of the world. In
her concern for the countryside and the fate of the peasantry,
Weil thought that Marxism is too exclusively interested in the
fate of the proletariat because it judges the proletariat to be the
force for historical change.[11] She thought that the relation
between social oppression and individual suffering required

keeping in mind the general "nature of the ties which keep the individual in material dependence" (103). So she was concerned to teach people not only about different modes of production but also about what relieves the subordination people suffer in their everyday lives:

> For example, a workman who has a large enough garden to supply himself with vegetables is more independent than those of his comrades who have to get all their food from the shopkeepers; an artisan who has his own tools is more independent than a factory worker whose hands become useless as soon as it pleases the boss to stop him from working his machine. (103)

Through examples such as this one she encourages us to identify differences where they exist as well as to appreciate the reality of our control in crucial areas of our lives. This control is not to be minimized but is to be appreciated both as the freedom it is and as a guide to what we should value in a transformation of work.

Progress in the true sense of the word is partly gained in appreciating the freedom of the building workers, a freedom that shows "progress in the order of human values" (97). People are not made to be the playthings of the blind collectivities they form with their fellows. People are born to freedom, and so they are born to live in a free community. The only hope for redemption from the power of collective strength over individual lives comes in the sphere of the mind for the mind is the key link between the collectivity and the definition of freedom. Since thought is the only "essentially individual" (98) thing we have and since "collectivities do not think" (98), the only way that "the individual surpasses the collectivity" (97) is through the mind. The force of this Kantian conception of the mind leads Weil to see it in a way that denies that the individual's bodily movements or emotional expression could be integral to the his or her self-definition, for "all the rest can be imposed from outside, including bodily movements, but nothing in the world can compel a man to exercise his powers of thought, nor take away from him the control over his own mind" (98). As she says, "If you require a slave to think, the lash had better be put away" (98).

Although she revises them later, two views mark Weil's early writings on liberty. The first concerned her understanding of the notion of force. It was crucial for her that, if people were to enjoy a genuine liberty, the mind could not be forced to conform to prevailing relations of power and subordination but would be able to judge them. Mind is essentially critical, though, as she acknowledges, to "the extent to which the mind soars above the social melee, it can judge, but it cannot transform" (98). "All forms of force are material," she explains in a way that limits the place of spirituality in her early writings; "the expression 'spiritual force' is essentially contradictory; mind can only be a force to the extent to which it is materially indispensable" (98). The second view of liberty concerns the place of thought in the conception of a free community. She insists on the need for thought to control human activities:

> Thus, if we wish to form, in a purely theoretical way, the conception of a society in which collective life would be subject to men as individuals instead of subjecting them to itself, we must visualize a form of material existence wherein only efforts exclusively directed by a clear intelligence would take place, which would imply that each worker himself had to control, without referring to any external rule, not only the adaption of his efforts to the piece of work to be produced, but also their co-ordination with the efforts of all the other members of the collectivity. (99)

Such a goal involves widespread technical education, a pre-occupation of Weil's since her years at the lycée, so that each worker could form a clear idea of all the procedures involved in work as well as the coordination of production and distribution. This understanding would give each individual the possibility "to exercise control over the collective life as a whole" (99), as in the case of building workers, and thus the "community of interests would be sufficiently patent to abolish competitive attitudes" (99). Each person would be in a position to verify the activities of all the rest by using his or her own reason, which would mean that "the function of coordinating would no longer imply power" (99). Weil thereby offers a vision of how work must be transformed to provide a truer freedom not only on the building site but in society more generally. We find different moods in different parts of *Reflections*, as if she is trying to sustain the core rationalism of the Enlightenment vision while seeking for ways genuinely to realize it in its full meaning. But in part hers remains fundamentally an Enlightenment vision:

> There is but one single and identical reason for all men;
> they only become estranged from and impenetrable to each
> other when they depart from it; thus a society in which the
> whole of material existence had as its necessary and
> sufficient condition that each individual should exercise his
> reason could be absolutely clearly understood by each
> individual mind. (99)

Where reason had replaced power in their relationship to material existence, people would be concerned to win the esteem of their fellows. With the removal of an outward constraint constantly pushing people to work, people would overcome fatigue, suffering, and danger and find within themselves the resources for personal motivation, for, as Weil optimistically felt, "the sight of the unfinished task attracts the free man as powerfully as the overseer's whip stimulates the slave" (99). Hers is a powerful vision of the free community. In its own way it carries insights from Marx, Kant, Christianity as well as the *Iliad*, as it searches for a definition of collective ties that excludes people treating each other as things. While these influences shifted radically in the significance and meaning they carried for her, the vision remained constant:

> Such a society alone would be a society of men free, equal
> and brothers. Men would, it is true, be bound by collective
> ties, but exclusively in their capacity as men; they would
> never be treated by each other as things. Each would see in
> every workfellow another self occupying another post, and
> would love him in the way that the Gospel maxim enjoins.
> Thus we should possess, over and above liberty, a still more
> precious good; for if nothing is more odious that the
> humiliation and degradation of man by man, nothing is so
> beautiful or so sweet as friendship. (100)

The experience of women is subsumed under the general category of "men." In its own way the identification of masculinity with reason, which was fundamentally a part of the Enlightenment vision, was an assertion of power to silence the influence of emotions and desires in moral life. In helping to deliver the world to reason, this identification worked to legitimate the power men had in relation to women, with the result that if the world is made in the image of men, it is at the cost of the experience of women.[18]

Nevertheless, we can begin to see that when Weil challenges us to think about freedom, it is not merely as an abstract concept to which we have an intellectual commitment. We consider different ways of living our lives and attempt to establish what is important in human life. Weil always starts from a consideration of living relations before she attempts to theorize more generally. So, for instance, in her thinking about freedom she encourages us to think more clearly than we seem used to doing about differences in the nature of work people do. She wants us to reassess what is significant in terms of these work situations, in terms of the real freedom and control it leaves to people challenging the ways a liberal-capitalist society normally ranks them accordifng to wages, power, or influence. In this way we can discover ethical distinctions we ignore if we think of work as simply reflecting individual abilities and choices. But of course, thinking in this way means challenging the conventional distinction between morals, as a first order enquiry into what people believe, and ethics as a second order enquiry into the concepts people invoke in "the language of morals"[19]—a distinction that freezes our moral thinking in its implication that there is a fixed number of concepts somehow central to our moral experience.

Weil thus regards a consideration of different kinds of work necessary to illuminate the idea freedom. This consideration will give a new grounding to moral thinking at it establishes new terms of moral criticism:

> It is clear enough that one kind of work differs substantially
> from another by reason of something which has nothing to
> do with welfare, or leisure, or security, and yet which claims
> each man's devotion; a fisherman battling against the wind
> and waves in his little boat, although he suffers from cold,

> fatigue, lack of leisure and even of sleep, danger and a
> primitive level of existence, has a more enviable lot than the
> manual worker on a production-line, who is nevertheless
> better off as regards nearly all these matters. That is
> because his work resembles far more the work of a free
> man, despite the fact that routine and blind improvisation
> sometimes play a large part in it. (101)

The fisherman is more free precisely *because* his thought is fully in control of his actions. For Weil there is something in this mode of life that we should learn to treasure, even if we have difficulty thinking about it. Weil does not imply that people would necessarily choose this life if they were given the chance; they might not be at all suited to this kind of work. But learning to identify what matters can help people to realize what is missing in their own work—that is, the way their own work does not help them live as free men and women. Against prevailing moral and political traditions it can help people to realize that freedom has to do with the *quality* of the experience of working and not just the choice of work or choice of factory. Weil focuses on one crucial aspect of freedom when she inquires whether thought can be exercised in particular jobs as a measure of "the individual's zones of influence over society" (101).

Weil was concerned to show that people with more power don't necessarily have more control over their lives. We should not distinguish people only according to the leisure, welfare, or security they have or whether they have a "higher or lower position in the social mechanism" (102) but also "by the more conscious or more passive character of their relationship with it" (102). For Weil to stress whether people's work is under the control of their own intelligence is more important in illuminating freedom. She is aware that in a society founded on oppression "it is not only the weak but also the most powerful who are bond-slaves to the demands of collective life" (102) so that we have to be careful to distinguish the reality of freedom people enjoy. This inevitably involves challenging the self-conceptions of the society that tend to legitimate the prevailing social hierarchies. Weil discovers a different order that is more realistically dependent on "ideas of servitude and of liberty" (101). So, for instance, even though fishermen are not rewarded with material comforts, they enjoy a life of freedom, for all its hardships. But Weil say that we cannot know this theoretically in advance. It is only through a practical involvement with different lives that we can gain a sense of their truer freedom and so renew our moral and political traditions.

Weil wished to return the notion of liberty to a central place in our lives. Our prevailing traditions of moral and political thought cannot make plain to us that people are "born for liberty" (83). Rather, as Weil says, "If one were to understand by liberty the mere absence of all necessity, the word would be emptied of all concrete meaning" (85). If this were the case, as it is in the liberal and utilitarian traditions, liberty, according to Weil, "would not then represent for us that which, when we are deprived of it, takes away the value from life" (85).

Weil constantly struggled to find ways of restoring a sense of what gives meaning to life and what "takes away the value from life". In her earlier writings she often does this through glimpses of different occupations, but in her later writings she searches for cultures that sustained a conception of the good and meaningful life, even if that conception has been destroyed. She grew firmer in her conviction that history does not bring progress and that what survives is not always the best or most humane of values and relations but is often the most brutal. Even though she changed her sense of what gives life meaning, giving less weight to freedom and substituting goodness as she found more space for a spiritual reality, this thought is always near the heart of her writings.

Weil was convinced that Marx was quite wrong to think that capitalist society would ever produce the conditions of a free and equal society. He should never have believed "that slavery could produce free men" (117). Rather, she reiterates the familiar view that "slavery degrades man to the point of making him love it" (117), and she goes on to say

> that liberty is precious only in the eyes of those who
> effectively possess it; and that a completely inhuman
> system, as ours is, far from producing beings capable of
> building up a human society, models all those subjected to
> it—oppressed and oppressors alike—according to its own
> image. (117)

This might well be one of the reasons that in her thinking about liberty and oppression Weil stressed the importance of restoring the sense of dignity and self-respect to working people. People had to learn to treasure whatever remnants of liberty were left to them. And so it was important to conceive of liberty as a matter not simply of opening up options but crucially of offering people effective control over their lives. This was the only way that liberty could be made precious to people.

The strength of Weil's commitment to fulfilling the conditions of liberty is, then, sustained through her commitment to identifying the structures of oppression. As we have seen, Weil was acutely aware of the dangers of understating the depths to which people are touched by the forces that run counter to liberty. Part of oppression consists in the dispossession of the capacity to treasure or even to conceive properly of liberty, an oppression compounded through the silences in our inherited traditions. Weil was clear that we do not bring ourselves nearer to the conditions through which we can realize our liberty if we allow ourselves a simplified understanding of the dimensions of oppression. She felt that Marxism had allowed itself to lapse into such an oversimplification and that in doing so, it betrayed the most vital of its insights. It is, then, to Weil's analysis of the complexities of the levels on which oppression operates that we must now turn.

5
Oppression

Not to laugh at what human beings do, nor to be disgusted
by it, but to understand it.
—Baruch Spinoza, *The Ethics*

Weil's concern to develop a substantive conception of liberty
through her critique of Marxism in *Reflections* not only provided
her with a meaningful engagement with twentieth century social
reality but also helped her conceive of a social theory able to
address the nature of modern forms of social oppression, the
other main theme of *Reflections*. In this work Weil wished to
"bring everything into question again", (37), partly by pointing to
the poverty of inherited traditions to identify precisely the nature
and experience of oppression in contemporary society.

In her early writings, as we have seen, Weil drew heavily on
Marx's understanding that socialism was to be above all the
abolition of "the degrading division of labour into intellectual and
manual labour" (quoted in *Reflections*, 41)—a view that become
the cornerstone of her thinking about oppression. Yet Weil also
believed that this division was not merely a mechanical reflection
of the categories of class provided for in Marx's theory. For Weil
the division between conception and execution ultimately was not
reducible to class divisions, and the assumption that it could be
marginalized the force of Marx's own insights on the all-
pervasiveness of the degradation with which capitalist society had
infused human experience. She thought that the dimensions of

oppression could not be conflated but had to be considered systematically in turn, so that the questions that could illuminate the new historical situation could be formulated.

It was crucial for Weil to recognize the implications of the fact that the division between intellectual and manual labor had not been transcended in the Soviet Union;[1] this division had to be given critical attention in and of itself. Weil also thought that science could not be seen as a neutral or ahistorical form of enquiry but had to be regarded in its interrelationship with that division and therefore as woven into contemporary relationships of dominance and subordination. These concerns and their consequences for human dignity form the framework within which Weil considered the potential for transformation of oppression to liberty, seeing that it is crucial that "we do not seem to have understood what the conditions of such a transformation are" ("On Lenin's Book *Materialism and Empiriocriticism*, 34). Weil changed her mind about the nature of these conditions, but their analysis remained a constant goal throughout her writings, helping her to correct her thinking about the crisis in the nature of work in relation to the place of science in modern consciousness.

1 Science, oppression, and social theory

Since liberty involves the mind's confronting necessity, liberty is centrally connected in Weil's thinking with the nature of work. Work and the conception of necessity that is inseparable from it create the structure within which liberty can be defined. But the fragmentation that separates people into those who plan and those who carry out orders destroys the necessary balance between thought and action in the individual, a balance that is essential in Weil's notion of liberty. This fragmentation is reflected in the increase of the sum total of human knowledge in modern science at the cost of subordinating the individual mind to the sum total of knowledge.

Weil recognized that since the seventeenth century science has played a crucial role in enforcing the distinction between intellectual and manual labor and making it an aspect of the "common sense" of bourgeois society. By 1934 she was convinced not only that technological progress had failed to produce a prosperous and egalitarian society but also that the Enlightenment hopes that the growth of scientific knowledge would lead to the general diffusion of knowledge and the development of the powers of thought within people had been proven quite false. If specialization in intellectual fields had vastly increased the sum total of human knowledge it was at the cost of reducing and fragmenting the individual by deepening the split between intellectual and manual labor. As far as Weil was concerned, the accumulation of scientific knowledge simply added to the domination of the intellectuals. These are central themes in her analysis of oppression. Furthermore, she warned against certain conceptions of Marxism as a science while showing the need to extend Marx's criticisms of religion to science. Within modern culture science had replaced religion as a corpus of knowledge that people are "compelled to believe just in the same way as they are forced to obey" ("On Lenin's Book *Materialism and Empiriocriticism*, 35):

> just in the same way as the worker, in modern industrial production, has to submit to the material conditions of his work, so the mind, in scientific research, has nowadays to submit to established facts; and science, which was to have made all things clear and unveiled all mysteries, has itself become the outstanding mystery . . .
> Science has become the most modern form of the consciousness of man who has not yet found himself or has once again lost himself, to apply Marx's telling dictum concerning religion. . . . More generally, the conditions of all privilege, and consequently of all oppression, is the existence of a corpus of knowledge essentially closed to the working masses, which thus find themselves compelled to believe just in the same way as they are forced to obey. Religion, nowadays, no longer suffices to fill this role, and science has taken its place. . . . Socialism will not even be conceivable as long as science has not been stripped of its mystery. (35)

In her early writings Weil tends to connect oppression with

privilege and sees the condition of both as being related to "the existence of a corpus of knowledge essentially closed to the working masses." Her view of the place of science in modern consciousness helped her extend her thinking about oppression beyond the relations of power within the workplace and so beyond an orthodox reading of Marx's account of exploitation. To the extent that Marxism itself tended to foster belief in the ideas of technical and scientific progress, it was caught up in this vision of science and was therefore very much part of the problem. Thus Weil introduced her analysis of oppression within a critique of Marxism.

As Weil points out in terms that find a new resonance in post-World War II Europe, science and technological "progress" have brought us to the point where "We are living through a period bereft of a future. Waiting for that which is to come is no longer a matter of hope, but of anguish" (*Reflections*, 38). One passage in *Reflections* seems to encapsulate that despair and provide the setting for her thinking about the modern forms of socal oppression:

> Work is no longer done with the proud consciousness that one is being useful, but with the humiliating and agonizing feeling of enjoying a privilege bestowed by a temporary stroke of fortune. . . . The leaders of industry themselves have lost that naive belief in unlimited economic progress which made them imagine that they had a mission. Technical progress seems to have gone bankrupt, since instead of happiness it has only brought the masses that physical and moral wretchedness in which we see them floundering. . . . As for scientific progress, it is difficult to see what can be the use of piling up still more knowledge on to a heap already much too vast . . . and experience has shown that our forefathers were mistaken in believing in the spread of enlightenment, since all that can be revealed to the masses is a miserable caricature of modern scientific culture, a caricature which, far from forming their judgment, accustoms them to be credulous. Art itself suffers the backlash of the general confusion, which partly deprives it of its public and by that very fact impairs inspiration. Finally, family life has become nothing but

anxiety, now that society is closed to the young. The very generation for whom a feverish expectation of the future is the whole of life, vegetates, all over the world, with the feeling that it has no future, that there is no room for it in our world. But if this evil is felt more sharply by youth, it remains common to the whole of humanity today. (38)

In her challenge to the dominance of Enlightenment thought and the ideas of science and progress it fosters, Weil argues that far from forming our judgment, this mode of thought leaves us credulous. To the extent that Marxism depends on a belief in the progressive victory of productive forces and their power to generate a realm of freedom and equality, its place within a radical consciousness also had to be challenged, critically reassessed in the light of historical experience. To do so was in fact to be true to the historical nature of Marx's writings. Weil could not accept that Marx's analysis of bourgeois society had "demonstrated the ineluctible necessity of an early upheaval, in which the oppression we suffer under capitalism would be abolished" (39). "Scientific socialism" had assumed the status of a dogma "exactly in the same way as have all the results of modern science, results in which each one thinks it is his duty to believe, without ever dreaming of enquiring into the method employed" (40).

Weil's criticism of science is built on a conviction that a different kind of science could be created, one with a more organic relationship to people's everyday experience of work. For her "it would be enough if man were no longer to aim at extending his knowledge and power indefinitely, but rather at establishing, both in his search and in his work, a certain balance between the mind and the objects to which it is being applied" (94–96). Without this balance real thought is not possible. Our capacity for thought is not something we can take for granted but depends on what we are exercising our minds in relation to. As if trying to return to the core meaning of Kant's rationalism, Weil says, "Thought is certainly man's supreme dignity, but it is exercised in a vacuum, and consequently only in appearance, when it does not seize hold of its object, which can be none other than the universe" (105).

The absence of real thought was for Weil a profoundly

disturbing feature of post-Enlightenment culture. She did not believe it was a necessary consequence of Cartesian science since Cartesianism does not imply a separation between scientific thought and ordinary human thought. Rather, she believed that Descartes' work could provide the basis for a science quite different from the science that has actually developed from it, one that would relate scientific knowledge to practical activities and craftsmanship and that would thereby be much more organically connected to work. Her vision of the building workers getting together to solve a problem on the site is not only a vision of freedom but also of science and knowledge, as Dorothy Tuck McFarland notes: Weil's vocabulary "repeatedly uses 'to seize, to grasp' as synonyms of 'to know'—emphasizes that knowledge of the world is a physical as well as a mental act, that it involves deliberate bodily action—work—in the world."[2] Or, as Weil says in a passage in *Sur la science*, "The Pilot who in the tempest directs the tiller, the peasant who swings his scythe, knows himself and knows the world in the way expressed by the saying 'I think, therefore I am'; and the whole cortege of ideas that goes with it" (95).[3]

As she later challenged the distinction that an Enlightenment culture draws between science and religion, Weil consistently challenged the antagonism between science and metaphysics, claiming that rather than illuminating a search for truth, this distinction has darkened our path. McFarland is quite right to stress that

> In this notion that knowledge of the world (science) is not
> separate from Socratic or reflective self-knowledge
> (knowledge of the realm of value) is a view of man and his
> relation to the world in which there is no antagonism
> between science and metaphysics, and Weil traces this view
> to the very Descartes who is usually considered responsible
> for the unbridgeable gulf between them.[4]

In Weil's view Descartes "regards every mind, as soon as it applies itself to think *comme il faut*, as equal to the greatest genius" (*Sur la science*, 44). In her recognition of the capacity of every individual to think Weil identifies an egalitarian emphasis in rationalism. Weil also considered this view practical since for

Descartes true philosophy was to the mind "what the eyes are to the body" (45), a way of grasping the world.

According to Weil, when science is separated from work, the mind no longer has the world as its object and the idea of necessity is lost. The accumulation of scientific knowledge becomes an end in itself, and, insofar as the body of knowledge is too vast to be grasped by the individual mind, the individual is subordinated to it. The Enlightenment vision that saw the growth of knowledge as a precondition for the development of a free and equal society thereby turned into its negation as science became an instrument of domination.[5] While Marx never developed a critical analysis of the place of science in capitalist society—though he was aware of its role within production in reinforcing and legitimating the power of capital in its relation with labor—Weil thought that any understanding of the workings of the modern forms of social oppression has to give a central place to an analysis of science not only in terms of the abuse of science by the prevailing powers, but also in terms of the very form of scientific knowledge in the modern world. As she says, "Science is a monopoly, not because public education is badly organized, but by its very nature; non-scientists have access only to the results, not to the methods, that is to say they can only believe, not assimilate" (41). This idea that people are forced to "believe, not assimilate" is central to her connection of liberty with oppression, and it is an integral aspect of the "reversal of the relationship between subject and object" that characterizes her sense of oppression. When "the scientist does not use science in order to manage to see more clearly into his own thinking, but aims at discovering results that will go to swell the present volume of scientific knowledge" (111) when the body of scientific knowledge is too large to be grasped by the individual mind, and the proper relationship between the thinking subject and the object of thought is inverted. For Weil maintaining the proper relationship between the mind and its object is far more important than the piling up of knowledge, for "where the mind cannot embrace everything, it must necessarily play a subordinate role" (94). But this again is to challenge the Enlightenment vision of science.

We can see, then, that, though critical of the role and conception of science in modern Western society and of its use within orthodox Marxism, Weil was far from hostile to science itself. In particular, as Anne Reynaud-Guerithault's notes of the lectures Weil gave at the girls' lycée at Roanne during the school year 1933–1934 (published as *Lectures on Philosophy*) show, Weil had no hestitation in thinking about a science of society. She searched, in fact, for a basis for such a science in which the notion of oppression would have a central place:

> A scientific study of society should enable us to see what kind of society it is that would be the least oppressive in the given conditions. If one could understand on what oppression depends, one would no longer be in that unbearable situation of having to submit to it by being forced into a state of complete disorder. The idea of inequality between the oppressors and the oppressed would disappear. The oppressors would no longer think of themselves as the instruments of God; they would think of themselves as the tools of necessity. The oppressed, for their part, would no longer think of the oppressors as a race set apart. (129).

This quest to understand "on what oppression depends" so that people need not submit without fully understanding what it is they submit to remained with Weil to the end of her life. For Weil, it is as if a situation of subordination becomes "bearable" once people grasp the necessities behind it. Marx wanted workers to grasp the nature of exploitation in capitalist society, but he promised that the end of exploitation would bring the end of necessity. But in Weil's view "A state of things in which man has as much enjoyment and as little fatigue as he liked can, except in fiction, find no place in the world in which we live" (*Reflections*, 84).

Weil thought that what we "should ask of the revolution is the abolition of social oppression" (55) but that we have to be "careful to distinguish between oppression and subordination of personal whims to a social order" (55). While she was aware that any social order has to insist on certain restrictions to individual desires, she wanted to be sure that these restrictions were necessary and that they were fully understood by those who were being asked to hold to them. This would make certain forms of authority and subordination bearable if not clearly legitimate. The need to make the initial distinction between oppression and necessary restriction was always clear to her:

> So long as such a thing as a society exists, it will circumscribe the life of individuals within quite narrow limits and impose its rules on them; but this inevitable constraint does not merit the name of oppression except in so far as, owing to the fact that it brings about a division between those who exercise it and those who are subject to it, it places the latter at the disposal of the former and thus causes those who command to exert a crushing physical and moral pressure over those who execute. Even when this distinction has been made, nothing entitles us to assume *a priori* that the abolition of oppression is either possible or even simply conceivable by way of limit. (56)

According to Weil, oppression occurs when those who are subject to constraint are "at the disposal" of those who exercise constraint. But her thinking about what it really means for one person to be at the disposal of another was left abstract. Before she could connect oppression to issues of human dignity and individual worth, she needed to experience it for herself in the factory. In her early writing she was still very much thinking about oppression as a sociological concept within a renewed form of social theory capable of illuminating the realities of both capitalist and socialist societies.

As we have seen (in Chapter 2, sections 2 and 4), Marxist theory tends to argue that since capitalist society is the source of all oppression, the end of capitalism will inevitably bring the end of oppression. Weil thought that this view was crude and misleading and that it created all kinds of false expectations in working people. Marx had taken great trouble to show that individual capitalists should not be blamed since they are caught up in a system that could easily destroy them if they acted differently. So it was inappropriate to think of individual capitalists as the source of all evil and oppression. But Marx had also taught something whose implications for our understanding of oppression, Weil thought, was never fully recognized:

> Marx demonstrated forcibly, in the course of analysis of
> whose far-reaching scope he was himself unaware, that the
> present system of production, namely, big industry, reduces
> the worker to the position of a wheel in the factory and a
> mere instrument in the hands of his employers; and it is
> useless to hope that technical progress will, through a
> progressive and continuous reduction in productive effort,
> alleviate, to the point of almost causing it to disappear, the
> double burden imposed on man by nature and society. (56)

Marx's analysis of the ways the worker is reduced to "mere
instruments in the hands of his employers" informs Weil's
discussion in *Reflections* of one person being at the disposal of
another, which is one of her central characterizations of
oppression. But she also saw that Marx's demonstration of how
deeply embedded this form of oppression is in the capitalist mode
of production (though not in the system of private property *per
se*) should have undermined the hopes Marx sometimes put in
technical and scientific progress for creating the conditions for a
free and equal society.

If Weil thought that oppression could be reduced, she was
always suspicious of those who felt it could be abolished. She
seemed to share, almost instinctively, the Christian image of
people being born into the world with a burden to carry. She
welcomed some of these "necessities," thinking that, as in
creative work, they called forth people's best efforts. Perhaps this
was one reason she was happier with syndicalists who were often
more grounded in their own experience of work than with
Marxists who held faith in a different future. She was always
more of a materialist than many Marxists. Even in her later
writing saintliness was always something people could struggle for
in the everyday realities of life. There was little abstract in her
notion of saintliness. Weil saw that detached thought, which
emphasizes the necessity of directing one's attenton to the good
that is outside this world, "has as its object a way of living, a
better life, not elsewhere but in this world and immediately."[6]

Simone Weil never promised to imagine a system of production that could vastly limit oppression. But if we are forced to the
conclusion that a certain level of oppression is inevitable, then at
least we gain the advantage of "being able legitimately to resign

ourselves to oppression and of ceasing to regard ourselves as accomplices in it because we fail to do anything effective to prevent it" (56). In a period of such economic misery as she lived through this was a crucial issue. Weil recognized that "to have grasped this problem clearly is perhaps a condition for being able to live at peace with oneself" (56). If she could develop a clear analysis of the limits and character of oppression she could set the terms for a more realistic discussion of socialism—a discussion that would not create false hopes in working people. The task was not only one of answering clearly formulated questions, but also one of discovering the meaningful questions themselves. Weil was concerned to contribute both to the theory of socialism and to its practice:

> The problem is, therefore, quite clear; it is a question of knowing whether it is possible to conceive of an organisation of production which, though powerless to remove the necessities imposed by nature and the social constraint arising therefrom, would enable these at any rate to be exercised without grinding down souls and bodies under oppression. (56)

Weil retained the Marxist emphasis on the organization of production as the central element in oppression, but she did not share the traditional Marxist (as well as liberal) view that oppression is an issue of economics and politics rather than morality. Rather, Weil wanted to rethink the relation between morality and politics as part of her showing that oppression is fundamentally an issue of social theory and politics. She was forced to acknowledge that morality and religion are themselves powerless to change social relations of power and subordination: "Society does not depend upon reason and virtue" (*Lectures on Philosophy*, 129). She recognized that Christianity, which "brought with it the most pure morality in the world, has brought no change at all" (129).

As we have seen (in Chapter 3, section 5) Weil felt drawn to a materialist method partly because she still felt that it was absurd to put hopes into morally changing individuals, as if this could bring about a change in social relations. Her rationalism, which fostered a dualistic mode of thought, made it difficult for her to understand individual moral change as an integral aspect of transforming social relations. Weil tended to think at this early period of her writing that if she could not look towards individuals' changing, then she would have to look for a different form of society. This search demanded a purely rational inquiry that did not need to refer to individual needs and wants; these would be largely shaped within the context of the new social relations. She thought that "one has to study society as one studies biology, by studying the conditions of equilibrium" (130). As in Emile Durkheim's thought, in Weil's the social is *sui generis*. The form of social organization could be studied without any appeal to ideas of virtue or good will. Thus, in her investigations into its causes social oppression is an issue of politics:

> The whole problem of politics comes to this: to find, in conditions as they are, a form of society which would conform to the demands of reason and which at the same time would take into account necessities of a less important kind. . .
>
> A method as materialist as this is absolutely necessary if good intentions are to be changed into actions. It is absurd to want to reform society by reforming individuals.
>
> How many individuals who are just and scrupulous in their individual lives do not hesitate to lie when they are diplomats, to exploit their workers when they are employers, etc. (*Lectures on Philosophy*, 130)

In Weil's view, therefore, we cannot think about oppression simply in terms of the ways one individual treats another; nor can we think about injustice by considering individual behavior. Even though in theoretical work Weil tended to define oppression as "the negation of Kant's principle" whereby "man is treated as a means" (136), she questioned Kant's individualism and the liberal assumption that individuals can live free, equal, and independent lives as long as they do not become dependent upon each other.[47]

But if Weil had learned to question the idea that society can be reformed by reforming individuals, she had also learned to doubt the kind of "mechanical" reform made in the Soviet Union.

The very way society functions prevents men from being virtuous; it is a machine for making slaves and tyrants. It is a vicious circle: those who want to reform things mechanically end up in the pitiable way they have done in Russia; those who want to reform society by reforming individuals, have ended up with some very fine individual lives, but with nothing as far as society is concerned. (130)

Her experience of the Soviet Union showed her that capitalists will be replaced by bureaucrats as long as big industry, in which "the individual counts for almost nothing at all" (149), survives. She questioned the idea that private property is central to defining oppression and the idea that the form of government is as critical as "what form of production system exists" (148). She showed little hesitation in her analysis of the role of big industry in her condemnation of the Soviet Union:

In Russia the employer is gone, but the factory is still there. It makes no difference. The law which governs economic life as it is, is accumulation of wealth. The employer has the power to think only of himself, but no power to be good.

So, what is central in this problem is big industry and not the institution of property. The interests of those who represent the power of the firm and of those who work are absolutely opposed to one another.

It is not a question of what form of government there is, but what form of production system exists. The state is for all practical purposes in the hands of the capitalists.

In Russia, it is at bottom exactly the same. (148)

Work had been organized on a smaller scale up to the time of the development of capitalism. The peasants were sometimes tenants of the land they cultivated, and craftsmen often owned their own tools and materials. It is with capitalism that "Method is taken away from men and transferred to matter" (147). Descartes had never foreseen that "those who are masters of machines are masters of men and of nature" (150). Because the machines need men less than men need machines, men have become "slaves of machines" (150). With Marx's crucial analysis of the development of capitalism there was no longer an excuse for people to hide the reality of social oppression. As Weil says, "The first duty that it places on one is not to tell lies" (139). We should not hide from anyone "that millions of people are crushed by the social machine" (140). This had to be the starting point for thinking about the nature of oppression in modern society. Weil's commitment to the truth that held the deepest hopes for socialist theory, which had so often in both theory and practice degraded the truth to serve its own interests, is striking.[8]

2   Industry and oppression

Simone Weil was deeply impressed with Marx's analysis of the workings of the capitalist mode of production, which helped set the terms for her own understanding of oppression. She was less impressed with his conviction that capitalism prepared the way for socialism and for his continuing commitment to technical progress.

It is partly because Marx "gives such a first-rate account of the mechanism of capitalist oppression" that, as Weil says, it is "hard to visualize how this mechanism could cease to function" (*Reflections*, 40). She felt that his analysis was so powerful that it rendered unconvincing his sense of the transition from capitalism to socialism. When she first read *Capital* in her youth she had been "immediately struck by certain gaps, certain contradictions of the first importance" ("On the Contradictions of Marxism," 147). But, as she says, their "very obviousness, at that time, prevented me from placing confidence in my own judgment" (147). It is this capacity to engage with Marx in such a selective and critical way that has been so rare in the Marxist tradition. So often questioning has been thought disloyal.

Weil also rethought the emphases in the orthodox interpretation of Marx that she believed had systematically missed the real strengths and core of his analysis of the nature of oppression in capitalist society. Such interpretation tended to concentrate exclusively on the economic aspect of oppression in a way that distorted its significance within Marx's overall understanding of the workings of capitalism:

As a rule it is only the economic aspect of this oppression that holds our attention, that is to say the extortion of surplus value; and, if we confine ourselves to this point of view, it is certainly easy to explain to the masses that this extortion is bound up with competition, which latter is in turn bound up with private property, and that the day when property becomes collective all will be well. (*Reflections*, 40)

Weil discovered difficulties "even within the limits of this apparently simple reasoning" (40), for as the experience of the Soviet Union shows about the nature of oppression, "what is central in this problem is big industry and not the institution of property" (*Lectures on Philosophy*, 148). Weil thus recognized the importance of the struggle for power between different firms within both capitalist and socialist societies, a view that has a central position in her writings and that derives from:

Marx showed clearly that the true reason for the exploitation of the workers is not any desire on the part of the capitalists to enjoy and consume, but the need to expand the undertaking as rapidly as possible so as to make it more powerful than its rivals. Now not only a business undertaking, but any sort of working collectivity, no matter what it may be, has to exercise the maximum restraint on the consumption of its members so as to devote as much time as possible to forging weapons for use against rival collectivities; so that as long as there is, on the surface of the globe, a struggle for power, and as long as the decisive factor in victory is industrial production, the workers will be exploited (*Reflections*, 40)

Weil had discovered an argument for the centrality of industrial production that also shows that relations of power extend to the different spheres of social life. She tended to see economic power as only one form of power in society. Significantly, economic power replaced military power with the development of capitalist society once there was a shift from individual to collective production, and big industry developed.

The power the bourgeoisie has to exploit and oppress is the power of big industry.

If we want to understand what forces workers to lose their grasp of a truer liberty and what explains their subordination, we have to look to the organization of the factory and not to the system of property. Her reading of Marx showed Weil that a transformation of property relations would barely touch the real sources of oppression in big industry. She also saw limitations to what any purely legal or political changes could effect with respect to oppression:

> The power which the bourgeosie has to exploit and oppress
> the workers lies at the very foundation of our social life,
> and cannot be destroyed by any political and juridical
> transformation. This power consists in the first place and
> essentially in the modern system of production itself, that is
> to say big industry. (*Reflections*, 41)

To elaborate further on the nature of capitalist oppression, Weil quotes the contrast Marx draws between the craftsmen and the factory worker in his *Grundrisee*:

> Among craftsmen who work by hand, the worker uses his
> tools; in the factory he is at the service of the machine. In
> the former case it is the worker himself who has control of
> the instruments used in work, whereas in the latter he has
> to follow the movements of the machine. In craftsmanship
> the worker's limbs formed a living machine; in the factory,
> there is dead machinery which is independent of the
> workers, of which they are part like living cogs in a
> machine. (*Lectures on Philosophy*, 147)

Marx's conception of capitalism as the enslavement of living labor to dead labor helped Weil to see oppression not simply as a feature of capitalist societies but as fundamental to the organization of big industry. In her view the relation of power between capital and labor is not an issue of the personal relationship of respect between employer and workers, a relationship that in fact barely exists in the organization of assembly line production in big industry where discipline is the task of the machine. Rather,

Weil argues, the power relations between capital and labor must be considered in the context of the organization of the labor process, in which the relationship between science and machinery embodies the power of capital over labor.

Weil investigated the workings of assembly-line production as a new phase in the organization of production that inevitably set new terms for the relation between capital and labor. She grasped the full significance of Frederick Taylor's "scientific management" in establishing a new order of discipline in the workplace. She also understood the immense damage that assembly-line production would do to the possibilities of a socialist transformation in work relations in the Soviet Union. As we have seen (in Chapter 2, section 3), Lenin was concerned to maximize production, thinking that the critical issues had to do with the distribution of the product rather than with the conditions of its production.[9] He saw the assembly-line as an advance of science that should be fully utilized since it promised to increase production and so make more goods available. But Marx showed that science is not neutral in the interests of capital and labor; the fundamental concepts of science have traditionally been forged in the interests of those who seek and control the domination of nature.[10] Weil thought this view evident in Marx's discussion of machinery in *Capital*:

> In the factory there exists a mechanism independent of the workers, which incorporates them as living cogs. . . . The separation of the spiritual forces that play a part in production from manual labour, and the transformation of the former into power exercise by capital over labour, attain their fulfilment in big industry founded on mechanization. The detail of the individual destiny of the machine-worker fades into insignificance before the science, the tremendous natural forces and the collective labour which are incorporated in the machines as a whole and constitute with them the employer's power. (*Reflections*, 41)

Following Marx, Weil recognizes "the degrading division of labour into manual and intellectual labour" as "the very foundation of our culture, which is a culture of specialists" (41). For Weil a society based on specialization "can only organize a perfect oppression, not lighten it" (40) since specialization "implies the enslavement of those who execute to those who co-ordinate" (42). She learned from Marx that state oppression depends on "the existence of organs of government that are permanent and distinct from the population, namely, the bureaucratic, military and police machines" (42), a perception that allowed her to see that "At all levels we are brought up against the same obstacle" (42)—that is, oppression mediated by specialization. In this way she was ready to generalize Marx's remark about the "degrading division of labour into manual and intellectual labor" to talk about different aspects of capitalist society.

Weil recognized that the ability of workers to attain know-ledge and culture was the condition for a real revolution. She saw not only that the "domination of those who handle words over those who know how to handle things is rediscovered at every stage of human history" but that "these manipulators of words, whether priests or intellectuals, have always been on the side of the ruling class, on the side of the exploiters against the producers".[11] As Simone Pétrement points out, Weil's deep commitment to working class education is absolutely clear: "it is not by inspiring them with contempt for culture, described here as bourgeois, that the workers can be freed from the intellectuals' domination."[12] It is only by giving workers the ability to handle language themselves that we can begin to undo what Marx identifies as "the degrading division of work into intellectual and manual labor." According to Pétrement, this meant for Weil that workers "must prepare themselves to take possession of the entire heritage from previous generations. Indeed, this act of taking possession is the revolution."[13] Thus science as it has been inherited would have to be transformed.

3   Forms of oppression

In what she read about the Soviet Union Simone Weil saw evidence for her contention that so often "The essential task of revolutions consists in the emancipation not of men but of productive forces" (*Reflections*, 42). She thought that despite himself Marx was unduly influenced by the divinity the rise of big industry had made of the productive forces. In substituting matter for mind as the motive power of history in his rectification of the Hegelian dialectic, he conceived history, "as though he attributed to matter what is the very essence of mind—an unceasing aspiration towards the best" (44). Weil argued that this tendency within Marxism was profoundly in keeping with "the general current of capitalist thought" since "to transfer the principle of progress from mind to things is to give a philosophical expression to that 'reversal of the relationship between subject and object' in which Marx discerned the very essence of capitalism" (44). So, while Marx challenged the mythological idea of human progress, he reintroduced it in his assumption that the forces of production progress, an idea confused by the assumption that moral progress necessarily follows from economic progress.

This emphasis on productive forces served to make the maximization of production the goal of Soviet planning. According to Weil, though, when production becomes an end in itself, socialism can only enter as an issue of the distribution of production. Thus issues about the quality of work experience necessarily disappear as what is significant about socialism is displaced beyond the realm of the quality of working people's lives—a displacement for Weil that is integral to the emergence of new forms of oppression, as discussed in Chapter 3, section 2. As capitalist production legitimated the subordination and oppression of working people in the name of "progress," so the shared emphasis on productive forces corrupted the very heart of socialism. Weil was aware that the "term 'religion' may seem surprising in connection with Marx" (44), but she was forced to think in these terms once she had reflected on her experience of the Soviet Union:

> This religion of productive forces, in whose name
> generations of industrial employers have ground down the
> labouring masses without the slightest qualm, also
> constitutes a factor making for oppression within the
> socialist movement. All religions make men into a mere
> instrument of Providence, and socialism, too, puts men at
> the service of historical progress, that is to say of productive

progress. That is why, whatever may be the insult inflicted
on Marx's memory by the cult which the Russian oppressors
of our time entertain for him, it is not altogether
undeserved. . . . Marx, it is true, never had any other
motive except a generous yearning after liberty and
equality. (45)

This religion of productive forces was connected in Weil's
mind to the damaging distinction Marx sometimes fostered in his
writings between the "moral" and the "historical." Weil saw that
Marx's assumption that the productive forces have an inherent
tendency to increase (as discussed in Chapter 3, section 5)
provided in part for the inadequacies within his writings to grasp
the nature of the relationship between the "moral" and the
"historical." When Marx talks about the "historical mission" of a
dominant class to carry "the productive forces to an even higher
level,"[14] he is not talking about a moral advance but of its
material destiny. The problem with Marx is that he assumes that,
while historical forces have nothing to do with morality, they can
bring moral "progress." Weil identifies this distinction, without
dwelling on its implications, when she says:

> The recognition of the fact that the capitalist system grinds
> down millions of men only enables one to condemn it
> morally; what constitutes the historic condemnation of the
> system is the fact that, after having made productive
> progress possible, it is now an obstacle in its way. The
> essential task of revolutions consists in the emancipation not
> of men but of productive forces. (42)

It is worth emphasizing this last point since it shows how
production becomes an end in itself. Weil remained deeply
impressed by Marx's insight into the ways capitalist production
reverses the relationship not only between subject and object but
also between means and ends: Production is no longer organized
to fulfill human needs but becomes an end in itself, and
simultaneously, people are reduced to the means of industrial
production. Weil illuminates the process of these reversals in a
systematic comparison between production in pre-capitalist and
capitalist societies, which forms the core of her analysis of

oppression in *Reflections Concerning the Causes of Liberty and Social Oppression.*

While challenging the conventional conception of historical progress, Weil wanted both to acknowledge the nature of the unfreedom inherent in people's relation to nature and to explain the character of freedom that they could gain. When she wrote *Reflections*, she tended to accept—albeit, with a certain ambivalence—that the domination of nature has brought a degree of freedom, and she wished to distinguish the effects of this domination in the quality of individual lives. This analysis involves the question:

> What makes primitive man a slave? The fact that he hardly orders his own activity at all; he is the plaything of need, which dictates each of his movements or very nearly, and harries him with its relentless spur; and his actions are regulated not by his own intelligence, but by the customs and caprices—both equally incomprehensible—of a nature that he can but worship with blind submission. (79)

Weil had an early recognition of the importance of people fully understanding and ordering their own activities. These onerous conditions she describes, however, cannot be considered oppressive—that is, as involving relations of power and subordination among people; rather, "such material conditions necessarily rule out oppression, since each man is compelled to sustain himself personally, is continually at grips with outside nature" (62).

In primitive forms of production—hunting, fishing, gathering—"action seems to receive its form from nature itself' (62), using methods that "have often succeeded without men's knowing why" (62). For Weil, this kind of work, which involves the domination of nature and a direct and unmediated contact with reality, "brings out the best" in people in the sense that it is through this kind of work that the individual's liberty is most fully asserted—an idea similar to Kant's belief that acting against obstacles is what certifies moral behavior so that being moral is not a matter of individual talent and ability but of a rational nature common to all. The emphasis on necessity and struggling with necessities as giving life its reality remained an abiding theme for Weil. It is in this sense that to the end of her life Weil had the deepest respect for fishermen who confronted nature; their work continued to provide her with a model of meaningful labor, though she also realized that many jobs could not be fulfilled according to this ideal.

Weil agreed with Marx's view that "social existence is determined by the relations between man and nature established by production" (71) and that this view is the only sound basis for historical investigation. She did not, however, accept the conventional picture that people seem "to pass by stages, with respect to nature, from servitude to domination" (63), nor did she assume that what was valuable in previous stages would somehow be retained in a new synthesis at the higher stage of development. Her opposition to this Hegelian influence in fact sharpened considerably in her later writings, where she is more prepared to acknowledge that what is of value in culture has often been destroyed forever. Weil instead stressed that the relations between man and nature "must be considered first of all in terms of the problem of power, the means of subsistence forming simply one of the data of this problem" (71). Hence, in her earlier writing she values primitive conditions of production:

> At this stage, each man is necessarily free with respect to other men, because he is in direct contact with the conditions of his own existence, and because nothing human interposes between them and him; but, on the other hand, and to the same extent, he is narrowly subjected to nature's domination, and he shows this clearly enough by deifying her. At higher stages of production, nature's compulsion continues certainly to be exercised, and still pitilessly, but in an apparently less immediate fashion; it seems to become more and more liberalized and to leave an increasing margin to man's freedom of choice, to his faculty of initiative and decision. (63)

Weil thus acknowledges that we have reached the epoch "predicted by Descartes when men would use 'the force and action of fire, water, air, the stars and all the other bodies' in the same way as they do the artisans' tools" (79) thereby making themselves "masters of nature." Now, according to Weil, "work is accomplished in such a way as to take charge of nature and to organize her so that needs can be satisfied. Nature has been reduced to inert matter that we have to learn how to handle, as we handle any other matter" (63). But for Weil, while such progress is generally acceptable at a collective level, it betrays itself with respect to the quality of individual lives. Her admiration for Descartes is such that Weil does not want to see the consequences for the domination of individuals as following even indirectly from the domination of nature.[15] She prefers to see a "strange inversion" through which "this collective domination transforms itself into servitude as soon as one descends to the scale of the individual, and into a servitude fairly closely resembling that associated with primitive conditions of existence" (79).

For Weil, then, we cannot escape the necessities of nature: "As long as man goes on existing . . . the pressure exerted by necessity will never be relaxed for one single moment" (84). Therefore, it is fundamentally misleading to conceptualize our relationship with nature solely in terms of a shift from servitude to domination. Weil seems to suggest that even after industrialization, nature continues to exercise constraint, though Marx's view tends to mask this. We can never really hope to escape from nature's constraint, nor should we aspire to since it is essential for our minds to face matter that is foreign to us and indifferent to our will. It is only because stable patterns of relationships exist in nature that methodical action in the world is possible. Only because necessities confront us can work, in the sense that Weil uses the term, exist.[16]

Given her paradoxical view of "progress," the surprising fact Weil wants to account for is "not that oppression should make its appearance only after higher forms of economy have been reached, but that it should always accompany them" (62). This means there is a difference not only of degree but also of kind among different modes of production. Since Weil recognizes that "from the point of view of consumption there is but a change-over to slightly better conditions," she concludes that production is the decisive factor that is "transformed in its very essence" (62). But she challenges the conventional notion that sees this transformation as a "progressive emancipation with respect to nature" (62):

In reality, at these higher stages, human action continues,
as a whole, to be nothing but pure obedience to the brutal
spur of an immediate necessity; only, instead of being
harried by nature, man is henceforth harried by man.
However, it is still the same pressure exerted by nature that
continues to make itself felt, although indirectly; for
oppression is exercised by force, and in the long run all
force originates in nature (63)

Although Weil admits that this notion of force "is far from
simple" (63), she leaves it relatively undeveloped in her earlier
writings. But at least she is clear at this stage "that it is not the
manner in which use is made of some particular force, but its
very nature, which determines whether it is oppressive or not"
(63). Her ideas about the nature of force at this stage were
formed in relation to Marx's ideas about the state. He
understood, according to Weil, that "this machine for grinding
men down, cannot stop grinding as long as it goes on functioning,
no matter in whose hands it may be" (63). Thus she invokes
Marx against those in the Soviet Union who argued that, as long
as the state was in the hands of the working class, it could be put
at the service of the whole society. Weil's conviction of the
inherent oppressiveness of the state was strengthened by her visit
to Germany in August, 1932. There she experienced the
demoralization caused by years of unemployment and widespread
fear and insecurity. She was depressed to discover how various
political groups, including the syndicalist organizations, were
pursuing socialism through state control of the economy. Besides
rank and file attempts at united action with socialist workers
against the consolidation of Hitler's power, the Communist
leadership refused to cooperate with socialists they had learned
under Moscow's control to dismiss as social fascists. By October,
1943, Weil concluded that "the German Communist party is not
the organization of German workers resolved to prepare the
transformation of the regime . . . it is propaganda organization in
the hands of the bureaucratic Russion State" ("La Situation en
Allemagne", 138).[17]
Without denying that the way managers treat workers is *part*
of the workers' oppression, Weil also criticized the liberal notion
that oppression has its *source* in the ways people treat each other,

as if it is always in the power of people to treat others equally. Instead, she says, "Oppression proceeds exclusively from objective conditions" (63), thus challenging the liberal view that regards oppression as "the usurpation of a privilege" that could be retaken (57). Seeing "privileges" as "objective conditions" and in Marx's terms that "you cannot abolish oppression so long as the causes which make it inevitable remain" (57), Weil questioned the idea that a transformation of legal or property relations would automatically bring about a fundamental change in social relations. For her the existence of privileges is one of the sources of oppression:

> [I]t is not men's laws or decrees which determine privileges,
> nor yet titles to property; it is the very nature of things.
> Certain circumstances, which correspond to stages, no
> doubt inevitable, in human development, give rise to forces
> which come between the ordinary man and his own
> conditions of existence, between the effort and the fruit of
> the effort, and which are, inherently, the monopoly of a
> few, owing to the fact that they cannot be shared among all;
> thenceforward these privileged beings, although they
> depend, in order to live, on the work of others, hold in their
> hands the fate of the very people on whom they depend,
> and equality is destroyed. (64)

In Weil's view it is when efforts need "to be multiplied and co-ordinated to be effective" in the "struggle against men or against nature" (64) that coordination becomes the monopoly of a few where those who are subject to this power are at the disposal of those who exercise it is the source of oppression. For example, when the religious rites people use to win over nature become "too numerous and complicated to be known by all" (64), priests create a monopoly of this knowledge and exercise their authority in the name of nature's powers. Oppression is the result. Likewise, scientific knowledge is a privilege and a source of oppression in modern society, according to Weil: "Nothing essential is changed when this monopoly is no longer made up of rites but of scientific processes, and when those in possession of it are called scientists and technicians instead of priests" (64).

Besides knowledge, Weil also mentions arms and money as

other sources of privilege. When arms become powerful and difficult to handle without apprenticeship, they become a monopoly of specialists who can enforce their power. This can place workers at the mercy of warriors. Similarly, when the division of labor is developed so that workers can no longer live off their own products, those who have money under their control can obtain for themselves the "products of others' labour, and at the same time deprive the producers of the indispensably necessary" (64). Except for money, which appears at a given moment in history, these sources of privilege "enter into play under all systems of oppression" (65). What changes is the way they are distributed and combined.

While noting that oppression is rested in privileges, Weil is careful to stress that "privileges, of themselves, are not sufficient to cause oppression" (65). Rather, the struggle for power is fundamental to oppression, and it is this struggle for power that makes any liberal dream fictitious. It makes it impossible to hope that "inequalities could be easily mitigated by the resistance of the weak and the feelings of justice of the strong" (65). Although she continued to give a central emphasis to the struggle for power in her writings, Weil came to think of the relations between strong and weak in Christian terms.

The *Iliad* deeply influenced Weil's thinking about power: Her reading of the epic helped her to clarify a defining feature of oppression, the substitution of means and ends, and thus further to formulate her objections to liberal theory.

[I]n this ancient and wonderful poem there already appears the essential evil besetting humanity, the substitution of means for ends. At times war occupies the forefront, at other times the search for wealth, at other times production; but the evil remains the same. The common run of moralists complain that man is moved by his private interest: would to heaven it were so. Private interest is self-centred and incapable of giving rise to unlimited evils. Whereas, on the other hand, the law of all activities governing social life, except in the case of primitive communities, is that here each one sacrifices human life—in himself and in others—to things which are only means to a better way of living. This sacrifice takes on various forms, but it all comes back to the question of power. (69)

Here Weil challenges the moral psychology of liberal theory, which offers a rational conception of decision-making and human action in terms of individual self-interest, a conception to which the realities of social life do not correspond. It is the very substitution of means for ends that defines the "rationality" of capitalist social relations, as Marx saw: Within capitalist accumulation consumption appears not as the fulfillment of human needs and satisfactions—as liberal moral theory would have it—but as a "necessary evil" to be reduced to the minimum, a mere means to the end of maximizing profit. For Weil it is "the profound absurdity of this picture which gives it its profound truth; a truth which extends singularly beyond the framework of the capitalist system" (68).

The substitution of means for ends concerns Weil in her analysis of power. For the powerful the maintenance of power is an end in itself, for which the struggle of the oppressed against their oppression can constitute "an aggravating factor in that it forces the masters to make their power weigh even more heavily for fear of losing it" (69). The only feature peculiar to capitalism is that "the instruments of industrial production are at the same time the chief weapons in the race for power" (68). Whatever the methods in the struggle for power, they impose themselves as absolute ends. Weil had already learned that "The real subject of the Iliad is the sway exercised by war over the warriors, and through them, over humanity in general" (68). She was convinced that "It is the reversal of the relationship between means and ends, it is this fundamental folly that accounts for all that is senseless and bloody right through history" (69).

It is partly the stress Weil gives to the reversal of means and ends that encourages us to see working people as caught up in an endless struggle, without any control. She lost any confidence in Marx's idea that people make their own history, even if it is not in circumstances of their choosing. I think this reflects a deeper uncertainty in her early writings. She is unsure what kind of control people can be imagined to have over their lives. She talks more easily of liberty in terms of control over one's actions or of the processes of one's work, not so much in terms of control over the shape of one's life. Part of her still sees the oppressed involved in an unavoidable struggle against the conditions of their oppression. This is when she stresses the human faculty for liberty and self-determination: "men are essentially acting beings and have a faculty of self-determination which they can never renounce, even should they so desire, except on the day when, through death, they drop back into the state of inert matter" (67). This means the powerful have to be continually engaged in reinforcing a power they can never be sure of. The domination they seek is essentially impossible to attain for it will always be resisted because the oppressed always desire freedom. Thus at this stage of her writings, Weil believed that those we think of as "upholders of order" are unrealistic in their hope of creating a "balance between those who command and those who obey" (66). Their vision of stability of power is a chimera "on the same grounds as the anarchists' utopia" (66); it fails to realize that all power is unstable. The paradoxical result, for Weil, is that those in power become oppressed by the very "instruments of domination": in her view, "Human history is simply the history of the servitude which makes men—oppressors and oppressed alike—the plaything of the instruments of domination they themselves have manufactured, and thus reduces living humanity to being the chattel of inanimate chattels" (69).

It is because "this reversal of the relationship between means and end" has such a deep grip over the historical process that Weil concludes that "it is things, not men, that prescribe the limits and laws governing this giddy race for power. Men's desires are powerless to control it" (69). People may dream of moderation but they are powerless to practice it. The struggle for power undermines any sense of limits or moderation.

Weil does acknowledge that the oppressed sometimes "manage to drive out one team of oppressors and replace it by another, and sometimes even to change the form of oppression" (69). They cannot, however, abolish oppression itself. To do so "would first mean abolishing the sources of it, abolishing all the monopolies, the magical and technical secrets that give a hold over nature, armaments, money, co-ordination of labour" (70). They could not succeed in this, even if they could decide on setting themselves these tasks, since they would be "condemning themselves to immediate enslavement by the social groupings that had not carried out the same change" (70). Weil seems to think that obstacles and illusions limit the oppression people suffer—"Power is always running up against the actual limits of the controlling faculty," she says (72)—and that oppression "would know no bounds were these not by good fortune found in the nature of things" (70). In her view, people cannot really look to themselves to transform their situation. But it is important to realize that this view is out of spirit with much of *Reflections*, which holds out a possibility of mitigating oppression and sometimes reminds us that "if oppression is a necessity of social life, this necessity has nothing providential about it" (70).

According to Weil, we have to give up the idea that oppression will end when it becomes detrimental to production or that it will cease to be necessary "as soon as the productive forces have been sufficiently developed to ensure welfare and leisure for all" (70). We have to be aware that this dream would only be true "if men were guided by considerations of welfare; but from the days of the Iliad to our own times, the senseless demands made by the struggle for power have taken away even the leisure for thinking about welfare" (70). She argues that an increase in production can in itself make little difference to the oppression suffered.[18] This is how she summarizes her fundamental challenge to a conception of progress argued for in both liberal and socialist thought:

> The raising of the output of human effort will remain
> powerless to lighten the load of this effort as long as the
> social structure implies the reversal of the relationship
> between means and ends, in other words, as long as the
> methods of labour and of warfare give to a few men a
> discretionary power over the masses. . . . Once society is
> divided up into men who command and men who execute,
> the whole of social life is governed by the struggle for
> power, and the struggle for subsistence only enters as one
> factor, indispensable to be sure, of the former. (71)

In Weil's view, the critique of the idea of progress in liberal-democratic society involves thinking critically about material progress, which we too easily accept "as a gift of the gods, as something which goes without saying" (80), and exploring the costs at which it takes place. When she contrasts "primitive tribes, organized practically without inequality, with our present-day civilization," Weil is struck by the tragic realization that

> it seems as if man cannot manage to lighten the yoke
> imposed by natural necessities without an equal increase in
> the weight of that imposed by social oppression, as though
> by the play of a mysterious equilibrium. And even, what is
> stranger still, it would seem that if, in fact, the human
> collectivity has to a large extent freed itself from the
> crushing burden which the gigantic forces of nature place on
> frail humanity, it has, on the other hand, taken in some sort
> nature's place to the point of crushing the individual in a
> similar manner. (79)

Weil acknowledges that modern industry has solved critical issues of privation, incentive to effort, and the coordination of labor. But the solutions are only established at the cost of the people's fuller liberty for "social oppression provides an immediate solution, by creating, to put it broadly, two categories of men—those who command and those who obey" (82). This division inevitably involves people being driven "beyond the limits of their strength, some being whipped by ambition, others, in Homer's words, 'under the goad of a harsh necessity'" (82). Under modern conditions the worker has been systematically deprived of a freedom to innovate that people used to be able to take for granted. According to Weil, we should be careful not to confuse the power industrialized society has achieved in its domination of nature with the fate of individual workers; we should be wary of talking about "progress" before we have carefully considered the quality of individual lives. Although she does attend here to the quality of individual experience, in her earlier writing, Weil is more concerned to dispel liberal assumptions of material progress as having benefitted the whole community:

> The efforts of the modern worker are imposed on him by a
> constraint as brutal, as pitiless and which holds him in as
> tight a grip as hunger does the primitive hunger. . . . And

as for the sequence of movements in work, that, too, is
often imposed from outside on our workers; what is more,
in this respect, the constraint is in certain cases
incomparably more brutal today than it has ever been.
However tied and bound a primitive man was to routine
and blind gropings, he could at least try to think things out,
to combine and innovate at his own risk, a liberty which is
absolutely denied to a worker engaged in a production line.
(79–80)

Technical developments that have promised people "the
mastery over the forces of nature" have necessitated cooperation
on such an enormous scale that it is beyond even the capacity of
governments to control. As if intuiting the future role of
multinational companies and nuclear power, Weil concludes that
"humanity finds itself as much the plaything of the forces of
nature, in the new form that technical progress has given them,
as it ever was in primitive times" (83). We live in a society that
seems too complex for us to understand, let alone control. There
is no longer the relation between human effort and satisfaction
that made primitive society "easy to understand" (81), where
people were spurred into action by their hunger. Hunger still
drives working people, but it pushes them into a labor process in
which the "efficacy is indirect and often separated from the actual
effort by so many intermediaries that the mind has difficulty in
covering them" (81). They might be working in a factory where
they are not only deprived of any genuine freedom and control
but where "the utter fatigue, physical pains and dangers
connected with these labours are felt immediately, and all the
time" (81).

Weil fundamentally agreed with Marx, then, about the
centrality of work and production in forming people's experiences and relations with others. In industrial society the division
between the rulers and the ruled can be so deep and enduring
that these groups live in quite different worlds. This is what
fundamentally undermines any genuine sense of equality in
society and makes it difficult to believe in an effective democracy
in which people have control over their lives.[19] Weil was
concerned with realities of people's lived experiences in industrialized societies, both capitalist and socialist, rather than with

the rhetoric of freedom and equality that presents people with the illusion of a power and control that in most of their lives is not theirs. She believed that people cannot participate effectively as equal citizens in the political life of society if they are treated so fundamentally differently within work:

> . . . when the division between social categories is deep enough for those who decide what work shall be done never to be exposed to feeling or even knowing about the exhausting fatigue, the pains and the dangers of it, while those who do it and suffer have no choice, being continually under the sway of a more or less disguised menace of death. Thus it is that man escapes to a certain extent from the caprices of blind nature only by handing himself over to the no less blind caprices of the struggle for power. (83)

Weil had to experience this condition for herself in order to discover the reality of class relations of power and subordination.

4   Factory work

Reflections is a product of Simone Weil's profoundest observations on the civilization of her time and the movements for change within it. Yet, while Weil had by this time decisively abandoned the utopian hope she found in Marx of a society entirely free from oppression, *Reflections* nevertheless contains an important and unresolved tension regarding the nature of oppression and the possibilities for its mitigation. Weil by no means worked out the degree to which she thought oppression a necessary part of advanced industrial society. Sometimes she implies that because coordination entails a distinction between those who coordinate and those who execute, oppression is inherent in the indispensable task of coordination itself. At other times, however, Weil seems to hope that this function of coordination could be carried out, in a fashion absent under both capitalism and Soviet communism, in a generally non-oppressive way—that is, one that could accord dignity to the worker without undermining the difference between manager and worker.

Throughout *Reflections* these two threads interweave. There Weil seems to be exploring a set of concerns she has not yet fully got a grip on, yet the securing of answers to which is of the first importance for her.

The problem is, therefore, quite clear; it is a question of knowing whether it is possible to conceive of an organization of production which, though powerless to remove the necessities imposed by nature and the social constraint arising therefrom, would enable these at any rate to be exercised without grinding down souls and bodies under oppression. At a time like ours, to have grasped this problem clearly is perhaps a condition for being able to live at peace with oneself. (56)

Weil realized that part of this impasse in her thought stemmed from her own lack of a real familiarity with factory organization and thus with the real possibilities and alternatives for a minimally oppressive form of work organization. It was in part to remedy this ignorance that in the summer of 1934, as she was writing *Reflections*, Weil applied to the Ministry of Education for a leave from her teaching for the 1934–1935 academic year, giving this rationale: "I want to prepare a philosophy thesis concerning the relationship of modern technique, the basis of large industry, to the essential aspects of our civilization—that is, on the one hand our social organization and on the other our culture."[20] Her intention was to seek employment in a factory, where she thought she could learn some of what she needed to know to address these concerns.

There were certainly other reasons why at this time Weil wanted to work in a factory. She had decried the failure of the political groups with which she was familiar and with whom she had worked, to keep their political efforts focused on the actual work conditions within mine, field, and factory. The writing of *Reflections* moved her further from these political groups and from organized political activity in general. In 1934, disgusted with the drift toward militarism, nationalism, and fascism in Europe and despairing over the failure of the left in France and Europe, she wrote, "it is my firm decision to take no further part in *any* political or social activities, with two exceptions:

anticolonialism and the campaign against passive defense exercises" (*Seventy Letters*, 8). Weil did not really hold to this
resolve. In 1936 she was drawn into the factory sit-ins, and this
activity resulted in a renewed interest in trade unions. In fact,
Weil was never for very long removed from political activity of
some sort or other. Nevertheless, in 1934 she saw no satisfactory
direction for her efforts, and this is in part what made the notion
of working in a factory particularly attractive and imperative at
that time.

Moreover, the nature of Weil's criticisms of the political
movements of her time demanded that as a politically serious and
conscientious person she herself not maintain distance from what
she regarded as the true locus of human oppression—the work
place and especially the factory. This is not to say that by seeking
factory work she was attempting to set a political direction for the
Communist and syndicalist organizations; partly as a result of
developing the thoughts that became *Reflections*, she had ceased
by this time to identify with those groups. Instead, her sense of
what she took to be her moral and political commitment made
working in a factory a natural step for her. Thus, while for many
university-educated and privileged persons a retreat from organized political activity would lead to a withdrawal into more
"private" or professional pursuits consonant with their position in
society, for Weil this same retreat led in an entirely opposite
direction: to sharing at least for a time the life of a factory
worker.

Simone Weil had sought manual work since her university
days. We have seen that she had spent part of a summer picking
potatoes, and another working with fishermen in a Breton fishing
village. Since 1931 she had, in fact, formed the intention to work
specifically in a factory, the most characteristic form of work
organization under capitalism, and had tried (unsuccessfully) to
enlist her friend Simone Pétrement in this plan. She had not
acted on this intention earlier (during the height of the
Depression) because she did not want to deprive a worker who
might really need it of a job.

Furthermore, Weil was never comfortable working on behalf
of an oppressed group without in some way herself sharing their
plight. (This same sentiment is evident in the 1940s, when she
was anguished by her parents' pressuring her to flee with them to

the United States while she wanted to remain in France during the nazi occupation and to share that oppression with her fellow countrymen.) This was the deeper feeling underlying her criticism of the leadership of the workers' movement for becoming too distant from the workers. She too clearly saw the danger of the arrogance of the intellectual who thinks he or she "understands" the plight of the oppressed and knows what is good for them without actually sharing their condition. This particular stance of the "outsider" was a morally uncomfortable one for Weil. For her working in a factory would at least to some extent overcome the gap of privilege and experience.

Weil also felt that manual work was "real life" in a way that intellectual work was not. In a letter to a former student, written in 1935 while she was working in a factory, Weil says (with perhaps a slight trace of ironic self-recognition as an intellectual here), "This is the 'contact with real life' about which I used to talk to you" (*Seventy Letters*, 10). And, as she wrote to her friend Albertine Thévenon, "What a factory ought to be is something like what you felt that day at Saint-Chamond and what I have so often felt—a place where one makes a hard and painful, but nevertheless joyful, contact with real life" (20).

Finally Weil certainly desired to test herself, to see if she could "take" the hard work of an unskilled factory hand. She wrote, retrospectively, again to Albertine Thévenon: "I suffered a lot from those months of slavery, but not for anything in the world would I have avoided them. They enabled me to test myself and to touch with my finger things which I had previously been able only to imagine" (19–20).

So for Weil a combination of personal, moral, political, and intellectual reasons, along with the completing of *Reflections*— with the questions it raises without answering and the views it espouses—led her in late 1934 to seek work in a factory.

Weil's first job was at the Alsthom electrical works in Paris, where she worked as an unskilled laborer, running various power-presses making metal buttons and rivets and inserting metal bobbins in and out of a very hot furnace. This job lasted four months (until April 1935), when Weil suffered an injury to her hand. Several days later Weil began work at the Carnaud et Forges de Basse-Indre (in Billancourt). Her work at a stamping press was much harder than at Alsthom, and she stayed only four weeks when she was fired without explanation. Weil then looked for work for a month or so. She finally found a job at the Renault factory in Boulogne-Billancourt, on a milling machine. She worked there from early June until late August. In the fall she went back to teaching, in the lycée at Bourges.

6
Work

To take a youth who has a vocation for physical labour and
employ him at a conveyor-belt or as a piece-work machinist
is no less a crime than to put out the eyes of the young
Watteau and make him turn a grindstone. But the painter's
vocation can be discerned and the other cannot.
—Simone Weil, "Human Personality"

Simone Weil's experience of factory work transformed her
understanding of oppression and her sense of herself. She came
to see oppression as more firmly rooted in the experience of
indignity and humiliation. Factory work reinforced her sense of
the power of big industry to crush human life and consolidated
her belief that working people could not overthrow capitalist
relations of power and subordination.

Labor is a central category in Simone Weil's moral and
political theory. For her it is directly related to the issue of liberty
in modern society, where labor so easily takes on the aspect of
servitude and, in disconnecting the worker from reality,
engenders false dreams and values:

Everywhere, in varying degrees, the impossibility of relating
what one gives to what one receives has killed the feeling
for sound workmanship, the sense of responsibility, and has
developed passivity, neglect, the habit of expecting
everything from outside, the belief in miracles. Even in the

country, the feeling of a deep-seated bond between the land
which sustains the man and the man who works the land has
to a large extent been obliterated since the taste for
speculation, and unpredictable rises and falls in currencies
and prices have got countryfolk into the habit of turning
their eyes towards the town. The worker has not the feeling
of earning his living as a producer; it is merely that the
undertaking keeps him enslaved for long hours every day
and allows him each week a sum of money which gives him
the magic power of conjuring up at a moment's notice the
ready-made products, exactly as the rich do. . . . Generally
speaking the relation between work done and money
earned is so hard to grasp that it appears as almost
accidental, so that labour takes on the aspect of servitude,
money that of a favour. (*Reflections*, 117–18)

Modern labor, then, not only involves servitude, it also
disconnects workers from reality and thus from an understanding
of the social world. For Weil, however, work should do precisely
the reverse. This is why it was so important for her to consider
the ways the labor process could be transformed in order to
restore work to its proper place in human life. And thus it is that
she granted labor a central position in her thought.

In spite of its brutality, Weil saw a lack of resistance to
modern labor organization. She also recognized that our
potential for freedom is limited. Thus she identified and sought to
understand crucial issues of passivity that remain undeveloped
within Marxism. These problems provide the focus of discussion
in this chapter. The first section discusses Weil's attempts to
appreciate the different levels of degradation in the factory and
their interconnection. She was anxious to grasp what the
suffering involved in factory work means to people and what the
day-to-day experience of that suffering feels like. Weil thereby
brought moral issues to the center of her political theory and
through a development in her thinking directly related to her own
experience of this suffering developed the terms of a critique of a
Kantian tradition she saw as unable to grasp the sense in which
personal dignity is an issue of social relations. Weil identified as a
central moral and political issue the ways in which the worker
comes to count for nothing in his or her own eyes. The second

section develops this theme by looking at the ways in which the division between intellectual and manual labor are enforced through factory organization and the consequence of this division for working people in terms of the way their relation to time and space becomes impoverished and thereby disposseses them of control of their own experience. Weil sees that these dimensions contribute to a reversal of the proper relation between means and ends and extends this insight into her analysis of the form of technology in modern society, which is the focus of the third section. For Weil science could not be regarded as neutral but had to be thought about in terms of its adequacy to meet human need. The final sections of this chapter focus in more detail on the meaning Weil's own experience of factory work had for her and the ways in which living this experience of subordination contributed towards a shift in her thinking, enabling her to challenge dominant conceptions of justice in Western culture, both those that draw on a utilitarian conception of pleasure and those that draw on a concept of right.

2 A type of servitude

Simone Weil was aware that profound changes were taking place in the organization of work—that a second industrial revolution involving rationalization or new scientific methods of organizing work had occurred. As she notes in "La Rationalisation," "The first was defined by the scientific utilization of inert matter, and of the forces of nature. The second was defined by the scientific integration of living matter, that is to say of men."[1] In opposition to bourgeois society, which is more interested in production than in the producer, Weil explicitly took the position of the worker, which meant for her that "the study of rationalization becomes part of a very large problem, the problem of an acceptable order in industrial enterprise." In these new terms she developed some of the issues raised in her earlier *Reflections*. Apart from a few hints at the thought of Pierre Joseph Proudhon, Weil saw herself as breaking new ground in the socialist movement.

Weil acknowledged that "we are all experiencing a certain deformation which arises because we live in the atmosphere of

the bourgeois society, and even our aspirations towards a better
society feel the effects of it . . . nothing has value except that
which can be calculated in francs and centimes." (85) This
explains "why in the reproaches that we address to the economic
regime, the idea of exploitation, of money extorted to expand
profits, is almost the only one that is expressed clearly." (85).
Weil, however, learned for herself that "The worker does not
suffer only from the insufficiency of his pay. He suffers because
he is relegated by present-day society to an inferior rank, because
he is reduced to a type of servitude. The inadequacy of salaries is
only one consequence of this inferiority and of this servitude."
Weil thus wanted to shift concern to the experience of suffering
and humiliation within the workplace, knowing as she did that
"The suffering experienced in the factory because of the boss's
arbitrariness weigh as much on the life of the worker as do the
privations experienced outside the factory because of the
inadequacy of his salary."

Skilled work calls on the intelligence and cooperation of
workers. Unskilled work is more often a matter of obeying the
discipline of the machine. Such no longer involves the motives
and intentions of individual workers, and, with their personal
qualities making no difference, workers are often left feeling
replaceable.[2] In assembly-line production the speed of work is
given by the machine and, in having to keep up with it, workers
have no control themselves. In this context the idea of moral
behavior as having to do with distinguishing the motives with
which people act has little place. The worker simply has to
subordinate him- or herself to the machines, which not only
precludes any means for expressing individuality but also it
negates individual feelings and emotions. It is this latter point
that Weil dwelled on since she was always less concerned with the
expression of individuality than with the opportunities work can
give for direct contact with reality. But she is very aware that it is
women who are made to suffer most through unskilled work:

> For a man, if he is very skilled, very intelligent, and very
> tough, there is just a chance, in the present conditions of
> French industry, of attaining to a factory job which offers
> interesting and humanly satisfying work; and even so, these
> opportunities are becoming fewer every day, thanks to the

progress of rationalization. But as for women, they are restricted to purely mechanical labour, in which nothing is required of them except speed. (*Seventy Letters*, p. 11)

Weil warned that we should not think that mechanical labor allows for daydreaming or thought. Rather, "the tragedy is that although the work is too mechanical to engage the mind it nevertheless prevents one from thinking of anything else" (*Seventy Letters*, 11); "One's attention has nothing worthy to engage it, but is constrained to fix itself second by second, upon the same trivial problem" (15). She makes it clear that the temptation to give up thinking altogether is difficult to resist:

One feels so clearly that it is the only way to stop suffering. First of all, to stop suffering morally. Because the situation itself automatically banishes rebellious feelings: to work with irritation would be to work badly and so condemn oneself to starvation; and leaving aside the work, there is no person to be a target for one's irritation. One dare not be insolent to the foreman and, moreover, they very often don't even make one want to be. So one is left with no possible feeling about one's own fate except sadness. And thus one is tempted to cease, purely and simply, from being conscious of anything except the sordid daily round of life. And physically too it is a great temptation to lapse into semi-somnolence outside working hours. (16)

This is an important insight that Weil constantly returned to. It is as if the factory leaves people no space within which to have their own feelings. If anything, these feelings themselves are threatening to people's meeting the targets set for them. So they are turned against themselves and in subtle ways made to betray, or at least subdue their feelings and emotions, and this is the way the work situation "automatically banishes rebellious feelings." If people consciously realize that they have to swallow their frustrations and anger since otherwise they would be out of jobs, their strength and resolution are weakened and they feel ashamed. More often, people have to repress their feelings unconsciously to function effectively: a worker has to learn to "annihilate his soul" (22), as Weil says: "One *cannot* be conscious" (22).

Weil's discussions of factory work inevitably recall Marx's insights into the nature of alienation in capitalist production. But the fact that Weil is not drawn to Hegelian notions that stress work as an important expression of a human essence and so to see capitalist work as the denial of our very humanity enables her to isolate different ways in which individuals are forced to suppress themselves in the labor process. She thereby gives us a concrete sense of the damage people do to themselves that can potentially enrich our understanding from Marx. And she also thereby acknowledges that our emotions need some "outlet in word or gesture" (22), a view that involves some limited notions of expression. She makes us aware of how people must swallow their feelings of irritation and bad humor—though significantly for feminism she does not illuminate the ways this might be taken out on others, say in the family.

Sometimes, however, Weil does talk specifically about the experience of women workers. Although she never explicitly discusses the way the sexual power relations between men and women operate in the factory, she hints at the ways male foremen use their power over women workers. In a letter to Boris Souvarine, a political comrade, she shows a sensitivity to the condition of women in the factory:

> There is a conveyor belt (the first time I've seen one and it hurt me to see it) at which they have doubled the production flow, so one of the women told me, in the last four years. And only today the foreman took the place of one of the women at this belt and kept her machine working full speed for 10 minutes (which is easy if you can rest afterwards) to prove to her that she should work even faster. . . . As you know, the foot action required by a press is very bad for women; one of them told me that she had had salpingitis, but had been unable to get work anywhere except at the presses. Now at last she has a job away from the machines, but with her health definitely ruined. (18)

Weil was astonished to discover that while she herself felt completely exhausted after a day's work, the other women "could still prattle away and did not seem to be consumed with the concentrated fury" (18) she felt. The only women who did express fury of a sort were the ones who were ill, but had to go on working. She wanted to understand how women had learned to live with such situations without seeming to suffer. Weil wondered whether it was the possibility of earning good money that kept these women from expressing and even feeling fury and suffering. The money seemed to be the only thing that mattered, and the women put up with anything to get more, even when they were earning enough and earning more involved enormous efforts. Sometimes this money was not absolutely needed, but somehow it had become an end in itself. Weil had understood this abstractly in her writings about oppression, but it was very difficult to confront this attitude in reality. Had money degraded and corrupted the working class?

As Weil explained to Sóuvarine:

> a woman who works at the conveyor-belt told me on the
> way home in the tram that after a few years, or even a year,
> one no longer suffers, although one remains in a sort of
> stupor. This seems to me to be the lowest stage of
> degradation. She explained to me (what I already knew
> very well) how it was that she and her comrades let
> themselves in for this slavery. 5 or 6 years ago, she said, one
> could get 70 frs a day, "and for 70 frs we'd have to put up
> with anything, we'd have killed ourselves". And still today
> there are some who don't absolutely need it who are glad to
> work on the line for 4 frs an hour with bonus. Why did no
> one in the workers' movement, so called, have the courage
> to think and say during the high wages boom that the
> working class was being degraded and corrupted? It is
> certain that the workers have deserved what has happened
> to them; only the responsibility is collective, while the
> suffering is individual. Any man with proper feelings must
> weep tears of blood to find himself swept into this vortex.
> (18)

Where money had become an end in itself, working people had been assimilated into capitalist forms of life. Their no longer being able to think clearly about what made up their basic needs was the measure of their corruption for Weil. But once this corrupting process of substituting means for ends was in motion, people felt powerless to control it since they had assumed all kinds of financial responsibilities. This was the crucial importance of credit and hire purchase in tying working people into the disciplines of work. But Weil also appreciated that, since the element of skill had been transferred to the machines themselves in the modern factory, only fear and the lure of pay could remain as incentives for the workers. Corruption thereby became much harder to resist, and dignity became much harder for workers to retain.

Recognizing that these difficulties belong to the modern factory itself, Weil criticized liberal individualism for suggesting that workers should always be able to sustain a sense of themselves, and resist pressures to undermine their individual dignity, without comprehending the difficulties this involves. Liberal individualism leaves people feeling they only have themselves to blame, which is why it is so much easier to simply suffer in silence. The factory becomes the dead area in people's lives, a place they never want to be reminded of. Even militant workers "scarcely have the opportunity nor the appetite for theoretically analyzing the constraint that they experience every day: they need to flee from it" ("La Rationalisation").

Furthermore, Weil challenged liberal individualism it creates a myth that workers can identify with as a means of escaping the realities of their daily lives at work: it encourages people to discount their experience at work so as to identify with the equality in legal and political rights that they are promised within civil society. It makes it more difficult to understand the resources available "to the slaves of modern industry":

> It is true that a man of strong soul, if he is poor and dependent, has always the resource of courage and indifference to suffering and privation. It was the resource of Stoic slaves. But that resource is not available to the slaves of modern industry. The work they live by calls for such a mechanical sequence of gestures at such a rapid speed that there can be no incentive for it except fear and the lure of the pay packet. The Stoic who made himself proof against these incentives would make it impossible for himself to work at the required speed. The simplest way,

therefore, to suffer as little as possible is to reduce one's
soul to the level of these two incentives; but that is to
degrade oneself. So if one wishes to retain human dignity in
one's own eyes it means a daily struggle with oneself, a
perpetual self-mutilation and sense of humiliation, and
prolonged and exhausting moral suffering; for all the time
one must be abasing onself to satisfy the demands of
industrial production and then reacting, so as not to lose
one's self-respect, and so on indefinitely. This is the horror
of the modern form of social oppression; and the kindness
or brutality of one's superiors makes little difference. You
will perceive clearly, I think, that what I have just described
is applicable to *every* human being, whoever he is, when
placed in such a situation. (*Seventy Letters*, 38–39)

With control shifted systematically from the worker to the
machines work has been deskilled, "The rights that the workers
can achieve in the workplace do not depend directly on property
or profit, but on the relationship between the worker and the
machine, between the worker and his bosses, and on the more or
less great power of the administration" ("La Rationalisation").
This is not a situation workers have created, but it is one they
have had to learn to live with. They have no alternative but to
abase themselves to meet the demands of industrial production.
Since, according to Weil, our Kantian tradition presents respect
as an issue of relationship, say, between manager and worker, it
makes invisible the fact that one's retaining any sense of personal
dignity involves "exhausting moral suffering" because one is
locked into submitting to the demand of production while
"reacting so as not to lose one's self-respect." The Kantian
tradition fails to illuminate the moral reltions within production
itself, the way people can be degraded through the very
organization of the labor process. For Weil the labor process is
undermining and degrading "to *every* human being," and so this
issue is not dependent on individual moral qualities. Weil shifts
the weight of moral theory away from any idea that the individual
is to blame if undermined and degraded through the process of
production. What is more our individualistic moral traditions
inevitably make matters worse for it makes this suffering
invisible, and, as Weil notices, "For the unfortunate, their social

inferiority is infinitely harder to bear for the reason that they see it everywhere treated as something that goes without saying" (*Seventy Letters, 25*).

When Weil thinks of working conditions in the modern factory, she thinks of them in terms of slavery in which two factors are crucial: the necessity for speed and passive obedience to orders. What she thinks about the nature of obedience gains a greater depth when we realize she is often talking about the experience of women. The experience of subordination and powerlessness often makes more sense of the experience of women in a society in which they are denied power in both public and private realm. Although Weil rarely talks specifically about how women are brought up for a life of submission and obedience, her remarks sometimes seem to trade on this insight, as the example she gives for the "feeling that it is not normal in a factory to expect any consideration at all" shows:

> [A]t another factory, one was not allowed in until the bell rang, ten minutes before the hour; but before the bell a little door forming part of the big entrance was opened and any chiefs who arrived went through it. Meanwhile the women workers—with me among them more than once—waited patiently outside, before that open door, even in pouring rain. (33)

Weil recognized that the factory is alien territory, even though workers spend most of their lives there. She saw that factory workers are in a sense truly uprooted beings, exiles in their own land, an insight that seemed to help her to a deeper understanding of her own experience in the factory, though it did not really help her think about the relations between gender and class. She did not, for instance, see that women might feel this estrangement more sharply at work, since they were supposed to "identify" with the home and the family. This is a weakness in her writing about factory work since it encourages her to make generalizations that only make it harder to clarify sexual relations of power within the factory.

Weil's refusal to draw sharper distinctions between the experience of working-class men and women grew out of her sense that both men and women were subject to "the sense of inferiority which is necessarily induced by the daily assault of poverty, subordination, and dependence" (24). Even though she was already suspicious of the notion of "class struggle," she sustained a strong sense of the reality of class feelings, which "can hardly be stimulated by mere words, whether spoken or written" but which are "determined by actual conditions of life" (24). Weil, then acknowledged the importance of these feelings, but she thought that only in "exceptional moments" (24) would they lead to a challenge to the prevailing order. It is important to realize that she held these views during a period of mass unemployment. Daily resistance in the plants was bound to be less because of the power of capital in a period when workers were grateful to have jobs at all. This reality encouraged her to see the power of capital as almost invincible. She did not discuss ongoing resistance in the plants nor did she speculate whether firms choose women workers because they are brought up to submissiveness. Rather, she talks in more general terms about class feelings:

> What stimulates [feelings of class antagonism] is the
> infliction of humiliation and suffering, and the fact of
> subordination; but it is continually repressed by the
> inexorable daily pressure of need, and often to the point
> where, in the weaker characters, it turns into servility.
> Apart from exceptional moments which, I think, can
> neither be induced nor prevented, nor even foreseen, the
> pressure of need is always more than strong enough to
> maintain order; for the relations of power are all too
> obvious. (25)

Because she learned that subordination more easily leads to servility than to resistance, Weil was concerned to challenge the naive optimism of orthodox Marxism. She also wanted to distinguish between class feeling and a spirit of revolt, as she does in her response to Bernard, the manager of a stove factory near Bourges, when he refused to publish her article in the factory newspaper, saying that it encouraged a spirit of class, as opposed to a spirit of collaboration:

> Let us be clear about it: when the victims of social

oppression do in fact revolt, they have my sympathy,
though unmixed with any hope; when a moment of revolt
achieves some partial success, I am glad. Nevertheless, I
have absolutely no desire to stir up a spirit of revolt—not so
much because I am interested in preserving order as
because I am concerned with the moral interests of the
oppressed. (41)

At some level this remained her position. As she explains it, "I
know too well that those who are in the toils of a too hard
necessity, if they rebel at one moment, will fall on their knees the
moment after" (41). Weil goes on to draw a distinction that
assumed a crucial position in her writing after her experience of
factory work: "The only way to preserve one's dignity under
inevitable physical and moral sufferings is to accept them, to the
precise extent that they are inevitable. But acceptance and
submission are two very different things" (41).

Her insight that working people cannot be expected to revolt,
let alone bring about equal social relations, encouraged Weil
sometimes to exaggerate the conditions of the modern factory
worker as slavery. But her sense of how people are led to
experience themselves as "counting for nothing" is important in
her understanding of the workings of power in terms of class
relations and in her learning to make dignity and self-respect
central to issues of oppression and liberty. As she wrote to
Bernard:

To sum it up, my experience taught me two lessons. The
first, the bitterest and most unexpected, is that oppression,
beyond a certain degree of intensity, does not engender
revolt but, on the contrary, an almost irresistible tendency
to the most complete submission. I verified this in my own
case—I, whose character, as you have guessed, is not a
docile one. The second lesson is that humanity is divided
into two categories—the people who count for something
and the people who count for nothing. When one is in the
second category one comes to find it quite natural to count
for nothing—which is by no means to say that it isn't
painful. I myself found it natural; in the same way that now,
in spite of myself, I am beginning to find it almost natural to

count for something. (I say in spite of myself, because I am trying to resist; I feel so ashamed to count for something in a social system which treads humanity down.) The question at present is whether, in the existing conditions, one can bring it about, within a factory, that the workers count, and have the feeling that they count, for something. For this purpose it is not enough that the manager should try to behave well to them; it needs something quite different. (35)

This "something" can only become clear once we grasp how the detailed organization of production attacks a person's dignity and self-respect. As she comments in "La Rationalisation," noting the conflict between the needs and aspirations workers want to satisfy and the necessities of production, "If tomorrow the bosses are sent packing, if the factories are collectivized, that will not change in any way the fundamental problem, namely that what is required to put out the greatest number of products, is not necessarily what can satisfy the men who work in the factory." For Weil, mass production itself entails the annihilation of a person's dignity and the eradication of the control that derives from a clear grasp of reality. This process necessitates annihilation or total suppression of the self, which is one facet of the process whereby workers come to count for nothing, even to themselves. It creates a condition of total passivity.

For Weil, "It would be very beautiful if the most productive work procedures were at the same time the most agreeable. But one can at least approach such a solution by looking for methods which reconcile as much as possible the interests of the enterprise and the rights of workers." This is not simply a matter of looking for the middle ground between capital and labor. But it is in line with the desire Weil sometimes had to separate the question of the exploitation of the working class, which is defined by capitalist profit, from the oppression of the working class in the place of work. Even if it meant sidestepping some crucial issues for a while, this distinction allowed Weil to raise within the socialist movement crucial issues about the most desirable order in industrial enterprises.

3 Time and control

In 1934 Weil thought that "a factory ought to be . . . a place
where one makes a hard and painful, but nevertheless joyful,
contact with real life. Not the gloomy place it is, where people
only obey orders, and have all their humanity broken down, and
become degraded lower than the machines" (*Seventy Letters*, 20).
Eight years later, in "Human Personality," she observed:

> a modern factory reaches perhaps almost the limit of
> horror. Everybody in it is constantly harassed and kept on
> edge by the interference of extraneous wills while the soul is
> left in cold and desolate misery. What man needs is silence
> and warmth; what he is given is an icy pandemonium. (17)

As Weil notes in another essay, "Factory Work," which is based
on her 1935 experiences but reflects her Christian concerns of the
1940s, "material circumstances of living do not in themselves
necessarily account for unhappiness" (64). But it is difficult, she
explains, to gain a truthful understanding of the humiliations and
indignities of factory work. Existing political traditions cannot
help this understanding: liberal social theory treats these feelings
as contingent and individual responses to situations, while
Marxist theory dispenses with them in its account of the social
relations of power and subordination. Weil thus worked towards
her own conception of the miseries of work, one she sometimes
thought true to the spirit of Marx:

> It is the feelings bound up with the circumstances of living
> then, that make one happy or unhappy; but these feelings
> are not arbitrarily determined. They are not put over or
> effaced by suggestion. They can be changed only by a
> radical transformation of the circumstances themselves. But
> to change circumstances, they must first be known. Nothing
> is more difficult to know than the nature of unhappiness; a
> residue of mystery will always cling to it. For, following the
> Greek proverb, it is dumb. (64)

She then goes on to explain the difficulties in simply accepting what people say about their situations. This is not because people do not feel their own misery, but because it is easier to endure sometimes if it is held in silence. We need to be sensitive if we are to hear people voicing the nature of their discontent; we have to listen to what is going on behind their words:

> To seize [misery's] exact shadings and causes presupposes
> an aptitude for inward analysis which is not characteristic of
> the unhappy. Even if that aptitude existed in this or that
> individual, unhappiness itself would balk such an activity of
> thought. Humiliation always has for its effect the creation of
> forbidden zones where thought may not venture and which
> are shrouded by silence or illusion. When the unhappy
> complain, they almost always complain in superficial terms,
> without voicing the nature of their true discontent;
> moreover in cases of profound and permanent unhappiness,
> a strongly developed sense of shame arrests all lamentation.
> (64)

In Weil's view it is not simply that people are ashamed of their unhappiness but that they feel they have been forced to forsake expectations of a life truer to some deeper sense of themselves. Even those who have been forced to "sell out" cannot forgive themselves. And, since they cannot forgive themselves, they certainly are not ready to share their experience with others. Thus for Weil not only existing political theories but also the workers themselves cannot explain the condition of unhappiness created in the modern factory.

Weil investigates the nature of the unhappiness in the knowledge that "All systems of social reform or transformation seem to miss the point. Were they to be realized, the evil would be left intact" (66), for "They would change too little what underlies the evil, too much the circumstances that are not its cause (66). She thought, for example that the promise in reducing the hours of work was exaggerated and further that "the conversion of a people into a swarm of idlers, who for two hours a day would be slaves, is neither desirable nor morally possible, if materially so. No one would accept two daily hours of slavery" (66). If this statement reveals her conception of the work ethic, it also shows her impatience with schemes that were not immediately realizable. She recognized that if "there is a possible remedy, it is of a different order, less easily conceivable" (66). But she was prepared to make the "inventive effort": "It is necessary to transform incentives, to reduce or abolish what makes for disgust with one's work, to transform the relation of worker to factory, of worker to machine, and to make possible a radically changed awareness of the passing of time while working" (66).

In "Factory Work" Weil rethinks the notions that form part of her analysis of oppression in *Reflections*. She had to find her way back to the theoretical significance of workers' own experience of oppression to discover the terms of this renewed analysis. One result is her fuller recognition that those aspects of factory life that undermine a person's sense of dignity and self-respect had to be changed. Another is the realization that class relations of power and subordination dispossessed working people of their very means of expression, providing them instead with a public language of rights that could often mislead them about the sources of their suffering. But Weil could only grasp this once she had learned how the details of factory organization make it difficult for workers to sustain a sense of personal dignity.

The assembly line denigrates work by making the incentives of individual workers, who must subordinate themselves to the demands of the machinery, irrelevant. According to Weil, one of the most powerful incentives to work is "the feeling of an end to be accomplished and a job to be done" (66). Depriving workers of this incentive, the assembly line thereby deprives them of whatever meaning or dignity they might otherwise find in their work. Such undermining of the worker has nothing to do with his or her attitude to work, but with the nature of the tasks the worker is being forced to do. For Weil, though, it is not work itself that gives life dignity, as we are conventionally led to think; it is the quality of work. If people can feel proud at the speed they have attained or the ease with which they do their monotonous and routine work, this only shows the deep need they have to sustain a sense of pride, their determination in face of the fact that "one's attention has nothing worthy to engage it" (*Seventy Letters*, 15). But Weil is clear that as long as workers "are limited over long periods of time to repeating identical sequences of 5 or 6 simple movements, they cannot be said really to be manufacturing objects. As long as this is true, there will be an abased and malevolent proletariat at the heart of society, whatever else is done" ("Factory Work," 68).

Weil recommended that when an operation calls for simple repetitive movements an automatic machine should be used—but this would be "the diametric opposite of most machines now in use" (68). As she comments on modern factory work, in a way that recalls her analysis of oppression in *Reflections*, "Things play the role of men, men the role of things" (60).[3] There is no place for the discipline of the assembly line within Weil's vision of socialism. To reverse the unnatural and injurious relationship between people and machines we accepted as "normal" within both capitalist and socialist societies, Weil thought a fundamentally new technology was necessary. She recognizes this need in *Reflections*, but in "Factory Work" she understands what it means in practice:

> A specialized machine worker now has for his share in a manufacturing process only the automatic repetition of certain movements, whereas to the machine that he serves goes the whole share, stamped and crystallized in its metal, of synthesis and intelligence that an assembly-line process may imply. Such a reversal is unnatural, criminal. But if a person had for his task the regulation of an automatic machine and the contriving of the cams appropriate to the varying parts to be turned or machined, he would assume, on the one hand, his share of the synthetic and intellective efforts required, and on the other, a manual effort involving, like that of the artisan, real skill. Such a relationship between man and machine would be entirely satisfactory. (69)

Such machinery would be designed, then, "not only to make objects, but also not to destroy men" (72). It would not make people happy, but nor would it "force them to abase themselves" (72). Weil constantly sought for examples of what she calls real rationalization—that is, "technical progress which does not oppress the workers and does not constitute a greater exploitation of their strength" ("La Rationalisation"). She thus recognized the moral reality of both machinery and the work situation it creates, liberal moral theory makes invisible.

Weil searched for a more satisfactory relationship between people and machines as a way of extending their realm of true liberty. She rejected the idea that a transformation in ownership will itself guarantee a shift from a realm of necessity to a realm of freedom. This vision is merely an illusion for her because "if tomorrow we took possession of the factories, we would not know what to do with them and we would be forced to organise them exactly as they are organised at present after a more or less long time of wavering." Weil had no solutions herself, knowing that only in the factories could a new organization of production be tested, a new organization that could only be created after a careful analysis of what is good or bad in the present order. Adopting a less radical tone than he does in *Reflections*, in "Rationalization" Weil is convinced, partly as a result of the factory occupations that spread through France in 1936, that "It is necessary to begin with the present order to conceive a better one."

To extend the freedom and control over work Weil recognized as necessary meant challenging a pervasive tendency in the present order of industry towards rationalization or Taylorization. She criticized the language of rationalization or "scientific" organization of work for only *seeming* to satisfy the demands of reason. She thought instead that a rational organization of work ought to respond of necessity to the interests of the worker, the boss and the consumer." Because it does not do so, Weil refused to see Taylorism as a possibility for progress, as a means of increasing productivity. Rather, she saw Taylor attacking the possibilities of extending any meaningful freedom of work, for "His goal was to take away from the workers the possibility of determining for themselves the procedures and the rhythms of their work, and to place back into the hands of management the choice of movement to be carried out in the course of production." This process was perfected with assembly-line production, where the repetition of mechanical gestures takes from the worker the choice of method and the intelligence of their work. For Weil, Taylor's "primary concern was to find the means to force the workers to give the factory the maximum of their capacity for work. The laboratory was for him a means of research, but above all a means of constraint." He was not really interested in a method for rationalizing work, but in a method of controlling workers.

In *Reflections* Weil sees that "We are living in a world in which nothing is made to man's measure; there exists a monstrous discrepancy between man's body, man's mind and the things which at the present time constitute the elements of human existence; everything is disequilibrium" (108). This insight developed through her experience of factory work, which revealed to her the importance of issues of time, space, and rhythm and set her conceptualization of work on a new basis.

She saw that "Time and rhythm constitute the most important factor of the whole problem of work" ("Factory Work," 69). Since thought is supposed to master time, in some sense thought is the source of human dignity:

> This world into which we are cast *does* exist; we are truly
> flesh and blood; we have been thrown out of eternity; and
> we are indeed obliged to journey painfully through time,
> minute in and minute out. This travail is our lot, and the
> monotony of work is but one of the forms that it assumes.
> But it remains not the less true that our thought is intended
> to master time, and this vocation, for such it is, must be
> kept inviolate in every man. (69)

Here it is evident that her factory experience was beginning to blend with her deepened involvement with Christianity, which confirmed her sense that we cannot really expect to find happiness in this world, nor is happiness what matters. This belief helped her feel that "It is at once inevitable and fitting that work should involve monotony and tedium" (69).[4]

Increasingly absorbed in revealing a wider order in the universe that human beings had to learn to respect, Weil developed new terms for criticism of labor practices. Like the movement of seasons, Weil thought that "Everything that is in some degree beautiful and good reproduces in some way this mixture of uniformity and variety; everything that does not is bad and degrading" (69). Unlike the peasant's toil, which is necessarily obedient to the world's rhythm, factory work is relatively independent of it; it interrupts natural rhythms of life, according to her; work time apes clock time, and it loses its meaning:

> The futurity of one working in a factory . . . is empty
> because of its absolute unforeseeableness, and deader than
> the past because of the identity of the moments, which
> succeed one another like the ticking of a clock. A
> uniformity that imitates the movements of a clock, not that
> of the constellations, a variety that recognises no rule and
> consequently excludes all possibility of foreknowledge,
> makes for a time that is uninhabitable and irrespirable to
> man. (70)

Since workers can be interrupted at any moment and shifted to a new job they have no control over their time. Workers cannot afford to get too absorbed in what they do since this only makes it harder to respond to orders the instant they are given. In this situation workers can have no specific ends themselves unless the end is to reach quitting time. But since "one working day gives rise to another, no more than that, the achieved end in question is nothing less than a form of death" (70).

Weil therefore argues that workers need some control of their time if they are to have control over their work. And for any sense of a future to be opened up, they would have to know at the very least what they are expected to achieve over the next week and be left to organize the necessary work themselves. But as it is, a worker has "no way of visualizing achievement except under the form of wages, especially in the case of piece-work, which bends him to an obsession with money" (70). In more immediate terms, with workers performing five or six simple, high-speed movements, indefinitely repeated "until the exact second when a foreman comes up to move them like so many objects to another machine where they remain until moved again" (60), there can be no rhythm. Rhythm implies moments of pause, however short, as when a peasant swings his scythe. The better and swifter the peasant works, the more he leaves the impression with the onlooker that he is taking his time. But the "spectacle presented by men over machines is nearly always one of wretched haste destitute of all grace and dignity" (61). Again

Weil appeals to some sense of what is natural for people, to give force to her criticsim:

> It comes natural to man, and it befits him, to pause on having finished something, if only for an instant, in order to contemplate his handiwork, as God did in Genesis. Those lightening moments of thought, of immobility and equilibrium, one has to learn to eliminate utterly in a working-day at the factory. (61)

In a modern factory manual operations have to follow one another uninterruptedly "in something like the tick-tock succession of a timepiece, with nothing to mark the end of something concluded and something about to begin" (61). What is more, the worker is obliged to reproduce this barren monotony with his or her body without falling asleep, since the worker "must remain ever alert to confront the unexpected" (60). The worker is not free, but has to learn to obey the rhythms of machines; the machines do not belong to the worker in any sense; rather, he or she serves them according to the latest order received. As Weil says, "They are not for him a means of turning a piece of metal to a specified form; he is for them a means whereby they will be fed the parts for an operation whose relationship to the ones preceding and the ones following remains an impenetrable mystery to him" (63). The parts have their history since they have passed from one stage of development to another. "But he counts for nothing in that history, he has not left his mark on it, he knows nothing of what has gone on" (63), while "each physical annoyance needlessly imposed, each show of lack of respect, each brutality, each humiliation, however trivial, appears as a fresh reminder of his alien status" (63).

Whereas Marx saw that the factory *reduces* the worker to the status of an object, Weil demonstrates the ways this happens. Drawing on a Christian tradition, she identifies the dynamics whereby the power relations of the factory present the worker with a particular version of her or himself that is confirmed over and over again through the actuality of performing the work. For Weil, as we have seen, factory work undermines the worker by violating the equilibrium that can sustain a core of human dignity. It destroys inner unity by disrupting the proper relation between thought and its object, between conception and execution. Her growing sensitivity to issues of time, space, and rhythm allowed her to specify the dynamics of this process of inner erosion in more detail:

> the same muffled and permanent dread that inhibits his thought from travelling through time also keep it from wandering through the plant and fixes it to a point in space. The workingman does not know what he produces and consequently, he experiences the sensation, not of having produced, but of having been drained dry. In the plant he expends—occasionally to the uttermost—what is best in him, his capacity to think, feel, be moved. He squanders it all, since he leaves the plant emptied; and yet he has put nothing of himself in his work, neither his thought, feelings, not even, save in a feeble measure, movements determined by him, ordered to some end. His very life ebbs from him without having left a trace behind him. (63)

The rare moments in which unskilled workers do not feel "drained dry" but can feel proud in successfully overcoming some difficulty leave an incomplete feeling of joy since there are rarely "companions or superiors to judge and appreciate what has been successfully overcome" (59). People are only concerned with completing their own work or with handling the products. The firm is only interested in what production levels have been reached. And for Weil, "Such indifference is a privation of that human warmth which will always be in some degree necessary" (59).

It is impossible for people to avoid that suffering by "hushing and lulling the mind to a point where it may become insensitive to pain" (58). The constant possibility of accidents such as a stalled machine or a lost tool creates an intolerable awareness of the monotony of work. As Weil says, "Nothing is worse than a mixture of monotony and accident. They are mutually aggravating, at least when accident is bound up with anxiety" (58). Since there is no place for "accident'" within the flow of production and every slowing down is the worker's fault, thought has to remain in constant readiness to "find within itself resources to cope with the unexpected" (59) while the worker repeats the same monotonous movements indefinitely. "Such an obligation is contradictory, impossible and exhausting" (59). The ordeal that drains the soul can be "read in the eyes of nearly all the workmen filing out of a plant" (59).

Sometimes people argue that workers do not suffer from the monotony of work since otherwise they would not be so annoyed by a change of work. But changes of work are more wounding than comforting because they always seem to involve some loss of earnings and because the anxiety of not working fast enough, which is diffused through every working moment, becomes concentrated at such times. Thus "second nature, a convention, to attach more importance to money, which is something clear-cut and measurable, than to obscure, inpalpable, inexpressible feelings that possess one while at work" (56).[5] Even when work is paid by the hour there is annoyance because change of job is suddenly imposed, as a command that must immediately and unquestioningly be obeyed. This can only leave workers feeling that their time "is incessantly at someone else's beck and call" (57).

But since orders to change jobs are the sole factor making for variety, "to eliminate them in thought is to condemn oneself to imagining an unbroken succession of ever-identical movements, to visualizing monotonous desert regions of experience that thought has no way of exploring" (57). And the alternative is equally bleak since it forces workers into direct experience of their subordination:

> If thought seeks to sidestep that monotony by imagining a
> change—namely an unexpected order—it can effect its
> passage from present time to futurity only by way of a new
> humiliation. Thus, thought draws back from the future.
> This perpetual recoil upon the present produces a kind of
> brutish stupor. (57)

For Weil the illumination of the actual nature of the unfreedom workers suffer and the discovery of new moral relations of production involved a recognition of the symbolic nature of the material, which she explains in a letter to the factory manager at Bourges:

There is nothing unpleasant in contemplating the walls of a
room, even a poor and bare one; but if the room is a prison
cell one cannot look at the walls without a pang. It is
exactly the same with poverty, when it is combined with
complete subordination and dependence. Slavery and
freedom are simply ideas; what causes suffering is actual
things. Therefore what hurts is every detail of daily life
which reflects the poverty to which one is condemned; and
not because of the poverty but because of the slavery. The
clanking of chains must have had this effect, I imagine, for
convicts in the past. In the same way too every image of the
well-being one lacks is painful if it presents itself in such a
way as to recall the fact that one is deprived of it; because
this well-being also implies freedom. The thought of a good
meal in pleasant surroundings was as haunting for me, last
year, as the thought of oceans and plains for a prisoner, and
for the same reasons. I felt a yearning for luxury that I
never felt before or since. (*Seventy Letters.* 37–38)

Weil often thinks of the modern factory as a prison, where
people cannot forget that they are not free "for the vice of their
servitude grips them through the senses, their bodies, the
thousand and one little details that crowd the minutes of which
their lives are constituted" ("Factory Work," 55). Rare moments
of freedom can only be sustained if people cut off or somehow
displace themselves from their everyday experience. This does its
own damage. It infuses life with an abiding sense of unreality.
But this also explains why workers will often just want to get on
with their own jobs and will feel so pained if an accident or
change of work forces them to turn to a foreman or warehouse
keeper.

The time-clock is the first detail in the daily life of the factory
that makes a worker's servitude apparent. It dominates the trip
from home to plant and "since arrival 5 or 10 minutes ahead of
time is of no avail, the flow of time appears as something pitiless,
leaving no room for the play of change" (55). There is no place
for anything except the ceaseless demand that the worker get on
with the job. Workers are not supposed to question: "Never
mind the reasons," the foreman says, and as Weil points out
wryly, "Contradictory orders are not such according to the logic

of the factory" (55). In an early letter to her friend Albertine
Thevenon, she isolated this necessity to obey without a word as a
basic factor, along with the necessity for speed, in making for the
slavery of workers:

> The order may be an unpleasant or a dangerous or even an
> impracticable one; or two superiors may give contradictory
> orders; no matter, one submits in silence. To speak to a
> superior—even for something indispensable—is always to
> risk a snub, even though he may be a kindly man (the
> kindest men have spells of bad temper); and one must take
> the snub too in silence. (*Seventy Letters*, 22)

She explains this further in her argument with the manager at
Bourges who can't understand why workers won't complain if
they feel something is wrong, especially when he has made it
clear they won't be punished. She knows that the very
"possibility" of a snub is enough to remind workers of their
subordination, that they count for nothing in the modern
organization of production:

> I was unable to give you any concrete example of a superior
> resenting a legitimate complaint by a workman. But how
> could I have risked the experiment? To submit in
> silence—as I should probably have done—if my complaint
> had been badly received, would have been an even more
> painful humiliation than the subject of the complaint. To
> make an angry reply would probably have meant looking
> for a new job straight away. Admittedly, one cannot be sure
> beforehand that one's complaint will be resented, but one
> knows it is possible, and that possibility is enough. It is
> possible because the superior, like everyone else, has spells
> of bad temper. And anyway one has the feeling that it is not
> normal in a factory to expect any consideration at all. (33)

Weil thought that society must be corrupted to its very core
"when workingmen can feel at home in a plant only during a
strike, and utter aliens during working hours" ("Factory Work,"
64). She also saw that as long as workers are "homeless in their
own place of work, they will never feel at home in their country,

never be responsible members of society" (64). Weil's later work on the regeneration of France, *The Need for Roots*, centers on healing this sense in workers, both in towns and the countryside. This meant transforming social institutions so that workers could begin to value themselves not only as workers but as citizens of the larger community. For, under the current system, workers could not value themselves:

> It is as though someone were repeating in his ear at every passing moment and with all possibility of reply excluded: "Here, you are nothing. You simply do not count. You are here to obey, to accept everything, to keep your mouth shut." Such reiteration becomes irresistible. One comes to acquiesce down deep that he counts for nothing. All or nearly all factory workers, even the most free in their bearing, have an almost imperceptible something about their movements, their look, and especially in the set of the lips, which reveals that they have been obliged to consider themselves as nothing ("Factory Work," 56).

In considering how to help working people retain their sense of dignity, Weil returned to what she thought of as the first principle of education: that "in order to 'raise' anyone, whether infant or adult, one must begin by raising him in his own eyes"—a principle she thought a "hundred times truer still when the chief obstacle to his development is the humiliating conditions of his life" (*Seventy Letters*, 24). It is in the context of this central task that the degrading conditions of life had to be changed. If workers could be helped in identifying those aspects of their everyday conditions that are humiliating and under-mining, they could learn to extend the realm of freedom and control in relation to their work. The effect would not be a matter of a once and for all transformation of capitalist property relations. A new organization of work involving the development of a different form of technology would have to be patiently explored. Yet this inquiry would involve shifting the relations of authority and power in a way that would continually extend the conscious control that workers have over the processes of work. Although Bernard had talked about collaboration with workers at Rosieres, his vision of collaboration was inadequate because it did not touch the power relationship between management and workers. Weil could only discern a complete subordination since even the workers' own co-operative was not in fact controlled by them, while for her the very benevolence and generosity of the Rosieres management only served to underline the workers' passivity.

Well aware that all organizations imply the giving and receiving of orders, Weil emphasized that she was not against subordination as such. She did not think that true liberty exists as the ending of all forms of authority relations. But she did object to a subordination in which one human being is treated as a tool at the disposal of another. She wanted constantly to extend the specifically human capacities of responsibility and intelligence as the souce of freedom at work, so she objected to any situation in which a worker "has only to obey passively, with his mind and heart totally uninvolved" (47). On the other hand, she says,

> there are circumstances in which subordination is something fine and honourable—for example: when orders confer a responsibility upon the recipient; when they make demands upon those virtues of courage, will, conscience, and intelligence which are the definition of human value; when they imply a certain mutual confidence between superior and subordinate and only a small degree of arbitrary power in the hands of the former. (47)

But as she knew for herself workers could rarely have this kind of confidence shown in themselves.

to understand the entrenched character of relations of dominance and subordination, Weil knew that it was crucial to scrutinize the form of science and technology and to grasp its relationship to our inherited traditions. We have seen that the reduction of issues of dominance and subordination to issues of ownership was deeply inadequate for her. Thus in developing her understanding of the ways in which people are undermined in their working lives, Weil was drawn to address directly the relationship between our historically emergent form of science and its implications for relations of subordination; it is partly through this enquiry that we can grasp both the roots of subordination and the limits on our capacity to transcend it.

4 Science, technology, and control

For Weil the idea of labor is the "only spiritual conquest achieved by the human mind since the miracle of Greece" (*Reflections*, 106). She discovered numerous signs in the religious traditions of antiquity, including the Old Testament, that "physical labour was pre-eminently a religious activity and consequently something sacred" (*The Need for Roots*, 295). But with her reverence for Ancient Greece it as hard for her to acknowledge that at the height of Athenian democracy work had come to mean the exclusion from public life. By the time of Plato, money had become crucial in Athenian life, and work had been divorced from all religious inspiration. Since public life was the arena for citizenship, a life of physical labor was reserved for prisoners of war, foreign workers, women, and children, according to Alfred Sohn-Rethel, this division between intellectual and manual labor served to reinforce the class divisions within Greek society.[6] The temptation to see work as some kind of punishment was reinforced in Western culture, as Weil saw it, through aspects of the biblical tradition. This left a tradition of disdain for physical labor.

Weil looked to the seventeenth century for traditions that could underpin a demand to reinstate the centrality in moral and political theory of the category of physical labor. It is significant she looks to Francis Bacon as the first to put forward "the idea of labour considered as a human value".

> For the ancient and heart-breaking curse contained in Genesis, which made the world appear as a convict prison and labour as the sign of men's servitude and abasement, he substituted in a flash of genius the veritable charter expressing the relations between man and the world: "We cannot command Nature except by obeying her." This simple pronouncement ought to form by itself the Bible of our times. It suffices to define true labour, the kind which forms free men, and that to the very extent to which it is an act of conscious submission to necessity. (*Reflections*, 106–107)

While Weil saw Bacon's dictum as a way to formulate the inner connection between labor and freedom, she was also ambivalent about seeing progress as the domination of nature, which is very much the framework set by Bacon. His "simple pronouncement" is made in terms of command and control of nature: We obey in order to command. Although Weil thought that this "simple pronouncement" could define the kind of labor "which forms free men," she seems blind to some of its implications. This is because Weil often seems to have been thinking of the sailor who by means of a tiller and sail can use the wind to move his boat in the opposite direction from that in which the wind is blowing. In a sense he can be seen as commanding the forces of nature. But this involves a working with nature rather than against it. Bacon often implies that nature has to be attacked to force it to reveal secrets that it would keep for itself, a view that is deeply masculinist since it conceives of nature as a woman who has to be put on a rack to make sure that "she" gives up "her" knowledge.[7] Weil never completely escaped from this vision of the progress as involving the domination of nature. It creates a tension in her writings that she never fully resolved. It is present in her understanding of freedom as it is in her formulations of women's experience.

Although Weil drew from Bacon to indicate the possibility of a deeper connection between labor and science, she realized that "After Descartes, scientists progressively slipped into considering pure science as an end in itself' (107). It was significant to Weil that this idea of a life devoted to some free form of physical labor was sustained in literature. Goethe's Faust, who exists for Western culture as "a symbol of the human soul in its untiring pursuit of the good, abandons with digust the abstract search for truth, which has become in his eyes an empty and barren occupation" (107). He long to be stripped of his magical power, which for Weil can be "regarded as the symbol of all forms of power" (274), to spend a life among free people taken up in hard and dangerous physical labor. This vision guided Weil throughout her life and writing. It is to be found in Rousseau, Shelley, and above all in Tolstoy; it is crucial in grasping the truth in Proudhon and Marx. And, "As for the working-class movement, every time it has managed to escape the demagogy, it is on the dignity of labour that it has based the workers' demands" (107).

But it is a vision that has to be restored to science, which has to return to Descartes to learn again to "place at the core of the social problem the dignity of the producer as such" (108). The originality of modern civilization lies in this conception of labor as a source of spiritual value.

For Weil, it is crucial in developing an appropriate relation to the world through work that the workers know they are not all-powerful; work is not a realm of transcendence of necessity but of engagement with it and thus gives freedom a sense of reality. But it is equally important for Weil that people know that they are not totally without power in relation to the world. Through the use of our bodies and minds, we can act on the world and change it, albeit only partially. This is integral to her appreciation of Marx, who "set down as man's essential characteristic, as opposed to the animals, the fact that he produces the conditions of his own existence and thus himself indirectly produces himself" (108). Weil, however, is ambivalent about the nature of control. She says, for example:

> [T]hough astronomy does not give us any real power over the sky, still it makes the sky enter into our realm, to the point that the pilot dares to use these stars—which the power of all humanity together could not cause to deviate from their course by a hair's breadth—as his instruments" (*Sur la science*, 94).[8]

For Weil there is nothing nobler than for a person to be brought "directly to grips with naked necessity, without his being able to expect anything except through his own exertions, and such that his life is a continual creation of himself by himself" (*Reflections*, 87). This view corresponds to Marx's, but she gives it a somewhat different significance when she emphasizes that "Man is a limited being" who unlike the God of the theologians is not given to be "the direct author of his own existence" (87). He would, however, "possess the human equivalent of that divine power if the material conditions that enable him to exist were exclusively the work of his mind directing the effort of his muscles. This would be true liberty" (87). But it was also clear to Weil that "labour would . . . become conscious" only when science "would . . . become concrete" (107).

It is in this context that a critical understanding of modern science becomes crucial for Weil. She sought to restore the relation between science and labor, and thereby bring theory and practical activity into relation. According to her, "Science is today regarding by some as a mere catalogue of technical recipes, by others as a body of pure intellectual speculations which are sufficient unto themselves; the former set too little value on the intellect, the latter on the world" (105). Thought will be exercised in a vacuum unless it can "seize hold of its object, which can be none other than the universe" (105). It is the possibility of application that gives scientific thought its connection with the universe and so its concrete value, in Weil's vision:

> On the day when it became impossible to understand
> scientific notions, even the most abstract, without clearly
> perceiving at the same time their connection with possible
> applications, and equally impossible to apply such notions
> even indirectly without thoroughly knowing and
> understanding them—on that day science would have
> become concrete and labour would have become conscious;
> and then only will each possess its full value. (105)

But until this moment comes, "there will always be something incomplete and inhuman about science and labour" (105). Weil acknowledges that those who have argued that applications are the goal of science have "meant to say that truth is not worth seeking and that success alone counts" (105). She argues instead for a different conception of science "whose ultimate aim would be the perfecting of technique not by rendering it more powerful, but simply more conscious and more methodical" (105). She thought Descartes conceived science as "a method for mastering nature" (105) that could be organized in such a way as to be clear to any individual. Descartes wanted to found a workers' university and was concerned to show that with a proper method mental effort alone, not intelligence or skill, would lead to knowledge.

But Weil also realized that Descartes' initial attempts to bring knowledge within the grasp of all people in his *Discourse on Method* was subverted when he allowed for the domination of algebra over science. As Paul King argues, "It was precisely his materialist orientation which resulted in his objectifying a conceptual device." [9] He quotes an early letter of Weil's to prove his point:

> Descartes never found a way to prevent order from
> becoming, as soon as it is conceived, a thing instead of an
> idea. Order becomes a thing, it seems to me, as soon as one
> treats a series as a reality distinct from the terms which
> compose it, by expressing it with a symbol; now algebra is
> just that . . . (*Seventy Letters*, 3)

This realization helped Weil grasp one source for the "total abyss" that separates the scientist and the uneducated in modern society and is similar to that which separates the free man from the slave. In recognising that science had come to play a central role in the organization of big industry, she saw the ways science could be harnessed to the interests of capital in the exploitation of human labor.

Weil was aware, then, that despite his desire to democratize knowledge, Descartes helped to father a technology which remained in the hands of "intellectual workers." Even if we managed to subject all forms of work to methodical thought, we would still be left with a "profound difference in kind which separates theoretical speculation from action" (*Reflections*, 91). With the development of machinery, "he who applies method has no need to conceive it in his mind at the moment he is applying it" (92). Thus when a difficulty arises, the scientist is brought in to solve it as a theoretical problem using the concepts and symbols of science. Only afterwards would the solution be applied to the action. As Weil says "what is carried out is not a conception but an abstract diagram indicating a sequence of movements, and as little penetrable by the mind, at the moment of execution, as some formula resulting from mere routine or some magic rite" (92). In this way Weil sees the development of algebra in Descartes' work, whatever his conscious intention, as enforcing the distinction between intellectual and manual labor. It prepares the central place of science in the domination of human labor and brings us to the situation in modern industry where "there is method in the motions of work, but none in the mind of the worker" (92). For Weil it is not simply that science is used to enforce the rule of capital in the modern factory, but that science and labor have been regarded along with freedom through one and the same path. This is why we cannot think of the reorganization of work without investigating the foundations of modern science.

Throughout the different periods of her writing Weil sustained the view presented in *Reflections* that "the most fully human civilization would be that which had manual labour at its pivot, that in which manual labour constituted the supreme value" (104). But she is careful to distinguish this from the "religion of production" she saw as supreme in both the United States and the Soviet Union, for, as she says, "the true object of that religion is the product of work and not the worker, material objects and not man" (104). Under these conditions it was more important for Weil to think about the nature of the labor process than about the traditional socialist concern with the distribution of production. For her the "religion of production" also affects the nature of modern technology since "Up to now, technicians have never had anything else in mind than the requirements of manufacture. If they were to start having always present before them the needs of those who do the manufacturing, the whole technique of production would be slowly transformed" (*The Need for Roots*, 57). Therefore Weil thought it crucial to change the very notions of science underpinning the use of technology in modern industry.[10]

For Weil, especially in the later *The Need for Roots*, this meant more directly challenging the dominant Cartesian tradition—though she believed that many of Descartes' intentions had been lost in the development of "Cartesianism." Since the scientific revolution of the seventeenth century people have believed "that force rules supreme over all natural phenomenon (230), though, somewhat paradoxically, people have also wanted to believe that they could somehow escape the rule of force to "base their mutual relations upon justice, recognised as such through the application of reason" (230). Weil eventually placed herself in fundamental opposition to both modern science as founded by Galileo and Descartes and to the Renaissance humanism that she saw as having triumphed with the French Revolution in 1789. But her challenges to the framework established by the reconciliation between science and humanism—which itself sets the boundaries of an Enlightenment culture in general opposition to religion—grew from her fundamental desire to grasp the place of science in the oppression of working people.

Weil challenged the conception of science as a branch of study whose object is somehow placed beyond good and evil. She saw that the conception of science as simply concerned with the facts has served to place it at the service of capital. In this light scientists are simply people "who are paid to manufacture science" (245). For Weil unless the ways working conditions of life, which are systematically ignored by technologists focusing on maximizing production and profit, were analyzed, the nature of technical research and scientific education with respect to the conditions of working people could not be reoriented and manual labor could not become a central value. Weil was critical of socialism for not having his central task on its agenda

> Speaking in general terms, a reform of an infinitely greater social importance than all the measures arrayed under the title of Socialism would be a transformation in the very conception of technical research. So far, no one has ever imagined that an engineer occupied in technical research on new types of machinery could have anything other than the following double objectives in view: first, to increase the profits of the firm which has ordered the research, and secondly to serve the interests of the consumer. For in such a case, when we talk about the interests of production, we mean producing more and at a cheaper rate; that is to say, these interests are really identical with those of the consumer. Thus, these two words are constantly being used the one for the other.
>
> As for the workmen who will be spending their energies on this machine, nobody thinks twice about them. Nobody even thinks it possible to think about them. The most that ever happens is that from time to time some vague security apparatus is provided, although, in fact, several fingers and factory stairs daily splashed with fresh human blood are such a common feature. (54)

She realized that "what is essential is the idea itself of posing in technical terms problems concerning the effects of machines upon the moral well-being of the workmen" (55). In this way she showed that a genuine sociology of work is inseparable from moral theory, a profound challenging to disciplines that did their best to keep them apart. But if this was part of her larger program in *The Need for Roots*, it had yet to be clearly formulated at the time of writing her *Reflections*.

As we noted earlier (Chapter 3), Weil felt that Bolshevik leaders were no more aware than the capitalist world that a true liberation of workers required a transformation in the technical and organizational conditions of work. They had barely appreciated what Weil took to be a central conviction in Marx that "any change in the relationship between the classes must remain a pure illusion, if it is not accompanied by a transformation in technical process, expressing itself in entirely new types of machinery" (54). Weil cannot resist asking cynically, "what use can the partial or total nationalisation of economic production be to workers, if the spirit of these research departments hasn't changed?" (54).

Even in the Soviet Union, where labor was held to be a central social value, there was in reality only a concern with "the religion of production." There was hardly an inkling of the transformations that would be necessary for a more genuine liberty and for labor to assume its central position in social life. As Weil says, "It is not in relation to what it produces that manual labour must become the highest value, but in relation to the man who performs it" (*Reflections*, 104). She thinks labor "must constitute for each human being what he is most essentially in need of if his life is to take on of itself a meaning and a value in his own eyes" (104). This is a clumsy formulation that can easily be misconstrued to suggest that work is akin to each individual's finding a way of expressing his or her true individual self. Instead, Weil was convinced that the labor can give us a way of "getting directly to grips with the world" (104) and in so doing could help us feel—in contrast to Rimbaud's complaint that "we are not in the world" and that "true life is absent"—that "in those moments of incomparable joy and fullness we know by flashes that true life is there at hand, we feel with all our being that the world exists and that we are in the world" (104). This explains how manual labor could serve as the pivot of a fully human civilization,[11] a conviction Weil never lost, in spite of the consequences to liberty of the Cartesian scientific tradition.

It is no accident that when Simone Weil reflected on what working in a factory meant for her personally, she focused on the issue of dignity and self-respect. It is as if at last she had found a way of making Kant's injunction—first notes in her Lecture at Roanne during the school year 1933–1934—that "Oppression is an insult to the dignity of human nature" (*Lectures on Philosophy*, 138) her own. She had had to find a way back to Kant "in and through slavery" to discover what it meant for dignity to be truly grounded within the self.

But at the same time she learned to question Kant's confidence that dignity and self-respect are "inner values" that can be sustained in the face of relations of power and subordination; she learned, on the contrary, how *vulnerable* are our dignity and self-respect. Not only does dignity depend on "external reasons" but it can be "radically destroyed" with the "daily experience of brutal constraint" (*Seventy Letters*, 21). This realization led her in later writings to a much deeper grasp of the interrelationship between the "internal" and "external" of a person's sense of self and the social relations of power and subordination he or she lives out. In this sense her thinking became much more dialectical, though in a dialectic deeply influenced by Christian notions. This is the way Weil expresses her own struggles with herself in a letter to Albertine Thévenon:

> What working in a factory meant for me personally was as follows. It meant that all the external reasons (which I had previously thought internal) upon which my sense of personal dignity, my self-respect, were based were radically destroyed within two or three weeks by the daily experience of brutal constraint. And don't imagine that this provoked in me any rebellious reaction. No, on the contrary; it produced the last thing I expected from myself—docility. The resigned docility of a beast of burden. It seemed to me that I was born to wait for, and receive, and carry out orders—that I had never done and never would do anything else. I am not proud of that confession. It is the kind of suffering no worker talks about; it is too painful even to think of it. When I was kept away from work by illness I

became fully aware of the degradation into which I was
falling, and I swore to myself that I would go on enduring
the life until the day when I was able to pull myself together
in spite of it. And I kept my word. Slowly and painfully, in
and through slavery, I reconquered the sense of my human
dignity—a sense which relied, this time, upon nothing
outside myself and was accompanied always by the
knowledge that I possessed no right to anything, and that
any moment free from humiliation and suffering should be
accepted as a favour, as merely a lucky chance. (22)

Her sense of the difficulty of people's sustaining a sense of
dignity profoundly affected her understanding of the nature of
oppression and can help to explain the appeal for Weil of the
Christian notion of affliction, which for her expresses human
vulnerability to relations of subordination. Weil had a sense of
unease as she struggled with a tension between a conception of
humanity as born to liberty and her developing sense that
aspiration could itself be undermined through the brutal processes of social relations. With a concrete experience of the
subordination through which this happened, she could no longer
expect people continually to struggle to assert their humanity.
Thus she broke with the Hegelian tradition, which bases its sense
of the dialectic on the necessity of people's struggles against the
conditions of oppression. This necessity was no longer assured as
the rational core of the historical process.

In discovering a way to make dignity and self-respect central,
Weil recognized sources of power not usually acknowledged
within traditional conceptions of materialism. Although at the
time of her factory experience she probably still believed that,
because "all forms of force are material," "the expression
'spiritual force' is essentially contradictory" (*Reflections*, 98) she
began to give a different sense to the idea that "mind can only be
a force to the extent to which it is materially indispensable" (98).
It is as if she recognized that a force need not be material and
that, possibly under the influence of Marxism, she had accepted
too narrow a conception of materialism. Challenging the
Renaissance humanist tradition, developed by Kant, which
sought to guarantee to human beings alone a freedom to escape
the rule of force and to order their relations according to

conceptions of justice, Marx sought to be "scientific" in his attempt to extend Descartes' conception that "force rules supreme over all natural phenomena" (74) to human relations. Within Marxism, as Weil notes in *The Need for Roots*, "force is given the name of history; it takes the form of the class struggle" (231). Significantly for Weil, this means that "justice is relegated to some future time which has to be preceded by a sort of apocalyptic cataclysm" (231). But as Weil learned, "Force is not a machine for automatically creating justice. It is a blind mechanism which produces indiscriminately and partially just or unjust results, but, as by the law of probability, nearly always unjust ones" (232).

This idea is not foreign to her *Reflections*. It is part of what makes her vision so depressing, since she could not then recognize anything else. But if her experience of factory work made her in many ways even less hopeful, it also opened up a different vision of human life in which the importance of people sustaining a sense of human dignity and self-respect could be more easily accepted as an end in itself. Her thinking was brought closer to the quality of working people's everyday lives. Even if she did not discover a tendency to rebel against oppressive social conditions—rather, the reverse—she did discover a yearning for justice that she had not recognized in her earlier analysis. She came closer to grasping how a concern with justice was entwined with relations of power and subordination.[12] Justice had a place within the social world, and, if the materialism inherited from Marx could not acknowledge this, then materialism had to be reformulated. It was a deep flaw in Marxism that it seemed to relegate justice to some future time and so was unable to discover it at work, however dimly and painfully, within everyday social relations. To the extent that Marxist theorists have wanted to interpret Marxism as a theory of social forces, they have inevitably missed some of the profoundest insights of Marx's materialism. As Weil expressed in *The Need for Roots*, where her thinking carries the deep influence of Christianity:

> Where force is absolutely sovereign, justice is absolutely
> unreal. Yet justice cannot be that. We know it
> experimentally. It is real enough in the hearts of man. The

structure of a human heart is just as much of a reality as any other in the universe, neither more nor less so than the trajectory of a planet. (232)

For Weil, justice or love is exempt from the mechanism of force, and in this sense materialism does not extend to the heart. Thus, according to her, alongside the truths of materialism, the heart must be clearly taken account of. What became more important for Weil, however, was the recognition of the place of justice not simply as an idea but as affecting the relations among people and our sense of ourselves. Her spirituality was nourished by the same sources. She never saw the spiritual as an independent and autonomous realm but as something whose reality has to be expressed in the relations between people. In this way her spirituality was essentially material. But it is quite misleading, I think, to imagine that her concern with justice and truth came with her conversion to Christianity. Rather, it was there that she found they had the centrality she wanted for them and a moral language in which they were firmly grounded.

While in *Reflections* Weil is convinced that mind gives life its dignity and meaningfulness, her experience of factory work opened her to the importance of the heart. One could say it made her thinking less "masculine," less tied to traditional notions of rationality. It is the awakening of the heart that helped her understand the nature of human dignity and self-respect. She broke with traditional Kantian notions, which identify our capacity for morality with our reason, while insisting on giving reason and the mind their due importance for understanding of human dignity. This experience also changed her sense of human suffering in conditions of subordination and oppression. For her it was no longer adequate to think of human liberty exclusively in terms of giving mind control over action—or in terms of the reversal of the relationship of subject and object, means and ends. She thus developed a different way of revealing what is so damaging to people in their subordination. She could no longer hope that damaging processes could be reversed in a different order of social relations without first understanding the nature of the injury, damage, and injustice done to people. Out of a sense of these injuries would come a grasp of the significance of the structures of power and subordination. This new way of thinking—similar to that developed by feminism—marked a profound shift in emphasis for Weil, and it helps explain how her experience of factory work opened her to Christianity.

Weil's experience of factory work also forced her to revise the rationalism she had been brought up to assume. Thought remained central to her understanding of what gives human life its dignity, but the place of thought had to be conceived within a changed understanding of human life; it could not in and of itself grasp suffering. In her earlier thought she deals with the heart in a more or less Kantian framework, in which feelings and desires are seen as "interferences" in the proper tasks of life given by reason. Certainly she maintained a deep hostility to those, such as André Gide, who were concerned with the cultivation of the sensations. For Weil, "the reality of life is not sensation but activity—I mean activity both in thought and in action. People who live by sensations are parasites, both materially and morally, in relation to those who work and create—who alone are men" (*Seventy Letters*, 12).

The factory made Weil aware that people are not individually in the same relation to morality. The universalism that the Enlightenment had assumed and that helped form the idea of equal citizenship had no reality within the modern forms of social oppression. Even if each person is equally capable of living a moral life, each is not in an equal position to act morally. Thus Weil criticized some deep assumptions of this moral tradition in order to come to terms with the realities of factory life. What made this a little easier was her sense that somehow working-class life offered people more genuine contact with reality. She did not believe, however, that the factory allows for the solidarity and comradeship socialists often imagine and in which Marx sees the promise of a transcendence of class society.

Her shift to the language of a Christian tradition led Weil to see that the alienating conditions of factory work can provide for an anchoring of experience in reality and a quality of experience that necessarily escapes the privileged. It also led her to think about working peoples' experience of the factory possibly for the first time in terms of a conception of goodness. As Weil wrote to a pupil while she worked at a factory,

Above all, I feel I have escaped from a world of
abstraction, to find myself among real men—some good and
some bad, but with a real goodness and badness. Goodness
especially, when it exists in a factory, is something real;
because the least act of kindness, from a mere smile to
some little service, calls for a victory over fatigue and the
obsession with pay and all the overwhelming influences
which drive a man in upon himself. (11)

For similar reasons, "if ever you recognise a gleam of intelligence
you can be sure that it is genuine" (12).

In the university, on the other hand, "one is paid to think, or
pretend to think" (12). So in seeking out factory work for herself
she was leaving the "world of abstractions" for a fuller contact
with real life. She knew that in the relative ease of middle-class
life, where people are often more concerned with behaving in the
socially approved ways, people are more likely to betray their
inner sense of themselves. This isn't to say that working people
are likely to have more connection with this inner sense of
themselves, but that the hardships of their everyday lives can
mean that they are less artificial or false, less likely, for instance,
to show kindness when they do not feel it.

Weil spent her last weeks of factory work in a state of physical
and nervous exhaustion and was plagued by bad headaches. As
she wrote in her journal, "I got up with anguish, I went to the
factory with fear, I worked like a slave" ("Journal d'ucine," 144).
Weil discovered "crushing, bitter fatigue, at times so painful that
one wished for death. Everyone, in every situation, knows that it
is to be fatigued, but for this fatigue there needs to be a separate
name" ("La Vie et la grève des auvières metallos," 225–26). This
experience had penetrated her so deeply that even outside of
work she had completely lost any sense that she could count for
anything. Getting on a bus while working at Renault, she found
herself struck by a feeling that shook her sense of self and her
understanding of the power of social institutions over people's
lives. "How is it that I, a slave, can get on this bus and for my 12
sous use it like anyone else? What an extraordinary favour! If I
had been brutally made to get off, told that such comfortable
means of travel were not for me, that I could go only on foot, I
believe that that would have seemed to me entirely natural"

("Journal d'Ueine," 124). Not to be treated brutally seemed purely gratuitous, "a gift of chance" (124).[13]

Simone Pétrement makes the point that just as Alain had found that the worst of war was not the danger or the physical discomfort but the slavery, so Weil in the factory above all suffered from humiliation:[14] "The capital fact is not the suffering but the humiliation" (107). The feeling of personal dignity as it has been formed by society is shattered. One must forge another kind" (107). Immediately on leaving work, she attempted an assessment of her experience. The central concern was the same.

> What did I gain from the experience? The feeling that I do not possess any right, whatever it might be, to anything whatever. . . . The ability to be morally self-sufficient, to live, without feeling inwardly humiliated in my own eyes, in a state of lament and perpetual humiliation; to taste each moment of freedom or comradeship to the full. (106)

According to Pétrement, Weil certainly concluded—she had doubted this—that a certain slavery is to the material conditions and the very instruments of work: the machines. As Weil says, "In all the other forms of slavery, the slavery is in the circumstances. Only here it is carried into the work itself' (124).[15] She still hoped to find ways of changing this state of affairs, possibly through inventing machines of a different kind. But her discovery from her own example that "an obviously inexorable and invincible oppression does not engender rebellion as an immediate reaction but rather submission" (107) helped reinforce her doubts about the future of liberty. As Pétrement sees it, "So long as one thinks that oppression automatically engenders rebellion, one is sure that oppression can never last for long. But when one sees that this is not so, one realizes that for liberty there are dark nights that can last very long."[16]

To regain some strength after her experience of factory work, Weil was sent by her parents on a trip to Portugal, to Viana do Castelo. It was in witnessing a procession around the fishermen's huts somewhere between Viaa and Porto that she made the first of "three contacts with Christianity that have really counted," as she described in a letter to Father Joseph-Marie Perrin, who was known for his help to Jews and other refugees and helped Weil get work as an agricultural laborer. She was in a wretched state physically, and, as she says,

> I entered the little Portuguese village, which, alas, was very wretched too, on the very day of the festival of its patron saint. . . . The wives of the fishermen were, in procession, making a tour of all the ships, carrying candles and singing what must certainly be very ancient hymns of a heart-rending sadness. . . . There the conviction was suddenly borne in upon me that Christianity is pre-eminently the religion of slaves, that slaves cannot help belonging to it, and I among others. (*Waiting for God*, 66–67)

So it was her experience of herself as a slave within the factory that seemed to open her to Christianity. It was part of an inner process of transformation that provided her with a language that seemed to illuminate what she had experienced both about herself and others in the factory. She was invoked a Chrtistian language to reach a deeper contact with realities that prevailing modes of thought and feeling continually evaded.

6 Morality, justice, and subordination

On September 22 Simone Weil left Portugal with her parents and returned to Paris. She then taught philosophy at the girls lycée in Bourges, south of Paris, in the fall of 1935. One of her students was the daughter of the owner of the Rosieres Foundry, and through her Weil met the chief engineer and technical manager, M. Bernard, whom she visited a number of times between December 1935 and June 1936. She wanted to learn more about the operation of the factory from the management's point of view, and she wanted to share her experience of what it was like to be a worker. She wanted some form of collaboration between the two groups because she had become convinced that "After a so-called working-class revolution, just as much as before it, the workers at R. will go on obeying passively—so long as the system of production is based on passive obedience" (*Seventy Letters*, 40).

What we can justifiably expect from people much depends on their situation within the relations of power and subordination. Liberalism tends to blind us to this reality in its assumption that people can abstract themselves from such relations and act towards others as equals in their "personal relations." So it is one of the centrally legitimating claims in a liberal-democratic society for an individual who, for instance, has worked his way up from a working-class background to a position of social power to believe that if he or she has done so, there is no reason why anyone else should not be able to. Accordingly in this view social differences in power and wealth flow directly from individual differences in ability. But Weil challenges this claim in correspondence with Bernard in which she demonstrates issues of inequality have an important moral aspect:

> The fact that you yourself in the past were bolder with your superiors gives you no right to judge. Not only was your economic position totally different, but also your moral position—if, at least, as I think I understood, you were at that time holding more or less responsible jobs. I myself, I think, would run equal or even greater risks in resisting my university superiors if necessary (supposing we had some kind of authoritarian government) and with far more determination than I would show in a factory against the overseer or manager. And Why? . . . In the university I have rights and dignity and a responsibility to defend. What have I to defend as a factory worker, when I have to renounce all rights every morning at the moment I clock in? All I have to defend is my life. It would be too much to be expected to endure the subordination of a slave and at the same time to face dangers like a free man. To compel a man in that situation to choose between incurring a danger and fading away, as you put it, is to inflict a humiliation which it would be more humane to spare him. (33–34)

In Weil's view, then, we have to learn to organize our expectations of people according to our understanding of their moral positions. If men and women are forced to endure a subordination akin to slavery in the assembly-lines of modern factories, they are bound to have an ambiguous relationship to their legal and political rights in public life. Even if working people strongly identify with these rights, it will often be difficult for them to have the confidence and self-assurance to assert them.[17] This is something a middle-class person can more often do, because he or she does not carry the same fears of being put down and humiliated. So issues of individual dignity, confidence, worth, and self-assurance all gradually found a secure place within Weil's moral and political thinking.

The experience of factory work seemed to lead Weil to give up thinking in terms of the "oppression" of working people. For Weil this language was too tied to the discovery of the social sources of oppression, which in the light of her understanding of inherited traditions seemed to foreclose the possibility of giving full recognition to the moral issues involved—to how people are hurt, the depths to which they are made to suffer within work. It is as if Weil felt that the conception of oppression was too tied to traditions of thought that believe in the possibility of its transcendence through an unjustified faith in history. Weil also felt that the liberal language of rights was quite inadequate to illuminate the moral issues faced within factory work. Marx's discussion of exploitation seemed to offer greater depth but was too often translated into a quantitative language of wages. Weil was more concerned with Marx's critique of the institution of wage labor itself.

Thus Weil needed "a new language to convey what needs to be said" (14), and she found in Christianity a conception of affliction that could acknowledge the moral centrality of suffering without promising a vision of the human agent as free to break through the structures which bring suffering about. It was from within a reformulated Christianity that Weil discovered a language that could begin to illuminate the truth of factory work. Consequently, she saw that, while "Physical labour may be painful, but it is not degrading as such" ("Human Personality," 17), for her it became true that "it is sacrilege to degrade labour in exactly the same sense that it is sacrilege to trample upon the Eucharist" (18). That modern factory systematically degrades labor she had already grasped in *Reflections* where she concludes that "The present social system provides no means of action other than machines for crushing humanity; whatever may be the intentions of those who use them, these machines crush and will continue to crush as long as they exist" (119). She was thinking that this had little to do with conscious intentions and motives with which capitalists or state bureaucrats worked. People could only grasp the moral realities of these "industrial convict prisons constituted by the big factories" (119) if they challenged assumptions that individuals are free to act morally towards others unless they are constrained physically.

Weil came to feel that it mattered enormously how workers understood their situation in the factory. It would make all the difference to the ways they would challenge their suffering. She thought that Marx's emphasis on whether workers had a "correct analysis" of the workings of capitalist exploitation could too easily shift workers' focus away from their conditions and themselves. Rather, Weil wanted each worker to understand this suffering for him- or herself, believing that such understanding could only help the worker grasp the need to gain greater control of the labor process. As Weil learned, workers understood that exploitation is not simply an issue of economics but reaches deep into every soul. But she also discovered that there was no public language that could help make this experience and suffering concrete to them. Thus in her later writing she seeks to give voice to affliction:

> If the workers felt . . . that by being the victim they are in a certain sense the accomplice of sacrilege, their resistance would have a very different force from what is provided by the consideration of personal rights. It would not be an economic demand but an impulse from the depth of their being, fierce and desperate like that of a young girl who is being forced into a brothel; and at the same time it would be a cry of hope from the depth of their heart.
>
> This feeling, which surely enough exists in them, is so inarticulate as to be indiscernible even to themselves; and it is not the professionals of speech who can express it for them.
>
> Usually, when addressing them on their conditions, the selected topic is wages; and for men burdened with a fatigue that makes any effort of attention painful it is a relief to contemplate the unproblematic clarity of figures.
>
> In this way, they forget that the subject of the bargain,

which they complain they are being forced to sell cheap and
for less than the just price, is nothing other than their soul.
(18)

As Weil learned in the factory, often it is too difficult and
painful for people to express what they know. They prefer to
suffer in silence or to collude with a story that helps them think
better of themselves, even though they know it is not true. It is
only in rare moments that people can accept the truth. Weil did
come to believe that we crave truth because it offers us a much
truer and fuller contact with reality, however painful this may be.
But the time and place for recognizing and expressing truth have
to be appropriate and require deep trust, in ourselves and one
another, an ability to share pain, which is rare. As far as Weil
was concerned, the working-class movement had done little to
earn this trust and much to betray it. It had failed to appreciate
that in wage-labor the subject of the bargain "is nothing other
than [the] soul."

Within a liberal-capitalist society people think of the sale of
labor as a contract that is negotiated between equal partners,
each of whom has rights. Thus trade-unionists see themselves as
"negotiators"—a view that supports Weil's identification of the
"bargaining spirit" already "implicit in the notion of rights"
(*Seventy Letters*, 18). Further, the idea of the contract legitimates
the conception of wage-bargaining as an economic issue about
the sale of a commodity, which happens to be human labor. In
her rejection of the idea of human labor as a commodity Weil
agreed with Marx's analysis of wage-labor, though she felt that
the point of his critique has largely been lost within the working-
class movement, partly because Marx himself was too ready to
forsake moral language. Weil's experience of factory work taught
her the centrality of a revitalized moral language in grasping the
nature of wage-labor in capitalist society.

Weil also criticized the liberal tradition's conception of harm
done to others as a matter of infringement of rights, for this
assumes that the integrity of the individual is somehow left intact.
As long as justice is conceived in exclusively distributive terms, it
fails to illuminate the injustice involved.[18] As Weil says, "if a
young girl is being forced into a brothel she will not talk about

her rights. In such a situation the world would sound ludicrously inadequate!" ("Human Personality," 21).

In this deeper sense Weil can perhaps be thought of as preparing the ground for a feminist philosophy. I do not think it is an accident that she invokes the situation of a young girl who is being forced into a brothel to make clear to herself the meaning of "violation:" it is not understandable simply as a matter of infringing a person's rights but concerns the damage that is being done. When we damage someone in this way, we damage his or her trust in life, his or her self-confidence, self-respect, and ability to relate to others. Weil never fully explores these effects, possibly because of a deep suspicion of any seemingly "psychological" language. She felt that the idea of the violation of something sacred should suffice.

As well as criticizing the silences of the liberal tradition's concept of right, Weil challenged utilitarian assumptions that underpin notions of justice with individual wants and desires. This is another facet of a liberal tradition that fixes issues of justice in a language of distribution. Weil's essay "Human Personality" shows that damage can be done to more than "the personality and its desires" (12) but to the very integrity of the individual. In some important sense something sacred is being violated when this kind of injustice is being done:

> It is not the person which provides this criterion. When the infliction of evil provokes a cry of sorrowful surprise from the depth of the soul, it is not a personal thing. Injury to the personality and its desires is not sufficient to evoke it, but only and always the sense of contact with injustice through pain. It is always, in the last of men as in Christ himself, an impersonal protest.
>
> There are also many cries of personal protest, but they are unimportant; you may provoke as many of them as you wish without violating anything sacred. (12)

Here we can begin to see now Christianity became a rich resource for Weil, sharpening her sense of the depths of the injustice that people suffer. Yet in her anxiety that we might miss the full force and significance of the distinctions she wants to draw, Weil slips into polarities that can make it difficult to think through the relationship between the different levels of justice she is aware of. So she makes us strikingly aware that our traditional discussions of distributive justice in terms either of rights or of the satisfaction of personal desire tempt us into making "ludicrously inadequate" analyses that only distort our understanding, making it harder to come to grips with the moral realities of a situation; yet she fails to see that it is partly through becoming aware of situations in which it is appropriate to think in terms of rights or desire that we sharpen our sense of the "inappropriateness" of this language in other situations.

It is important to recognize that Weil's antagonism to the "personal" has to do with her specific opposition to the influence of Emmanuel Mounier and the Personalist movement developing in France at the time.[19] The movement, generally socialist but convinced of the importance of spiritual values, emphasized the individual rather than the state as the locus of responsibility and reform. For Weil its emphasis on the "personal" could preclude a grasp of the workings of the impersonal, which grew in significance in her later writings. Her essay "Human Personality" was in part a critical response to the influence of Personalism. Her antagonism pushed her into drawing an important distinction between the "personal" and the "impersonal" as somehow indicating different levels of protest. This helps us understand how she can see agitating for rights as usually involving a "personal" assertion which has a "commercial flavour" (18). She did not really want to acknowledge that rights can be invoked in any other way. Her choosing the example of the violated young girl, as if it demonstrates once and for all the deeper truth about the notion of rights that would otherwise have eluded us, reveals one of the problems in her method—presenting issues too absolutely. Had she explored a series of different situations, she might have been less dogmatic in her presentation. It is as if she wants to banish the very notion of rights from our moral and political discourse as carrying the contamination of the Romans. I feel the same way about her antagonism to the "personal," though I can recognize the strength of the particular point she is making.

At least Weil shows us the poverty of our inherited traditions to illuminate, for instance, the moral realities of wage-labor. A different conception of justice is needed if we want to truly illuminate the suffering done to people:

This profound and childlike and unchanging expectation of
good in the heart is not what is involved when we agitate for
our rights. The motive which prompts a little boy to watch
jealously to see if his brother has a slightly larger piece of
cake arises from a much more superficial level of the soul.
The word justice means two very different things according
to whether it refers to the one or the other level. It is only
the former one that matters. (10)

In spite of her new emphases, Weil did not forsake her earlier
political concerns. In a letter she wrote to Bernard on March 16,
1936, to make clear her political feelings, she declares, "I long
with all my heart for the most radical transformation of the
present regime in the direction of greater equality. I do not at all
believe that what is nowadays called revolution can bring this
about" (*Seventy Letters*, 40). She was clear that

> Whether the manager at R. takes orders from a managing
> director who represents a few capitalists or from a so-called
> "State Trust" makes no difference, except that in the first
> place the factory is not in the same hands as the police, the
> army, the prisons, etc., and in the second case it is. The
> inequality in the relations of power is therefore not lessened
> but accentuated. (40)

The problem, as she saw it after her experience of factory work,
"quite independently of the political regime, is to progress from
total subordination to a certain mixture of subordination and
cooperation, with complete cooperation as the ideal" (40).
Working people thus had to learn to rediscover their own sources
of strength, but she saw that "Many indispensable truths, which
could save men, go unspoken for reasons of this kind; those who
could utter them cannot formulate them and those who could
formulate them cannot utter them. If politics were taken
seriously, finding a remedy for this would be one of its most
urgent problems" ("Human Personality," 22).

For Weil, then, a precondition of the development of a politics
adequate to human need is the institution of a voice for the
oppressed at its center. Yet Weil's is a pessimistic vision that does
not offer guarantees, and her own experience reinforced her

sense that any hope for such transformed politics was misplaced. While stressing the importance of the articulation of truth, Weil recognized the limits of what could be expected from working people in the context of a process structured to undermine the power of reflection.

Whether it was right to expect workers to develop such a capacity was central to Weil's reflections on the nature of power. She wanted to learn where subordination had to be accepted as inevitable and where it could be meaningfully challenged so that the realm of true liberty could be extended. This could not simply be a matter of extending the options available to people but of discovering ways of giving people effective control. Weil did everything in her later writings to help this process, which involved her furthering her understanding the sources of power in modern society in new terms, such as her meditations on the *Iliad* and her understanding of Christianity provided.

7
Power

> But power-seeking, owing to its essential incapacity to seize
> hold of its object, rules out all consideration of an end, and
> finally comes, through an inevitable reversal, to take the
> place of all ends.
>   It is this reversal of the relationship between means and
> end, it is this fundamental folly that accounts for all that is
> senseless and bloody right through history.
> —Simone Weil, *Reflections*

In her early writings Weil is concerned with the complexities of the
operations of power. Her awareness of power and of the ways it
pervades the social body constituting human experience in ways
that render it inaccessible to control is part of what establishes a
continuity in her writings. It is this property of the operation of
power that gave Weil an early sense of the inadequacies of a
Kantian conception of morality—however bound she remained to
it in crucial respects—located as it is in the tenet that rational
beings live in a condition of freedom that provides for the
possibility of moral decision. Weil could not refuse to notice that
any capacity for freedom we have is cut across by the presence of
power. She was therefore concerned to articulate a conception of
the nature and consequences of power.

If, however, an awareness of power pushed Weil beyond a
Kantian framework of reference and helped to draw her thinking
towards the influence of radical traditions of thought in her early
work, by the time she produced her later work her sense of

power as the inevitable and irresistible condition of social life was paradoxically drawing her deep into pessimism. Weil's moral commitment to the oppressed is at times all that prevents a feeling that the train of her thought leads logically to capitulation. As her awareness of power intensified, so she came to look to Christianity to provide for any sustenance of a conception of the good. Her vision became increasingly bifurcated into a realm of the evil where power reigns and a realm of the good outside human experience.

This chapter concerns the development in her conception of power, focussing in particular on the significance of her rereading of the *Iliad* for her understanding of power. It is in her thinking about power that the great themes of her work—the diversity of levels of oppression, the reversal of a proper relation between means and ends, the question of the potentiality, or lack of it, for the actualization of liberty—finally fuse. If her vision lacks any real sense of hope, nevertheless through these later developments Weil found a way of articulating the actuality and depth of human suffering through a sensitivity that is fundamental to any truly radical thought. Weil's experience of factory work—in which, as we saw in the previous chapter, she pushed herself through the experience of her own degradation to appreciate a level of knowledge of which she believed her contemporary radicals to be wholly unaware—opened the way for her development of a Christian language that gave a voice to the condition in which the realm of power has so violated and silenced the individual that the self is all but annihilated: the condition of affliction.

Weil's willingness to engage with and draw on past sources is part of what provides for the continuing significance of her work. In her thinking on power, Weil offers us a revitalized sense of our relationship with the past, which, as we shall show, gives a way of subverting historical relativism. Weil's readings of the *Iliad* heightened her awareness of the importance of language and recast her sense of the relationship between the body and the mind. Weil came to understand that power mediates our relationship to our language, to our silence, and to our own bodies. She saw that an understanding of the character of power is essential if we are to take seriously the processes that underpin human passivity and sustain unfreedom.

1   The struggle for power

Because Weil believed that it is only due to the "intervention" of
the struggle for power that the resistance of the weak and the
feelings of justice of the strong are unable to mitigate inequalities, she gave the struggle for power a central position within her
analysis of oppression. In her writings she is concerned to show
that "Oppression proceeds exclusively from objective conditions"
(*Reflections*, 63), but like Marx she leaves us generally dis-
oriented about the place of moral critique within her form of
historical analysis in her early writings. She felt that Marx
accounts so thoroughly for the mechanism of capitalist oppression
that "one can scarcely visualise how, with the selfsame cogs, the
mechanism could one fine day transform itself to the point where
oppression should progessively begin to disappear" (140). Thus,
even in her early writings, she can place no confidence in Marx's
assertion that "the regime would produce its own gravediggers";
she feels this assertion "is crucially contradicted every day" (117)
and wonders, incidentally, how Marx could ever have believed
that slavery could produce free men since "Never yet in history
has a regime of slavery fallen under the blows of the slaves"
(117). So Weil could never really share Marx's hopes. Nor could
she dispense with moral discussion, even in her early writing,
probably because she could never, like Marx, replace it with any
trust in the historical process.[1] Rather, her sense of the centrality
of the struggle for power undermined any sense of rationality
within the historical process, and this led her later to focus on the
lessons of *Iliad* as she was consolidating a vision inspired by
fundamentally Christian sources.

In the struggle against nature the confrontation of certain
necessities and limits gives reality to human life. But in the
relations of power between people limits are undermined and
power becomes an end in itself:

> It is altogether different as soon as relations between man
> and man take the place of direct contact between man and
> nature. The preservation of power is a vital necessity for the
> powerful, since it is their power which provides their

sustenance; but they have to preserve it both against their
rivals and against their inferiors. (65)

Rulers are "ceaselessly compelled to reinforce their power for
fear of seeing it snatched away from them, are for ever seeking a
domination essentially impossible to attain" (67). This would not
be so if "one man could possess in himself a force superior to that
of many other men put together; but such is never the case" (67),
because the instruments of power such as arms, gold, machines,
magical, or technical secrets always "exist independently of him
who disposes of them, and can be taken up by others" (67).

Weil thinks there is always an "irredemiable disequilibrium" in
the relations between rulers and ruled but that, insofar "as the
very methods of labour and of warfare rule out equality" (67),
they "seem to cause madness to weigh down on mankind in the
manner of an external fatality" (67). Weil's language here in
Reflections shows the deep influence of the *Iliad* on her thinking
about power, though she only later gave full expression to how
relations of power reduce people to things. In her early writings,
however, the emphasis is more directly on the ways power-
seeking reverses the relation between means and ends as power
becomes an end in itself. War thereby becomes an end in itself,
and in this sense war tends to provide a model for Weil's thinking
about the workings of capitalist production. She thought the fact
that Marx and Engels never really analyzed the phenomenon of
war beyond thinking that capitalist greed is the cause of wars was
an enormous omission, especially "since industrial production is
nowadays not only the chief source of wealth but also the chief
means of carrying on war" (151).[2] Production had come to hold
sway over people's lives; likewise in the *Iliad* Weil saw the "sway
exercised by war over the warriors, and, through them, over
humanity in general" (68).

A central dilemma for Weil is that, though power is by
definition only a means, "power-seeking, owing to its essential
incapacity to seize hold of its object, rules out all considerations
of an end, and finally comes, through an inevitable reversal, to
take the place of all ends" (69). It is this reversal of the
relationship between means and end that forms Weil's conception
of human history, in which people become "the plaything of the
instruments of domination they themselves have manufactured,

and [this] reduces living humanity to being the chattel of inanimate chattels" (69). Because people no longer have any control over their lives, Weil could no longer look with any great confidence to social relations for a limit to the struggle for power; for her, "it is things, not men, that prescribe the limits and laws governing this giddy race for power" (69).

Within this context, according to Weil, we cannot think in terms of moderate goals people set for themselves for there is no place for moderation, especially where maintaining power becomes an end in itself for the rulers. Nor can we think of limits the oppressed might place on "this giddy race for power" through their resistance to subordination since resistance "can operate in such a way as to aggravate the evil as well as to restrict it," forcing the masters to "make their power weigh even more heavily for fear of losing it" (69). For both these reasons Weil concludes that "it is things, not men, that prescribe" whatever limits exist. This is a radical conclusion that minimizes the place of consciousness and activity in working people's resistance to oppression, a view that grew in significance with her meditations on the *Iliad*. People are reduced to matter through the workings of the relations of power. The tyrannical character of relations of power "would know no bounds were these not by good fortune found in the nature of things" (70).

Weil attempts a sketch of "a list of the inevitable necessities which limit all species of power" in the full knowledge that "although power depends on the material conditions of life, it never ceases to transform these conditions themselves" (71). Firstly, she mentions the way all sorts of power rely on instruments that have a given scope, illustrating this notion by saying that "you do not command in the same way, by means of soldiers armed with bows and arrows, spears and swords as you do by means of aeroplanes and incendiary bombs" (71). Secondly, power is always "running up against the actual limits of the controlling faculty" (72), and collaboration carries its own problems. Working with others presents its own problems of organization: misunderstandings between people, different goals, purposes, and intentions that put individuals at odds with each other. Collaboration "is never absolutely free from rivalry" (72). Weil stresses that since the faculties necessary for exerting control—such as examining, comparing, weighing, deciding, and combining—are essentially individual, they inevitably limit the exercise of power. Lastly, the exercise of power depends on the creation of surplus production sufficient to feed all those engaged. Significantly in Weil's thought developing these factors together "enable one to conceive political and social power as constituting at each moment something analogous to a measurable force" (72).

But these limits to power and oppression Weil identifies remain hidden when "every oppressive society is cemented by this religion of power" that "falsifies all social relations" (73):

> The powerful, be they priests, military leaders, kings or capitalists, always believe that they command by divine right; and those who are under them feel themselves crushed by a power which seems to them either divine or diabolical, but in any case supernatural. Every oppressive society is cemented by this religion of power, which falsifies all social relations by enabling the powerful to command over and above what they are able to impose; it is only otherwise in times of popular agitation, times when, on the contrary, all—rebellious slaves and threatened masters alike—forget how heavy and how solid the chains of oppression are. (73)

Weil, however, rarely underestimated "how heavy and how solid the chains of oppression are." She knew how rare are the moments like the factory occupations of 1936, when workers can realize that the power is in their own hands. The immediate cause of the strikes was the victory of the Popular Front in the May elections. Long overdue reforms were expected with the election of a socialist government, and all over France there were spontaneous occupations of factories. But even though those days brought feelings of unspeakable joy to Weil, she immediately stressed the new responsibilities workers had in the new situation. Possibly it was because she was still aware of the power capitalists maintained that she wanted to challenge any easy illusions of power the workers might have had. In an open letter to one of the four million unskilled workers who had recently come into the trade unions, she warned of a need for vigilance:

When you had no rights, you recognized no obligations.
Now you are somebody, you have strength, you have
received some advantages; but in return you have acquired
some responsibilities. . . . Now you must work to make
yourself capable of assuming them; otherwise these newly-
acquired advantages will vanish one fine day like dream.
One preserves his rights only if he is capable of exercising
them properly. ("Lettre Ouverte à un syndiqué," 244)[3]

Her vision is generally much more pessimistic.

But she never ceased to treasure those rare moments when the
relations of power are upset. The occupations in June 1936
allowed the workers the chance to feel at home in their places of
work, even to show their families around. This gave Weil a sense
of what their relationship to their factories could be, though she
had never expected that it could be brought into existence
through such an uprising. As she says in "Meditation on
Obedience and Liberty," which was written in the second half of
1937, four years after *Reflections*, and carries the flickering
influence of this moment of hope:

Such moments do not last, although the downtrodden
ardently hope to see them last for ever. They cannot last,
because that unanimity which is produced in the heat of a
quickening and general emotion is incompatible with any
form of methodical action. Its effect is always to suspend all
action and arrest the daily course of life. This temporary
stoppage cannot be prolonged; the course of daily life has to
be taken up again, and daily tasks have to be performed
. . . it is always the same ones who have to obey. (144)

The powerful do their best to prevent this "crystallization of the
subject masses," and "as a rule this emotion has barely had the
time to awaken when it is repressed by the feeling of an
irredeemable impotence" (144).

Infused as it is with a practical understanding of how relations
of power work to crush people's individual sense of worth,
"Meditation on Obedience and Liberty" also bears the scars of
Weil's experience in Spain. Her initial enthusiasm and identification with the cause of the Spanish Republic stemmed partly from

the strength of anarcho-syndicalism within the revolutionary movement. She had always been deeply opposed to war, even when made by revolutionaries to defend their revolution. She always thought that war inevitably strengthened the power of the state at the expense of the people. In 1933 she wrote that "War is inconceivable without an oppressive organisation, without a system in which one group, which gives orders, has absolute power over those who carry out orders" (La Situation en Allemagne," 241). But on her arrival in Barcelona it seemed to her that she was actually living through one of "those historic periods—1792, 1871, 1917—which one reads books about . . . one of those extraordinary periods, which until now have not lasted, when those who have always obeyed assume respons-ibility" (209).[4] She made initial contacts with Partido Obrero de Unificación Marxista (POUM), the dissident Communist group whose founder, Joaquin Maurin, was the brother-in-law of her friend Boris Souvarine. She soon left Barcelona for the front in the Aragon region and made for the town of Pina to connect with one of the anarchist columns, drawn by what she saw as the love and spirit of brotherhood within the anarchist organizations. But she was soon deeply disillusioned by her experience, and she felt herself to be morally an accomplice to militia troop', unnecessary bloodshed.

In her *Journal d'Espagne*, Weil records some notes on conversations with peasants in Pina. As in her own experience of factory work she was constantly testing the ideas she had formed with the reality in terms of people's lives. So in Pina she wanted to understand their experience of farming collectively and the everyday changes that the revolution had brought in their lives. She was struck by the sharp feeling of inferiority many of the peasants continued to feel, but, as she notes in a letter to George Bernanos, "In a country where the great majority of the poor are peasants the essential aim . . . should be the improvement of the peasants' conditions; and perhaps the main issue of this war, at the beginning, was the redistribution of land" (*Seventy Letters*, 108). The war in Spain, however had somehow become an end in itself, and human life had inevitably been degraded and devalued in the process: What had started as a war of famished peasants against landed proprietors and their clerical supporters had become a war between Russia on the one hand and Germany and

Italy on the other. Weil was deeply struck by the fact that

> Although there was no insolence, no injury, no
> brutality—at least I saw none and I know that theft and
> rape were capital crimes in the anarchist
> militias—nevertheless, between the armed forces and the
> civilian population there was an abyss, exactly like the abyss
> between rich and poor. One felt it in the attitude of the two
> groups, the one always rather humble, submissive and
> timid, the other confident, off-hand and condescending
> (109)

Although Weil stayed in Spain for only two months before an accident forced her to leave, the experience affected her understanding of the workings of power not only within war but more generally. She was increasingly concerned that in France, as elsewhere in Europe, military preoccupations would more and more dominate all the everyday aspects of existence, and in the militarization of the economy she saw evidence of the growing power of the state in relation to the people themselves. She was convinced that keeping up with Hitler could only be done by undergoing privations and constraints "almost equal to those imposed by Hitler."[5] With the damage that is wrought by war fresh in her mind, from her experience in Spain, she was prepared to recommend concessions to Hitler if that would preserve peace. In a letter she drafted in 1937 she was clearly not prepared to go to war over Czechoslovakia: "I . . . affirm that a defeat without a war is preferable to a victorious war."[6] But in 1939, as she was led to think through the damage that would be done to moral and spiritual values in Europe with the victory of Nazism, she abandoned her pacifism.

Deeply pessimistic of the prospects for Europe as the military question became determining and doubtful of the new possibilities created by the recent factory occupations, Weil predicted that "Capitalism will be destroyed by the development of national defence in each country, and replaced by the totalitarian state. This is the revolution we shall have."[7]

Weil thought that the perpetual nature of the conflict between opposing social forces in Europe was not understood, and she was disillusioned with prevailing traditions of thought, both

liberal and Marxist, for being unable to illuminate the dark
realities people in Europe faced in 1937. Early in 1937, in "The
Power of Words" she wrote:

> Every social status quo rests upon an equilibrium of forces
> or pressures, similar to the equilibrium of fluids; but
> between one prestige and another there can be no
> equilibrium. Prestige has no bounds and its satisfaction
> always involves the infringement of someone else's prestige
> or dignity. And prestige is inseparable from power. (169)

In these new terms, Weil saw the essential contradiction in
society, an impasse "from which human society can only escape
by some miracle" (170).

At this time she tried to understand the nature of the power
Stalin held over the Soviet Union and Hitler was achieving in
Germany. She felt that no one could conceive even vaguely how
Stalin had "the power to cause any head whatever to fall within
the confines of the Russian frontiers" ("Meditation on Obedience
and Liberty," 141). Marxism could not adequately account for
the submissiveness of the oppressed in the factories and also
during war, when people seemed ready to die for ideas or orders
they did not comprehend. If she was to grasp the nature of power
such as Stalin's, she realized she must begin to take more
seriously the notion of prestige:

> The necessity for power is obvious, because life cannot be
> lived without order; but the allocation of power is arbitrary
> because men are alike, or very nearly. Yet power must not
> be seen to be arbitrarily allocated, because it will not then
> be recognized as power. Therefore prestige, which is
> illusion, is of the very essence of power. ("The Power of
> Words," 168)

Thus power can appear as something absolute and sacrosanct
both to those who wield it and to those who submit to it—an
example, for Weil, of how our "political universe is peopled
exclusively by myths and monsters; all it contains is absolutes and
abstract entities" (157).

So it is that in Weil's view the "glossy surface of our

civilization hides a real intellectual decadence . . . we seem to have lost the very elements of intelligence" (156). For Weil this is

> . . . illustrated by all the words of our political and social vocabulary: nation, security, capitalism, communism, fascism, order, authority, property, democracy. We never use them in phrases such as: There is democracy *to the extent that* . . . or: There is capitalism *in so far as* . . . The use of expressions like "to the extent that" is beyond our intellectual capacity. (157)

According to Weil, this intellectual decadence helps create conflicts with no definable objectives. As she says, "Words with content and meaning are not murderous" (156). But when "empty words are given capital letters, then, on the slightest pretext, men will begin shedding blood for them and piling up ruin in their name" for in these conditions "the only definition of success is to crush a rival group of men who have a hostile word on their banners" (156).

In her formulation of the power of language philosophy and politics are given a new relation to each other: "when a word is properly defined it loses its capital letter and can no longer serve as a banner or as a hostile slogan; it becomes simply a sign, helping us to grasp some concrete reality, or concrete objective, or method of activity" (156). And, for Weil, "To clarify thought, to discredit the intrinsically meaningless words, and to define the use of others by precise analysis—to do this, strange though it may appear, might be a way of saving human lives" (156). This was a task that Weil set for herself those dark times. But it was no easy task, for "the whole intellectual climate of our age favours the growth and multiplication of vacuous entities". Crucially for Weil "They stupefy the mind; they not only make men willing to die, but infinitely worse, they make them forget the value of life" (170).

In "Meditation on Obedience and Liberty" Weil reveals her most pessimistic vision of the social world. Marx cannot account for the submissiveness of the oppressed. "When an old working man, unemployed and left to starve, dies quietly in the street or some slum, the submission which extends to the very point of death cannot be explained by the play of vital necessities" (142).

The force that makes such an unequal situation possible, as Weil saw it, depends on maintaining the false notion that those at the bottom of the social scale are without value, which is partially accomplished because people are led to devalue their own experience and lives. Unable to look to the social order to sustain a sense of the value of their lives, people would have to learn to look towards a different source. Weil therefore concluded that there was an absolute opposition between the social order and both truth and justice. For her, since "Everything that contributes towards giving those who are at the bottom of the social order the feeling that they possess a value is to a certain extent subversive" (145), the values that would be created within the social order would not help people towards a sense of truth and justice.

Weil's "Meditation on Obedience and Liberty" marks a significant shift in her thinking about power and subordination: here society itself, rather than a particular form of society, demands obedience and submission. Struck by "the submission of the greater number to the smaller" (140) and by the ways this obedience is maintained, she thinks that we cannot have the crudest knowledge of this process "as long as we have not formed a clear notion of social force" (141). "Society cannot have its engineers as long as it has not first had its Galileo" (141). Weil was preparing the way for this Galileo, if she could not provide the analysis herself. It is in this meditation that she thinks so categorically of society as, in Plato's terms, a "great beast." In an implicit criticism of her concern in *Reflections* to relate oppression to the conditions of production, she shifted to thinking that "The social order, though necessary, is essentially evil, whatever it may be" (146). Collecting these themes together, Weil says:

> If one considers a society as a collective being, then this
> great beast, like all other beasts, can principally be defined
> by the ways in which it makes sure of its food, sleep, shelter
> from the elements—in short, its life. But society considered
> in its relation to the individual cannot be defined simply by
> the methods of production. . . . Obedience and command
> are also phenomena for which the conditions of production
> do not provide a sufficient explanation. (142)

Thus Weil concludes, "The notion of force and not that of need is the key to an understanding of social phenomena" (142). The fact that nearly everyone wants either to preserve or overthrow the present relations of power throws a "veil" over "the fundamental absurdity of the social mechanism" (143). In her work on the *Iliad* Weil sought "the secret of this machine" by attempting to look this "apparent absurdity fairly in the face" (143). But tensions remain since it can be difficult to make sense of her sense of subversion in the light of her theory of power. It sometimes seems to be invoked as an amoral concept, which just means subversion of the established order. Sometimes we can be left unsure whether something is being asserted as a timeless necessity or as a historically grounded insight.

Realizing that her early explanations relied too heavily on the substitution between means and ends within production, Weil's experience of work encouraged her to look for a different kind of explanation for the nature of obedience and command. She sought the objective limits of power within things themselves, rather than feeling the need to explore the nature of obedience and subordination themselves. She was clear, however, that if history was not to be seen as a "fairly-tale," it had to be admitted that there are limits to the ways power can extend the foundations on which it rests. As far as big industry is concerned, "each important advance in mechanization has created at the same time resources, instruments and a stimulus towards a further advance" (*Reflections*, 74) so that, for instance, the telegraph, the telephone, the daily press provided the means of control and information indispensable for the centralized economy "that is the inevitable outcome of big industry. Weil acknowledges that this phenomenon of "automatic development is so striking" (75), especially in the nineteenth century, but she also wants to stress that "the spur of competition forces it to go even farther and farther, that is to say to go beyond the limits within which it can be effectively exercised" (75). So already in her *Reflections* the central contradiction within capitalist society is not between capital and labour, but is "the internal contradictions which every oppressive system carries within itself like a seed of death; it is made up of the necessarily limited character of the material bases of power and the necessarily unlimited character of the race for power considered as a relationship between men" (76). The struggles of working people against their conditions of oppression has been displaced in this account which seeks to make the struggle for power central. But at some level people remain the playthings of historical forces, in a way not too dissimilar to the orthodox Marxism of the Second International. The productive forces can be seen to have been replaced by the struggle for power as an end in itself. But both conceptions find little place—though for quite different reasons—for the struggles of working people in their own liberation.

Weil loses confidence in the workings of this "internal contradiction" as a "seed of death." She talks less in her later writings about the limits assigned to power by the nature of things. She used to think that "By attempting to command where actually it is not in a position to compel obedience, it provokes reactions which it can neither foresee or deal with" (76). She thought that "capitalism is passing through a phase of this kind" (76). She seemed to think of this as the more or less automatic workings of some kind of justice. As she says, "Thus it is the nature itself of things which constitutes that justice-dealing divinity the Greeks worshipped under the name of Nemesis, and which punishes excess" (76). Though this faith in a "justice-dealing divinity" was to remain with her, it was to find a different source. She could fundamentally no longer believe in the limits set to power by the "nature of things." But, even in her *Reflections*, she didn't think that when a specific form of domination no longer has the resources to maintain its supremacy that it will begin to disappear progressively. Rather it is then that it often becomes more harshly oppressive as it struggles to discover new material resources to sustain its power.

But without Marx's confidence in the productive forces Weil is left with a view of history as the play of blind forces. Even though she resists drawing any conclusions she has to admit that "At first sight there seems to be no weak spot in this sinister mesh of circumstances" (78). It could be argued that her early writings lead her into an impasse so she has to look towards a different, possibly religious and transcendental source, if she is to imagine "an attempt at deliverance" (78). Certainly we can see the roots for her developing disillusionment with the social world in her conception of the struggle for power. Eventually she reached the point where she saw the social order, though necessary, as essentially evil in its relation to individuals:

> But whatever may be the patterns taken by social transformations, all one finds, if one tries to lay bare the mechanism, is a dreary play of blind forces that unite together or clash, that progress or decline, that replace each other, without ever ceasing to grind beneath them the unfortunate race of human beings. (*Reflections*, 78)

A similar emphasis in her later "Meditation on Obedience and Liberty" shows she has shifted to talk more openly about "the fundamental absurdity of the social mechanism," whatever underlying social patterns may emerge with a new balance of power between social forces. But in her later meditations on the subordination and submission of the many she declares that numbers, whatever we are led to think, constitute a weakness. This is a theme she reiterates in *The Need for Roots* and is part of developing a kind of geometry of social forces.[8] She argues that "The masses are not in subjection despite the fact of their being number, but because they are number" ("Meditation on Obedience and Liberty," 143):

> Since the many obey, and obey to the point of allowing suffering and death to be inflicted on them, while the few command, this means that it is not true that number constitutes a force. Number, whatever our imagination may lead us to believe, is a weakness. Weakness is on the side where people are hungry, exhausted, where they implore and tremble, not on the side where they live comfortably, bestow favours, and issue threats. (143)

It is precisely because it is a few that rule that they can form themselves into a more coherent group. Even the mass organization of people would not reverse this relation for "it is only possible to establish cohesion between a limited number of men" (143). She believed, therefore, that the solidarity of working people was only possible for a few rare moments. Mostly they were bound to exist as a "juxtaposing of individuals—that is to say weakness" (143).

Weil came to see history increasingly as a play of forces, in which participation, even from a distance, entails contamination and the risk of defeat. Still, for her it was not possible to take refuge in indifference. She returns to the formula of the "lesser evil," "provided it be applied with the coldest lucidity" (146). Although the *Iliad* helped restore her faith in some kind of divine justice, in her later writing she accepts that the one mode of domination is likely to be succeeded by another. For Weil it is as if the ways people behave in the social world can at best lighten the load of the oppressed or work to sustain them in their individual sense of worth and dignity. But this is very far from thinking that social relations can become moral relations among free and equal individuals. This is a vision that no longer made sense to Weil.[9]

Salvation thus could not come in the social order. "The struggles between fellow citizens do not spring from a lack of understanding or goodwill; they belong to the nature of things, and cannot be appeased, but can only be smothered by coercion" (146). But this does not mean that people should accept the social order as somehow organized in the interests of all. Weil fiercely rejected this liberal vision. She would never minimize the brutality and suffering entailed by the ongoing struggle for power, even though she wanted to place limits on them. Resistance had to be expected, but there could be no guarantee that it will not make the situation of working people even worse. She reproached the French capitalists in *The Need for Roots* not for being capitalists but for not carrying out the duties and responsibilities that could rightly be expected from them. In her later writing, where she returns to a vision of balance between different social forces, she stresses the duties that go along with power. If people abuse their positions, they should expect heavier punishment. She was seeking a different understanding of equality before the law since people should not expect to be treated equally if they are in unequal positions of power within society. Perhaps World War II gave her a flickering sense of the possibility of some kind of renewal in France. But her concern also flowed directly from her experience of workers' and peasants' lives in France. She had learned to focus directly on measures that would restore dignity and pride wherever she saw the possibility. Weil struggled for ways to define how a worker's pride and dignity could be sustained, the only goal she could fully and wholeheartedly believe in. She still wanted to understand the processes through which workers were reduced through "the reversal of the relationship between subject and object" (41). But in order to establish a new framework for her reflections upon the workings of power she turned again to the *Iliad*.

2 Power and value

Weil found in the *Iliad* the truest expression of the workings of power. For her it was "the only veritable epic of the western world", ("The *Iliad*, Poem of Might," 180) containing truths that are barely accessible to us, though of the utmost significance in grasping our own historical situation. Through meditating on the *Iliad*, Weil attempted to illuminate her own times—to find a way to reveal the meaning of the emergence of Hitler and fascism. Not simply looking to the past to find a relevant comparsion in destruction, she drew attention to the poverty of prevailing traditions of moral and political thought to illuminate contemporary reality.

Weil's essay "The *Iliad*, Poem of Might" was written shortly after "The Great Beast: Some Reflections on the Origins of Hitlerism", which has a direct connection with the war that had just begun. Weil realized that what threatened the world was not just Hitler's Germany but the condition of Western civilization that had made Hitler possible. She saw Hitler as aspiring for a universal domination that Rome, its conquests and its empire, had made admirable. This threat would not be abolished by a victory of the democratic countries. A deeper change was required to challenge the Roman inheritance. This is why Weil devotes such attention to describing in this essay the methods that Rome employed to extend and maintain its conquests.

Rome was centrally concerned with its power and prestige: Never discussing peace except after a crushing victory, it also invested its power with an appearance of legality. Weil explores "to what extent the Mediterranean basin was reduced to spiritual sterility by the totalitarian State" (130). She could not excuse the Romans on relativist grounds that somehow acts we regard as inadmissible were forgivable in the past. For Weil "There is no ground for believing that morality has ever changed" since the purest forms of morality have always been known. And even if morality has changed, this would not justify speaking of Rome with admiration in our epoch:

> If I admire, or even excuse, a brutal act committed two thousand years ago, it means that my thought, today, is lacking in the virtue of humanity. Man is not divided into compartments, and it is impossible to admire certain methods employed in the past without awakening in oneself a disposition to copy them. (133)[10]

Weil's developing concern with spiritual values in the late 1930s marks a shift in her writings as her vision expanded to consider Western culture in a new light. She no longer accepted the terms of reference established by the Western Enlightenment tradition for they could not explain the forms of oppression and liberty that exist within modern society. Her developing relationship to Christianity cannot be separated from this broadening of her vision. Simone Pétrement mentions how Weil's reading of the *Bhagavad-Gita* also had a burning relevance to the beginning of the German offensive in 1940. Because the dialogue deals with the question of whether Arjuna, a man who has pity for others and whom war fills with horror, must nonetheless go fight in the war, Weil saw Arjuna's problem as hers. She was concerned with Krishna's words that prove to Arjuna that if he fights in a certain way, he can still remain pure. Weil meditated on Krishna's teaching, for she was struck, as Pétrement explains it, "by the resemblance between the spirit of Gita and the Christian spirit, and instead of her admiration for this poem turning her away from Christianity, it brought her even closer."[11]

A deepened concern with spiritual values was an integral part of her rejecting her long-held pacifist position. She became convinced of the unimaginable destruction of human values that would result with Hitler's victory. In "Cold War Policy in 1939" she drew up a balance sheet between the terrible human costs of war and the costs of German hegemony in Europe. After a painful inner struggle she changed her view that the cost of war was greater, and she accepted an overriding obligation to work for Hitler's destruction. She became convinced "that spiritual values are really dead once they have been killed. . . . And nothing will replace what has been lost, as nothing replaces a precious human being cut off in the flower of youth" ("Three Letters on History." 80).

Hitler's attempts at the domination of Europe were in many crucial ways a repetition of the policy and methods of Rome. Rome always made it appear that it punished its enemies as a matter of duty, not for its own interest and pleasure. Using propaganda, which is essential for a policy of prestige, Rome gave an impression of legitimacy to its cruel acts. As Weil says, "The master must always be in the right and those he punishes must always be in the wrong" ("The Great Beast," 114)—an impression requiring considerable skill to maintain. We need to dispel two common ideas regarding the relation of power and justice if we are to grasp the situation. "One is that the just cause always continues to appear just even after it has been defeated; the other is that might by itself is sufficient to establish right" (115). The Romans were always careful to cover the actions of their might with plausible pretexts—as the Germans did too.

In Weil's view "By thus keeping up appearances one makes it impossible or difficult for one's opponents to draw upon the strength which comes from indignation" (115). Unlike the Romans, however, the Greeks were never able to believe that they were always in the right. When they perpetrated cruel abuses of power, they were aware that they were doing so. The Romans could only feel condescending pity if their subjects had suffered an excess of cruelty, but never remorse. It never occurred to them that their rebellious subjects or enemies might have had some right on their side:

> In a general way, the Romans enjoyed that tough, unshakeable, impenetrable collective self-satisfaction which makes it possible to commit crimes with a perfectly untroubled conscience. When conscience is impermeable by truth there must be a degradation of heart and mind which obscures and weakens thought; and that is why . . . the only Roman contribution to the history of science is the murder of Archimedes. In compensation, however, this complete

self-satisfaction, reinforced by power and conquest, is
contagious, and we are still under its influence today.
(116)

So it is that power has its human costs, though people can remain
blind to them. In a letter written at roughly the same time she
makes it clear that "To me it seems that all progress in the
direction of centralized power implies irreparable losses in the
realm of everything that is really precious" ("Three Letters on
History," 80).

This does not mean that Weil imagined a society without
constraints, but she had gone beyond a Durkheimian sociology in
which social life is impossible without constraints. Weil had
learned how to think about the nature of these constraints, and
she recognized that "some of these forms are consistent with an
atmosphere in which spiritual values (for want of a better term)
can develop. They are the good forms. Others kill these values"
(79). Weil knew that judgements of value were inescapable. But
they were not "subjective" or "personal" for "nothing concerns
human life so essentially, for every man at every moment, as
good and evil." For social theorists or writers to avoid
discriminations of value—or, like the surrealists, to set up the
"total absence of value as the supreme value" ("The Responsibility of Writers," 167)—is to betray their calling and forfeit all
claim to excellence. Weil had come to appreciate that "the
continuity of spiritual tradition is of infinite value and its loss is a
real loss" ("Three Letters on History," 80). She had escaped the
terms of moral relativism that have become the common-sense
assumptions within social theory and anthropology because they
seemed to be the only alternative to nineteenth century
rationalism, which tacitly judged other cultures in terms of the
values and institutions of Western culture, and thus the only way
in which the values and institutions of different cultures could be
given equal recognition and respect.

Weil did not accept uncritically the ideas of power and
greatness at the center of Western culture since the Romans.
Unless these values were fundamentally challenged within
Western culture, Hitler would not really be defeated. Thus Weil
demonstrates the necessity of accepting a broader responsibility

for Hitler in her willingness to understand him not as pathology but as living out Western ideals and values. For Weil,

> Bohemia is not more oppressed by Hitler than the provinces were by Rome. The concentration camps are not a more murderous affront to human goodness than were the gladiatorial games and the sufferings inflicted on slaves. The power of a single man is not more absolute, more arbitrary, or more brutal at Berlin than it was at Rome. ("The Great Beast," 130)

Weil did not know that the concentration camps were to become mass extermination camps, but she does reveal something important when she declares that "the spirit of the two systems seems to be very nearly identical and to merit praise or execration in identically the same terms" (131).

That people and values are vulnerable to the workings of power is central to the social theory Weil was reaching for in the late 1930s. Suspicious about the workings of centralized power that too easily fostered Roman ideals of power and greatness, she had a vision of decentralized power that she saw as the condition of a just peace:

> [I]n a given country, at certain times, there arise forms of social life which do not kill by constraint that delicate and fragile thing which is the medium that favours the development of the soul. It requires a social life that is not too centralized, and laws to control arbitrariness, and, in so far as authority is necessarily arbitrary, a willingness to obey which allows of submission without humiliation. ("Three Letters on History," 80)

So it was that her spirituality remained inseparable from her politics. This was a significant strand in her thinking that developed in the writing of *The Need for Roots*. But it is in tension with a much deeper pessimism in which salvation could only come in individual terms while society remained Plato's "Great beast." At different moments in her later writings she took up these separate strands with equal intensity, though without resolving the tension between them.

In "Cold War Policy in 1939" Weil recognized that "contrary to what is often said, spiritual values are very easily destroyed by force, even to the complete obliteration of all trace of them. Indeed if this were not so, why should anyone except the meanest self-seekers be much concerned about Politics?" (191). Thus for her a sense of the fragility of human values and relations required a concern with politics. She learned to dread the universalism of power and dominance, a dream to be feared rather than cherished, seeing how "all the freshness, originality, and vitality of a great part of the world was drained away by the tedium and the monotonous uniformity of the Roman domination" (191). She thought that because "We have colonized all the civilizations that differed from our own" so that "The whole world today, or very nearly, is either Europeanized or in direct subjection to Europe" (191), there was no hope for barbarians' breaking into this world and "bringing with them the variety and the life from which a new civilization could spring" (191). The danger of colonialism is still with us with United States' cultural and political dominance. But it is a dominance that is being resisted.

It has been the cult of power and grandeur, conceived after the Roman model, that has been handed down. This cult "has inspired us to acts as well as words" ("The Great Beast," 134). Weil knew that many still boasted of the use made of these methods in ruling their colonial empires, for, as she recognized, "The idea of the despised and humiliated hero, which was so common among the Greeks and is the actual theme of the Gospels, is almost outside our tradition" (134). With their conception of virtue the Greeks had grasped the tragic inevitability of people being subjected to force. They did not simply glorify those who wielded power triumphantly but knew to celebrate those who suffered under it without becoming base themselves.

The Romans, on the other hand, were intellectually subservient to the very force they wielded since their culture was "almost entirely subservient to propaganda and the will to domination" (133). This could not bring into being a genuine civilization for obedience was not freely given but always imposed by force and fear. Those who practised or celebrated domination, like the Romans, could never develop genuine spiritual or human values.

Weil recognized the extent to which French culture had to a

great degree been pervaded by the Roman ideal, even though it had "many minds of the first order that have been neither servants nor worshippers of force" (134). This was true in all democratic states that had turned themselves into nations by submitting to a centralized, bureaucratic, militarist state—a phenomenon was not connected with Germanic blood but with the very structure of the modern state. She believed that if Europe was ever to have a just peace, it would have to face the implications of the Roman spiritual and the political inheritance. Only if the ways in which the political crisis of the centralized state—that drains all life and vitality to itself—is tied up with a spiritual crisis involving notions of greatness and power were recognized, could a way forward be seen.

Weil did not, however, believe that Christianity could simply be a counterweight for it was deeply contaminated in its relationship to Rome. In fact, according to Weil, "the twofold Hebraic and Roman tradition has in great measure negated, for two thousand years, the divine inspiration of Christianity" (133). In this way Weil sought to spare Christianity a responsibility for its own history; she blamed others for its inhuman contempt for conquered enemies and its respect for force.[12] It was as if it was only with the careful reading of the *Iliad* (which she translated for herself) and the Greek tragedies that Weil could touch an incomparably humane accent that they shared with the Gospels, if not with Christianity more generally. For her it was through the *Iliad* that people might learn at last not to admire force, hate their enemy, or scorn the unfortunate. "It is this," she says, "which makes the *Iliad* a unique poem, this bitterness issuing from its tenderness and which extends, as the light of the sun, equally over all men" ("The *Iliad*, Poem of Might," 176).

Her essay on the *Iliad*, more than any other of Weil's works, treats the relations between the human soul and the suffering caused by might:

The true hero, the real subject, the core of the *Iliad*, is might. That might which is wielded by men rules over them, and before it man's flesh cringes. The human soul never ceases to be modified by its encounter with might, swept on, blinded by that which it believes itself able to handle, bowed beneath the power of that which it suffers. Those

who dreamt that might, thanks to progress, belonged
henceforth to the past, have been able to see its living
witness in this poem. (153)

This belief in the effects of "progress" was shared, as we have
seen, by both liberal and Marxist theory. Fascism challenged
both, but, to grasp its significance in the twentieth century, a new
moral and political language had to be forged.

For Weil it is an illusion to think that progress had brought us
into a world in which power and might have no part. Liberalism
would often have us believe that differences can be worked out
through reason alone. It fosters the idea that if an argument is
cogent and reasoned, it will inevitably be listened to since we
live, at least in the Western democracies, within a more or less
equal social world in which inequalities and injustices can always
be legitimated and explained. Marx knew that given the class
relations of power within capitalist societies, only the powerful
voice would be listened to. But through the *Iliad* Weil
understood, in a way Marx is often blind to, that "The human
soul never ceases to be modified by its encounter with might."
The *Iliad* helped Weil understand the workings of power. Thus
for Weil, because there are constant dangers that we will lose
touch with the values and relationships that we are struggling for,
the struggle for power cannot be an end in itself.

Spain had taught Weil what it meant to admire force and hate
the enemy. She could not forget how men "would retail with
cheery fraternal chuckles at convivial meal-times how many priests
they had murdered, or how many 'fascists', the latter being a very
elastic term" (*Seventy Letters*, 108). She saw thus that the whole
purpose of struggle is soon lost in an atmosphere of this sort,
where others are not recognized as fellow human beings. This
view is quite different from a liberal humanism that denies the
reality of suffering and humiliation with the idea that we can each
abstract ourselves from our social relations and face each other as
equal human beings—and thereby denies the reality of relations
of power and force, thinking they leave our integrity untouched.
The *Iliad* taught Weil something very different: force is a
universal phenomenon to which all beings, by the very fact of
being born, are subject. We are much more deeply vulnerable to
the workings of force than we take ourselves to be. It is only

through an awareness of shared suffering that we can recognize others as fellow human beings. This is not to minimize the distinctions that exist between us. This is not the facile pity of liberalism.

In the *Iliad* the human race is not divided up into conquered persons, slaves, and suppliants on the one hand and conquerers on the other. For Weil Marxism, conceived fundamentally as a theory of social forces, does not provide insight into *how* both oppressed and oppressor live and are damaged by relations of power. Although Marx recognized that both capitalist and worker are constrained within a capitalist mode of production, he did not have the language to illuminate this. Weil, however, saw that the powerless are crushed by force, while those who think they possess power are intoxicated with it. Further, she understood that "Might is that which makes a thing of anybody who comes under its sway. When exercised to the full, it makes a thing of man in the most literal sense, for it makes him a corpse" (153–154). This became the only way Weil could recognize misfortunate as the common human lot from which no one is spared.

Usually referring to injustice in terms of unfair distribution and assuming that unfair treatment does not harm a person, liberal moral theory too often tempts us into ignoring the effects of misfortune on the soul. Weil fundamentally challenged the liberal idea "that the soul can suffer and remain unmarked by it, can fail, in fact to be recast in misfortune's image" (177). For Weil the recognition of the inescapability of human misery is a "pre-condition of justice and love" (177). Such a recognition depends on a love of truth. We cannot separate ourselves from those who are impoverished and oppressed, thinking they have nothing to do with us. Nor can we lie to ourselves in order to protect ourselves from the knowledge of our own vulnerability. But this is what we are constantly learning to do, imagining that it is a sign of strength to hide our vulnerability. We do not want to touch the sources of our suffering, thinking that, if we turn our backs to it, we can show ourselves to be strong and independent in relation to others. As we disguise ourselves, we distance ourselves from the sufferings of others. Weil knew that only one who refuses to lie can perceive and describe misfortune justly. In the *Iliad* "nothing precious is despised, whether or not destined to perish" (177).

3   Power and suffering

For Weil an understanding of human suffering should be at the center of moral and political theory. In the displacement of this concern, according to her, our traditions have "hardly gone beyond the limit of Greek civilization. Of that civilization, since the destruction of Greece, only reflections are left" ("The *Iliad*, Poem of Might," 181). It was in Greece alone that, significantly for Weil, cruelty was not sanctioned or thought inevitable, nor did people exempt themselves from "the common misery of man" (181). In her view their "strength of soul" (181) preserved the Greeks from self-deception.

Weil thought that it is particularly in our reflections on human suffering that we are open to self-deception. We shun suffering; we try to excuse it by making it seem inevitable; we think it has to be endured to bring about a better future. So much of our moral and political theory has been shaped in the nineteenth century concern with progress that it is almost impossible to escape such assumptions. The *Iliad* helped Weil question the kinds of self-deception nourished in these traditions. It presents "a true expression of misfortune" (181), whereas an idea of misfortune usually involves two forms of self-deception: "first, that degradation is the innate vocation of the unfortunate; second, that a soul may suffer affliction without being marked by it, without changing all consciousness in a particular manner which belongs to itself alone" (181). For Weil, however, as she learned from factory experience, we are all equally open to degradation and humiliation and thus fool ourselves if we think we are specially protected.

Weil's insights into the varieties of self-deception derived from her reading of the *Iliad* extend to her more radical impulse to question the delusions of those who think that the poor and oppressed are only getting what is due to them. This view has taken different historical forms so that, for instance, in the nineteenth century poverty was often seen as the result of immorality and thus as deserved punishment. This still finds echoes in the view that people are poor because they show a lack of qualities such as ambition or initiative. These views work to legitimate the suffering people are made to endure and, crucially for Weil, make it difficult to see suffering for what it is.

In her view we cannot understand human suffering unless we relate it to justice. Weil thought this idea inspirational for the *Iliad* and also the Gospels. It had the deepest influence on her own thinking on human suffering:

> [T]he understanding of human suffering is dependent upon justice, and love is its condition. Whoever does not know just how far necessity and a fickle fortune hold the human soul under their domination cannot treat as his equals, nor love as himself, those whom chance has separated from him by an abyss. The diversity of the limitations to which men are subject creates the illusion that there are different species among them which cannot communicate with one another. Only he who knows the empire of might and knows how not to respect it is capable of love and justice. (181)

Human suffering can therefore only be grasped through love related to justice. As we have already argued, she is not simply talking about distributive conceptions of justice that occupy such a central position in utilitarian social theory, in which the exclusive concern with the distribution of goods makes human suffering essentially an issue of unfair distribution. Weil wanted to draw on aspects of the Greek conception of justice as injury and violation. These refer more directly to the suffering people cause each other in the way that they treat each other and so suggest how loving others is the condition of justice. Weil wanted to restore the connection between love and justice and create a space for it at the heart of moral and political discourse.[13]

In connecting justice with love, Weil implicity challenged liberal tradition. She saw in Attic tragedy, at least in that of Aeschylus and Sophocles, how "the idea of justice sheds its light without ever intervening" but also how "the humiliation of a soul that is subject to constraint is neither disguised, nor veiled by a facile piety; neither is it an object of disdain" (180). The idea that we can treat someone as an equal through showing them equal respect is often such an exercise in "facile piety." When we say that it does not really matter to us whether someone works down the mines or on a assembly line in a large car plant since we make sure to treat others equally, we are disguising "the humiliation of a soul." Such a view can encourage working people to think they should identify themselves as "equal citizens" and so put aside the humiliations they are often made to endure in everyday life at work. It is as if the experiences at work have to be suffered in silence if people are to expect to receive "equal respect" in the rest of their lives.

For Weil the *Iliad* also shows "just how far necessity and a fickle fortune hold the human soul under their domination" (181). If one moment we are the victors, then the next moment we can be the vanquished. This is as true of war as it is true of our position in "the modern forms of social oppression." In fact, it is by reflecting on the ways warfare is depicted in the *Iliad* that Weil thinks we can come to a truer understanding of the nature of social life, where she believes that "necessity and a fickle fortune" play the kind of overwhelming role she sees in the *Iliad*. In her view this is one of the important lessons we need to learn if we are to treat others as equals and learn to love them as ourselves. If fate can strike even the most fortunate, we cannot think that people are entirely individually responsible for the lives they live in society. It is an illusion for people to think they can have control over their lives, as the emergence of nazism in Germany showed. It is better to live without these illusions.

Building on her understanding of suffering from her exper-ience of factory work and the war in Spain, Weil further saw the *Iliad* as an illumination of the ways in which both victors and vanquished are made to suffer. As we have seen, her experience of factory work helped her to question a liberal tradition that blinds us to the damage being done to industrial workers through the indignity of subordination. If we simply think that some people earn more than others so they can buy more on the market, we fail to grasp the workings of relations of subordina-tion. Our utilitarian moral theory encourages us to think in terms of market criteria of distribution for our conceptions of equality and justice. The sufferings people endure amount to not having the means to afford satisfactions available to others. A person's individuality is supposedly left unscarred and people can always recover from whatever humiliation and indignity they have endured. These comforting delusions legitimate the inequalities of social life. But Weil understands that workers actually suffer rather than merely being deprived of the means to secure satisfactions; it is a delusion to believe that a soul may suffer affliction without being marked it" (181).

Weil's argument also amounts to a break with orthodox Marxist theory in its tendency to see the proletariat as unscarred by capitalist oppression—they have been denied surplus value which is rightly theirs—and so able to renew social relations through a revolutionary transformation. Weil's discussion of the relation of oppression and oppressor to power already anticipates this break. She thought Marx inconsistent in his understanding of the power of capital to crush human lives and yet continue to have faith in the proletariat. A more realistic social theory could only be developed if people faced more directly the power of social relations to mark the soul. Marx's theory remained curiously utopian in this crucial respect. The *Iliad* promised Weil deeper insights into the workings of relations of power.

4 Power, individuality, and violation

"Might is that which makes a thing of anybody who comes under its sway. When exercised to the full, it makes a thing of man in the most literal sense, for it makes him a corpse" ("The *Iliad*, Poem of Might," 153): This is an extreme that became a commonplace within Hitler's concentration camps. Even though Weil did not see the outcome of nazism, she did struggle for a way to understand it. Like Walter Benjamin, though in a radically different way, she increasingly looked to the epic and to remnants of a damaged past to illuminate a present,[14] for it was only with a break from contemporary traditions that present reality could be understood. Current modes of thought either colluded or had simply lost their power. She needed to grasp the workings of power in all their diversity:

> The might which kills outright is an elementary and coarse form of might. How much more varied in its devices; how much more astonishing in its effects is that other which does not kill; or which delays killing. It must surely kill, or it will perhaps kill, or else it is only suspended above him whom it

may at any moment destroy. This of all procedures turns a
man to stone. (155)

It was Christianity that gave Weil the image of turning people
to stone, but the *Iliad* helped her to a fuller expression of what it
means for people to be turned to stone. For Weil it became
necessary to think in terms of damage being done to the soul. She
saw that social life has the power to fragment and violate the
individual and therefore criticized the tradition of liberal moral
and political theory that, taking the integrity of the individual for
granted, is based on the decisions and choices individuals would
take.

For Weil the way that social life can reduce people to things
cannot simply be understood in terms of damage to the
"personality." She was not concerned with the ways people's egos
are hurt or offended, nor with individual happiness or sadness,
achievement or failure. These are experiences people can recover
from; they rest at a superficial level and do not inflict the kind of
deeper "damage" to people that so often remains without a
voice. Instead, Weil saw in the *Iliad* a tradition that fully
recognizes and articulates the kind of damage that people endure
in social life—the different ways people can be transformed into
things:

> From the power to transform him into a thing by killing him
> there proceeds another power, and much more prodigious,
> that which makes a thing of him while he still lives. He is
> living, he has a soul, yet he is a thing. A strange being is
> that thing which has a soul, and strange the state of that
> soul. Who knows how often during each instant it must
> torture and destroy itself in order to conform? The soul was
> not made to dwell in a thing; and when forced to it, there is
> no part of that soul but suffers violence. (155)

Yet, for Weil, a person reduced to this unnatural condition may
not necessarily be aware of or know how to talk about the pain
inflicted. This is a difficulty in the situation. The tragedy is partly
that our prevailing traditions have not helped to give this soul a
voice, a way of understanding what has happened. In the end
that is what Simone Weil takes herself to be doing. She seeks to

give language to the oppressed and afflicted. She wants to help them to know themselves, even if they can do little in their situation.

Even Marxism, which sets itself the task of being the instrument for relief of the oppressed, fails, as in Weil's view, in this essential task. It remains imprisoned within modes of thought that unknowingly reproduce and confirm important sources of oppression. Even its discussion of class oppression is not clearly enough focused on the experience and indignity of work to give working class people a full enough understanding of their situation within capitalist society. It leaves them often with the delusion that they remained "unmarked" by the relations of power. Regarding individual change as a sign of "bourgeois individuality" and as essentially a distraction from the major focus of taking power from the ruling class—which is often at the cost of individuality—Marxist theory does not acknowledge that individuals themselves have to change in order for relations of power to be substantially altered. Weil, however, recognized not only that power reduces people to things but also that it can make them invisible—and invisible within traditional modes of thought. By illuminating some of the tensions of class experience as they are lived out in individual lives, Weil helps us to focus on what has always been a weakness within Marxist theory.[15]

As Weil has learned from her experience of factory work, dignity and respect have to do with more than attitudes employers take towards workers, however much these attitudes might soften the situation of power and subordination. This situation is not simply a matter of the workings of personal relations, of the ways people choose to treat each other. Weil elaborates on this insight, through which she moves beyond Kantian morality, in her reading of the *Iliad*. In her view, Priam is reduced to a thing not by the attitude Achilles takes towards him or the feelings he has for him but by the power Achilles holds over him. Because of this power, Priam's life is no longer in his own hands, and this is what reduces him to the status of a thing. In his supplication Priam might thus move Achilles, affect his attitude, but this does not change the relations of power between them whereby Priam is merely an object for Achilles:

It is not for want of sensibility that Achilles had, by a

sudden gesture, pushed the old man glued against his knees
to the ground. Priam's words, evoking his old father, had
moved him to tears. Quite simply he had found himself to
be as free in his attitudes, in his movements, as if in place of
a suppliant an inert object were there touching his knees.
(157)

Could Achilles have acted differently towards Priam, especially if he "found himself to be" so "free in his attitudes"? No,
according to Weil. For her the Kantian vision that depends on
being able to universalize the situation—being able to put oneself
in the same situation as the suppliant—cannot really begin to
make sense in this situation. We are being misled if we construe
it in these terms. It is incapable of illuminating the reality of
relations of power and subordination in social life. As far as Weil
is concerned, it would take a "supernatural" gift for Achilles to
act differently.

The workings of the relations of power mean that when
Achilles meets Priam as suppliant he is not facing a person. It is
not simply "unrealistic" to think Achilles should abstract himself
from this relation of power so that he and Priam can confront
each other "person to person." Such a view suggests that moral
issues only enter when we think about how Achilles, as a person,
acts towards Priam, and, in so doing, this view omits to examine
the issue of the moral—and political—nature of a situation in
which one person is reduced to the status of an object. For Weil,
then, the Kantian conception of individual moral choice and its
assessment of whether individuals act out of a sense of moral
duty fails to illuminate such a situation. We need a different kind
of moral language.

Weil uses Priam's supplication scene to bring out the
difference between relating to a person and relating to an object.
Achilles faces an "object," not someone he chooses to treat as an
object as Weil indicates when she says that "he had found himself
to be as free in his attitudes, in his movements, as if in place of a
suppliant an inert object were there touching his knees." This is a
situation Achilles "had found himself" in—a situation created by
the power Achilles has over Priam's life, rather than a situation
of inequality created through the attitude he takes towards
Priam. Thus, in considering how different it would be for

Achilles if he were facing another person, rather than an object, Weil attends not to attitudes but to the *physical* experience of contact with a person:

> The human beings around us exert just by their presence a power which belongs uniquely to themselves to stop, to diminish, or modify, each movement which our bodies design. A person who crosses our path does not turn aside our steps in the same manner as a street sign, no one stands up, or moves about, or sits down again in quite the same fashion when he is alone in a room as when he has a visitor. (157)

This way of clarifying "this undefinable influence of the human presence" gives as much weight to our bodily movements as to the attitudes we take towards others. This itself is a move away from the Kantian emphasis on "respect" as the appropriate attitude towards others, as if we were free to bestow humanity on others through our attitude. Weil does not think we have such power. Rather, she provides a context in which bodily movements are acknowledged to have importance, if not priority, in how our attitudes towards others are given form. She thereby resolves the Cartesian duality of "mind" and "body," which, in conceiving relations of power and the affliction they create in either mental or physical terms, leaves aspects of those relations and their effects invisible.

Weil's argument appears to follow an approach similar to Wittgenstein's in his later writings, as an example from his *Culture and Value* suggests:

> The origin and the primitive form of the language-game is a reaction; only from this can the more complicated forms grow.
>   Language—I want to say—is a refinement: "in the beginning was the deed."[16]

If we are careful not to interpret the notion of "reaction" too crudely and mechanically, we can discern a similar shift in Weil's thinking. When she says that "human beings around us exert just by their presence a power," she tentatively displaces the priority of our concern with moral attitudes towards others and hints at the way these "attitudes" are grounded in our relations with others. Our conscious assessment of a situation is already building upon this reality of bodily movement. Again our attitude is not something we bring into conscious existence, though it is something we can become aware of.[17]

Since for Weil there is a difference between our facing a person and our facing someone who has been reduced to an object through the workings of the relations of power and subordination and since for her a person cannot freely choose between these contrasting positions, she fundamentally opposes existentialist conceptions of freedom that insist that a person can always resist being treated as an object. She is concerned to affect our thinking about human freedom by teaching us something important about the limits to freedom. Paradoxically, perhaps it is when we face objects—or people who have been reduced to objects—that we find ourselves to have a "freedom" we do not actually have in our relations with others. When we face "objects," we can do with them as we please; "objects" make it impossible for our behaviour to be influenced in the usual way. We have entered a different kind of moral situation:

> this indefinable influence of the human presence is not exercised by those men whom a movement of impatience could deprive of their lives even before a thought had had the time to condemn them. Before these men others behave as if they were not there; and they, in turn, find themselves in danger of being in an instant reduced to nothing, imitate nothingness. Pushed, they fall; fallen, they remain on the ground, so long as no one happens to think of lifting them up. But even if at last lifted up, honoured by cordial words, they still cannot bring themselves to take this resurrection seriously enough to date to express a desire; an irritated tone of voice would immediately reduce them again to silence. He spoke and the old man trembled and obeyed. ("The *Iliad*, Poem of Might," 157)

People reduced to objects through the workings of relations of power do not carry a "human presence." They can no longer communicate this in their relations with others. Although Weil is referring to an "extreme" situation in the *Iliad* in which a "movement of impatience could deprive" Priam of his life, she also wants this extreme to illuminate more familiar relations of power and subordination. When she goes on to say that "Before these men others behave as if they were not there" she echoes her observations on the workings of criminal justice. In another essay from the same period, "Human Personality," Weil speaks in similar terms of working class people caught up in the administration of justice. Thus, in an image to which she often returns, Weil describes "a vagrant accused of stealing a carrot from a field [who] stands before a comfortably seated judge who keeps up an elegant flow of queries, comments, and witticisms while the accused is unable to stammer a word" (25). It is important to appreciate that it is the very lack of control people have in their lives that makes them so "invisible." Even if the powerful change their attitude and the situation is changed, the oppressed "still cannot bring themselves to take this resurrection seriously enough to express a desire." They cannot therefore take the first step in rediscovering a sense of individual identity.

This marking of the soul by relations of power is particularly difficult to acknowledge within prevailing traditions of moral thought that seem to take for granted that individuals are always free to take a different course in their lives, that the future is always open and that people's moral decisions need never be determined by what has happened to them in the past. For Weil the Greek conception of character can give us a different way of thinking about the state of the soul and the possibilities of change.[18] The reality is that people cannot always recover from their experiences of subordination and powerlessness; recovery, at least, is far more difficult than we are conventionally encouraged to think:

> At least some suppliants, once exonerated, become again as other men. But there are others, more miserable beings, who without dying have become things for the rest of their lives. In their days is no give and take, no open field, no free road over which anything can pass to or from them. These are not men living harder lives than others, not placed lower socially than others, these are another species, a compromise between a man and a corpse. That a human

being should be a thing is, from the point of view of logic, a contradiction; but when the impossible has become a reality, that contradiction is a rent in the soul. That thing aspires every moment to become a man, a woman, and never at any moment succeeds. This is a death drawn out the length of a life, a life that death has frozen long before extinguishing it. ("The *Iliad*, Poem of Might." 158)

Class relations of power and subordination can bring about the condition Weil describes. The recognition that a "frozen" life is a form of living death is crucial for Weil, who forces us to think not simply about the satisfactions of life but fundamentally about the very quality of our lived experience. To express this recognition that a human being can live as a thing, Weil must speak in terms of a "rent in the soul"—in the only language available to her in which this experience can be expressed. Her conversion to Christianity helped her to find a language that not only illuminated the *Iliad* for her but also enabled her to understand an experience people otherwise remain silent about. It gave her a way to express and condemn the suffering of the oppressed and acknowledge the violation of a person that comes with being silenced while never betraying the depth of that suffering through a metaphysics of illusion.

5 Truth, power, and justice

While the suffering of working people remained a primary focus throughout her work, Weil's conversion to Christianity makes a profound shift of emphasis. As her understanding of the workings of power deepened so did her conception of justice change. In part this is reflected in the shift from a language of oppression to a language of affliction, in which the workings of justice are often to be left to a divine providence. But Weil is not consistent about this, and she sustains her political concerns. This does not mean her writings can be seen as a development from politics to theology in which her earlier writing is repudiated. This common interpretation, as we have stressed, distorts our understanding of the significance of her earlier political and thought its influence on her later Christian writings.[19] But it is also important to grasp the crucial shift in her thinking, which is also a result of her meditations on the *Iliad*. These meditations helped her to consolidate an important change in her thinking about power and the relation of justice to power. These meditations also mark a break with the Marxist view of capitalist society as fundamentally a class-divided society in which the working class, through its resistance to the rule of capital, can be sure of always having justice on its side.

Marx tends to see society as fundamentally divided and the history of society as the history of class struggle. Weil came to regard this conception as dangerously misleading in a number of respects. In considering power exclusively as a possession rulers use against those who are powerless, Marxism conceives of political change in terms of wresting this power from the hands of the rulers and thus revolution as fundamentally a transfer of power. This view assumes that rulers can handle power as if it were some kind of neutral instrument. Weil, however, saw with Lord Acton that "power corrupts and absolute power corrupts absolutely"—an idea that her reading of the *Iliad* helped her to articulate. This was an issue that had assumed enormous contemporary significance with the emergence of nazism in Germany and the overwhelming power of Stalin in the Soviet Union. In this context Weil's political ideas changed as she sought for a language that would not avoid the painful truths of historical realities by turning them into questions of interpretation. This involved reconsidering the relation between power, human suffering, and justice. It had been proven historically damaging to assume that one's enemy—including one's class enemy—only had to be destroyed for freedom and justice to be assured.

The Leninist tradition within Marxism concentrates Marxist thinking about the nature of power into an exclusive concern with taking state power. It tends to see the state as the source of all power in society so that control of the state automatically gives the power to transform society. Lenin felt no difficulty in importing the most advanced assembly-line technology of the West and in praising ideas of scientific management worked out by Taylor.[20] But this meant importing into a revolutionary society the latest techniques of management control and subordination.

The idea in Russia seemed to be that, if the working class was in power, any methods that could maximize production would, through distribution, benefit working people. Since power had been captured from the ruling class, it could be used in the interests of the whole society. In power, the working class could do no injustice to itself. Working people were denied grounds of legitimate protest for, unlike workers within capitalist production, they were not oppressed and were inevitably working in their own interests.

Weil's attraction to Trotsky was initially based on his readiness to admit that the Soviet bureaucracy had become a new ruling elite able to concentrate power into its own hands. But it did not satisfy Weil to place responsibility for everything that was wrong and unjust within Soviet society on the shoulders of a bureaucracy and so create the belief that if only this elite were removed a genuine workers' state would be brought into existence. The problems went much deeper. But, as we have argued, Weil could hardly formulate the issues within the traditional categories of Marxist theory, for some of the problems had their source also in some of Marx's own conceptions.

The Marxist conception of power as a commodity that can be exchanged and distributed, with which Weil disagreed, derives from liberal political theory, in which the issue of legitimacy and authority involves who controls this power and how its ownership can legitimately be transferred. Thus power appears to be a neutral instrument that can be controlled and used for whatever ends rulers have chosen.[21] But, as Weil learned from her reading of the *Iliad*,

> as pitilessly as might crushes, so pitilessly it maddens who ever possesses, or believes he possesses it. None can ever truly possess it. The human race is not divided, in the Iliad, between the vanquished, the slaves, the suppliants on the one hand, and conquerors and masters on the other. No single man is to be found in it who is not, at some time, forced to bow beneath might. ("The *Iliad*, Poem of Might," 161)

Thus Weil recognizes everyone's vulnerability to power, though, in doing so, she is aware that she is going against the grain of circumstances. Her understanding of the power of social circumstances to affect the ways we think and feel makes her suspicious of the effectiveness of certain forms of rational argument. People have to learn to experience a certain vulnerability in themselves—or even be shocked into recognizing the hurt being done to others—if they are to begin the difficult process of rethinking their ideas. One of the constant themes in both her early and later writing is a concern with how people are denied the time and space in which this thinking can take place. She never underestimates the power of thought, but she is always aware of the power of social institutions, not only the factory, to make this thought impossible. While Marx understood that people need activities through which they can express themselves, he did not really grasp people's need for the time and space to strengthen an inner relationship to themselves and to develop a clearer sense of control over their individual lives.

Weil believed in the power of truth, especially for those who are oppressed or afflicted, to nourish the soul. But she also saw that the truth is a food that people are deprived of. She learned the difficulty of speaking the truth, but she did not think this difficulty was simply the result of "class interests" distorting people's conceptions of social reality. For her this orthodox conception of class consciousness did not fully explain the place of untruth in people's lives. The idea of "false consciousness" provided too limited a framework within which to identify the important issues involved. Marxist theory was too easily identified with relativist notions of truth, as if each class carries its own independent truth, and this relativism thereby creates the problem of what gives the proletariat a "truer" understanding of capitalist society.[22] Recognizing these deficiencies, Weil saw the need for setting different terms for the relationship between truth and power.

She saw that all people are vulnerable to suffering violence; this is a truth social relations often protect people from. Social relations tend to deny the vulnerability of the powerful, making them feel they are stronger than they are, and to blind the oppressed to their own sources of power. Weil did not deny the reality of relations of power and subordination but her view does challenge the idea that the oppressed can only grab power from those who have power over their lives and cannot look to different sources of their own power. She sought to shake the confidence people have in their inherited conceptions of power and justice not so much through changing people's consciousness as through bringing people to recognize truths they would otherwise deny. Weil did not think that any group or class had a clear monopoly on the truth. She challenged conventional Leninist assumptions that saw the task of revolutionaries as bringing "political" consciousness to a working class otherwise limited to a trade-union consciousness. She deplored the elitism in this view. She thought the anarchists and syndicalists were often more aware of how much they had to learn from working people. So even if she felt that truths could be discovered or rediscovered, she never thought of truth as a "possession" that could be firmly held by a single class group. It was one of the strengths of her Christianity to make clear that both the strong and the weak had something to learn from each other.

Weil thereby showed that it is possible to reject the positions of Marxist theory that unless the proletariat has the monopoly on truth, we are left with a situation of moral relativism. She did not, however, think that Marx was so firmly caught within this false polarity. In her view he was rather trying to express the fact that the working class has a closer relationship to reality, through labor, but she also knew this to be very different from the ways "truth" and "consciousness" have usually been thought about within the Marxist tradition.

Simone Weil is rare in her grasp of the power of social relations to influence, even mold, our self-conceptions. She recognized how hard it is to challenge our self-deceptions, especially when our everyday relations seem to confirm them. We think that we are different from others, though we pay lip service to a vision of shared humanity. For her, all are vulnerable to power; all are vulnerable to self-deception:

> If all men, by the act of being born, are destined to suffer violence, that is a truth to which the empire of circumstances closes their minds. The strong man is never absolutely strong, nor the weak man absolutely weak, but each one is ignorant of this. They do not believe that they are of the same species. The weak man no more regards himself as like the strong man than he is regarded as such.

He who possesses strength moves in an atmosphere which offers him no resistance. Nothing in the human element surrounding him is of a nature to induce, between the intention and the act, that brief interval where thought may lodge. Where there is no room for thought, there is no room for justice or prudence. This is the reason why men of arms behave with such harshness and folly! (163)

The strong have to become aware of their own vulnerability if they are truly to be aware of others as fellow human beings. But Wcil was also concerned that the weak should realize that they are not "absolutely weak" but have their own sources of strength and dignity. People had to accept and value themselves in their own eyes, before they could feel genuinely equal with others; otherwise equality is only false. Orthodox Marxism fails to understand this, referring instead to people's gaining a truly scientific understanding of capitalist society, as some kind of external object. Such an understanding often does little to awaken people to their own situation and can, in fact, reinforce an already existing sense of intellectual inferiority. It rarely supports working people to a sense of their own individual and collective dignity and strength. Since in the orthodox Marxist view power is exclusively conceived of as something people lack or have been deprived of, it is often difficult for people to value what they still have in their own working-class traditions and culture. People are often left to judge themselves in terms that are not their own.

Marxist theory does argue that it is almost "natural" for people to abuse the power they have over others, and thus it recognizes that conceptions of justice must involve the realities of power. If this is a strength of Marxist theory, Marxism nevertheless too often assumes that justice is the exclusive possession of a single class. Weil was certainly opposed to Lenin's idea that the moral could be defined as whatever was in the interests of the proletariat. Nor, while critical of the workings of bourgeois justice, did she think the proletariat would automatically act with a sense of justice once it has assumed power or that justice was always in the hands of the proletariat. She learned this painful lession during the civil war in Spain, when she heard of the killing of a young fascist youth who refused to declare himself for the republic. As she wrote to George Bernanos,

> In a light engagement a small international party of
> militiamen from various countries captured a small boy of
> 15 who was a member of the Falange. As soon as he was
> captured, and still trembling from the sight of his comrades
> being killed alongside him, he said he had been enrolled
> compulsorily. He was searched and a medal of the Virgin
> and a Falange card were found on him. Then he was sent to
> Durruti, the leader of the column, who lectured him for an
> hour on the beauties of the anarchist ideal and gave him the
> choice between death and enrolling immediately in the
> ranks of his captors, against his comrades of yesterday.
> Durruti gave this child 24 hours to think it over, and when
> the time was up he said no and was shot. Yet Durruti was in
> some ways an admirable man. Although I only heard of it
> afterwards, the death of this little hero has never ceased to
> weigh on my conscience. (*Seventy Letters*, 107)

What becomes of the "beauties of the anarchist ideal" if it treats people in this way? Weil was always less concerned with ideals than with what their reality amounted to in everyday life. She was also puzzled because Durruti was "in some ways an admirable man." This made it more important to understand what had happened, rather than simply explain it as an exceptional happening. The deeper issue was, as she says, "the attitude towards murder" (108). She never heard a Spanish or French combatant "express, even in private intimacy, any repulsion or disgust or even disapproval of useless bloodshed" (108). Nor did she think that fear played the large part Bernanos assigned to it in this butchery. She felt the need for a different kind of explanation for the ease with which people murder when they have learned to see others as less than human, one she confirmed through her reading of the *Iliad*.

In this same letter to Bernanos, in a comment that illuminates how her relationship to Christianity stretches back, Weil says that "nothing that is Catholic, nothing that is Christian, has ever seemed alien to me" (105) and that if there was a choice on church doors forbidding entrance to those who have an income above a certain low figure, she "would be converted at once" (105). She seemed almost to sense then that Christianity could offer terms for an understanding of justice, power, and violence, if only she could dig deep into its original sources—to Greece, which she later claimed as the inspiration for the Gospels.

Weil's letter to Bernanos suggests how the shock of her experience in Spain might well have led to the transformation in her politics that was later consolidated through her reflections on war and her reading of the *Iliad*. In this letter she grasps for ideas that her later essay on the *Iliad* brings into sharper focus:

> Men who seemed to be brave—there was one at least whose courage I personally witnessed—would retail with cheery fraternal chuckles at convivial meal-times how many priests they had murdered, or how many "fascists", the latter being a very elastic term. My own feeling was that when once a certain class of people has been placed by the temporal and spiritual authorities outside the ranks of those whose life has value, then nothing comes more naturally to men than murder. As soon as men know that they can kill without fear if punishment or blame, they kill; or at least they encourage killers with approving smiles. If anyone happens to feel a slight distaste to begin with, he keeps quiet and he soon begins to suppress it for fear of seeming unmanly. People get carried away by a sort of intoxication which is irresistible without a fortitude of soul which I am bound to consider exceptional since I have met it nowhere. (108)

No doubt it was difficult for Weil to accept that "nothing comes more naturally to men than murder" once a certain class of people has been placed outside the ranks of those whose life has value. Once she had experienced this for herself in Spain, she could not excuse it but had to understand it. Certainly her politics always recognized the power of social influence on people, but such influence was not enough of an explanation. Men would do everything not to appear "unmanly", but it could no longer be said that if individuals showed a strength of character and will they would act differently. This Kantian theme no longer seemed credible. It could not help her grasp how people "get carried away by a sort of intoxication which is irresistible," though she later understood this "intoxication" through her reading of the *Iliad*. Particularly disheartening for Weil, however, was the recognition that anarchists and socialists seemed to act little differently in these situations. Political principles could not explain such behavior, and so Weil was forced to move away from the prevailing traditions of political thought.

It was crucial for Weil to understand how it was that the temporal and spiritual authorities could place a certain group of people "outside the ranks of those whose life has value." What gives the authorities the power to do this? In *The Need for Roots* Weil seeks to connect this power to the weakness in our inherited culture. It had long been her insight that, as long as we conceive of human dignity as guaranteed within a modern discourse of rights, when those rights are withdrawn—by the authorities that supposedly have the power to constitute them in the first place—people can be deemed as no longer existing as human beings. This is what happened to Jews in Nazi Germany. Their rights of citizenship were revoked and tragically there was little within a liberal tradition that could sustain them. Nor was this situation a failure of democracy as it has often been described, for Hitler was voted into power. Weil was strangely silent about this issue, though she had already learned these painful lessons in Spain.

In Spain Weil had met Frenchmen who were peaceable and who would never have dreamed of doing any killing themselves but "who savoured that blood-polluted atmosphere with visible pleasure" (108). She learned that for people to resist being carried away by this sort of intoxication required a "fortitude of soul" that was rare, yet she also saw that, given their complexities, making judgments and assigning responsibility in such situations had to be done carefully. This influenced Weil's assessment later of the difficulties facing the French under German occupation. In a letter to the philosopher Jean Wahl, written from New York in 1942, she asserts, "I don't much like to hear perfectly comfortable people here using words like coward and traitor about people in France who are managing as best they can in a terrible situation" (158). Although it often made her unpopular, she was not prepared to condemn out of hand those who are prepared to work with Vichy or even with the Germans;

she sought first to explore motives that could be justified within this and other situations. She saw that people can be constrained by pressures they could only resist if they were heroes. But, as Weil says, "Most of the people here, however, who set themselves up as judges have never had the opportunity to find out if they themselves are heroes" (159). And, she adds, "I detest facile, unjust, and false attitudes, and especially when the pressure of public opinion seems to make them almost obligatory" (159).

The Spanish Civil War broke her faith in the Confederación National de Trabajo (CNT), the anarchist trade union organization and the only organization she still had any sympathy with. As she makes clear in her letter to Bernanos, "From my childhood onwards I sympathized with those organizations which spring from the lowest and least regarded social strata, until the time when I realized that such organisations are of a kind to discourage all sympathy" (105). She learnt to face the fact that, even though the anarchists had different principles, their principles did not stop them from acting brutally. She also came face to face with the dominating influence of the Soviet Union on the Communist Party in Spain. Her experiences in Spain thus froced her into a new direction in her thinking.

Though Marxism understands there is a deep connection between morality and power, it tends to think that morality serves the purposes of a particular class, thereby breaking the connection between morality and justice and encouraging an instrumental view of morality in which different classes simply used different moral views to further their own interests. This was a reduction of morality Simone Weil could never accept. She wanted to grasp the full influence of relations of power to morality and justice *without* thereby forfeiting her understanding of the significance of morality in human life. Therefore she was gradually moved away from traditions on the Left that traditionally denigrate moral considerations. It was largely in the *Iliad* that she discovered a different way of thinking through the relation of morality to power. It is in this new context that her own individualism—if it is rightly called that—is to be understood.

6 Violence and justice

Weil's reading of the *Iliad* helped her understand how people get caught up in the vicious circle of violence, where there is no place for moderation or reasonable words. These "would demand a more than human virtue, one no less rare than a constant dignity in weakness" ("The *Iliad*, Poem of Might," 168). Violence comes to have an existence of its own:

> For violence so crushes whomever it touches that it appears
> at last external no less to him who dispenses it than to him
> who endures it. So the idea was born of a destiny beneath
> which the aggressors and their victims are equally innocent,
> the victors and the vanquished brothers in the same fortune.
> (168)

When violence takes over, people are almost inevitably caught up and lose themselves in it, in spite of the strength of their principles. For Weil, "Might is the only hero in this picture" (174); there are only brief moments in which the soul awakens, "only to lose itself again to the empire of might" (174). The few moments when men find their souls are the moments when they love—when the soul can realize itself whole, when "there is no room for ambiguous, troubled or conflicting emotions" (174). Such moments are rare in the *Iliad*, but the presence of friendship, of genuine hospitality, of love of a son for his parents, and of fraternal and married love "suffice to make what violence kills, and shall kill, felt with extremist regret" (176). For Weil,

> It is this which makes the Iliad a unique poem, this
> bitterness, issuing from its tenderness, and which extends,
> as the light of the sun, equally over all men. Never does the
> tone of the poem cease to be impregnated by this bitterness,
> nor does it ever descend to the level of a complaint. Justice
> and love, for which there can hardly be a place in this
> picture of extremes and unjust violence, yet shed their light
> over the whole without ever being discerned otherwise than
> by the accent. The destitution and misery of all men is
> shown without disimulation or disdain, no man is held

either above or below the common level of all men, and whatever is destroyed is regretted. The victors and the vanquished are shown equally near to us, in an equal perspective. (177)

This is a tone Simone Weil increasingly aspires to in her own writing. Not only does she think of this impersonal stance—if we can call it that—as more truthful, she also thinks it more effectively evokes a deepened sense of justice. Still, this stance, as Christian as it is Greek, does produce tensions in her writing for Weil never gave up her identification with the suffering of the oppressed.

From this stance, however, Weil saw the wrongness of the labor movement's continuing to think of injustice exclusively and contentiously in terms of rights. She came to think that the Left is impregnated with a "bitterness" that rarely rises above the "shrill nagging of claims and counter-claims" ("Human Personality," 21). From her perspective a social theory that builds on notions of justice and love rather than on rights became necessary. She thought the Left was wrong to seek justice simply through the agitation for rights, however significant this conjunction has been historically. She was thus moving away from ideas of "class war," from the idea that the bourgeoisie had to be overthrown as a class. She came to doubt this conception of a revolution, believing that, just as the peasants had lost in the civil war in Spain, so the working class would inevitably lose. Thinking that it was always more important to be concerned with improving the lot of the working people and to do whatever would support their dignity and self-esteem, she sought for a different conception of politics and justice which would somehow keep the interests of working people firmly in view. It was in this context that the notion of rights had to be replaced by a conception of love and justice, as she makes clear in her 1943 essays, "Human Personality":

If you say to someone who has ears to hear: "What you are doing to me is not just", you may touch and awaken at its source the spirit of attention and love. But it is not the same with words like "I have the right . ." or "you have no right to . . .". They evoke a latent war and awaken the spirit of

contention. To place the notion of rights at the centre of
social conflicts is to inhibit any possible impulse of charity
on both sides. (21)

If we are not to misinterpret this, we should be aware that
Weil talks about "charity on both sides" (21), by which she
means a matter not of the poor appealing to the rich for charity
but of a certain balance of power between different classes in
society. She sees justice in terms of a limit, balance, or
equilibrium that has to be respected. This means that different
classes must learn not to abuse their power. In *The Need for
Roots* she makes clear that responsibility goes together with
power and that the bourgeoisie have proved themselves incapable
of fulfilling the duties set for them within a capitalist society since
they have abused their power. She also makes clear her thinking
about the need for a certain balance between equality and
inequality in the organization of society. She never loses her
sense of the brutal workings of relations of power.

The Greeks confirmed Weil in her idea that justice is
inseparable from relations of power, both between individuals
and between classes. This partly explains why "The even balance,
an image of equal relations of strength, was the symbol of justice
from all antiquity, especially in Egypt" ("Forms of the Implicit
Love of God," 100). Using as a central example Thucydides'
account of the Athenians' ultimatum to destroy the ancient town
of Melos unless its inhabitants joined forces in the war with
Sparta, Weil articulates important insights into the possible
relations of justice to power. The people of Melos had invoked
justice, imploring pity for their town:

> Thucydides has put the lines in question into the mouth of
> these Athenians. They begin by saying that they will not try
> to prove that their ultimatum is just.
>> "Let us treat rather of what is possible. . . . You know it
>> as well as we do; the human spirit is so constituted that
>> what is just is only examined if there is equal necessity on
>> both sides. But if one is strong and the other weak, that
>> which is possible is imposed by the first and accepted by the
>> second."
> The men of Melos said that in the case of a battle they

would have the gods with them on account of the justice of their cause. The Athenians replied that they saw no reason to suppose so.

"As touching the gods we have the belief, and as touching men the certainty, that always by a necessity of nature, each one commands wherever he has the power. We did not establish this law, we are not the first to apply it; we found it already established, we abide by it as something likely to endure for ever; and that is why we apply it. We know quite well that you also, like all the others, once you reached the same degree of power, would act in the same way." (99)

Although Weil was generally in sympathy with thinking in terms of laws in social life, she argued that it was not a necessity of nature that "each one commands wherever he has the power." Nor did she think that truth and justice would win in history. She could not see much sense in Hegel's idea that history somehow maintained what was of value of significance in the past. Marx had also fallen for this misconception of progress in identifying history with the progress in human values, even though he had also worked for a more realistic sense of the part power plays in social life. For Weil, the fact that people have justice on their side was no guarantee that they can succeed in their struggle. She denied to people this consolation. At the same time, however, she thought that an appeal to justice in the face of power is an appeal that fundamentally matters.

Minimizing the significance of relations of power, liberalism tends to foster the notion that if a cause is just, it will have to be listened to. Simone Weil saw no evidence for this, either in her own life or in her reading of history. There was no reason to think that justice would prevail. Liberalism also does a deep disservice to the poor and oppressed in encouraging them to think that, if they are not listened to, either their reasons have not been clearly enough presented or they cannot really have justice on their side. She far preferred the "lucidity of mind in the conception of injustice" she found in Greek thought. This made her more sympathetic to Marxism or even to the conservative ideas of Bernanos, who refused to pretend that justice exists where it does not. She criticized both the Romans and the

Hebrews for legitimizing a belief, as she saw it, in which "the strong sincerely believe that their cause is more just than that of the weak" (99).

Weil could never take seriously the liberal idea that in a democratic society people have equal power because they are all guaranteed the right to vote. She did not minimize the importance of the electoral vote, but she insisted on placing it in the context of the effective power people had over their lives. As far as she was concerned we can't truthfully *begin* to think about justice unless we have first assured that a situation of rough equality exists. As she learned from Thucydides, "what is just is only examined if there is equal necessity on both sides," a truth equally applicable to the relations between individuals and social groups. For Weil it is as if relations between individuals have a more or less homologous structure with relations at the social level. Certainly she was constantly moving between these different levels, constantly drawing insights from one to illuminate the other:

> When two human beings have to settle something and
> neither has the power to impose anything on the other, they
> have to come to an understanding. Then justice is
> consulted, for justice alone has the power to make two wills
> coincide. . . . But when there is a strong and a weak there
> is no need to unite their wills. There is only one will, that of
> the strong. The weak obeys. Everything happens just as it
> does when a man is handling matter. There are not two
> wills to be made to coincide. The man wills and the matter
> submits. The weak are like things. (99)

In her Christian writing she thinks of true justice in terms of "the image of that Love which in God unites the Father and Son" (99). Rather than causing a complete shift in her thinking, her Christianity allowed her to look more deeply into the relations between strong and weak, powerful and powerless. It gave her, for example, the image of people being turned to stone, which was for her a more accurate representation of the workings of power and subordination she experienced in factory work. Similarly, in shifting her thinking from oppression to affliction, she was enabled to express issues of human suffering she had failed to illuminate adequately within secular moral and political modes of thought. She discovered that Christianity could reach a deeper level of understanding, one that had become generally unavailable in social and political thinking, and she sought to restore its insights to a central position where she felt it could illuminate the realities of human suffering that would otherwise remain invisible.

7 Affliction and justice

Paradoxically, Weil's Christianity brought a new realism to her political thinking. It helped her grasp why it can be wrong to expect the strong to help the poor and oppressed, who, she believed, would always be forsaken, even by those who pretend to make their interests central. The peasants of Aragon, like the workers in the factories, could expect little help from many of their supposed traditional defenders. In her important essay "Forms of the Implicit Love of God" Weil often refers to the good Samaritan who turns his attention towards "a little piece of flesh, naked, inert and bleeding beside a ditch" (103) to illuminate by contrast the reality of relations between the strong and those who are "reduced by affliction to the state of an inert and passive thing" (102). Rather than simply being an "extreme" version of "loving our neighbor," this example is supposed to help us grasp why it is so hard for the strong to really come to the help of the weak. For, as Weil explains, "The sympathy of the weak for the strong is natural, for the weak in putting himself into the place of the other acquires an imaginary strength. The sympathy of the strong for the weak, being in the opposite direction, is against nature" (104).

Because it is "against nature," the sympathy of the strong for the weak has to derive from what Weil came to think of as "the supernatural virtue of justice" (100). Thinking of it as supernatural helps us to an awareness of how difficult it is for people to achieve, so that we cannot really expect it. Against this liberalism can create a false sense of life in presenting moral relations as matters of individual will and conscience. It assumes that we have a freedom in our relations with others, but this freedom is often largely fictitious. In a form of moral collusion the weak accept this pretence that the weak and the strong can put themselves in each others' places since it gives them "an imaginary strength." But if the reality of moral life is to be restored we have to reorganize our expectations of others. "Almsgiving when it is not supernatural is like a sort of purchase. It buys the sufferer" (104). Perhaps the first step is to *acknowledge* that, if we are in an unequal power relationship, we do not have the freedom to relate to others in any way we choose.

Weil's understanding of the supernatural virtue of justice opens up the possibility of equality and sense of community within an unequal society. Although this vision is no longer really a socialist one, it is informed by an abiding sense that justice is owed to people to the extent that it can be within an injust society:

> The supernatural virtue of justice consists of behaving
> exactly as though there were equality when one is the
> stronger in an unequal relationship. Exactly, in every
> respect, including the slightest details of accent and
> attitude, for a detail may be enough to place the weaker
> party in the condition of matter which on this occasion
> naturally belongs to him, just as the slightest shock causes
> water which has remained liquid below freezing point to
> solidfy. (100)

There is a sensitivity in this passage to the complexity and injury that can so easily be done to people within unequal relationships that opens the possibility of hope, while not for a moment understating the dangers in the situation or excusing or legitimating these unequal relations of power. There is constant recognition of the tension that is inevitable as long as these unequal relations exist. Weil recognizes—in a way that liberalism cannot—how easy it is for the strong and powerful to patronize and condescend. Liberalism so often leaves people blaming themselves for the injuries and humiliations they suffer at the hands of institutions and people who have power over their lives without even realizing what they are doing.

In "Forms of the Implicit Love of God," which she sent to Father Perrin just before she left France in 1942 to join her parents briefly in the United States, Weil illustrates the relationship between justice and power in the workings of criminal justice. Setting out her understanding of just treatment, she shows that even where "there is no intentional unkindness" (110), condescension and cruelty are an "automatic effect of professional life" (110). She shows how contempt for the afflicted is an understandable consequence of relations of power that has become institutionalized and thus rendered almost invisible within liberal society:

> Men think they are despising crime when they are really despising the weakness of affliction. A being in whom the two are combined affords them an opportunity of giving free play to their contempt for affliction on the pretext that they are scorning crime. He is thus the object of the greatest contempt. Contempt is the contrary of attention. (109)

Weil then turns to give full attention to the experience of the person caught up in the penal machinery who is so often forgotten and rendered invisible. This prepares us to consider what it is like for soldiers caught up in the machinery of violence portrayed in the *Iliad*. We find the same appreciation of gesture and detail in Weil's perceptions:

> No state is beaneath that of a human being enveloped in a cloud of guilt, be it true or false, and entirely in the power of a few men who are to decide his fate in a word. These men do not pay any attention to him. Moreover, from the moment when anyone falls into the hands of the law with all its penal machinery until the moment when he is free again—and those known as hardened criminals are like prostitutes, in that they hardly ever get free until the day of their death—such a one is never an object of attention. Everything combines, down to the smallest details, down even to the inflections of people's voices, to make him seem vile and outcast in all men's eyes including his own. The brutality and flippancy, the terms of scorn and the jokes, the way of speaking, the way of listening and of not listening, all these things are equally effective. (109)

So that we do not condemn these people individually but learn something about the institutional workings of relations of power, Weil makes us realize that we can expect nothing else, for in "a professional life which has as its object crime seen in the form of affliction . . . such a contact, being uninterrupted, necessarily contaminates, and the form this contamination takes is contempt" (110).

Even if we question the usefulness of this not altogether clear idea of "contamination," the example shows how the notion of "attention" comes to have a particular significance for Weil. The source of attention is supernatural, though it is connected to an idea of justice that was always important for her. Initially it was in her reflections on the *Iliad* that she discovered a way of thinking about what it means for individuals to be caught up in a machinery of power. The strong, rich, and powerful can always ignore, overlook, and patronize those they have power over. They never really need to look directly at or make eye contact with them when they give their orders or instructions. This is not expected of them. Weil's contribution to our understanding of institutional power brings into focus the inadequacy of our inherited traditions. She is able to illuminate the moral issues involved if we are to sustain the poor and oppressed in their dignity and self-respect.

8 The machinery of violence

Simone Weil's meditations on the *Iliad* both echo and deepen her reflections on factory work. War presents people with a different kind of necessity, but, as in the factory, it is a necessity they have to come to terms with each day. In both she sees "a denial of nature" ("The *Iliad*, Poem of Might," 170), and her description of the condition of the soldier echoes her analysis of the effect of factory work on the laborer:

> That men should have death for their future is a denial of
> nature. As soon as the practice of war has revealed the fact
> that each moment holds the possibility of death, the mind
> becomes incapable of moving from one day to the next

without passing through the spectre of death. Then the
consciousness is under tension such as it can only endure for
short intervals. But each new dawn ushers in the same
necessity. Such days added to each other make up years.
That soul daily suffers violence which every morning must
mutilate its aspirations because the mind cannot move
about in a time without passing through death. In this way
war wipes out every conception of a goal, even all thoughts
concerning the goals of war. (170)

It is as if Weil's experience of factory work gave her the capacity
to understand the effects of war. Just as the factory crushes the
worker's soul, so the "day comes when fear, defeat of the death
of beloved companions crushes the warrior's soul beneath the
necessity of war" (171). Just as the factory blots out the
possibility of all thought, so war permits only flashes of thought
about death. And just as factory workers are deprived of any
sense of future, so for "warriors death itself is their future, the
future assigned to them by their profession" (170). She
understood how it is that the soul obliterates itself in the face of
this necessity as she grasps the tensions in the situation.

But her meditations on the *Iliad* also helped deepen her
reflections on the lack of resistance to the organization of work.
She knew it was more than fatigue that drained away the energy
to resist, but the *Iliad* allowed her to sense more of the weight of
both servitude and war, so acknowledging connections between
them, in spite of the difficulty of fully entering into the
experience of such situations:

The possibility of so violent a situation is inconceivable
when one is outside it, its ends are inconceivable when one
is involved in it. Therefore no one does anything to bring
about its end. The man who is faced by an armed enemy
cannot lay down his arms. The mind should be able to
contrive an issue; but it has lost all capacity for contriving
anything in that direction. It is completely occupied with
doing itself violence. Always among men, the intolerable
afflictions either of servitude or war endure by force of their
own weight, and therefore, from the outside, they seem

easy to bear; they last because they rob the resources
required to throw them off. (170)

Through the *Iliad* Weil was able further to reflect on how the
mind is deprived of all its capacity in both servitude and war, an
issue that appears in her earlier writings, but which she could
never fully explain. She needed to withdraw from active politics
to think for herself about the realities that faced her in order to
arrive at a fuller articulation of such concerns.

Such insights as the comparison of war to factory work gave
Weil also confirmed the shift in her political views. She saw that
just as soldiers come to focus on the destruction of the enemy as
a means to their own salvation, so the proletariat in the "class
war" imagines that the complete destruction of the bourgeoisie as
a class will bring an end to the proletariat's misery at work. But
she also understood, through the *Iliad*, why the kind of moderate
reforms she was concerned with, such as helping to initiate a
factory newsletter, are resisted with such vehemence:

A moderate and reasonable end to all its suffering would
leave naked, and exposed to consciousness, memories of
such violent affliction as it could not endure. The terror, the
pain, the exhaustion, the massacres, the deaths of
comrades, we cannot believe that these would only cease to
ravage the soul if they were drowned in the intoxication of
force. The thought that such vast efforts should have
brought only a negative, or limited profit, hurts too much.
(171)

The worker cannot afford to see the capitalist as a fellow
human being when he gets caught up in the language of class war;
he or she sees the capitalist only as the incarnation of all evil, as
the warrior sees the enemy, and as the enemy must be killed, so
the capitalist has to be destroyed to liberate the condition of the
working people. People have suffered too much and been hurt
too deeply for compromises and reforms to appear reasonable.
We cannot expect things to be different. But at the same time we
have to appreciate the injury people do to themselves in
sustaining these beliefs, however necessary they might be.
Believing that if only the enemy is destroyed, all difficulties and

problems will automatically be removed, people are blinded to the sources of misery and unhappiness that lie within themselves. This is an effect that can be intensified to silence the doubts that might emerge from within—as Freud understood, though psycho-analysis too often accepts the other side of the dilemma, blinding itself into thinking that all misery has its source in childhood relationships and that external structures of power and oppression are essentially projections of an inner reality yet to be resolved.[23] This is something the *Iliad* also sees clearly. As much as the damage done by others, it records the damage people do to themselves:

> The Soul, which is forced by the existence of an enemy, to destroy the part of itself implanted by nature, believes it can only cure itself by the destruction of the enemy, and at the same time the death of beloved companions stimulates the desire to emulate them, to follow their dark example. (171)

In destroying part of themselves, "the very thought that these may be joy in the light," people become incapable of showing respect to others. They cannot really listen to the pleas of others or assess their situations realistically. Claude Landzmann in his film *Shoah* (1985) suggests that anti-Semitism continued in Poland after World War II because of the way such feelings enabled Poles to block any recognition of the suffering they were responsible for causing to the Jews during the war. Weil similarly recognizes that "Whoever has had to mortify, to mutilate in himself all aspiration to live, of him an effort of heart-breaking generosity is required before he can respect the life of another" (173). Showing further the implications of the *Iliad*, she contrasts the soldier with the slave who is emblematic in her thinking for different forms of labor:

> the vanquished soldier is the scourge of nature; possessed by war, he, as much as the slave, although in quite a different way, is become a thing, and words have no more power over him than over inert matter. In contact with might, both the soldier and the slave suffer the inevitable effect, which is to become either deaf or mute. (173)

When Weil argues that might "petrified differently but equally the souls of those who suffer it, and of those who wield it" (173), she again recognizes that both vanquished and victor—both worker and capitalist—are caught up in a process they cannot control. As workers become the instruments of a capitalist process of production they do not control, so soldiers barely exist as autonomous individuals able to make rational decisions for themselves when it comes to the realities of war:

> The winning of battles is not determined between men who
> plan and deliberate, who make a resolution and carry it out,
> but between men drained of these faculties, transformed,
> fallen to the level either of inert matter, which is all
> passivity, or to the level of blind forces, which are all
> momentum. This is the final secret of war. This secret the
> Iliad expresses by its similes, by making warriors
> apparitions of great natural phenomena: a conflagration, a
> flood, the wind, ferocious beasts, any and every blind cause
> of disaster. Or else by likening them to frightened animals,
> trees, water, sand, to all that is moved by the violence of
> external forces. (173)

So in one of the many such extended similes in the *Iliad*:

> As when destructive fire runs through the depths of a wood;
> everywhere shirling, swept by the wind, when the trees
> Uprooted are felled by pressure of the violent fire;
> Even so did Agememnon son of Athens bring down the
>   heads
> Of the fleeing Trojans.[24]

For Weil, if the "ability of turning men to stone is essential to might" (174), "The art of war is nothing but the art of provoking such transformations" (174). It is in this more or less automatic "turning to stone" that people have to kill within themselves the ability to see the enemy as fellow human beings. As the Vietnam War brought home to a generation in the 1960s what Weil learnt for herself in Spain, the logic of "kill or be killed" takes over in the training of soldiers, and the enemy in this case became the 'Cong" or the "gooks." The war became an end in itself, as people lost grip of what it was supposed to be about in the first place. That no longer seemed to matter. The destruction of the enemy came to promise the only hope for redemption and thus the only hope that people might be able to live with themselves in the future. It seemed to make the killing and brutality bearable. So, for Weil, in any war.

When she says that in such situations the Soul has "to destroy the part of itself implanted by nature" (171) or, at another moment, that a person has to destroy "in himself the very thought that there may be joy in the light," she does not simply think in liberal Kantian terms of our attitudes towards others, but grasps the crucial insights that our ability to respond to others is not simply an issue of individual will and attention. If a person has been forced to destroy certain capacities within himself, "how should he respect such humble and vain pleadings from the vanquished?" (172). The implication is that we are quite wrong if we expect people to react with understanding and respect. If we do so, we only betray our own lack of understanding of the difficulties that people face.

This meditation about war also offers insights for Weil into the workings of capitalist production. It helped her to develop a moral understanding of the damage done to the oppressed and afflicted that would otherwise be legitimated or at the very least rendered invisible. In her early writings she realized that Marx had recognized the power of the capitalist labor process to damage lives but at the same time wanted to believe that the proletariat was somehow free from the injuries of capitalist society and able to make a revolutionary transformation. She felt this was a deep contradiction in Marx's writings, involving confusions about the relationship of morality to power. Because he thought the proletariat potentially had the economic power to challenge the power of capital, he wanted to think it must automatically be in a moral position to do this. Weil came to think that this is a delusion that blocks clear historical analysis and that it entails expecting too much from working people. It does not help people acknowledge the difficulties they face or the reality of their powerlessness and lack of confidence. It tends to assume a sense of equality people find it hard to feel, and it does not help people really to sustain a sense of dignity and pride.

When Weil talks about "the horror of the modern form of

social oppression" she makes it clear that "the kindness or brutality of one's superiors makes little difference" (*Seventy Letters*, 39). She also makes it clear that this suffering does not depend on individual qualities, since it is the social relations in a modern factory that make everyone suffer. It is the inescapability of this situation that the *Iliad* helped to sharpen for her. It gave a different edge to her insight that in the factory "if one wishes to retain human dignity in one's own eyes, it means a daily struggle with oneself' (38). In this way Weil undercuts liberal inclinations that tempt us into thinking that a "freely chosen" situation cannot injure so deeply, while leaving us speechless in face of this everyday horror. Our inherited liberal traditions seem to render this suffering invisible.

But Marxism also fails to analyze the correct causes and nature of this suffering, thinking it has its source in ownership. This forced Weil to develop her own path. She eventually came to feel that class feeling did not have to be exacerbated before any change could happen—although at the same time she thought that "the continual repression of class feeling—which to some extent is always secretly smouldering—is almost everywhere being carried too far" (25). If she was concerned to give an occasional outlet to this feeling, as for instance in her proposal to help the manager at Bourges with a factory newspaper, this "would not be to excite it but to soften its bitterness" (25), a bitterness she thought only encouraged workers to blame capitalists for all their ills without thinking about the unavoidable aspects of their suffering. This is the insight with which Weil initiates her analysis of oppression in *Reflections*. She never lost her sense that class feeling is not determined by the attitudes we take up towards others but by "actual conditions of life. What stimulates it is the infliction of humiliation and suffering, and the fact of subordination" (24). Weil did not care whether people regarded her writings as "reformist" as long as she did not leave working people with a false expectation of the future. After her experience of factory life she was concerned to do everything that would help working people recover or retain their sense of dignity, and this remained the center of her moral and political vision.

It is this feeling for restoring the dignity and self-respect of workers initially in their own eyes and then as part of a challenge to the denigration of work in modern society that Weil develops in her later writings. Certainly she deepened her suspicions of Marxism, especially when it pretended to hold the monopoly of truth. She learned to seek the truth and challenged traditions that deride its centrality to human experience. She sought a strength in the notions of truth, beauty, justice, and compassion, which she thought "are always and everywhere good" ("Human Personality," 24). These are the only words that she considered pure enough to voice affliction. She knew that while the "afflicted silently beseech to be given the words to express themselves," they are often given ill-chosen words "because those who choose them know nothing of the affliction they would interpret" (23). Weil knew to choose her words carefully because she had learned for herself what she was talking about. It was because she had experienced the way relations of power so easily turn people to matter that she was drawn to thinking of affliction rather than oppression. But it was her deepened understanding of the nature of power, especially as it was illuminated for her in the *Iliad*, that fundamentally transformed her sense of politics in her move towards Christianity.

One of the pressing issues for Weil in her reflections on the *Iliad* was undoubtedly the defeat of the working-class movement in Germany and the support of working people for fascism. This had been an integral part of the reorientation of her thinking for some time. She wanted to understand the nature of a mass movement such as fascism and found that the *Iliad* could help her understand the nature of Nazi leadership and the nature of the power and authority it involved. Again she had to seek new terms of analysis to come to terms with the machinery of violence the Nazis had created.

From the beginning the Nazis turned the Jews into an internal enemy who were portrayed as less than human. The existence and growth of anti-Semitism could not be convincingly understood in traditional Marxist terms. But while Weil saw what was happening and had formulated the terms for understanding such a situation, she did not speak out openly or directly about the fate of the Jews in Germany. Was she struggling for that "extraordinary equity" she saw inspiring the *Iliad* so that "One is hardly made to feel that the poet is a Greek and not a Trojan" ("The *Iliad*, Poem of Might," 179). Or did her own feelings about being Jewish somehow affect her understanding? Did this make it difficult for her to really feel the preciousness of what was being destroyed in the destruction of the Jews in Germany?

I am not sure what the answers are, though I cannot help missing this concern in her writing. Even though Weil cared deeply about the ways in which peoples and cultures became uprooted—it is the central theme in *The Need for Roots*, written for the regeneration of France after the war—she never seemed to care in the same way about the fate of the Jewish people. In this she seems to fail to emulate the stance of the *Iliad*:

> By whatever means, this poem is a miraculous object. The bitterness of it is spent upon the only true cause of bitterness: the subordination of the human soul to might, which is, be it finally said, to matter. That subordination is the same for all mortals. . . . No one in the Iliad is spared, just as no one on earth escapes it. None of those who succumb to it is for that reason despised. Whatever, in the secret soul and in human relations, can escape the empire of might, is loved, but painfully loved because of the danger of destruction that continually hangs over it. Such is the spirit of the only veritable epic of the western world. (180)

It was this spirit that Weil wanted to make her own. It helped her come to terms with the armistice, which she saw as "a collective act of cowardice and treason" the whole nation bore responsibility for. Thus, as if learning from the *Iliad*, she knew "that all the French, including myself, are as much to blame for it as Petain" (158). Likewise, in *The Need for Roots*, she refuses to blame Hitler individually for the atrocities of nazism. She saw that to blame individuals is an evasion of responsibility that is tantamount to a refusal to learn from historical experience. The ideas of power and greatness that Hitler was acting out were the ideas that he had learned to admire within Western culture, which emulated the deeds of Caesar and Napoleon. In Weil's view, we cannot disown the fruits of our inheritance, however bitter they turn out to be, and we must, indeed, take responsibility for them and their sources.

With all her acute observations, however, Weil could also be blind and dogmatic. She was a selective thinker who too often divided the world between the forces of good and the powers of evil. Despite her growing understanding of how peoples have been uprooted both within the towns and in the countryside, she could not imagine that she could have been uprooted from a relationship with a Jewish culture and history. These had nothing to do with her. Nor did she see in the Christianity she had come to identify with any responsibility for what was happening with Jews in Germany. If Hitler's ideas of power and greatness were to be laid at the feet of Rome, so his anti-Semitism could have been seen as connected to the relationship between Christian and Jew in Western culture. But Weil was silent about this. She found it hard to love the Jews or to accept her own Jewishness; sometimes she seemed to despise them and this part of herself. She even denied her Jewishness when it seemed to stand in the way of her getting a teaching job.[25] In some sense the Jews had become her enemy, seeming to threaten the security of a France she wanted to identify with. But in this way she had also become her own enemy, according to her own reading of the *Iliad*. Being reduced to matter, in her later Christian writing, is the means for salvation, while in her thoughts on the *Iliad* it is still "the only true cause of bitterness." If being reduced to matter as a means of salvation was a constant temptation for her, it only became a direction in her religious writings towards the very end. Her own end came very soon. Towards the end it was in affliction that "the splendour of God's mercy shines" ("The Love of God and Affliction," 90).

8
Morality, truth, and politics

1 Truth and politics

Simone Weil was relieved to arrive in England from New York in November of 1942. In a letter to her parents she described herself as being "infinitely and completely glad to have crossed the sea again" (*Seventy Letters*, 162) for she had regretted ever having left France, which had been occupied by the Germans while she was away. She had felt that she had run away, and this she could not endure. She was well received by Maurice Schumann and Louis Closon in London but soon realized that it would be difficult to put into effect her plans to return to France on a dangerous mission to see a front-line nurses' corps implemented behind enemy lines. This was refused her, but she was offered a job examining documents concerning the reorganization of France after the war that were sent to London by the Resistance committees.

A period of intense writing activity ensued in which her spiritual understanding continued to illuminate her politics. She strove to outline a doctrine that could nourish and support the thinking of the Resistance groups, recognizing that, while "a doctrine does not suffice. . . . it is indispensable to have one, if only to avoid being misled by false doctrines" (*Ecrits de Londres*, 151). But she was not prepared to make compromises in her belief. She did not intend to deviate from her Christianity but rather to express its very depths. As she describes it, "To gather people behind Christian aspirations . . . it is necessary to try to define them in terms that an atheist might adhere to completely, and to do this without depriving these aspirations of what is specific to them" (169).

Weil's spirituality involved a clear separation between good-ness and the realm of necessity, God and the world. With Plato she had learned to criticize those who do not know "how great is the real difference between the necessary and the good."[1] This separation of the two domains also expresses her rigorous conception of the Good, which, according to Kant, must never be identified with what is presented to us within the empirical realm. As Simone Petrement explains, "What especially moves her is the idea that to put good in the world—'in front of the curtain', as she expresses it—would mean to fail in the respect and compassion that one owes to the unfortunate; for it would mean that one believed that misfortune is always a just punishment."[2] I do not think this conclusion follows, but it helps us grasp that for Weil where necessity itself reigns, good is, as it were, prevented from reigning directly. This profound duality allowed Weil to preserve the pure scientific vision of the world as concerned with the realm of necessity, yet she admires and loves this necessity, seeing it, as we have discussed, as a precondition for giving shape and meaning to human life.

Weil's sense that the necessities that science presents us with are to be accepted and loved is in tune with Greek conceptions of science. But the post-Renaissance science we have inherited sees the world as "blind necessity which constrains us," and it thus "appears to us as a thing to overcome" ("Classical Science and After," 21). It has lost its relation to art or religion and is oriented towards the mastery and domination of nature. To the Greeks, in contrast, that same necessity, which is revealed in geometry, "was a thing to love, because it is God himself who is the perpetual geometer" (21). Weil knew how the picture of the world elaborated by a science affects how we conceive our relation to the world. She was concerned, as we have argued, about the loss of any analogy between the laws of nature and the conditions of work in the development of twentieth century science. Science no longer recognized an identity of structure between the human mind and the universe. Having forsaken the link that had existed in the popular mind in the eighteenth and nineteenth centuries between science and the idea of truth, however erroneous this association had been, our culture was in danger of losing the very idea of truth: "The disappearance of scientific truth amounts, in our eyes, to the disappearance of truth itself, accustomed as we are to take one for the other" ("Reflections on Quantum Physics," 63).

Weil saw a deep and abiding danger in this loss of the idea of truth. While she recognizes that it is impossible for people not to have a representation of the truth that is not defective, she argues "they must have one—an imperfect image of the non-representable truth which we once saw, as Plato says, beyond the sky" (62). The mind needs this to direct its efforts or to use as its guide, for without it "utility at once takes its place, because man always directs his effort towards some good or other" (62). The effect, according to Weil, is a deep impoverishment within our culture reflected in the shallowness of our relations with ourselves and others. She sees a symptom of this condition in the arguments of social theory and historical understanding that truth is relative to a particular culture or historical moment.[3] The idea that truth is socially and historically produced makes it even harder for people to face the truth about themselves. People will constantly learn to displace and avoid truths that fit uneasily with the images they have created for themselves. This is an option Weil always refused herself.

The intelligence can judge utility only if it is judging it against something higher. It is in this sense that truth is not of this world—it cannot be bent to fit in with prevailing fashions and propaganda. Weil was aware of how advertising slogans, publicity, propaganda meetings, the press, the cinema, and radio had taken the place of thought in the modern world. It is as if our thinking is done for us through these modes—as structuralism has sensed uncritically in its notion that our individualities, our subjectivities, are articulated through the dominant discourses within a culture. Individual subjects are the results of these processes they no longer control. Protest is rendered almost impossible for it means attempting to appeal to a sense of "experience" that is somehow prior to language, to a realm that, according to structuralism, does not exist. Morality itself is reduced to a manipulation of appearances for there is only a void where there would be criteria for judging between the different moral accounts of a situation. Structuralist theory becomes impotent as it is left to describe these different accounts, unable to explain them.[4]

As long as public opinion reigns supreme, we are left bereft of a vision of truth within which to guide public life. Within democratic regimes we see politics as a competition among interest groups using whatever power and persuasion they have at their disposal and must assume that the "public interest" will somehow be served through this process. Weil, however, knew that the powerless, weak, and impoverished will continue to suffer, though she was aware of the difficulties of thinking justly in the realm of politics. "Human intelligence—even in the case of the most intelligent—falls miserably short of the great problems of public life" (*Ecrits de Londres*, 90). But this difficulty does not abolish the duty to seek solutions or at least to work to establish certain guiding ideas. She had long recognized that the idea of rights is too weak to serve as a guiding notion, as the revolutionaries of 1789 had hoped. A right that goes unrecognised is not worth very much. Weil makes this point clearly in the early pages of *The Need for Roots*, where she argues that the idea of rights must be replaced by the concepts of justice and obligation.

For Weil "Rights are always found to be related to certain conditions. Obligations alone remain independent of conditions. They belong to a realm situated above all conditions, because it is situated above this world" (*The Need for Roots*, 4). Thus Weil wanted to show that an important source of confusion in our moral and political culture lies in our refusal to acknowledge a realm of values situated above all conditions. She thought this something Plato could teach. But as long as we continue to think of rights as if they exist as absolute principles we make our confusion worse. This is how Weil explains the situation we still largely inherit:

> The men of 1789 did not recognize the existence of such a realm. All they recognized was the one on the human plane. This is why they started off with the idea of rights. But at the same time they wanted to postulate absolute principles. This contradiction caused them to tumble into a confusion of language and ideas which is largely responsible for the present political and social confusion. (4)

While John Rawls and Ronald Dworkin, among others, have recently attempted to reinstate a language of rights,[5] this notion is incapable of the tasks that are being set for it. Tragically, the rights that Jews enjoyed in the Weimar Republic did not protect them from injustice and humiliation in Hitler's Germany. Their rights were withdrawn.[6]

The reassertion of a language of rights in recent moral and political theory has partly developed because of the perceived weaknesses of utilitarianism to provide such a general theory. Without a higher standard, according to Weil, "utility becomes something which the intelligence is no longer entitled to define or to judge, but only to serve. From being the arbiter, intelligence becomes the servant, and gets its orders from the desires" ("Reflections on Quantum Physics," 64). What is more, we are without the terms that might illuminate this situation because we are so used to it that we take it for granted. Nobody thinks of defining utility. "And, further, public opinion then replaces conscience as sovereign mistress of thought, because man always submits his thought to some higher control, which is superior either in value or else in power" (64). If Weil was talking about Europe in 1941, she was touching something we can still dimly sense as a loss of the idea of truth. The difficulty is that the loss of intelligence that goes along with this loss of truth can make it even harder for us to recover from this situation. It matters less if we accept the options Weil sets before us than if we can recognize this cultural impoverishment as our own.

The loss of truth, then, implies for Weil the establishment of a pervasive passivity in people's relationship to their experience, a passivity that is at some level inescapably painful. In her view, it is connected to the degradation of work in modern society, and she argued that "No society can be stable in which a whole stratum of the population labours daily with a heart-felt loathing. This loathing for their work colours their whole view of life all their life" ("Factory Work," 71). It cannot be adequately grasped in sociological terms as a shift in people's orientation towards work, as if it were a matter of recording a shift from people's seeking satisfaction in their work to their looking for this satisfaction in leisure activities and home lives.[7] To say that work has simply become a means of earning money rather than a source of fulfillment in itself is to fail to grasp the place that work occupies in people's lives. Weil provides the resources for the insight that consumer commodities could not fill the void left in people's lives by a loathing of their experience at work and that the frustrations and humiliations of work under such conditions extend to the home, where they may be taken out on the family. Work has to be returned as a source of human dignity and self-respect if some sense of balance is to be restored to working-class life. Otherwise false hopes and expectations are generated to fill this void.

Marxism can create compensations for the daily humiliations of work by fostering a belief that the working class is destined to dominate history. This view can minimize the significance of working-class consciousness and self-activity when it leaves people convinced that history will bring its own salvation. For Weil Marxism had become part of the problem as much as part of the solution when she considered Marx's writings again, on her return to Europe in 1942. She thought that Marx had never really developed what she called his early "philosophy of labour" ("Is There a Marxist Doctrine," 64) and saw such a philosophy as "perhaps more particularly a need of our time" (169). For Weil this task had to take into account the conclusions of her essay on "Factory Work." Marx had been checked in his thinking, according to Weil, because he had begun to take himself too seriously. His sense, common enough in the nineteenth century, that he had been chosen to play a decisive role in the salvation of mankind, weakened his thinking. Weil did everything to provide a corrective to what she took as his messianic illusions:

> Were a bolt-maker to experience a legitimate and limited pride in the making of bolts, there could be no question of infusing him with a factitious, unlimited pride by holding before him the thought that his class is destined to make and dominate history. Similar considerations are applicable to private life, notably family life and relations between the sexes. The dreary exhaustion from factory work leaves a gaping void that clamours to be filled. It can be filled only by rapid, violent gratifications the resulting corruption of which is contagious for all classes of society. The correlation is not immediately obvious but it does exist. The family can expect no consideration among the people of this country as

long as a part of that people continue to work in loathing
and disgust. (71)

2   Goodness and materialism

Weil appreciated that Marx was capable of ideas of genius, but
she concluded in 1942 that he had been unable to create a
doctrine. "Is There a Marxist Doctrine?" shows that her
movement towards Christianity in some ways helped her to a
renewed interest in Marx's work. She believed that the orthodox
current of thought which claims to stem from Marx had proven
itself unable to work with the truths he had discovered: "Truth is
too dangerous to touch. It is an explosive" (170). In taking these
truths from Marx, she did not think she was drawing anything
that was incompatible with her Christianity. In her own way she
was setting the terms for a dialogue between Marxism and
Christianity that is still of living significance in Central and South
America. In Marx's writing Weil recognizes that "there are
compact fragments whose truth is unchanging, and which
naturally have their place in any true doctrine. Thus it is that they
are not only compatible with Christianity, but of infinite value to
it" (170). As we have shown, she was taken with his twin idea of
"taking society as the fundamental human fact and of studying
therein, as the physicist does in matter, the relationship of force"
(171).

According to Weil, materialism should be extended to explain
social relations, but it becomes ruthless if "the relationships of
force that define the social structure entirely determine man's
destiny and his thoughts" (171). If force accounts for everything
so that our thoughts can only reflect relationships of force, there
is no hope for justice. As Weil says, "It does not even leave the
hope of conceiving justice in its truth" (172). This is why it was
crucial for Weil to sustain, at least initially, a sharp distinction
between the realm of necessity and the realm of good.
Materialism was to be adhered to as long as it clearly dealt with
the realm of necessity and did not assert that this realm is all
there is. Such an assertion, for Weil, denied that "the very being
of man is nothing else but a perpetual straining after an unknown

good" (173). Materialism would be consistent if all concern with morality and goodness could be done away with. The absurdity of all materialism is shown as soon as we regard "matter as a machine for manufacturing the good" (173).

Plato had taught Weil that contradiction, far from being a criterion of error, is sometimes a sign of truth. She did not think we should remove all sign of contradictions but that we should learn how to face legitimate ones. If we cannot eliminate either of two incompatible thoughts, we must learn to use them "as a two-limbed tool, like a pair of pincers, so that through it direct contact may be made with the transcendental sphere of truth beyond the range of the human faculties" (173). That such a realm exists is beyond doubt for Weil in her later writings. It was part of her faith that, corresponding to this reality, "at the centre of the human heart, is the longing for an absolute good, a longing which is always there and is never appeased by any object in this world" ("Profession of Faith," 219).

Our thinking cannot escape contradictions for in Weil's view there is an "essential contradiction in human life" whereby "man, with a straining after the good constituting his very being, is at the same time subject in his entire being, both in mind and in flesh, to a blind force, to a necessity completely indifferent to the good" ("Is There a Marxist Doctrine?" 173). Weil discerned which religious and philosophical traditions are authentic according to whether they sustain this fundamental contradiction between the good and the necessary, or their equivalent, justice and force, but she was dogmatic in doing so, refusing to think that the good and the necessary might be brought into a different relation with each other. Having been convinced by Plato that an infinite distance separates the good from necessity and that they have nothing in common, Weil leaves us with the categorical assertion that "the whole of materialism, in so far as it attributes to matter the automatic manufacture of the good is to be classed among the inferior forms of the religious life" (174). This kind of assertion shows both the limits of Weil's grasp of materialism and the direction of her powerful critique of it. It allows her to identify a common weakness of Marxists and the apostles of liberalism, the bourgeois economists of the nineteenth century "who adopt a truly religious accent when they talk about production" (174). At the same time we can be left feeling that

Weil's sense of materialism is at some level fixed as undialectical.

For Weil materialism accounts for everything, with the exception of the supernatural. Or, as she also puts it, "only a shade of difference, something infinitely small, separates a spirituality like Plato's from materialism" (174). As Weil came to understand Plato,

> He does not say that the good is an automatic product of necessity, but that the Spirit has domination over necessity through persuasion; it persuades necessity to cause most of the things that take place in turn towards the good, and necessity is overcome by means of this wise persuasion. (175)

Weil was drawn back in her later thought to a more or less orthodox Marxism because, separated from its vision of progress, it seems to confirm that "This universe, minus the supernatural, is only matter" (177). She thought that in describing the universe solely as matter, one seizes upon a particle of truth. So it is that she believed Marx's writings to be of greater value for a Christian than those, for example, of Voltaire and the Encyclopedists, who "found a way of being atheists without being materialists" (177). She came to set herself against any idea that justice is of this world. She objected to any description of the universe "as a combination of matter and of specifically moral forces belonging to this world, that are on a level with nature" (177) and believed that such a description falsifies both politics and spirituality. In this way she also separated herself from interpretations of Marx that have fundamentally challenged orthodox Marxism. A brief comparison can help illuminate the difficulties of situating Weil within the tradition of Western Marxism.

In the writings of Karl Korsch and, for example, Georg Lukács there is a return to the inspiration of Hegel (see Introduction). For them Marx's work cannot be grasped as outlining the laws of capitalist development that exist over and above the experience of people themselves. The revolution cannot be delivered to working people but somehow has to be made by them. It is because people make history, even if not in conditions of their own choosing, that it was important for Korsch and Lukács to stress the development of working-class activity and consciousness. But despite his philosophical grasp of these issues in *History and Class Consciousness*, Lukács remained trapped in a vision of progress like most of Western Marxism before the questioning of the Frankfurt School. For Lukács the historical mission of the proletariat is established because of its objective position within the capitalist mode of production. So it is that the coming to subjective consciousness of the position working people have within the capitalist system of exploitation yields an objective grasp of capitalist social relations. Lukács could only sustain this vision through a sense that contradictions within the economy will inevitably provoke a revolutionary transformation. He could not adequately escape from a theory of economic crisis, although Korsch eventually made this radical break. For Weil the weakness of this idea traditionally lies in their attempt to acknowledge the crucial significance of the subjective moment in the totality and their introduction, thereby, of the importance of morality in political theory—an introduction made by something of a sleight of hand, as in Lukács' understanding of the relation between the subjective and the objective that ultimately conflates the moral and the economic. He did not think about morality outside the framework of economic relations, and these are the terms for discussion of morality in Western Marxism. If within this tradition moral forces belong to the struggles of this world, Weil believed that we could never really learn their significance.[8]

Like theorists in this tradition, Weil was also deeply concerned with working class education and culture. She did not underestimate the importance of ideology and consciousness and appreciated that if people were taught that revolution was inevitable it would make them passive. She had wanted people to control their work by giving their minds effective control over their actions. But this vision of freedom plays a less significant role in her later writing, where she is guided by the distance between necessity and goodness—although this is less true of *The Need for Roots* than of the later writing dealing specifically with Marxism. But significantly she did not attempt to develop what she took to be Marx's idea of non-physical matter as a way of exploring the place of thought. She wanted to formulate a notion of psychological matter, knowing that Marx really only explores society "as being the human fact of primary importance in this world" (177). It is central for Weil that "Under all the phenomena of a moral order, whether collective or individual, there is something analogous to matter properly so called" (178). This is the way Weil wanted to show that our thoughts are subject to necessity—although she did reduce our ideas and beliefs, as orthodox Marxism does. She shared with Marx a disdain for what he called mechanical materialism—the idea, still prevalent in the philosophy of mind, that we can explain human thought on the basis of physiological mechanisms. For Weil, "Thoughts are subject to a mechanism which is proper to themselves; but it is a mechanism" (178); thoughts have their own laws of necessity.

Our thoughts are not subject to physical necessity, but they are subject to necessity. According to Weil, "Everything that is real is subject to necessity" (178), but unless we know that this specific necessity for mental life exists, we will mistakenly think that moral phenomena are exact copies of material phenomena. So it is common for orthodox Marxism to ridicule moral concerns on the assumption that moral well-being results automatically from physical well-being. We might also think that moral attitudes and behavior are arbitrary and can be brought about by mere suggestion or indeed by an act of will. In this view, our feelings of jealousy or possessiveness, for instance, will automatically change if we change the situation we are living in. In the early years of the Soviet Union it was commonly believed that moral changes, in, say, the family and divorce, would follow automatically from changes in property ownership.[9] Weil, however, acknowledged the workings of necessity in areas where we are not used to recognizing it. Weil made striking use of materialism in order for us to learn to take more seriously aspects of our being that traditional materialism often teaches us to despise. She broadened the orthodox Marxist vision of experience in her recognition that "The relation between cause and effect is as rigorously determined in this field as it is in that of gravity. Only it is harder to know" (178). She refused reductionism and helped to establish the integrity of our beliefs, thoughts, and imagination, to make the inner life and spirituality, which Enlightenment culture has taught us to despise or ridicule, acceptable realities.

Taking seriously these neglected areas of our experience opens us up to a deepened psychological awareness—though Weil was deeply suspicious of a psychological language. Failure to grasp the significance of the areas of experience that we do not easily express, is, as Weil recognizes, "the cause of countless sufferings in daily life" (179). Her sensitivity to the workings of human energy is clear in her example that

> if a child says he isn't feeling well, is kept away from school, and all of a sudden finds the strength to play with some little friends, his indignant family think he has been lying. They say to him: "Since you had the strength to play, you had the strength to work". But the child may very well have been sincere. He was held back by a genuine feeling of exhaustion which the sight of his little friends and the attraction of playing with them have truly dissipated, whereas school lessons did not contain a sufficient stimulus to produce this effect. (179)

Similarly Weil thinks we should not be astonished when we firmly make a resolution and yet do not stick to it. She points out that "the very act of making the resolution may have exhausted the stimulus and thus prevented even a start being made in carrying it out" (179). If we go against ourselves with the resolution, we might well drain ourselves, even make ourselves quite ill. But if we are ignorant about the ways energy works, we might have only the barest inkling of what has happened. Our inherited liberal moral culture does not help us to this understanding of ourselves. If we think in Kantian terms that we are simply weak in will, we will never learn that we can be setting the wrong tasks for ourselves. At some level we are out of touch with what we need for ourselves.

This type of ignorance produces its own kind of difficulties in relationships of power. For example, industrialists can only think of making their workers happy, as Weil says, "either by raising their wages, or else by telling them they are happy and sacking the wicked communists who assure them to the contrary" (179). They lack the political and psychological understanding that could show them the importance of attitudes of mind. Weil perhaps was reaching for an appreciation of a more dialectical relation than could be made clear within her own language. For her industrialists are

> . . . unable to understand that, on the one hand, a workman's happiness consists above all in a certain attitude of mind towards his work; and that, on the other hand, this attitude of mind can be brought about only if certain objective conditions—impossible to know without making a serious study of the subject—have been fulfilled. (179).

As Weil sees it, "This twin truth, suitably transposed, is the key to all the practical problems of human existence" (179).

So it is that Weil challenged the suggestion of liberalism that people can take up attitudes to work as a matter of individual will. It is useless to carry on telling people that they should be happy and take up a positive attitude towards their work. While she also questioned the reductionist argument of orthodox Marxism that these attitudes flow directly from material conditions, at the same time she sustained her fundamental sense that Marx was right to begin by "positing the reality of social matter, of a social necessity" (179). She is clear that "In the operation of this necessity which governs men's thoughts and actions, the relations between society and the individual are very complex" (179).

Plato was important in helping Weil understand some of the nature of this complexity. For, in her view, he had felt very strongly that "social matter is an infinitely greater obstacle to overcome between the soul and the good than the flesh properly so called" (180). She had learned to shift the terms of discussion away from the individualistic framework established for liberalism by Kant. It is no longer our desires or our inclinations that can explain why we are not constantly aspiring to do the good. Nor can we account for this in terms of the weakness of our individual wills. We have to search for a social explanation that can take full account of the power of society in relation to individual lives. We have to recognise—as Weil thought Christianity does in its idea that the devil is on his own ground in social matter—"That social matter is the cultural and proliferating medium par excellence for lies and false beliefs" (180). Society for Weil had become Plato's "Great Beast," though at some level it remained a beast she hoped to tame when she did not despair of it completely. It is from society that we draw our ideas of good and evil. Weil acknowledgcd that this theme is not developed by Plato, even though she sensed its presence behind all his writings.

Weil often asserts her position dogmatically. The very clarity of her dualism somehow seems to block off further exploration even of her own insights. The relationship between power and morality does not leave us with a contradictory moral inheritance. Within the social world we are blindly subject to the opinions of society, even when we are in violent disagreement with others about good and evil. As Weil says, it is easy to see others as trapped within the conventions and ideas of socicty while still seeing ourselves as having a correct view of justice and the good. But one can only understand the truth that Plato has formulated "when one has recognized it as true of oneself' (181).

Weil escaped by appealing to a source that exists beyond the social world. She thinks that the difference between Marx and Plato is that Marx is "unaware of the possibility of exceptions brought about through the supernatural intervention of grace" (182). Weil agrees with what she takes as the central conception in Plato "that all men are absolutely incapable of having on the subject of good and evil opinions other than those dictated by the reflexes of the beast, except for predestined souls whom a supernatural grace draws towards God" (180). But she also knows that people are differently placed in relation to power— "since the beast is huge and men are tiny, each one is differently placed in relation to it" (181). Still, this does not mean her thinking can capture the complexity of the relations between society and the individual. It is as if in thinking about the nature of Marxism again, some of her insights about power derived from her meditations on the *Iliad* were no longer available to her. At moments her thinking becomes almost mechanical as if trapped by her own interpretations of Marx. She recognizes that "society is composed of groups which interlock in all sorts of ways, and social morality varies from group to group" (181). Since it is impossible to find individuals with exactly the same backgrounds, each being composed of a different network of groups, "the apparent originality of individuals does not contradict the proposition that thought is completely subordinated to social opinion" (182). This is reminiscent of much earlier writing.

3 Morality and power

Marx understood the mechanism of social opinion by recognizing that each social group manufactures a morality for itself. Weil knew that every professional group produces a morality so that those who conform to the rules are placed outside the reach of evil. The moral atmosphere of a given society reflects the power exercised by each group, although it is also true that the moral atmosphere of a society reflects elements from former ruling classes that have since disappeared or been displaced from power. But people will often be blind to the workings of particular conceptions, assuming that they reflect a way of thinking inherent in human nature. Weil cites the example of the importance attached to theft in the French penal code. Theft is more severely punished than the rape of children, even though the men who drew up the code would no doubt have preferred to lose part of their wealth than to have their children defiled. Weil points out that when drawing up the code, they were, unknowingly, "simply the organs of social reflexes; and in a society based on commerce, theft is the prime anti-social act" ("Is There a Marxist Doctrine?" 1983). Likewise, it is because the white slave traffic is a kind of commerce that people have only with difficulty come to punish it.

Weil thought that Marx's view of social necessity could have plunged him into despair "since it is a necessity powerful enough to prevent men, not only from obtaining, but even from conceiving justice" (190), but Weil also saw that Marx considered people's desire for justice far too deeply rooted to be refused. Weil felt something like this herself but she could only make sense of it as a feeling for something transcendent. She thought that Marx "took refuge in a dream wherein social matter itself takes charge of the two functions that it denies man, namely, not only to accomplish justice, but to conceive it" (190). She could no longer identify with the morality of a particular class or to hold out hopes of justice prevailing. She knew that the common characteristic of social morality had been formulated by Plato in definitive terms: "They call just and beautiful things that are necessary, for they do not know how great in reality is the distance which separates the essence of the necessary from that of the good" (183).

Weil conceives Marx's social world in terms similar to Kant's conception of the empirical world as a world governed by necessity and determination. Kant looks to an independent intelligible world as the source of morality and goodness. So Weil thinks that, for Marx, "Since society is vitiated, poisoned, and the social poison permeates all men's thoughts without exception, everything that men imagine under the name of justice is simply lies" (192). For Weil as long as justice is absent, the individual cannot conceive it, and "it can only come to him from outside" (192). Marx thus gets trapped into containing his conception of justice within a framework of property relations so that it appears to him that the only way to serve justice "is to hasten forward the operation of the that mechanism, inherent in the very structure of social matter, which will automatically bring men justice" (192). This conflation of morality and production serves to marginalize the moral character of questions about the means to attain a just society within Marx's theory. At some level it necessarily implies a form of pragmatism. This is the way Marx could regard as just and good "not that which appears to be so to minds warped by the social lie, but solely that which could hasten the appearance of a society without lies" (193). As Weil says in one of the "Fragments" written in London in 1943, "It matters little what means he employs to this end; they are good, provided they are effective" (158). For Weil this meant Marx fell into the very weakness that he tried to avoid: Having no adequate grounding for his conception of justice, he "placed the social category to which he belonged—that of professional revolutionaries—above sin" (158).

If one accepts as an absolute value the specific morality of the social group to which one happens to belong, "One's mind is then at rest; but morally speaking one is dead" (156). For Weil only by escaping the sphere of relative moralities can we know the absolute good. We have to learn ways of entering indirectly into contact with the sphere of transcendent truth inaccessible to our intelligence. Our thoughts do not lay hold of the good. Marx had failed to understand that force is a stranger indifferent to the good and that, in any case, good is not always and everywhere the stronger. Weil is convinced in her later writings that the "true road" exists and that Plato and others have followed it. As she explains the Christian position she reached towards the end of her life, "it is open only to those who, recognising themselves to be incapable of finding it, give up looking for it, and yet do not cease to desire it to the exclusion of everything else. To these it is given to feed on a good, which, being situated outside this world, is not subject to any social influence whatever" (157). This is the only way open to people to escape from the falsehoods which poison social life to reach a knowledge of justice and truth. Marx, however, had wanted to assume that society, "by an automatic process of growth, would eliminate its own toxins" (157).

Weil sustains an orthodox reading of Marx in her view that Marx's revolutionary materialism "consists in positing, on the one hand, that force alone governs social relations to the exclusion of anything else, and, on the other hand, that one day the weak, while remaining the weak, will nevertheless be the stronger" (159). For Weil this meant that Marx believed in miracles without believing in the supernatural. It is a Christian idea that weakness as such, while remaining weak, can constitute a force. But as she makes clear at the end of "Is There a Marxist Doctrine?" weakness has to do with a force of quite a different kind from that wielded by the strong; it is a force that is not of this world, that is supernatural" (194). As far as Weil was concerned, "Marx accepted this contradiction of strength in weakness, without accepting the supernatural which alone renders the contradiction valid" (195). Weil, however, puts the issue too sharply for it can be more generally acknowledged that in facing our vulnerability we can tap a different source of strength. It has been a significant insight of recent feminism to refuse to contrast strength and weakness.[10] Weil knew that to sustain their dignity and self working people had to see both the actuality and the limits of their resources in work situations, but she tended to lose touch with this in her more theoretical engagement with Marxism, a level on which she never found an adequate way of integrating what she had learned from her own experience of factory work.

As Weil knew, but could not examine, the conceptions that are current in any society are influenced by the specific morality of the group that dominates the society. Since she assumed a position she believed Marx established, that all social relations are governed by force, Weil had to look beyond the social world for any genuine vision of goodness and justice. In the end it was her Platonism that governed her reading of Marx and influenced her attitude to the social world. As Iris Murdoch says of Plato, "There is in all his work, and not only in the later dialogues, a recurring tone of sometimes almost vehement rejection of the joys of this world."[11] Human life is not anything much. Not only is the flesh moral trash but we are shadows, chattels of the gods. Weil took on this fairly grim view of the human situation, believing that we cannot escape from the lies we inherit from the groups within which we live and that our efforts will be of no avail as we stumble from one false version of goodness to another. This pessimism is deeply ingrained in the later Weil as it is a Plato and creates a tension like that Murdoch sees in Plato and Kant, who she thinks temperamentally resemble each other "in combining a great sense of human possibility with a great sense of human worthlessness."[12] According to Murdoch,

> Kant is concerned both with setting limits to reason, and
> with increasing our confidence in reason within those limits.
> Though he knows how passionate and how bad we are,
> Kant is a moral democrat expecting every rational being to
> be able to do his duty. Plato, on the other hand, is a moral
> aristocrat, and in this respect a puritan and a different type,
> who regards most of us as pretty irrevocably plunged in
> illusion.[13]

Both these attitudes exist in Weil. The vast distance they both establish between the necessary and the good makes them both quite alien to Hegel. Thus there is a limitation in Weil that prevents her from fully exploring the origin and character of our illusions in ways that Hegelian-influenced Marxism, such as Antonio Gramsci's, has been more able to do.

Gramsci's interpretation of Marx in his *Prison Notebooks* draws heavily from Hegel. Writing in the shadow of the Russian Revolution, he argues, as Korsch and Lukács do, that it is only in the context of Hegel's thought that Marx can be properly understood. Gramsci rejects an orthodox interpretation of Marx in which Marxism is centrally concerned with establishing the laws of development of capitalist society that would lead inevitably to a socialist revolution. According to Gramsci, this vision produces passivity and fosters a false conception of history as "progress." Weil, however, accepted a more mechanical interpretation, as we have seen, of the conception of progress in Marx. She saw a tension between Marx's perception of the centrality of force and his faith in progress, but rather than rethinking the conception of progress, Weil looked for the authentic source of justice outside the social world. Her commitment to justice as a value is in tension with her conviction about the pervasiveness of force. It is surprising that this did not consistently sap her sense of the need to make changes in the prevailing relationships of power and subordination.

Gramsci, like Weil, acknowledges that we grow up "to take part in a conception of the world mechanically imposed by the external environment, i.e. by one of the many social groups in which everyone is automatically involved from the moment of his entry into the conscious world."[14] Gramsci recognizes that we are all conformists. But unlike Weil, Gramsci also sees that "it is better to work out consciously and critically one's own conception of the world."[15] We can choose to be our own guides, determining our own spheres of activity as we refuse to accept the external molding of our personality. If we can learn to identify the conceptions of the world we have inherited, recognizing that we belong to a multiplicity of human groups we can begin to develop a different sense of ourselves that does not involve, as it does sometimes for Weil, replacing one form of illusion for another.

Despite these differences between Weil and Gramsci, at another level the distance perhaps is not so great. Both Weil and Gramsci recognize that the egoistic personality has the need to preserve and aggrandize itself—although for Gramsci this egoistic personality has to be understood as growing out of the contradictory powers of social relations—and both welcome a necessity that allows us to overcome our egoistic fantasies. In Weil's terms, even though the good exists outside the world, the necessities we face in this life are themselves the tool of the good because they can teach us to submit our person to an impersonal order.

Weil, however, retained a strong sense that the self is essentially egoistic. In her view we cannot distance ourselves from an egoistic self to establish a fuller relationship with a core sense of self. Gradually the vision of freedom in Weil's later writing involves our destroying whatever sense of personal autonomy remains as we learn to reduce ourselves to matter. There is a deep strain of self-denial that gains ascendancy as it turns inward to punish the self. But there are other times when Weil might have sympathy with Gramsci's idea that "The starting-point of critical elaboration is the consciousness of what one really is, and is 'knowing thyself' as a product of the historical process to date which has deposited in you an infinity of traces, without leaving an inventory"[16]—a view that challenges a liberal conception that takes self-knowledge to be a matter of discerning our pre-given desires and goals. We have instead to grasp the historicity of our consciousness—of how the ways we think and feel have been influenced by our class, ethnic, and gender relations. This is the way we can truly understand ourselves, and as a result we will no longer experience ourselves as isolated individuals whose place in the world is uniquely defined by our individual qualities and abilities. We will come to realize and value the ways that our experience has been shared by others who have a similar history and culture. But for Gramsci this was significantly a matter of strengthening a sense of individuality, rather than reducing it to a shared class identity, as in more mechanical interpretations of Marx.[17]

Weil understood the importance of workers' coming to trust their own perceptions of social relations, rather than those presented to them by management. This was essential if people were to recover and sustain a sense of dignity and self-worth. She had an acute sense of the importance of finding exactly the right words that would illuminate, without betraying, the reality of working people's experience. She knew how "In the worker's mind the struggle 'against the boss' is confused with the assertion of human dignity" ("The Power of Words," 167). She recognized a danger of tilting at windmills unless workers learned not to blame instinctively their employers for all the hardships of work in a factory. Weil never lost her sense that "The society in which we live includes forms of coercion and oppression by which those who suffer from them are all too often overwhelmed; it includes the most grievous inequalities and unnecessary miseries" (164). She had, however, grown weary of talking in general terms about the "destruction of capitalism" for "the slogan can only imply the destruction of capitalists, and more generally, of everyone who does not call himself an opponent of capitalism" (165). Weil wanted to go beyond the terms of traditional Marxist discussion, arguing that workers have to learn to consider whether under any other property system the management would not inflict some of the same hardships as well as whether some hardships might not well be abolished without any alteration of the existing property system. It is in asking these questions that workers take more control of their situation, learning to set their own terms rather than submitting to an externally established orthodoxy. For her, there is a danger inherent in Marx's refusal to theorize seriously about the character of socialism, on the assumption that it is impossible to do so realistically while living within a capitalist society. The Left has continued this reserve, and it has had disastrous historical consequences, as the historical experience of Stalinism makes plain. Militants contemptuously dismiss as "reforms" any modifications to the regime.

Weil held to the idea that the most serious and legitimate conflict that sets groups of men against one another "is what is called today the *class struggle*," but, she adds, that is "an expression which needs clarifying (162). For Weil, the notion of class struggle involves "the eternal struggle of those who obey against those who command when the mechanism of social power involves a disregard for the human dignity of the former" (162). Since only rarely can the function of command be exercised in a way "that respects the personal humanity of those who carry out orders" (162), the struggle is "eternal" "because those who command are always inclined, whether they know it or not, to trample on the human dignity of those below them" (162). This is a view with which Gramsci would have agreed. He was also aware that as long as there is a stable social hierarchy, in Weil's words, "those at the bottom must struggle so as not to lose all the rights of a human being" (162). Writing in a way that can equally illuminate Gramsci's notion of hegemony, Weil notes that "The tension between pressure from below and resistance from above creates and maintains an unstable equilibrium, which defines at each moment the structure of a society" (163).[18]

Weil and Gramsci also share a sense of the importance of working-class education. Gramsci knew, as Weil did, how relations of power work so that some group

has, for reasons of submission and intellectual

subordination, adopted a conception which is not its own
but is borrowed from another group; and it affirms this
conception verbally and believes itself to be following it,
because this is the conception which it follows in "normal
times"—that is when its conduct is not independent and
autonomous, but submissive and subordinate.[19]

For Gramsci this is "the reason why philosophy cannot be
divorced from politics."[20] Gramsci was as suspicious as Weil of
revolutionaries who thought that it was their task to bring truth
to the people. Like Weil, he saw his task as being grounded in
finding the words to give expression to workers' own experience
of oppression. If intellectuals were to be organically related to
the people, they would be working out and making coherent "the
principles and the problems raised by the masses in their practical
activity."[21]

Weil, however, found it difficult to explain how working-class
people often take the conceptions of others as their own when
she thought in more general terms of social relations as relations
of force. It is hard for her to sustain in her more theoretical voice
the importance of social relations to individual dignity. These are
the times in her writings when the language of force takes over
and when the story of the interminable and useless massacres
around Troy seem to be the only legacy from antiquity for her, as
they were in her experience in Spain and in her fear of war. But
she is closer to Gramsci when she remembers that there are also
different legacies, recognizing, for instance, that "there is also the
vigorous and concerted action of the Roman plebians who,
without shedding a drop of blood, escaped from a condition
verging upon slavery and obtained the institution of tribunes to
guarantee their new rights" ("The Power of Words," 163). This
was also the way French workers, in occupying the factories
without violence, enforced the recognition of certain elementary
rights.

As Weil focussed more on the notion of social relations as
relations of force, she became less capable of recognizing the
contradictions that exist in our experience. If contradictions exist,
they seem to exist at the level of our consciousness as levers that
can bring us to an awareness of a realm beyond. Such is the
dominant tone in her Christian writings. Thus she was less aware

than Gramsci of how the consciousness people have inherited from the past and uncritically absorbed can prevent them from developing a sense of their own autonomy. It has been a central insight of recent feminism that women have to separate their own visions of themselves from the dominant visions of men, to learn to live for themselves, rather than in the shadow of others. Women have begun to develop their own conception of the world, even if only embryonic, "a conception which manifests itself in action, but occasionally and in flashes," as Gramsci says.[22] As women gain a clearer sense of themselves, they can act with greater clarity and authority. But if they remain divided, unable to make out their own beliefs and values, then often they suffer, what Gramsci calls "the contradictory state of consciousness" that does not permit of any action, any decision or any choice, and produces a condition of moral and political passivity."[23]

The question of the extent to which Weil gives her grasp of human dignity and freedom a full enough place in her theoretical writing has to do with an ambivalence concerning the importance of individuality in Marxist thought. Gramsci thought it most useful to think of "human nature" as a "complex of social relations" "because it includes the idea of becoming (man 'becomes', he changes continuously with the changing of social relations) and because it denies 'man in general.' "[24] Thus for Gramsci "If one's own individuality is the *ensemble* of these relations, to create one's personality means to acquire consciousness of them and to modify one's own personality means to modify the *ensemble* of these relations."[25] Weil, however, was more concerned to bring us into relation with necessity so that we can combat an inflated and egoistic sense of self. Assuming that the concern with individuality inevitably fostered a false and inflated sense of self, she did not really think that coming to consciousness of ourselves can bring us into relation with necessity.

Weil's conviction that the self is inherently egoistic, then, sets her in tension with a Hegelian Marxist tradition. But at another level she might have been impressed by Gramsci's insight into the relation between morality and power. In learning to investigate oppression not simply as a matter of "social analysis," as she had done in her earlier *Reflections*, but in terms of dignity and self-respect, she was looking for ways of bringing moral and structural features into relation with each other. Like Gramsci, she saw that they could be investigated adequately not as independent structures but only in relation to each other. Weil had to learn to think of freedom not simply as giving the mind control over our actions but as also concerned with dignity and self-respect. So freedom connects to justice, but not simply to a conception of justice conceived in distributive terms. Justice instead has to do with the treatment that is owed to people as human beings, a treatment that does not unwittingly violate them. This does more than make space for the individual within a social analysis of oppression. It fundamentally connects in a renewal of social theory issues of oppression to questions of dignity and justice. But it is unclear to what extent Weil could really develop this focus. In her more Christian writings her concern with oppression finds expression within a language of affliction, while her concern with freedom tends to be displaced by a focus on goodness from an independent realm.

Like the Frankfurt School, Weil was impressed with the shift of power in the relations between individual and state that had taken place in the twentieth century. Plato's vision of society as the "Great Beast" helps express the power held over individuals in modern societies and shows why it difficult to think of justice in distributive terms exclusively, since that conception assumes the integrity and independence of individuals. Our discussion of justice has to take into consideration the change in balance between state and civil society as well as the power of the social machine to crush individual lives. We can no longer accept as an adequate basis for our social and political theory the market assumptions of nineteenth century capitalism and the language of rights that went along with it. It is because individuals can be reduced to matter by the prevailing relations of power that Weil could not share some of Gramsci's early hopes. In many ways we face a bleaker reality in which we have to illuminate the injuries and impoverishment of individual lives. For the Frankfurt School this meant turning to Freud, while for Weil it was only Christianity that could illuminate the nature of the suffering and affliction which would otherwise go without a voice.

In her later writing, including *The Need for Roots*, Weil examines the injuries done to people when their fundamenta human needs fail to be recognized, let alone fulfilled, within society. She gives particular stress to the injustice that is done to people when they are uprooted, an idea she developed from her experience of factory work. She recognized that workers were often made to feel like strangers in the workplace whose presence was being suffered. She never forgot the memory of women having to wait outside in the rain because they did not feel they could take refuge in the factory before the time for their shift. As we have attempted to explain, it was her attempt to illuminate the forms of degradation and violation she came to know in the factory that drew her to Christianity. A similar motivation may well be at work in Central and South America where Christianity and Marxism are being brought into a new and vital relation.

We can see here the development of a tradition that sees Christianity and Marxism not as mutually exclusive bodies of thought as mutually illuminating in a process of emancipatory struggle. For Weil an understanding of the relationship of morality to power was connected to the importance of truth for both morality and politics. It was truth that we were to learn to live by.

4   Affliction, truth, and justice

In her haunting essay "Human Personality" Weil writes that "The intelligent man who is proud of his intelligence is like a condemned man who is proud of his large cell" (267). With Plato's cave replaced by the prison cell here, she thought the mind, which is enclosed in language, can possess only opinions and that "the only way into truth is through one's own annihilation; through dwelling a long time in a state of extreme and total humiliation" (27). These are dark moments in which Weil is turned sharply against the self. For her the self has to be annihilated, not simply the ego. It is not enough in her later writings for us to accept our own suffering as a way of being able to feel the suffering of others.

Her interpretation of the *Iliad* had helped Weil to an understanding of affliction, and for a while understanding and responding to affliction was the only task for her, a task through which she revealed that often we avoid truth as we avoid the knowledge of affliction and so revealed something important about the relationship of truth to justice. From this point of view Weil virtually identifies truth with affliction, for, as she says, "It is the state of extreme and total humiliation which is also the condition for passing over into truth. It is a death of the soul" (27). But this is an identification that we do not have to make if we are to learn from her.

For Weil the same barrier that keeps us from truth keeps us from understanding affliction. She sees a natural alliance between truth and affliction:

> Just as a vagrant accused of stealing a carrot from a field stands before a comfortably seated judge who keeps up an elegant flow of queries, comment, and witticisms while the accused is unable to stammer a word, so truth stands before an intelligence which is concerned with the elegant manipulation of opinions. (25)

Weil thinks that "Just as truth is a different thing from opinion, so affliction is a different thing from suffering. Affliction is a device for pulverizing the soul; the man who falls into it is like a workman who gets caught up in a machine. He is no longer a man but a torn and bloody rag on the teeth of a cog-wheel" (27).

Weil takes it as her task to find the words that will help to express the truth of workers' affliction, "the words which can give resonance, through the crust of external circumstances, to the cry which is always inaudible: 'Why am I being hurt?' " (24). For, as we have seen, according to Weil,

> Affliction is by its nature inarticulate. The afflicted silently beseech to be given the words to express themselves. There are times when they are given none; but there are also times when they are given words, but ill-chosen ones, because those who choose them know nothing of the affliction they would interpret. (23)

Even if people are not far removed from affliction by the circumstances of their lives, they automatically distance themselves from it. They do not want to know. The task of knowing and articulating that Weil took for herself put her on the path of extreme and total humiliation. She accepted this as her lot, believing that it is only saints and geniuses who can help the afflicted. But in this way she separated herself from others and made it harder for others to learn from what she had to give. This has often blocked an appreciation of her writings.

Weil wants us to face the reality of affliction, knowing that this is a condition people can be reduced to by relations of power. This is one of the lessons of the *Iliad*. It challenges liberal visions of social equality through which can instinctively, as it were, turn away from facing some of the realities of poverty and oppression. As if to shock us into a recognition that we would otherwise resist, she insists on drawing a sharp distinction between suffering and affliction. Suffering can inspire a tender feeling of pity in generous souls, but people often shiver and recoil when confronted with the reality of affliction which, as Weil describes it, is a "corrosive force, a mutilation or leprosy of the soul" (28). She also knows that the afflicted themselves feel the same horror at their own condition.

While we learn within a liberal moral culture to think of equality as a matter of being prepared to put ourselves in the situations of others, we are not helped to recognize the difficulties we face in doing so. We often become surprised at the rage and bitterness that underly relationships of power and subordination; we cannot face the sufferings of the innocent. We fail to appreciate and even tend to minimize the injuries done to others. We do not want to accept that the damage is beyond repair, having invested in the idea that whatever damage we have suffered in our individual and social relations can always be repaired or made good. At best all we often do is pretend to listen, but really we do not want to know. We want to keep this affliction at a safe distance for we sense that it would cost us a great deal to open up to it. "To put oneself in the place of someone whose soul is corroded by affliction, or in near danger of it, is to annihilate oneself. It is more difficult than suicide would be for a happy child" (28). This is why the afflicted are very rarely listened to. As Weil has it, "They are like someone whose tongue has been cut out and who occasionally forgets the fact. When they move their lips no ear perceives any sound. And they themselves soon sink into impotence in the use of language, because of the certainty of not being heard" (28).

This is why there is no hope for the vagrant who stands before the magistrate: "Even if, through his stammerings, he should utter a cry to pierce the soul, neither the magistrate nor the public will hear it. His cry is mute" (28). Nor can the afflicted easily look to each other for support and solidarity for they are equally deaf to one another. They suffer from general indifference, finding ways "by means of self-delusion or forgetfulness to become dead to his own self' (28). During the writing of this essay Weil seemed to have had little hope for any social change. She came to believe that only through the supernatural workings of grace could one gain the capacity to truth and to affliction:

> Because affliction and truth need the same kind of attention
> before they can be heard, the spirit of justice and the spirit
> of truth are one. The spirit of justice and truth is nothing
> else but a certain kind of attention, which is pure love. (28)

It is through an intense and disinterested attention, which is love, that we can come close to grasping the truth of the situation the vagrant finds himself in. And this is to do him justice to give him what is owed. At some level we cannot begin to do justice to others unless we fully understand the reality of their condition. The judge does not really have to listen or to acknowledge the affliction that is being endured, for all he has to know is that a law has been broken. We easily assume that suffering must be deserved—that it is some kind of punishment. This is one way that we turn our faces from the suffering that is around us. In insisting on a qualitative difference between suffering and affliction, Weil asks us to appreciate a mutilation and damage to the soul that cannot be easily repaired. She also asks us to acknowledge that in giving love and attention to others we also injure ourselves. We lose something of ourselves. This is a reality which liberalism protects us from. We cannot easily repair, even if we can identify and name the damage done to others within an unjust society. Souls are mutilated and bodies are bent. Innocents are made to suffer.

In "The Importance of Simone Weil" the Polish writer Czeslaw Milosz argues that with million killed or tortured in the twentieth century, European thinking has been circling around the problem of who can justify the suffering of the innocents. He knows that sometimes "old enigmas of mankind are kept dormant or veiled for several generations, then recover their vitality and are formulated in a new language."[26] Weil helps us come closer to the heart of this issue in her challenge to notions of progress and her grasp of a relationship of truth to politics, though she does not really expect to be listened to. As in Shakespeare's *King Lear*, it is only the fools who tell the truth. In one of the last letters she wrote to her parents, Weil explains that

> What makes the tragedy extreme is the fact that because the
> fools have no academic titles of episcopal dignities and
> because no one is aware that their sayings deserve the
> slightest attention—everybody being convinced a priori of
> the contrary, since they are fools—their expression of the
> truth is not even listened to. (*Seventy Letters*, 200)

For centuries people have been unaware that what they say is true. "And not satirically or humorously true, but simply the truth. Pure unadulterated truth—luminous, profound, and essential" (200).

In *King Lear* it is striking that even Kent and Cordelia constantly manoeuver to evade the truth. They attenuate, mitigate, and constantly veil the truth, as Weil grasps it. For Weil the truth cannot simply be handled as a gift from one person to another; people have to struggle for it themselves, and they have to earn it through their own suffering and experience. Towards the end of her life Weil came to realize that

> There is a class of people in this world who have fallen into
> the lowest degree of humiliation, far below beggary, and
> who are deprived not only of all social consideration but
> also, in everybody's opinion, of the specific human dignity,
> reason itself—and these are the only people who, in fact,
> are able to tell the truth. All the others lie. (200)

Weil felt a deep affinity for these fools. She knew that the "eulogies of my intelligence are positively *intended* to evade the question: 'Is what she says true?' And my reputation for 'intelligence' is practically equivalent to the label 'fool' for those fools" (201). Weil had a growing inner certainty, as she put it in an earlier letter to her parents, "that there is within me a deposit of pure gold which must be handed on" (196). But she also felt that there was no one to receive it, that people were not prepared to make the effort of attention. With attention being fragmented by the nature of modern experience, people seem to have almost lost a capacity to concentrate their attention. People are in danger of losing the very power of thought.

But this could never mean giving up. As Milosz says:

> Willing or not, we are committed. We should throw our act
> into the balance by siding with the oppressed and by
> diminishing as much as possible the oppressive power of
> those who give orders. Without expecting too much: hubris,
> lack of measure, is punished by Fate, inherent in the laws of
> iron necessity.[27]

Weil never lost her commitment or her identification with the suffering and oppressed. She refused any easy compromise or attempts at escaping an inevitable contradiction by patching it up. Thus she rejected attempts to solve what had become the fundamental contradiction in her later writings between a longing for the good and the cold universe governed by relations of force absolutely indifferent to any values. Rationalists thought they could solve this by placing good in this world, in matter, and usually in the future. Because her efforts were directed to making this contradiction as acute as possible, she has been accused of being too rigid and having lacked a dialectical touch. As Milosz says, though Weil was hostile to the notions of the dialectic, her thinking was dialectical in a significant sense: Dialectical thought is so often debased "into an art of compromise," but Weil refused to unify "opposites too cheaply."[28]

But we are left with a stark vision. We have to refuse any consolations. As Milosz quotes Weil, "We have to be in a desert. For he whom we must love is absent"; "To love God through and across the destruction of Troy and Carthage, and without consolation. Love is not consolation, it is light."[29] At the center of his vision is the idea of the wilful adbication of God from the universe. So it is for Weil that the source of goodness lies outside of this world. We lose the possibility of drawing upon this goodness if we identify with the conventional ethics of national or class interests. Industrialization is itself undermining the belief in the magic blessings of history for, as Milosz points out, "It is more and more obvious (in the countries of Eastern Europe as well) that refrigerators and television sets, or even rockets to the moon, do not change man into God. Old conflicts between human groups have been abolished but are replaced by new ones, perhaps more acute."[30]

The starkness of Weil's vision has often prevented people from learning from her and using her work to illuminate contemporary historical contradictions. Weil's turn to Christianity can be seen as a strength as well as a weakness—as a refusal to accept "the unity of the opposites too cheaply." It can help us to understand the significance of religion in radical movements. It can also teach us not to be dismissive of that dimension of human experience which is too easily construed and diminished in a polarity between illusion and actuality within a Marxist tradition fed by Enlightenment conceptions of reason and science.

When Milosz translated some of Weil's work into Polish in 1958, it was partly because he lamented the division of Poland into two camps, the nationalistic Catholic and the Marxist. He suspected that non-nationalistic Catholics had more in common with unorthodox Marxists—using that term for lack of a better one—than was suspected. He was concerned to show that the "choice between Christianity as represented by a national religion and the official Marxist ideology is not the only choice left today."[31] I think Milosz was also right to sense in the present world a much more serious religious crisis than appearances would have us guess. Years later some of this became clear with the emergence of Solidarity as a mass movement in Poland, which rejected the simple alternatives that had been traditionally offered and insisted on asking new questions about the relation of state and civil society. Politics and spirituality came together in Solidarity. It was part of the strength of the movement and partly explains its rootedness within Polish society.

When the shipworkers of Gdansk wanted to erect a monument to remember the deaths of people in an earlier rising, ten years before, they chose three colossal crosses on which three anchors—symbols of hope—are nailed. At the foot of the crosses is a sculpture reminding us of events past and a fragment of a poem by Milosz:

You, who have wronged a simple man
Bursting into laughter at the crime
. . . .
Do not feel safe. The poet remembers.
You can slay one, but another is born.
The words are written down, the deed, the date.[32]

As Józef Tischner, a priest and supporter of Solidarity, explains:

In this monument, there is *truth*. First there is the truth of recollection. Ten years ago the first workers of this shipyard perished here. . . . But this is only one motif, only the first raising of the curtain. Immediately after it, or even with it, comes the second, deeper one . . . the anchor is associated with what was crucified here—work and hope.[33]

So it is that the work of art "takes us by the hand and leads us to what is deeply hidden, leads us to essential truth."[34] In these words we can sense how some of Weil's reflections found an acceptance in the formative moments of Solidarity in Poland.

Lech Walesa, a leader of the Solidarity movement, gives testimony to Józef Tischner's idea that "A life is a disease of speech."[35] In September of 1981, during the Solidarity Congress in Gdansk, there was a great deal of talk about lies and liberation from the falsehoods and propaganda of the state machine might be possible. Echoing Weil's distrust of conventional moralities, members of Solidarity sought to recall the proper meaning of words that had been deprived of their truth content by propaganda. When a general strike broke out in August of 1980, the media used deceptive terms to refer to the event, referring to how "An irregularity of supplies had been noticed" or noting that "There are certain breaks in production."[36] As Walesa says, "Obviously, the issue here was not only about words; words simply manifested a fear of the truth—truth, suppressed for so long, that it exploded with great force."[37] An aim of the propaganda was to leave the impression that those "disruptions" and "irregularities" were not caused by the workers but by the "workforce," an anonymous and impersonal entity. Against this Walesa talks of Solidarity as a "communion of people who did not wish to participate in a lie."[38]

Weil knew how precious are the words we can depend on. She also understood the vulnerability of the content of words to relations of power and subordination. Yet if it is true that we cannot allow all morality to be conflated with language, it is also true that we cannot afford to underestimate the force of language in a movement which aspires to freedom. This is something that Solidarity has understood in stressing the conception of solidarity as itself a spiritual resource. For, as Tischner says in "Solidarity of Consciences," a sermon delivered by Wawel, on October 19, 1980:

> History creates words in order that, in turn, they may create history. The word solidarnosc has joined the other, very Polish words to give new form to our days. Here are just some of these words: *freedom, independence, human dignity*—and today *solidarity*. Each of us feels the awesome gravity of meaning within this word.[39]

As Tischner explains it, the ethic of solidarity is an ethic of conscience. Significantly we cannot explain the workings of conscience simply as an internalization of social norms. Nor can we adequately account for it in Freud's terms as the internalization of parental authority, particularly the authority of the father. To an important extent conscience also constitutes an independent reality within an individual. We can listen to our conscience that calls from within, or we can stifle, or even deny it. But for Tischner "It is impossible to be in solidarity with people who have no conscience."[40] As he says:

> This is clear because to be in solidarity with a person means to rely on that person, and to rely on a person means to believe that there is something permanent in a person, something that does not fail. For this, however, one thing is needed: one must want to have a conscience.[41]

It might be more reliable and less risky not to depend upon conscience but rather on writing road signs that people have to comply with on the path of life. But this is not the way to build morality. As Tischner has it, "It is not a question of a military drill but of behaviour that issues from within."[42]

As in Weil, there is a recognition in Tischner's views that humans have the power to destroy in themselves the very thing that determines their humanity. Weil had learned from the *Iliad* how easily people can be reduced to matter through the conditions of their lives, but she was less clear whether conscience can always be restored if only one wants it enough. Her Christianity sometimes helped her to think that if people only turned towards God with the right spirit, they might be offered grace. But she had few illusions about what it would cost to help people in affliction. Strikingly the story of the Good Samaritan is at the heart of Weil's account of responding to affliction, as it is in Tischner's formulation of the relation of solidarity with politics:

> Take the parable of the Good Samaritan; he also lived in a particular society, in a world of a particular religion and politics. Nonetheless, his deed somehow breached the limits of this world, reached beyond the structures that this world imposed upon people. The good deed of the Samaritan was a response to the specific cry of a specific man. It is simple; someone is crying for help.[43]

It is important that the pain of this wounded man, for Tischner, is not the result of disease or advanced age but is a pain caused by someone else. It was one person who devised this lot for another. And, as Tischner says, "It is precisely this fact that is of importance; it is this that in a particular way stirs conscience and calls for solidarity. Nothing outrages one more than a gratuitous wound, a wound inflicted on one person by another."[44] This does not preclude solidarity with all who suffer, but our solidarity is particularly vital, strong and spontaneous, according to Tischner, with those who suffer pain that could be avoided— accidental, needless pain. Politics thus connects fundamentally with justice because, as Tischner asks, "Is it not the aim of politics to organize the arena of human life in such a way that one person does not inflict injury on another?"[45] For Tischner, "The communion of solidarity differs from many other communions in that 'for him' is first and 'we' come later."[46] Thus solidarity establishes specific bonds whereby one person joins with another to tend to the one who needs care.

Weil anticipated concerns about the nature of freedom and justice that spoke both to the difficulties of liberal moral theory and to the developing crises within Eastern European countries. For a time Solidarity seemed able to tap a similar vein of concern. Both recognized the need to go beyond distributive conceptions of justice.

Weil knew that an injustice is being done when a gratuitous wound is inflicted on one person by another. She recognized, as we have shown, that the word "justice" means two very different things: On the one hand, it touches "this profound and childlike and unchanging expectation of the good in the heart" ("Human Personality," 10); on the other, "the motive which prompts a little boy to watch jealously to see if his brother has a slightly larger piece of cake arises from a much more superficial level of the soul" (10). But the latter is the only level that we seem ready to acknowledge and give expression to within prevailing distributive conceptions of justice. It is as if we have lost a capacity to recognize the injustice done to people when it is not a matter of rights or unequal distribution. But Weil reawakens an older vision of justice that was known to the Greeks and to a biblical tradition:

> Every time that there arises from the depths of a human
> heart the childish cry which Christ himself could not refrain,
> "Why am I being hurt?", then there is certainly injustice.
> For if, as often happens, it is only the result of a
> misunderstanding, then the injustice consists in the
> inadequacy of the explanation. (11)

As it is, there are many people who get a positive pleasure from the cry while many others simply do not hear it, for "it is a silent cry, which sounds only in the secret heart" (11). But she also recognizes that these two states of mind are closer than they appear to be since often "deafness is complacently cultivated because it is agreeable and it offers a positive satisfaction of its own" (11). The recent movement towards solidarity in Poland was a precious moment in which people learnt to hear this cry and it was important because those who still have the power to cry out hardly ever express themselves, either inwardly or outwardly, in coherent language. Often the words through which they seek expression are quite irrelevant. This is all the more inevitable, as Weil has it, "because those who most often have occasion to feel that evil is being done to them are those who are least trained in the art of speech" (11). For Weil, it is important to hear the suffering behind the words.

For Weil what is sacred in every human being is an indomitable expectation "in the teeth of all experience of crimes committed, suffered, and witnessed, that good and not evil will be done to him" (10). This is important for Weil for "Although it is the whole of him that is sacred to me, he is not sacred in all respects and from every point of view" (10). As she explains it, "He is not sacred in as much as he happens to have long arms, blue eyes, or possibly commonplace thoughts. Nor as a duke, if he is one; nor as a dustman, if that is what he is" (10). So it is that we can understand the Psalm "So show us how to spend our time and acquire a heart of wisdom" (Psalm 90: 12). Perhaps this idea expressed in the Psalm was not unknown to Kant who felt awe before the moral law—but the tradition that we have inherited from him, which conceives morality in terms of a more superficial conception of reason, has found it impossible to sustain this insight.

Morality cannot be a matter of learning rule governed behavior. This is what encouraged Weil to place goodness beyond conventional morality, but also beyond a sense of rules or prescriptions that we legislate for ourselves. These ideas came alive within the spirit of solidarity for, as Tischner has it, solidarity does not need to be imposed from the outside by force. "This virtue is born of itself, spontaneously, from the heart. Did anybody force the Good Samaritan to bend over the wounded man who lay by the roadside?"[47] For Tischner "The virtue of solidarity is an expression of human goodwill. In essence we are all in solidarity, because in the depth of our souls we are people of goodwill. Solidarity is born out of goodwill and awakens the goodwill in human beings."[48] Echoing an image that was close to Weil's heart, he says, "It is like a warm ray of sun; wherever the ray falls, it leaves a warmth that radiates spontaneously."[49]

5 Dignity and freedom

Like Weil, who challenges the distinction between politics and
morality that is a feature of both liberalism and orthodox
Marxism, Tischner also challenges prevailing theories of exploitation for being too closely associated with a vision of political
economy separated from ethics. Often theories that refer to
ethics do so in an abstract way that does not illuminate concrete
realities. We have to realize that, along with the social and
economic changes that affect work in society, the nature of
exploitation changes too. Working people recognize exploitation
relatively easily—its basic sign is needless suffering. Solidarity,
like Weil, has recognized the natural good in work. As Tischner
has it, "Work is an expression of human goodwill. The one who
'exploits' and 'abuses work' is aiming at what is most human in a
person—at the very goodness of human will. . . . Exploitation
aims at human goodwill by demeaning it, belittling it, betraying
it."[50] So it is that an exploited person has every right to feel that
he or she has been betrayed.

Solidarity has sought to recover the dignity of human labor. It
has understood, as Weil did, that physical labor may be painful,
but it is not degrading, in her later writings she says that "Exactly
to the same extent as art and science, though in a different way,
physical labour is a certain contact with the reality, the truth, and
the beauty of this universe and with the eternal wisdom which is
the order in it" ("Human Personality," 17). It is a crime to take a
youth who has a vocation for this kind of work and "employ him
at a conveyor belt or as a piece-work machinist" (17); it is no less
a crime than to put out the eyes of the young Watteau and make
him turn a grindstone. But she also saw that the degradation of
any labor is sacrilege. Tischner likewise identifies the moral
suffering involved in such work, knowing that this does not
preclude physical suffering. However, as he explains it, "moral
suffering is something different, distinct and specific. To tiredness, fatigue, and exhaustion, to menacing hunger, something
else is added, like a dull burden, a pain of the soul, a pressure on
the heart."[51]

The Solidarity movement in Poland has challenged the moral
exploitation of work. Its members knew that in the final analysis

exploitation is not simply an economic issue. It concerns not only what happens to the product, but what happens to a human being. For Tischner, then, "To rebel against moral exploitation is a basic duty of conscience."[52] This is particularly significant within a state socialist regime that takes itself to be organized around the dignity of labor. As Walesa remembers it, through such rebellion millions of people in Poland were "shedding the invisible veneer of a lie and breaking the equally invisible barrier of fear."[53] While the continuous references in all the media "to production and its plunging levels demonstrated the role assigned to the workers: that of a tool that cannot strike, after all, since tools do not strike,"[54] workers knew the reality of their lives, whatever words of praise the regime used about the dignity of labor. Thinking back after the movement had been brutally suppressed, Walesa could still say that "Today's Solidarity is a communion of the people who do not wish to participate in a lie. This is the simplest ethic of the common working people."[55]

Solidarity has learned in practice what Weil had learned from her experience of factory work: the importance of sustaining workers in their sense of dignity. Tischner points out that "A mutiny of conscience against the moral exploitation of work brings to the forefront the question of human dignity. The question of dignity comes before the questions of work and compensation."[56] Workers know that neither hunger nor tiredness nor physical exhaustion is the worst. People feel a deep sense of betrayal as their goodwill in the work is treated with contempt. As Tischner describes it and as Weil knew from her own experience, "The worst thing is the sullen gust of treachery that disquiets each working day, each working hour."[57] But she was in many ways less hopeful than Tischner who could say that "Since treachery has occurred, fidelity must follow. Since humiliation has been inflicted, respect must ensue. Since there was degradation, equality must come."[58]

For Solidarity the democratic character of a given social movement is decided by an idea that gathers around itself the energy and hearts of people. Such was the idea of human dignity as a condition of meaningful freedom and equality in their new vision of democracy. For Tischner,

The obviousness of human dignity expresses itself in the

saying "They can starve us, but they may not dishonor us."
Freedom expresses itself thus, "Let us be ourselves."
Today, everybody finds within himself a sense of dignity,
workers, farmers, intellectuals, and scientists. The idea of
dignity is the background for all concrete hopes. Even in
the call for bread, there is a call for the recognition of
dignity. This is why today dignity is our democratic idea.[59]

This involves a fuller principle of absolute respect for human
beings than we can find within a liberalism that identifies respect
with an acknowledgement of legal and political rights. As Weil
knew, this version of respect often does not touch the injustice
that is done to people. We have to fear a situation where the very
injustice that destroys people goes under the name of justice. The
injustice of social structures is based on a fundamental lack of
respect for the human person.

A recognition of human dignity helps us appreciate the
importance of people learning to value themselves in their own
eyes. We can no longer separate an external transformation of
relations of power and subordination from an inner transformation of the self. In this sense psychology cannot be separated
from politics. Weil realized that the control people have over
their lives and the development of the inner resources to sustain
that control are crucial moral issues; but she also identified as
central to moral theory the inadequacy of seeing these resources
as the properties of individual personalities. That is, our
individual experience is in part a shared social and historical
experience. Often liberalism has led us to internalize and
privatize our pain, teaching us to blame ourselves for an
experience that is shared with others. At the same time,
however, it is inadequate and inappropriate to transfer responsibility from the individual self to the larger structures of power
and subordination.

Resisting the polarities of a liberal sociological understanding
that roots blame either in the individual or in the society. Weil
recognized that we have to shift the terms in which we think
about responsibility. She argued that people had to learn to take
responsibility for their own lives, rather than constantly blaming
others because people entirely lose responsibility by projecting it
onto an abstraction called "society". Nevertheless, as she saw,

people lose contact with reality if they underestimate the power of the 'Great Beast' to distort their moral consciousness and disposses them of the capacity for conscience. This is part of what Weil learned in Spain, where she did "not hear anyone express, even in private intimacy, any repulsion or disgust or even disapproval of useless bloodshed" (*Seventy Letters*, 108). With the appalling historical experience of regimes of power still fresh in our memories, it is important to repeat Weil's words that "once a certain class of people has been placed by the temporal and spiritual authorities outside the ranks of those whose life has value, then nothing comes more naturally to men than murder" (108).

It is a sad reflection on revolutionary politics in the twentieth century that it has been so easy for movements of liberation to think that if only their enemies could be destroyed, then a reign of goodness and peace could be established. This is a dangerous radicalism that takes us back to Robespierre. It is haunted by an abstract vision of the "enemy" who are no longer "like us." It can lead us to lose a sense of the enemy as living out their lives in contradictions that are often difficult for them to identify, let alone resolve. It is this tendency towards abstraction and the legislation of principles divorced from experience that has taken such a deep hold. In liberal culture we are encouraged to establish what is right in the abstract and then to praise or condemn people by reference to it, rather than focussing on the historical reality of people's lives. Weil saw the importance of this process of abstraction in Spain, but it is also part of the politics of the factory. Her movement towards Christianity gave her a way of preserving the sense of a realm of absolute goodness without losing sight of the moral significance of people's particular difficulties and suffering. Yet, at the same time, on another level a movement towards categorical judgment was an inescapable part of her own thinking. The influence of Christianity in her thinking reflected a struggle that was going on within herself. Ultimately it led to her own self-negation—the need to turn herself to matter to be somehow worthy of the religious vision she was increasingly held by.

This theme of the complexity of morality, which Weil can help us to focus, can be paralleled to a contemporary understanding of the personal as the political. It can make us aware of the contradictions within our lives—as we learn to acknowledge our different feelings, we learn of the complicated relation between feelings and ideals. It has been too tempting to simplify the issues we face in changing ourselves, as if change could be a matter of learning to put our own interests aside as "egoistic" and "selfish" and of accepting our duties and obligations. This notion of change, however, is a continuous strain in Weil's writings, fostering its own forms of moralism. But partly because Weil resisted any easy resolution of this tension, she can help us develop a sensitivity to the different levels of people's experiences. It is obvious that some will often go to great lengths to present the difficulties they face in changing as a way of defending the powers or privileges they have. But we also have to be wary of the sacrifices that some people make, knowing the resentments they often harbor at another level.

We have often ceased to be able to think meaningfully about what has value or meaning for us. We learn to adapt to what is expected of us, thinking this a sign of healthy citizenship. The danger of such conformism, as John Stuart Mill points out, is that often it leaves us with an abstract and attenuated grasp of our individuality.[60] For liberal individualism too often leaves us with a sense that we have to prove ourselves constantly to others to ward off feelings of inadequacy and failure so deeply rooted in the Protestant ethic. We can be wary of differences, only feeling secure if we are alike. It is as if we have lost our substance. We assume that all values are on the same level, reflecting individual choices. Where previously we might have talked about what was good, virtuous, worthy or desirable, we are now reduced to abstract speculation about values, and our language is in danger of losing contact with important realities. It comes to feel empty and abstract, unable to illuminate the tensions in our lived experience. Weil's discussion of uprootedness, the heart of *The Need for Roots*, addresses some of these issues.

Christianity helped Weil understand that, in their struggle against oppression, people must begin to reverse the structure of injustice by uprooting injustice from their own hearts. She understood that when we are tempted to project our sense of evil onto an enemy we move further away from grasping the truth about the levels of human suffering. In an interview with *The Catholic Worker*, Jean Goss-Mayr, a Christian pacifist who has worked for many years in Latin America, seems to echo an idea that had become central to Weil:

> We like to think that all the good is on our side, all the bad on the other. But it is not like that in reality. There is evil present in those who perform injustice, and also in those who submit to it. But from the moment that our primary concern becomes the human person, even the one who does evil, then our methods will change radically. No longer will I wish to attack another man's body, but rather his heart and his conscience. For everyone has a heart and a conscience.[61]

Thus contemporary liberation movements can help us appreciate the force and significance of Weil's view that it is a central moral and political task to reinstate a proper relationship between means and ends wherein the human person becomes the core value. This would be central to a meaningful vision of socialism.

Following the assassination of Benigno Aquino in 1983, Hildegard and Jean Goss-Mayr were invited to the Philippines to share their experiences in promoting Christian nonviolence. They knew that we have to learn to face the truth about ourselves if we are to challenge injustice. Dictatorship is possible because we submit to it. As Cory Aquino said when they first met her, "If I were to campaign, I'd campaign against the corruption, because I feel this is really the slavery of our people."[62] If this corruption starts at the top it very quickly descends to all levels of society as people allow themselves to be purchased for power, for privileges, for money. In any capitalist society, when money becomes a sign of virtue—as it has in Margaret Thatcher's England—people lose any sense of discretion as they flaunt their wealth as a sign of individual moral virtue. As the Goss-Mayrs say with reference to the Philippines, "This is why, from the very beginning, it is important to struggle against this corruption right among the people, to speak the truth, to denounce injustice, to refuse to participate in the corruption of the regime."[63] So it is that truth becomes a source of dignity and self-respect. People are no longer prepared to compromise with what they know in their hearts to be wrong just because others are doing so.

In the Philippines people were refusing to participate in the corruption any longer. They would say to their comrades, "If you play along with this, if you accept payment for your vote, then you are part of the corruption. You have to learn to say no, even if it costs you." As Jean Goss-Mayr knows,

> It was really a conversion that was necessary inside the people. Not to lie, not to steal, and not to kill. Very simple. And yet, when it comes, it is a source of terrific strength in the people. It allows them to fight to the death. It brings a spirit of joy because people feel that real life is springing up. They accept their suffering with more joy than the money that the corrupt government would have given them. And they feel themselves becoming fully human.[64]

So it is that people can learn to believe in themselves again. Dignity is the source of a radical transformation of people and of structures, as the Goss-Mayrs teach it in the seminars for opposition politicians, labor union leaders, and representatives of the religious base communities. The movement formed out of this in the Philippines worked courageously in the midst of great social misery, exploitation, and harsh repression. Its participants coined a word in their language, Tagalog, to give expression to nonviolence according to their understanding: "Alaydalang," offer dignity.

The suffering of the people, as well as their conviction that truth and justice are a strength, brought the people together, as Jean Goss-Mayr learned in his youth, when he joined the French army to kill Hitler, having learnt from the media that Hitler was the devil—if he killed Hitler then everything would be OK. As he says:

> I killed day and night for many weeks—but I never killed Hitler. I killed so well that I received medals. I was a war hero, but within myself I became more and more destroyed because I saw that I was killing peasants and workers, sons of families like my own, the people who I had wanted to defend.[65]

These were issues that had also deeply worried Weil. They connected to her desire for justice, which entailed learning through involvement. Yet in Weil's later writings involvement is necessarily tied for her to pushing herself into the annihilating condition of affliction. She was deeply hurt living in London in 1942 that she could not participate in the war. She was sure that affliction and a certain kind of death were her vocation. She desired affliction, but at the same time she wanted to be driven to it by necessity. She could not choose it for herself:

> If affliction were defined by pain and death, it would have been easy for me, while in France, to fall into the enemy's hands. But affliction is defined first of all by necessity. It is only suffered by accident or by obligation. And obligation is nothing without an opportunity for fulfilling it. It was to find such an opportunity that I came to London (*Seventy Letters*, 178–79)

But the war machine refused to send her on a mission to France. She reproached herself more and more grievously for having left occupied France. She did not want to kill, but she wanted to be part of the effort to defeat Hitler. But she was disappointed.

6 Spirituality and politics

In thinking about affliction we touch a deeper ambivalence in Weil's writings. Since affliction exists in the word, Weil found it difficult to go without her share of it. She found it almost unbearable to be separated from those who were suffering under the German occupation. More generally she had come to believe that only through affliction can one come to know the truth. This was true both in her Marxism and in her Christianity. As she says in her letter to Schumann, "Leaving aside anything I may be allowed to do for the good of other people, life for me means nothing, and never has meant anything, at bottom, except as an expectation of the revelation of the truth" (*Seventy Letters*, 178). At different moments in her life she got caught up with a particular form of self-negation, connected to her abiding hostility to notions of individuality and expression, which had originally separated her, as we have explained it, from Marx's conception of labor and had marked her spirituality. In Weil's thought there is no space within which to connect individuality with truth and thereby to bring us into a deeper relation with aspects of ourselves. I think this is a deep flaw in her writing, which is in tension with the intensity of her insight into human needs that often go unrecognized. She seems to have been torn between a sense of the value of human life rooted in community and a sense that we can only suffer in this world and torn by the thought that truth would only be revealed to her at the moment of death. As she writes to Schumann,

> I feel an ever increasing sense of devastation, both in my intellect and in the centre of my heart, at my inability to think with truth at the same time about the affliction of men, and the perfection of God, and the link between the two.
>
> I have the inner certainty that this truth, if it is ever granted to me, will only be revealed when I myself am physically in affliction, and in one of the extreme forms in which it exists at present.

She also says that even as a child "I always had the fear of failing, not in my life, but in my death" (178). In her last year in London this fear grew more and more intense. This is a tragic aspect of her spirituality. It brought her to the edge of an identification with death. It was as if she was punishing herself, turning her feelings against herself, because she was unable to find a way back to France on an all-important mission.

In 1938, Weil, to use her own words, had been "captured by Christ." But as Milosz argues, her biography is not a pious story of conversion. "Conversion," he says, is an inappropriate term for Weil. It is true, she said that before that she had never believed that such a thing, a personal contact with God, was possible. But she also says that through all her conscious life her attitude had been Christian: "One can be obedient to God only if one receives orders. How did it happen that I received orders in my early youth when I professed atheism?"[66] It was not simply a matter of professed faith for she knew that "Religion, in so far as it is a source of consolation, is a hindrance to true faith: in this sense atheism is a purification."[67] A rejection of any form of consolation is part of the continuity of her thought. For Milosz,

> The unique place of Simone Weil in the modern world is
> due to the perfect continuity of her thought. Unlike those
> who have to reject the past when they become Christians,
> she developed her ideas from before 1938 even further,
> introducing more order into them, thanks to the new
> light."[68]

The central aspect of this continuity was Weil's identification
with the afflicted. It was a commitment to the suffering and the
poor that mattered. This is also crucially understood by Fernando
Cardenal, a Trappist monk and activist as well as a minister of
culture in the Sandinista Revolutionary government, who thinks
that it is politically self-serving to accuse priests in Nicaragua of
legitimating a revolution that brings communism and atheism to
Nicaragua through their partisanship. Nicaragua, he says, is not a
country in which priests join an established political party in
order to come to power and not to serve the people. This vision
of politics as the competition of interests groups for power was
equally alien to Weil, who wanted to transform politics to a
concern with morality and the everyday conditions of people's
lives. As Cardenal has it—invoking again the story of the Good
Samaritan—"We're taking sides, yes—with the good Samaritan.
Here you have to take sides, you have to be 'partisan'. Either
you're with the slaughtered or you're with the slaughterers. From
a gospel point of view I don't think there was any other
legitimate option we could have made."[69] Nicaragua had been
governed for nearly half a century by an unjust, murderous, and
bloody dictatorship. In the final fifty-two days of the offensive
against Somoza's regime alone, fifty thousand persons died.

For Cardenal the revolution is legitimate in its own right and
does not need a priest to come and "give his blessing." As he
says, "Its legitimacy stems from the search for justice and
liberation of the exploited."[70] He is critical of a self-serving
anticommunism that distorts Marxism because it has not the
courage to see what Marxism really is—an approach to the social
sciences. It is inappropriate simply to identify Marxism with
atheism and then to accuse the Nicaraguan revolution of being
atheist. The reality is more complex. Often accusers do not know

what Marxism is, but "distort it and use a caricature of it to denigrate, to cheapen, and to malign, effortlessly and under-handedly, anything that's done for the poor."[71] Nor do people stop to think about who the atheists in Nicaragua are. As Cardenal has come to see it, the biblical concept of the atheist is the correct one for in the Bible the atheist is the one who does not love.

> That's who really denies God. I have comrades who say that they "don't believe", that they "don't have the faith". But they've been living a life of love, a life of commitment—they've given the gift of self and of sacrifice—for twenty years now in the cause of the poor. Certainly this will be acknowledged on the Last Day as geniuine faith. And I know others who, in the name of God, are slitting peasants' throats out on our border, to create panic.[72]

Cardenal, like Weil, prefers to be "with those who, without putting God's name on their lips, and perhaps without even formally knowing God, are doing all God asks to be done for a suffering people. They carry God's love, yes, and God's tenderness, in their hands and in their lives."[73] This cannot be said for those who with the name of God in their lips are sending their investment out of the country because they say the revolution is Marxist and atheist. For Cardenal they are attacking their own people in the name of God. Nor can he identify with those who, in the name of God, think themselves summoned to be a dominant class others should serve. As he says, "This is their faith. And this is their God, whittled down to the level of their privileges and interests."[74] It is an identification with the suffering of the poor that has returned what has been called liberation theology in Central and South America to a concern with truth and justice.

Hildegard Goss-Mayr lived in Latin America when liberation theology was first evolving. She learned

> You have to bring together your faith and the situation in which you live. You have to know your situation—know it well—and then you must ask yourself how the word of God,

how the Bible, helps you find an answer in this situation. So the old dilemma of the separation between faith and life is overcome. It is a matter of reincarnating Christian faith and love in the historical situation of the continent. From this perspective, it became very clear that the Church had to stand on the side of the poor.[75]

From this concern with the poor grew an involvement with the writings of Marx. But even though Marx can be read as challenging the separation of theoretical understanding from the everyday practice of living, Marx is not often interpreted in this way. Weil did not see Marx in this way. Understanding Marx's challenge involves grasping the importance of Hegel for Marx, but this is not the kind of reading of Marx that Weil reached. Rather, both Weil and liberation theology look to the Gospel for the vision and goal of society and to Marx for a social science to help in the practical building and understanding of the workings of society. Marx provides an analysis of the larger society within which the vision is to be realized. If the poor are to have justice, the structures of society must be transformed.

Fernando Cardenal is one of those Nicaraguan priests who believes "we can reach God in Nicaragua only through the mediation of the struggle for and with the poor."[76] They refuse to make a choice between politics and spirituality, knowing how these are connected in the historical experience of suffering and oppression. As Cardenal says:

> I think that those who are asking us to "define ourselves"
> are asking us to put asunder something that we feel God has
> joined together here in Nicaragua. What they want is for us
> to either abandon the priesthood or abandon the popular
> revolution—two things that I feel to be profoundly united in
> my life, in my faith, and in my spirituality.[77]

Thus Cardenal rejects the idea that the concern of priests can only be with the well-being of souls and not with the material struggles of people in this life. Weil was not consistent about the nature of this mission, but in many ways she prepared important ground for a relationship between spirituality and politics. She lived in dark times often without the support of a movement that could sustain her trust in people. She knew too well how the social machine can crush individual lives.

Part of what drew Weil to Christianity is its identification with the cause of the poor. Yet, although she went to great lengths to experience the lot of the poor, she was often isolated in her work. Still, she might well have welcomed a revolution, such as in Nicaragua, in which Christians have been so deeply and positively involved. It has given people like Cardenal a chance to make his faith more his own, he says, rather than something borrowed from others. He talks of being renewed from within by the love he sees practiced around him. The revolution has given him something that was often denied to Weil in her life—which possibly could have renewed her sense of hope and trust in people: For Cardenal, "The Sandanista Front provided me with the opportunity of daily risking my life for the cause of the poor—flesh-and-blood persons I see and esteem."[78] Weil had also constantly felt the need to be in touch with the reality of people's struggles. But often she was isolated in the insights she reached. Having suffered deeply because of her experiences in Spain, she might well have been suspicious of the heroism described by Cardenal, of people "going to their death with such courage, and with no wish but to fight to the death rather than place their fellow Sandanistas in danger."[79] But she might also have been affected by his sincerity in saying "All this was a great inspiration for me, and has been truly precious for me, for my faith and my religious life."[80]

Extending the place of thought in our lives is a constant theme in Weil's work, though it can also be in tension with what she writes about obedience and necessity. This tension is also present in Fernando Cardenal. He knows that any sort of "blind obedience" is foreign to everything that he stands for. In a truer liberty people have to be free to think for themselves; anything else is beneath human dignity. Expressing the truth as people is a duty, the truth is not an area in which people can compromise themselves. To do so would be to injure one's relationship to oneself, as Pascal grasped it. It is in this deeper sense that we can grow in our own authority. We cannot simply accept the beliefs of others as our own without undermining the weakening our very sense of self. So it was crucial for Weil to express the truth as she had seen it in Spain, even if this lost her her friends. She had to be true to herself. In this deeper freedom of expression is crucial. It does not simply exist as one value among others. But we have generally lost touch with a philosophical grasp of personal identity that could illuminate this for us. It comes to exist as a right we are ready to defend—but we are often bereft of ways of justifying the rights which we claim.[81]

For Cardenal the freedom to express truth does not have to conflict with his deep feeling for obedience to God. As he says, "there is something more complex and deeper here"[82] for in his thirty years of religious life he has never understood more profoundly, as he has with the revolution, the importance of "obedience in faith," which is obedience to the will of God. As he says, "I hear this call of obedience to God in the voices and cries of our people suffering in poverty."[83] "And my conscience tells me to obey God by being unconditionally faithful, always, every moment, to my people—to a people still suffering."[84] This is a vision of obedience Weil shared. Her commitment to the people was equally strong. It was only confirmed in her movement towards Christianity.

Weil's ideas were in large part also confirmed by her experience of factory work. Cardenal was changed by an experience of living with the poor in Medellin, Columbia, during the last year of his Jesuit training. As he describes his experience

[T]he ties of friendship, affection, and love that I was able to form with the people that lived in that slum, the discovery I made of their magnificent human values, right in the midst of the violation and deprivation of their rights, made their situation one I finally couldn't stand any more.[85]

In contrast Weil had experienced very little real fraternity in the factory, much more bitterness. It became hard for her, as a result, to sustain a belief that people would be able to make real changes in their lives. She was more impressed with the injuries done to people's lives. All the same, she did devote her life to fighting for the poor and afflicted. Her Christianity revealed to her, as it did to Cardenal, a God who is not neutral but a God who takes sides with the poor. Before Cardenal had left the shantytown of Medellin, as he says, "I swore to them I'd devote my life, all the life left to me, to fighting for the liberation of the poor."[86]

Weil helps us reconsider the relationship of politics to truth. We learn to identify politics with power and we expect morality to be compromised if it stands in the way of power. We do not expect politicians to tell the truth. We might even think them naive if they do so. For these reasons Ernesto Cardenal, a monk and poet who became Minister of Culture in the Sandanista government, says, "I don't consider myself a politician; I'm a revolutionary. By revolution, I understand the efficacious practice of love of neighbour, in society and individually. Politics, as it is traditionally understood—parties battling to gain power or keep it—is something of absolutely no concern to me."[87] Many people in Nicaragua do not identify the revolution with politics. They say that politics does not interest them but become enthusiastic when it is a matter of talking about what the revolution has done for their lives. Weil was working for a different conception of politics that would center on sustaining the dignity and self-worth of working people. It would have to listen to what people expressed as the truths of their lives, rather than assuming that injustice was only being suffered if rights were being infringed or laws broken.

While Weil shifted from reading Marx to reading the Gospel—though she never lost her involvement with Marx's writings or the sense of injustice informing them—Ernesto Cardenal was not drawn to Marxism by reading the Gospel. The Gospel made Marxists of him and many who have identified with liberation theology in Central and South America. As he describes himself, "I'm a Marxist who believes in God, follows Christ, and is a revolutionary for the sake of his kingdom."[86] Again, he sees no incompatibility between Christianity and Marxism because he sees them as concerned with different things: "Marxism is a scientific method for studying society and changing it. What Christ did was to present us with the *goals* of social change, the goals of perfect humanity, which we are to co-create with him. These goals are a community of brothers and sisters, and love."[87]

In Ernesto Cardenal's descriptions of how he came to the Christian faith there is a tension that we know from Weil, a tension concerning the importance of the self and the extent to which faith involves a renouncing of the self. We know the direction that Weil took, but it is important to recognize that there are different directions, though the temptation of self-negation remains deeply embedded even within a faith that defines itself in terms of love. This is how Ernesto Cardenal describes his experience of this tension and his resolution:

> First, I had a religious conversion, in which I discovered
> God as love. It was an experience of a loving faith, a falling
> in love. It made me want to live in the most isolated, lonely
> place I could find, to be alone with God. So I entered the
> Trappists. There I renounced everything, even my interest
> in poetry and my interest in politics. And my novice master,
> Thomas Merton, showed me that it shouldn't be this way.
> He showed me that just because I surrendered myself to
> God, that didn't mean that I was supposed to change my
> personality. I should keep being the same as before.[90]

It is a gift to have such a teacher, especially one like Merton who did not just say this conceptually but taught it in the way that he lived and acted. Merton had long grasped that the contemplative life would have to "go political." When he died in Bangkok, at a meeting of Eastern contemplatives, he had just given a talk on monastic life and Marxism.

Weil had also developed an interest in Zen and Eastern religions. She had gained an enormous breadth of vision that helped her provide a context for grasping changes in the quality of life in Western society. She was constantly concerned to understand the intellectual and spiritual ills of the twentieth century, with reconnecting science with the religious dimension of ancient Greek science and so restoring to Western thought its spiritual roots. It would end the division between religion and science, a division that distorted both. Equally, it would reconnect spirituality and politics, for her commitment was always with the poor and the afflicted. She took it to be her unique task to help give a truthful expression to their experience. She could be dogmatic and blind, as I think she certainly was in relation to Judaism, but her sympathies could also be generous and tender. She had an acute intelligence, sometimes it did not save her from turning inwards against herself. Her vision was often deeply pessimistic, but she never gave up. She was always seeking new directions. She refused to be morally defeated; she insisted on calling us to our own responsibilities—to think as truthfully and honestly as we can about the situation that faces us, as bleak as it might be. She did not underestimate the powers that we are up against if we are to realise truth, freedom and justice:

> The powerful forces that we have to fight are preparing to crush us; and it is true that they can prevent us from existing fully, that is to say from stamping the world with the seal of our will. But there is one sphere in which they are powerless. They cannot stop us from working towards a clear comprehension of the objects of our efforts, so that, if we cannot accomplish what we will, we may at least have willed it, and not just have blindly wished for it; and, on the other hand, our weakness may indeed prevent us from winning but not comprehending the force by which we are crushed. Nothing in the world can prevent us from thinking clearly. ("Prospects," 23)

We have to learn to tell the truth about ourselves as much as about the situation of others. Truth is inseparable from the quest for justice. So it is that morality cannot be separated from politics. We do not have to follow the path that Weil took to recognize the courage and truthfulness that there is in her voice. It is one of the rare voices that can illuminate predicaments that we still face.

Notes

Series editor's introduction

1 Some of these tendencies are discussed in Michael W. Apple, *Education and Power* (New York and London: Routledge and Kegan Paul, ARK Edition, 1985) and Ernesto Laclau and Chantal Mouffe, *Hegemony and Socialist Strategy* (New York and London: Verso, 1985).

2 See, for example, G. A. Cohen, *Karl Marx's Theory of History: A Defense* (Princeton: Princeton University Press, 1978).

3 Samuel Bowles and Herbert Gintis, *Democracy and Capitalism* (New York: Basic Books, 1986), p. 6.

4 *Ibid*, p. 3

5 *Ibid*, p. 18.

6 Among the best analyses of the weaknesses of traditional Marxist approaches of dealing with these social movements are Michael Omi and Howard Winant, *Racial Formation in the United States* (New York and London: Routledge and Kegan Paul, 1986) and Michele Barrett, *Women's Oppression Today* (London: New Left Books, 1980).

7 Andrew Levine, *Arguing for Socialism* (New York and London: Routledge and Kegan Paul, 1984).

Introduction

1 A useful account of the history of the publishing of Weil's works in English and the effect of this particular history on the common view of Weil is given in George A. White, "Simone Weil's Bibliography: Some Reflections on Publishing and Criticism," in George A. White, *Simone Weil: Interpretations of a Life* (Amherst, Ma.: University of Massachusetts Press, 1981).

2 The most comprehensive biographical account in English is Simone Pétrement's *Simone Weil: A Life*, Raymond Rosenthal, trans. (New York:

Pantheon, 1976). An excellent recent (and much shorter) account is Dorothy Tuck McFarland's *Simone Weil* (New York: Frederick Ungar, 1983). Still very good and an exception to the failure to take Weil's early political life and writings seriously is Richard Rees's *Simone Weil: A Sketch For a Portrait* (Carbondale, Il.: Southern Illinois University Press, 1966).

In the final stages of preparation of this manuscript (unfortunately too late for us to make use of in this work), two other books on Simone Weil came to our attention, both of which raise the level of (Anglo-American) academic consideration of Weil to a distinctly higher level. They are Mary Dietz, *Between the Human and the Divine: The Political Thought of Simone Weil* (Totowa, NJ.: Rowman and Littlefield, 1989); and Peter Winch, *Just Balance: Reflections on the Philosophy of Simone Weil* (Cambridge: Cambridge University Press, 1989)

3   The major texts in the Anglo-American revival of Marxism are Gerald A. Cohen, *Karl Marx's Theory of History: A Defense* (Princeton: Princeton University Press, 1978); William Shaw, *Marx's Theory of History* (Stanford: Stanford University Press, 1978); John McMurtry, *The Structure of Marx's World-View* (Princeton: Princeton University Press, 1978); Melvin Rader, *Marx's Interpretation of History* (New York: Oxford University Press, 1979); Allen Wood, *Karl Marx* (London: Routledge and Kegan Paul, 1981); Richard Miller, *Analyzing Marx: Morality, Power, and History* (Princeton: Princeton University Press, 1984); and Jon Elster, *Making Sense of Marx* (Cambridge: Cambridge University Press, 1986). See also Andrew Levine, *Arguing for Socialism: Theoretical Considerations* (London: Routledge and Kegan Paul, 1984).

1   *Early life and politics*

1   There are two elements of Simone Weil's biography that bear mention but are beyond the scope of this book. One is the vexing matter of her relationship with Judaism. Her parents, though offspring of religious Jews, were freethinking nonbelievers who raised their two children with no religious identification. It appears to have been only in her teens that Weil was told of her family's Jewish roots, and she claimed later never to have identified with the Jewish faith or people. Her later study of the Old Testament and Hebrew civilization, on which she passed an almost wholly negative judgment, evidences no indication that this assessment had any bearing on anything having to do with herself. In a life dedicated to understanding and combating oppression and affliction, Weil seemed notably insensitive to the plight of Jews in increasingly fascist-dominated Europe. While quite aware of the anti-Semitic core of nazism and right-wing nationalist movements in Europe, she never seems to have been particularly moved by this form of oppression, and she wrote in 1938 that a German domination of France would involve discriminations against Jews (and Communists) that in her eyes "would hardly matter in itself" (*Seventy Letters*, 99, letter to Gaston Bergery, a leftist member of the Chambre des Deputes). (For more on this, see Chapter 7, notes 12 and 25.)

The second biographical matter is Simone Weil's femaleness. She always regarded it a misfortune to have been born a girl, and, given the times in which she lived and what she wished to do with her life, she was not much mistaken; only in 1924 were women admitted to the highest rung of the French higher education system, the Ecole Normale Supérieure (which Weil entered in 1928). The world of trade union activity and workers' education, with which she became so involved in the 1930s, was virtually entirely male. Weil's mother, whose own role in life was quite a traditional one, brought Weil up to eschew "feminine" dress and manners. Simone Weil was not insensitive to the plight of women; when she later worked in a factory, she noticed that women were more badly treated than the men. And it can be argued that certain aspects of her developed outlook reflect an importantly "female" sensibility. But Weil did not identify with women, and she can even be seen as having tried hard, at least implicitly, to dis-identify with them. (For more on Weil's awareness of women as a distinct group of workers and some thoughts on the implications for feminist thought of some of Weil's ideas, see Chapters 6 and 8.)

Both the Jewish and the gender-identification issues are intelligently discussed by Mary Dietz, *Between the Human and the Divine: The Political Thought of Simone Weil* (Totowa, N.J.: Rowman and Littlefield, 1989). Robert Coles's recent biography, *Simone Weil: A Modern Pilgrimage* (Reading, Ma.: Addison-Wesley, 1987) contains an important chapter on Weil's anti-Semitism.

2   Regarding relations to their family backgrounds, it is interesting to compare Simone Weil to her illustrious contemporary Simone de Beauvoir. For de Beauvoir rejection of and rebellion against the confines of her conservative, traditional family was an integral part of her rejection of bourgeois society. While Weil's rejection of that culture was a good deal more extreme, her deep attachment and loyalty to her parents and brother was one of the fixed emotional points of her life.

An extended and illuminating comparison between Simone de Beauvoir and Simone Weil is very nicely drawn by John Hellman, *Simone Weil: An Introduction to Her Thought* (Waterloo, Ontario: Wilfrid Laurier University Press, 1982), ch. 1.

3   Anarcho-syndicalism expressed specifically French conditions. Compared to Britain and Germany, France industrialized late; in the late nineteenth century the French labor movement was still dominated by relatively small-scale production, a setting in which the syndicalist dream of industry without bosses could seem viable. Labor's hostility to the state and to political organization in general was fostered by the particularly brutal actions of the French state in repressing the 1848 uprising and the Paris Commune in 1871.

The trade union movement in France reflected this syndicalist sentiment. Unions were organized into *syndicats*, small units based in a town, a craft, or an industry; only slowly did they federate at the national level. Compared to British and German unions they were poorly organized.

The history of French socialism prior to World War I also contributed to a much stronger separation between the workers' movement and the specifically political struggle for socialism than existed in Germany, Italy, or Great Britain. First, in Germany liberal or republican sentiment had no place to go but the workers' movement, thus pulling the latter in a reformist direction absent in France, where the independent source of republican sentiment freed the working class movement to be more revolutionary. Second, the French socialist movement predated the workers' movement and took a separate and relatively independent trajectory.

4 The quotation from Simone Pétrement, *Simone Weil: A Life*, Raymond Rosenthal, trans. (New York: Pantheon, 1976), p. 58, about Simone Weil at the Ecole Normale Supérieure is from V.-H. Debidour, *Simone Weil, ou le transparence* (Paris: Plon, 1963), p. 24.

5 A lycée is a high school that extends into what would be the first two years of college in the United States.

6 The quotation about Simone Weil as a teacher is from "Simone Weil professeur" written by four of her students, cited in Pétrement (*op. cit.*), p. 78.

7 In the courses she taught for workers at St.-Etienne, Weil worked with Urbain Thévenon, a leader of the union movement in the area. Weil became very close to him and to his wife Albertine, to whom she wrote some of the letters that provide an important window to Weil's thinking and that we cite below.

8 Quoted in Pétrement (*op. cit.*), p. 146.

9 Quoted in Pétrement (*op. cit.*), pp. 76–77. On the contrast between the true bonds created by common work and the ephemeral ones of shared political opinion, see Pétrement (*op. cit.*), p. 76, and Geraldi Leroy, "Simone Weil et le parti Communiste," in *Cahiers Simone Weil*, Septembre, 1980, p. 208 3:208.

10 Quoted in Pétrement (*op. cit.*), p. 118.

11 Quoted in Pétrement (*op. cit.*), p. 151.

12 Quoted in Pétrement (*op. cit.*), pp. 87–88.

13 Quoted in Pétrement (*op. cit.*), p. 161.

14 Quoted in Pétrement (*op. cit.*),.. pp. 147–48.

15 Quoted in Pétrement (*op. cit.*), p. 122.

16 For a history of the Third International in the 1920s and 1930s see Fernando Claudin, *The Communist Movement: From Comintern to Cominform*, Brian Pearce, trans. (New York: Monthly Review Press, 1975), vol. 1; Albert S. Lindemann, *A History of European Socialism* (New Haven: Yale Univesity Press, 1983); and Leszek Kolakowski, *Main Currents of Marxism* (Oxford: Oxford University Press, 1978), vol. 3.

7 Until 1933 or 1934 Marx's early writings, especially the *Economic and Philosophical Manuscripts*, were not available in French. It is not clear when Simone Weil read them; she refers to them directly in her writings on Marxism only in 1937. (See Chapter 2, section 2, and Chapter 3, section 5).

8 Quoted in Pétrement (*op. cit.*), p. 118.

19 Quoted in Pétrement (*op. cit.*), p. 118.

20 Pétrement (*op. cit.*), p. 118.

21 Some of Weil's ambivalence toward political organizations—and the PCF in particular—is illuminated in Mary Dietz's book, *Between the Human and the Divine: The Political Thought of Simone Weil* (*op. cit.*). Dietz penetratingly describes Weil's ambivalent attitude to social entities—that they are spiritually and humanly crushing, yet can nurture and provide a needed sense of belonging—as well as the ramifications of this ambivalence in her thought. Dietz describes (Chapter 4, section 3, and elsewhere) Weil's fear of collectivity, which is a major theme in her *Reflections Concerning the Causes of Liberty and Social Oppression*. Weil's remarks on this matter in *Reflections* are no doubt partly a product of her deep disillusionment with the Communist party and other left groups. But in the earlier period described in our account—up to 1932 or 1933—her antipathy to political organizations, and to the PCF in particular, was not so firmly established.

22 Quoted in Pétrement (*op. cit.*), p. 137.

23 Weil's perceptions of Germany and the role of the Communist party there are detailed in her series of articles translated as "The Situation in Germany."

24 Quoted in Pétrement (*op. cit.*) p. 159.

25 Boris Souvarine was a Trotskyite and a prominent PCF member in the early 1920s and then a prominent dissident Communist after his expulsion in 1924. He founded several journals, including *Critique sociale*, for which Simone Weil wrote in the 1930s. Weil met him in 1932, and he remained for her an important friend, political associate, and confidante. Like her, and in distinction from most Trotskyists of that time, Souvarine eventually became entirely and unqualifiedly hostile to Soviet-style communism.

26 Quoted in Pétrement (*op. cit.*) p. 151.

27 Quoted in Pétrement (*op. cit*), p. 176.

28 The quotation from André Weil about Trotsky and Simone Weil is from an interview with Malcolm Muggeridge appended to his collection of Weil's writings, *Gateway to God*.

29 Quoted in Pétrement (*op. cit.*), p. 198.

2 *Simone Weil on Marxism*

1 We will address the difficult problem of the gender of pronouns by sometimes using masculine and sometimes feminine forms. Weil herself always uses the masculine form when she is speaking of workers in general. And, though she has some perceptive things to say about women workers in particular situations, it seems evident that she thinks of the category "workers" in general as being male.

2 In Weil's last writings on Marx she adds a less flattering diagnosis to her

primarily generous assessment of the contradictions in Marx's thought. She suggests that Marx was drawn by the prestige accompanying the "appearance of force," which his theory claims is possessed by the proletariat in their role as the class representing the future ("Fragments, London 1943," 160). (See discussion of the moral effect of Marxism on the workers' movement, chapter 3, section 2.)

3 We do not mean to imply that all differences between Lenin and Kautsky are merely differences in emphasis, but only that some of the ones most relevant to Simone Weil's criticisms of Marxism are and also that there are important broad areas of agreement. The more historically significant disagreements— whether socialism could take place before capitalism had fully developed, and the legitimacy and necessity of a dictatorship of the proletariat (both of which Lenin affirmed and Kautsky denied)—are somewhat less central to the aspects of orthodox Marxism with which Weil grappled.

4 Translated by Larry Schmidt as "On Rationalization" (as yet unpublished).

5 See Rainer Traub, "Lenin and Taylor: The Fate of 'Scientific Management' in the (Early) Soviet Union," *Telos* 37 (Fall 1978), 84.

6 See Lenin, "The Taylor System—Man's Enslavement by the Machine," in *Collected Works* (Moscow, 1964), 20:153.

7 Weil was wrong in her supposition that Lenin never saw the inside of a factory, though she may well have been correct about Trotsky. Nevertheless, Lenin was never actually a factory worker, and Weil's central point here that neither great leader of the proletariat was deeply acquainted with the conditions that in Weil's mind were at the center of proletarian servitude still stands.

8 The position that power relations are to be included within "social relations of production" is taken by William Shaw in *Marx's Theory of History* (Stanford: Stanford University Press, 1978). Richard Miller, in *Analyzing Marx: Morality, Power, and History* (Princeton: Princeton University Press, 1978), also includes power relations within the social relations of production, but he is referring to power and control of economic life in society as a whole rather than specifically to work relations.

9 In implicit support of Weil's criticisms of Marx on this point (whether the impetus behind productive development is stronger than the social forces ranged against it), recent theorists of the labor process, such as Harry Braverman, in *Labor and Monopoly Capital: The Degradation of Work in the Twentieth Century* (New York: Monthly Review Press, 1974), have argued that capitalists often sacrifice efficiency of production in order to gain greater control over workers. That is, the social power of the capitalist class is stronger than the impetus to efficient use of the productive forces.

10 As this variability indicates, historical materialism need not take the form of a strict determinism and is thus broader than the economic determinism with which orthodox Marxism is usually associated. At the same time "historical materialism" has also been understood even more broadly and vaguely to mean that an understanding of history must be grounded in the economic

organization of society, including the means and relations of production. Such a view can be severed from many of the other tenets of orthodox Marxism with which it is historically connected.

11 Simone Weil's criticisms of the assumption of progress within the scheme of historical materialism are quite relevant to the contemporary revival within Anglo-American philosophy of an orthodox version of Marxism. For example both Gerald Cohen, in *Karl Marx's Theory of History: A Defense* (Princeton: Princeton University Press, 1978), and Allen Wood, in *Karl Marx* (London: Routledge and Kegan Paul, 1981), sympathetically expound and to some extent defend the notion that productive forces do tend to develop and increase throughout history and that they do so essentially *because* their doing so is conducive to human betterment. Wood and Cohen attempt implicitly to counter a Weil-like criticism of Marxism by trying to defend this view without any hint of appeal to spiritual or moral forces within history, relying only on the motivations of rational agents.

Although it is not possible to explore in any detail the complex arguments that Cohen and Wood offer in defense of the theory of productive forces, it is worth briefly indicating how Weil provides the resources to criticize such views. First, Weil would reject the view, sometimes implied by Cohen, that the greater level of material well-being created by capitalism itself is necessarily conducive to human betterment and (accompanying this view) that socialism will be superior both morally and productively in making such material well-being available to all. For Weil material well-being does not necessarily bring in its wake greater dignity or moral well-being.

Cohen and especially Wood sometimes link the development of productive forces and human well-being more intimately by saying that productive forces develop "human productive powers." But for Weil the most important productive powers are those used in the process of work; and, she argues, an increase in productive forces (in the sense of increased output, efficiency, and the like) is often very much at odds with the utilization of human powers of judgment, intelligence, and understanding in the work process. Many of the most impressive achievements of capitalist industry bring about a stultification rather than an enhancement of human productive powers of the sort Weil is concerned about.

Sometimes Cohen makes a different argument—that productivity advances human productive power in that it provides (the possibility of) much greater leisure time in which to develop one's human creative capacities. But for Weil this view severs human powers too much from the process of production itself. For her the important use of human powers is *within* work itself, not outside of it.

For an excellent critique of Cohen along Weilian lines—arguing essentially that his version of Marx's theory of history has not broken sufficiently with Hegelian assumptions of a "hidden mind" or "superintending agent" assuring that history progresses toward "the good"—see Joshua Cohen, "Review of G. Cohen, *Karl Marx's Theory of History: A Defense*," *Journal of Philosophy* 79 (1982): 253–73.

12 In a brief essay from 1937, "A Note on Social Democracy," Weil berates the

Popular Front government of Léon Blum for failing to institute appropriate reforms in light of the factory sit-ins of 1936 (discussed below). Mass consciousness (e.g., as manifested in the sit-ins) is, she avers, virtually never in touch with the real significance of a specific political conjuncture; and leaders who have the interests of the oppressed at heart (such as Blum) should not take the specific demands of the masses as a guide to the appropriate measures and reforms to be put forth at such times.

13 There is a somewhat significant philosophical difference between the theorists of the Second International (especially Kautsky) and Lenin regarding the significance of scarcity for politics and revolution. Kautsky argued that a true socialist revolution could not take place prior to the full development of all the productive forces of a society—hence prior to the full development of capitalism. For this reason Kautsky opposed the Russian Revolution, since in 1917 Russia was in only an early stage of capitalist development. Kautsky's view continues to be held by those who see the Soviet Union as a class society and who claim that such a development was inevitable since the Revolution took place before scarcity was conquered. Lenin, by contrast, argued that as long as the proletariat was the leading force, the Revolution would have a genuinely socialist character, even though the forces of production were not highly developed. The stage of capitalism could in a sense be skipped.

Despite this historically momentous difference between Kautsky and Lenin, there was a large measure of theoretical accord. Lenin agreed that the development of productive forces is a precondition for a truly nonoppressive society; prior to this, although the power of the bourgeoisie could be (and had been) undermined, the society could not yet truly be a Communist one. And so he saw one of the first tasks of the Revolution to be the development of the forces of production; this task was seen as an essentially bourgeois one, but one which in the Soviet Union was to be carried out by the proletariat.

Thus for both Kautsky and Lenin the conquest of material scarcity was an essential precondition for the building of a fully and truly non-oppressive society. Hence Weil's criticisms are applicable to both of them.

14 In fact Weil suggests a dialectic of power that is in some ways analogous to the Marxist materialist dialectic: Power can overreach its material base, and when it does so, it becomes less secure. This does not, however, mean that the oppressive power will be likely to disappear (and here the view is not analogous to Marxism) but only that that is at least a possibility. (See *Reflections*, 75–77.)

15 In her later essay "La Rationalisation" Weil makes even more explicit than she does in *Reflections* that the advantages of greater output must be given a legitimate role in determining the form of work organization, alongside concern with the workers' own well-being. She even implies—here going quite beyond the position taken in *Reflections*—that these two concerns are somehow to be given *equal* importance. In *Reflections* it is clear that the impact of the form of work on the worker's dignity and well-being should be the primary desideratum in the design of work organization; and this

emphasis is returned to in the Christian writings on work, such as "Factory Work" and *The Need for Roots*.

16 There seem to be two slightly distinct strands in Simone Weil's thinking about liberty and necessity. One is that human nature is too weak to be able to handle the situation in which necessities, obstacles, are absent. (See *Reflections* 84). The second is that liberty is strictly meaningless outside of the context of necessity (80). The second seems the more deeply grounded in the thought of *Reflections*.

17 The description given here is not meant to encompass all of the conditions that point toward a socialist revolution, but only those—sometimes called "subjective" factors—concerning the forming of the proletariat into a revolutionary agent. Marx and Marxism of course present "objective" factors as well—economic crises, monopolization, and the like.

18 Lenin, "One Step Forward, Two Steps Backward," quoted in Russell Jacoby, *Dialectic of Defeat: Contours of Western Marxism* (Cambridge: Cambridge University Press, 1981), p. 69.

19 Weil's argument on this point is akin to a criticism of historical materialism given by Andrew Levine in *Arguing For Socialism: Theoretical Considerations* (London: Routledge and Kegan Paul, 1984), pp. 175–77. Levine suggests that orthodox Marxism has tended to assume too readily that the interests that the proletariat has in socialist revolution translated into a "capacity" to bring about that revolution. He argues, similarly to Weil, that the forces Marxists actually cite are not sufficient to instil these capacities.

A difference, at least in emphasis, between Weil's view and Levine's is that Weil claims that on Marx's own view the forces of capitalism positively *undermine* the capacity for revolution, whereas Levine makes the less radical argument that Marx fails to demonstrate that those capacities are being created under capitalism.

20 Rosa Luxembourg, "Organizational Questions of Russian Social Democracy," quoted in Jacoby (*op. cit.*), p. 70.

21 Weil's criticisms of the Marxist view of the proletariat as revolutionary agent yield a problem with labor process theorists, such as Braverman (*op. cit.*), who makes criticisms similar to Weil's of the theory of productive forces. For while like Weil Braverman decries the progressive severing of ties between conception and execution in work under advanced industrial capitalism, he does not examine the implications of these changes in work for the psychology of the worker—that is, for their effect on workers' abilities to bring about radical change. Weil would see the evidence offered by Braverman of the further diminution of judgment and intelligence in work within advanced industrial societies (including Communist ones) as a further confirmation of her pessimism about radical change coming from workers themselves.

This point may seem not to be a direct criticism of Braverman, who draws no implication for revolutionary strategy or possibilities from his analysis; in fact, Braverman claims to be abjuring a focus on "subjective" factors altogether. However, as Anthony Giddens points out in his critique of

Braverman ("Power, The Dialectic of Control, and Class Structuration," in *Profiles and Critiques in Social Theory* [Berkeley: University of California Press, 1982], p. 207), this seeming methodological principle has the effect of omitting any role workers themselves might have played—e.g., through resistance to the management initiatives that Braverman analyzes—in determining the final shape of work organization.

In omitting a concern with the moral psychology of workers, Braverman is enabled to preserve a sense of revolutionary hope, without examining whether the "de-skilling" he describes would have the effect of undermining, as Weil suggests, a truly "revolutionary psychology" in the workers; but at the same time, as Giddens points out, Braverman's view ignores the less revolutionary changes workers may have been able to effect in resisting this de-skilling. (See note 24.)

22 Weil fails to challenge one element of the Marxist picture of how the proletariat comes to develop solidarity and to become a revolutionary force—namely, the claim that the conditions of the working class are being made increasingly uniform—a claim that, especially since Weil's time, has seemed particularly doubtful.

23 Weil's views regarding the sit-ins of 1936 are here being inferred in good measure from letters she wrote to two factory managers, Bernard and Detoeuf. These letters may be thought to be suspect as sources of Weil's final views on these matters. Weil's acceptance of the role of management in these letters may be merely a matter of practicality; she is, after all, attempting to get these men to make actual changes in the organization of their factories, and it would thus behoove her to use arguments she thinks are likely to be successful with them. She might well be keeping her true and more radical sentiments out of these letters.

Yet, as Mary Dietz emphasizes in *Between the Human and the Divine: The Political Thought of Simone Weil* (Totowa,. N.J.: Rowman and Littlefield, 1989), Weil was not clear regarding acceptance or rejection of managerial authority nor of other forms of political authority. It is not only in the letters but in *Reflections* as well that she fails to make a wholesale challenge to the prerogatives of management. Dietz sees Weil's position as reflecting a deeply-rooted ambivalence regarding authority. While this may well be true, we are also trying to indicate that one can still find in Weil something like a consistent position regarding the dignity of the worker and the authority of management.

24 In *Making Sense of Marx* (Cambridge: Cambridge University Press, 1985), Jon Elster argues in detail that Marx specifies no mechanism by which optimal development of forces of production are brought about in history; in particular, Elster supports Weil's skepticism whether Marx provides any account of how class struggle is meant to contribute to developing the forces of production.

25 Since Weil's time a body of literature has developed that argues that the organization of work in the workplace has been a continuous source of struggle between workers and management, with the work organization at

any given time representing the outcome of this constant struggle. See for example Richard Edwards, *Contested Terrain: The Transformation of the Workplace in the 20th Century* (New York: Basic Books, 1979). This literature is itself a reaction (though also a tribute) to Harry Braverman (*op. cit.*) and others (see notes 9 and 21), who argue that changes in workplace organization and technology have been determined primarily by employers' desire for control of their workers (often at the expense of greater productivity). Edwards' response to this line of argument (in accord with the view of Giddens, above, note 21) is to emphasize the role that workers' own initiative and resistance has played in shaping workplace organization.

Both of these strands within "labor process theory" accord with Weil's focus on the importance of work organization in the well-being of the worker. Yet Weil's views are substantially closer to Braverman's, who sees power in this area as residing almost entirely in the hands of management and owners, than to Edwards' and Giddens'. Perhaps it was Weil's own historical experience of the time that led her to leave no theoretical space to the idea that struggles of workers could themselves decisively shape the direction of technology and workplace organization.

Yet surely the developments in this direction described by Edwards and others would have been welcome to Weil. Moreover, struggles of workers to shape workplace organization would have given concrete social and structural embodiment to Weil's theme of the workers' continuous struggle for dignity.

3 Simone Weil on Marx: Revolution

1 By virtue of its support for France's participation in World War I, the French Socialist Party had been written off by many leftists—Simone Weil among them—who had very strong antiwar sentiments.

2 In an essay from 1937, "The Power of Words," Simone Weil criticizes other terms (such as "fascism," "communism," "capitalism") that, like "revolution," generate intense political passions but that Weil believes have come to lose all meaning or, in any case, whose usage has come to block clear thinking in the political arena.

3 See also "Is There a Marxist Doctrine?": "A visible revolution never takes place except to sanction an invisible revolution already accomplished" (184).

4 The duality in a conception of revolution—that it has a "good" as well as a "bad" meaning—is preserved in Weil's *Need For Roots*, the major political work of the later, Christian period of her life, written in 1942–1943:

> Under the name of revolution, and often using identical slogans and subjects for propaganda, lie concealed two conceptions entirely opposed to one another. One consists in the transformation of society in which a way that the working-class may be given roots in it; while the other consists in spreading to the whole of society the disease of uprootedness which has been inflicted on the working class. It must not be said or supposed that the second operation can ever form a

prelude to the first; that is false. They are two opposite roads which do not meet. (46)

5 We characterized the viewpoint with which Marx's materialism is to be contrasted as "idealist" or "moralistic," But "idealism," associated in Marx's eyes with Hegel, cannot be identified with "moralism" and in Hegel even constitutes a criticism of it. For Hegel agrees with Marx that abstract moral criticism is not effective in changing reality; thus, though himself an idealist, Hegel too is critical of moralism. However, in contrast to Marx, Hegel believes that the ultimate motive force behind real social change lies in the realm of ideas (but ideas rooted in the real movement of history, not abstract moral ideas of right and wrong)—that is, in manifestations of the World Spirit. Thus Marx's materialism, with which Weil is in agreement on this point, contrasts with both Hegel's idealism and with a moralism of which Hegel is critical.

6 Interestingly, in the beginning of "Is There a Marxist Doctrine?" Weil reiterates her sense of a difference between the early Marx and the "orthodox" Marx. The young Marx was not a materialist, she says: "As a young man he had set out to work out a philosophy of labor in a spirit very closely akin, at bottom, to that of Proudhon. A philosophy of labor is not materialist. . . . Man is not reduced to [matter]; he is placed in opposition to it" (169). The approving tone of Weil's statement of this position seems not entirely consistent with the rest of her analysis in this essay, which seems to imply that man as a laborer *is* in fact social "matter," subject to the unrelenting operation of force and necessity. While Weil continues to seek a way to make labor a sphere of human dignity, the source of that dignity had by the end of her life come increasingly to lie in contact with the supernatural, rather than in any concrete change in institutions—or, to be more precise, in social formations that have been infused with the appropriate religious and spiritual meaning. (Exploring this further lies beyond the scope of this book, but throughout Weil's writings in the 1940s there is a tension between a continuing search for forms of reorganizing the structure of work so as not to degrade the worker and the thought that labor inevitably means suffering and affliction so that dignity can only lie not in changes in the way work is organized but rather by infusing work with a religious and spiritual sense that involves, in part, the laborer's consenting to and even embracing the necessity of his labor and the suffering that accompanies it.)

7 While for Weil humanity in its social and worldly being is subject to force that is indifferent to the good, at the same time she sees the *natural* world, when properly understood, as in some way "reflecting" the good. One of Weil's major criticisms of modern science is that its form, methods, and results fail to reflect this good, whereas Greek science (as exemplified, for example, in the notion of equilibrium) was "more concerned to comprehend the secret complicity of the universe in respect of the good" ("Classical Science and After," 12). We am grateful to Dorothy McFarland for reminding us of this passage.

4 *Liberty*

1 Weil did not engage systematically with liberalism in the sense that she was continually thinking in relation to Marxism. But if she did not treat it as a distinct and unified tradition of thought, she often engaged with challenging what we can recognize as central aspects of a liberal tradition.

2 Weil was fundamentally influenced by Descartes, on whom she wrote her diploma dissertation for the Ecole Normale during the 1929–1930 school year. Entitled "Science and perception in Descartes," it begins by asking whether there is a method for obtaining truth available to all. "Nothing is more important for each man to know for it is nothing less than a question of knowing whether I ought to submit the conduct of my life to the authority of scientific thinkers, or solely to the light of my own reason; or rather . . . whether science will bring me liberty, or legitimate chains" (quoted by Dorothy Tuck McFarland [New York: Frederick Ungar, 1983], p. 25).

3 The liberty typical of a strand of liberalism that stretches from Hume and Mill to the consensus dominant in Anglo-American thought and politics today sees wants or preferences, whatever they may be, irrespective of significance, as being constrained. It sees the subjects or agents of freedom as merely the loci of such wants and preferences. Steven Lukes thinks

> This explains why liberals are often drawn to an "opportunity" rather than an "exercise" conception of freedom, according to which my freedom is solely a matter of how many doors are open to me. For opportunities are external to agents and can be identified without reference to them or their purposes. (*Marxism and Morality* [Oxford: Oxford University Press, 1985], 76)

4 Karl Marx, *Foundations of the Critique of Political Economy (Rough Draft)*, Martin Nicolaus, trans. (Middlesex: Penguin, 1973), p. 464.

5 Lukes (*op. cit.*), p. 79.

6 Karl Marx, "Results of the Immediate Process of Production," in *Capital*, Ben Fowkes, trans. (Harmondsworth, Eng.: Penguin Books, 1976) vol. 1, p. 1033.

7 Jules Lagneau, *Célèbres leçons et fragments*, 2nd ed. (Paris: Presses Universitaires de France, 1964), p. 194.

8 Simone Pétrement, *Simone Weil: A Life*, trans. Raymond Rosenthal (New York: Pantheon, 1976), p. 32.

9 Quoted in McFarland (*op. cit.*), p. 22.

10 Weil never really broke with the orthodox vision of Marx throughout her writings on Marx, though she shifted her sense of what can be hoped from a social revolution. The source of moral insight does not come from a struggle against existing conditions of production but always from an independent source that in her later writings is conceived platonically—as coming from beyond this world. Some of the issues in this difficult history are raised by Lukes (*op. cit.*).

11 Issues within the liberal conception of freedom have recently centered on Isaiah Berlin's two concepts of liberty. Berlin's own second thoughts can be found in the useful introduction he wrote to his *Four Essays on Liberty* (Oxford: Oxford University Press, 1969). A useful discussion of freedom in terms of options is in John Gray's "Freedom, Slavery and Contentment," in *The Frontiers of Political Theory*, Micheal Freeman and David Robertson, eds. (Brighton: The Harvester Press, 1980).

12 An issue Victor Seidler has explored further in *Kant, Respect and Injustice: The Limits of Liberal Moral Theory* (London: Routledge and Kegan Paul, 1986).

13 In this discussion Weil is clearly drawing on Plato's discussion of the "tyrant" in *The Republic*, F. M. Cornford, ed. and trans. (Oxford: Oxford University Press, 1941), Book IX 5766.

14 An insight that has become familiar in the philosophy and social theory of the Frankfurt School, particularly in the writings of Adorno and Benjamin. For a useful account of their relationship to issues of individuality and autonomy see Susan Buck-Morss, *The Origin of Negative Dialectics* (Brighton: The Harvester Press, 1977).

15 A useful reassessment of this tradition is found in Martin Buber's *Paths to Utopia* (Boston: Beacon Press, 1962). That the relationship of Marx's writings to what he called the tradition of "utopian socialism" is more complicated and interesting than Marx himself initially presented is becoming more generally appreciated. An interesting example is provided by Barbara Taylor's *Eve and the New Jerusalem* (London: Virago, 1983).

16 Georg Lukács' discussion of reification in his *History and Class Consciousness*, Rodney Livingstone, trans. (London: The Merlin Press, 1917) is one of the defining insights of a renewed appreciation of Hegel within Western Marxism. It had an enduring influence on the writings of the Frankfurt School. If Weil reaches similar insights, it is from quite different sources. It is part of her originality but also part of the difficulty of positioning her work in relation to Western Marxism. A useful discussion of this tradition is provided by Russell Jacoby in *The Dialectics of Defeat: Contours of Western Marxism* (Cambridge: Cambridge University Press, 1981).

17 A similar insight appears in the writings of Raymond Williams in, for instance, his *The Country and the City* (London: Chatto and Windus, 1973) and the more recent writings of John Berger, who takes up this theme in *Pig Earth* (London: Writers and Readers, 1979).

18 Some of the implications of an identification of masculinity with reason are drawn in Susan Griffin's moving book, *Pornography and Silence* (London: The Women's Press, 1981). These issues are also treated in Victor Seidler's "Reason, Desire, and Male Sexuality," in *The Cultural Construction of Sexuality*, Pat Caplan, ed. (London: Tavistock, 1981).

19 A useful discussion of this distinction and its place in organizing moral theory in the twentieth century is provided by Bernard Williams in his *Ethics and the Limits of Philosophy* (Cambridge: Harvard University Press, 1985).

5 *Oppression*

1 This issue is dealt with in her 1933 essay "Prospects: Are We Heading for the Proletarian Revolution?" as well as in her essay "On Lenin's Book *Materialism and Empiriocriticism.*" These are both part of an assessment of the October Revolution in Russia.

2 Dorothy Tuck McFarland, *Simone Weil* (New York: Frederick Ungar, 1983), p. 28.

3 This and all subsequent translations of *Sur la science* are taken from McFarland (*op. cit.*). Page references in the text are to the French original. Parts of the work have been translated as "Science and Perception in Descartes."

4 McFarland (*op. cit.*), p. 28.

5 Although developed from quite different sources, there are some striking similarities with the Frankfurt School and its assessment of the nature of science as an integral part of the Enlightenment inheritance. See, for instance, Theodor Adorno and Max Horkheimer's *Dialectic of Enlightenment*, John Cumming, transl. (New York: Herder and Herder, 1972).

6 From an unpublished text entitled "Some Reflections on the Idea of Value," quoted in Simone Pétrement's *Simone Weil: A Life*, Raymond Rosenthal, transl. (New York: Pantheon, 1976), p. 405.

7 This theme in Weil's writings is explicitly drawn out in the concluding chapter to Victor Seidler's *Kant, Respect and Injustice: The Limits of Liberal Moral Theory* (London: Routledge and Kegan Paul, 1986).

8 Marxist theory has too often conceived truth to be relative to class interests or to a particular mode of production. This prepared the ground for Lenin's instrumental conception of truth, which is identified with whatever could bring the revolution closer. But while some kind of cultural relativism has almost become the "common sense" of contemporary social science, at some level uniting phenomenology and structuralist traditions, Weil stands firmly against this direction of thought and feeling. Her objection to it is part of the deeper significance of her work and connects her in part with similar impulses in the writings of the later Ludwig Wittgenstein; both took themselves to be standing against some of the entrenched ideals of science and progress within contemporary Western culture.

9 Lenin's commitment to Taylorism and the importation into the Soviet Union of advanced Western industrial techniques in the early 1920s is discussed in Chapter 2; see also Carmen Claudin-Urondo's *Lenin and the Cultural Revolution* (Brighton: Harvester Press, 1977).

10 This issue of the relation of science to production has been raised by the Frankfurt School and more recently in Harry Braverman's stimulating book *Labor and Monopoly Capital: The Degradation of Work in the Twentieth Century* (New York: Monthly Review Press, 1974). It has received continuous attention in the *Radical Science Journal*.

11 Quoted in Pétrement (*op. cit.*), p. 87–88, from Weil's "la Vie syndicale: en marge du Comité e'études," published in *Effort*, December 19, 1931.

12 Ibid., p. 88.

13 Ibid.

14 See *The Communist Manifesto*, in Marx and Engels, *Collected Works* (London: Lawrence and Wishart, 1971–), 6:482.

15 The Frankfurt School seems to argue for a direct connection between Marxism and morality. See, for instance, Adorno and Horkheimer (*op. cit.*). This has also been a feature of more recent feminist writing. See, for instance, Caroline Merchant's *The Death of Nature* (New York: Harper and Row, 1980) and Susan Griffin's *Women and Nature* (New York: Harper and Row, 1978). Brian Easlea's *Science and Sexual Oppression* (London: Weidenfeld and Nicolson, 1981) has attempted somewhat schematically to connect this to issues of masculinity.

16 This sets Weil in opposition to a central aspect of a Kantian epistemology and to its inheritance within social theory in the later work of Emile Durkheim as well as in a structuralist tradition that emphasizes the way in which nature is constituted through particular mental categories or through particular modes of classification. Her conception of knowledge is fundamentally realist in that for her there is an object material world that exists independently of consciousness.

17 From McFarland's (*op. cit.*) translations. Page in the text refers to French original. The essay has been published as "The Situation in Germany."

18 It is in this deep challenge to ideas of progress and constantly increased production that Weil challenges guiding ideas within orthodox Marxism. She shows that these notions do not have to be central to an appreciation of the forms of oppression within capitalist society. This gives her writing an ecological relevance while showing the continuing relevance of some of Marx's central ideas to an analysis of industrialized societies.

19 This was the source of her developing suspicion of a language of rights, which fostered the idea that if rights are not infringed, then injustice cannot really be done to people and thereby made it more difficult for liberal theory to face the reality of modern forms of social oppression. Weil may sometimes have disparaged civil and political rights, but it was the universalism of this language in presuming that it can equally illuminate all forms of injustice and violation that she most clearly objected to. See her "Human Personality."

20 Quoted in Pétrement (*op. cit.*), p. 205.

6 *Work*

1 The translation of Weil's essay "La Rationalisation," which was origianlly dated February 25th 1937 and appears as part of *La Condition ouvrière*, was

made by Larry Schmidt of the University of Toronto in Mississauga. All
subsequent quotations are from Schmidt's translation.

2 Harry Braverman's *Labor and Monopoly Capital: The Degradation of Work
in the Twentieth Century* (New York: Monthly Review Press, 1974) helps to
shift the concern, as Weil does, to the centrality of the labor process in
considering the oppression of working people within factories. But if this
insight is more generally shared, it has itself been presented as a technical
issue rather than as being centrally concerned with the quality of experience
at work. This is the profound shift Weil helps prepare. See Chapter 2,
notes 6 and 14.

3 So Weil reaches quite independently themes George Lukács makes central to
his discussion of reification in *History and Class Consciousness*, Rodney
Livingstone, trans. (London: The Merlin Press, 1971). These became
defining elements within a tradition of Western Marxism, especially in their
influence on the Frankfurt School. Weil stands quite separate from this
tradition maintaining contact with shifts in working-class experience of
production which has often seemed a weakness in the Frankfurt School
writing.

4 This vision of Weil takes greater hold in her Christian writing but it is by no
means consistent, for sometimes it is part of the relationship of work to
necessity and sometimes she is struck by the job of work. She often is not
consistent but she usually argues with such conviction, as if by the very force
of argument we lose a sense that she would have ever thought any
differently.

5 George Lukács developed this conception of "Seeing Nature" in his
discussion of reification in capitalist society. See his "Reification and the
Consciousness of the Proletariat," in *History and Class Consciousness* (*op.
cit.*)

6 Alfred Sohn-Rethel develops his analysis in *Intellectual and Manual Labour*
(London: Macmillan, 1976). His writing is infused with an understanding of
the labor process and its transformation that is not often found in those
writing more directly under the influence of the Frankfurt School.

7 Some useful insights are provided by Benjamin Farringdon in *The Philosophy
of Francis Bacon* (Liverpool: Liverpool University Press, 1964). The
connection with the treatment of women and feminist work is made by
Carolyn Merchant in *The Death of Nature* (New York: Harper and Row,
1980).

8 Translated by Dorothy Tuck McFarland in *Simone Weil* (New York:
Frederick Ungar, 1983). Page reference in the text is to French original.

9 Paul King, "The Social and Political Thought of Simone Weil," Ph.D.
dissertation (University of California, Los Angeles, 1975), p. 95.

10 A useful collection of articles that helps focus attention on these themes is
Science, Technology, and the Labour Process, 2 vols., Les Levidow and Bob
Young, eds. (London: Free Association Press, 1981 and 1984).

11 This vision of the dignity of manual labour has also been shared by such

people as Edward Gill and William Morris but within the twentieth century dominance of Soviet Marxism it has rarely made it to the heart of socialist theory and practice. An important exception—which is in sympathy with the direction of Weil's thought on labor—is provided by Peter Maurin's, *Easy Essays*, Dorothy Day's *Loaves and Fishes* and *The Long Loneliness* (New York: Harper and Row, 1952) and others' writings in the Catholic Worker Movement. It connects crucially to the relationship between Christianity and Marxism, especially as this has developed within liberation theology in Central and South America, a topic discussed further in the concluding chapter.

12 Some of the implications of this are presented, though not really developed systematically, in "Human Personality." It gives in a clear sense of some of the directions she is taking in her later writing, though some of these ideas were not really developed in *The Need for Roots*.

13 The translations of passages from "Journal d'usine" and "La Vie et la grève des ouvières metallos" are drawn from Dorothy Tuck McFarland's useful and stimulating biography *Simone Weil* (*op. cit.*), pp. 66–67. Page references in the text are to the French originals.

14 Simone Pétrement, *Simone Weil: A Life*, Raymond Rosenthal, trans. (New York: Pantheon, 1976), pp. 231–32.

15 Ibid., p. 246.

16 Ibid., p. 246.

17 Weil was suspicious of a language of rights, especially in the universal form it was given with the French Revolution, as if all forms of injustice can be meaningfully conceived as an infringement of rights. This is discussed briefly in "Human Personality."

18 It can be useful to connect this to John Rawls's *A Theory of Justice* (Cambridge: Harvard University Press, 1971), where he includes respect and self-esteem as "social goods" that also need to be more equally distributed. It may be that a problem that Rawls's distributive model will not actually work with self-esteem and human dignity because it assumes that individuals are autonomous, independent of each other, and thus the model cannot deal with the working relationships of dependency and subordination.

19 For a useful discussion of Mounier and the Personalist movement, which situates it in historical context, see John Hellman's *Emmanuel Mounier and the New Catholic Left 1930–1950* (Toronto: Toronto University Press, 1981).

7 Power

1 A defense of Marx's conception of history or at least of one way in which it could be construed (as a form of economic or technological determinism) is provided by G. A. Cohen in *Karl Marx's Theory of History: A Defense* (Princeton: Princeton University Press, 1978). One of the most useful critical responses is provided by Joshua Cohen in a review article in the *Journal of Philosophy* 79 (May 1982): 266ff.

2   Anthony Giddens has explored this deficiency within Marxist writings in his attempted reconstruction of historical materialism in *A Contemporary Critique of Historical Materialism* (London: Macmillan, 1981).

3   Translated in Dorothy Tuck McFarland's *Simone Weil* (New York: Frederick Ungar, 1983). Page reference in the text is to the French original.

4   I have drawn the translation of these passages from Dorothy Tuck McFarland's *Simone Weil* (*op. cit.*), p. 77. Pages in the text refer to the French original. The essay has been translated as "The Situation in Germany."

5   Quoted in Simone Pétrement, *Simone Weil: A Life*, Raymond Rosenthal, trans. (New York: Pantheon, 1976), p. 294.

6   Quoted in Pétrement (*op. cit.*), p. 294.

7   Quoted in Pétrement (*op. cit.*), p. 296.

8   In *The Need for Roots* Weil in part returns to a recognition of the importance of social and institutional changes. She is more doubtful in the closing sections, but then Weil is not really a consistent thinker in this sense, which can be stimulating but also makes it extremely difficult to write about her without feeling that you are not doing justice to the complexity of her thinking in its different moments.

9   Weil recognizes complexities in the relationship between the individual and the collectivity as part of her refusal to think of "individualism" as "bourgeois" and "collectivity" as socialist. She argues that this is a naive and historically damaging view that has kept socialist theory from developing. For some discussion of this see Russell Keat, "Individual and Community," in *Marxism and Philosophy*, D.-H. Ruben and J. Mepham, eds. (Brighton: Harvester Press, 1974) vol. 4; and Victor Seidler, "Trusting Ourselves: Marxism, Human Needs and Sexual Politics," in *One-Dimensional Marxism*, Simon Clarke et al., eds. (London: Allison and Busby, 1980).

12   Her attitude to the Hebrews could only be sustained by separating Christianity, particularly Jesus, from his Jewish heritage and culture. She wanted to conceive Christianity as essentially an expression of Greek thought. Gustav Thibon mentions her dogmatism on this issue and notes her refusal to consider seriously evidence that was set before her in *Simone Weil as We Knew Her* (London: Routledge and Kegan Paul, 1983), which brings together the reflections of J. B. Perrin and Thibon, who both knew her when she was living in the south of France before leaving for the United States in May 1942.

13   This impulse is partly shared by Iris Murdoch in *The Sovereignty of Good* (London: Routledge and Kegan Paul, 1970) and by Michael Ignatieff in *The Needs of Strangers* (London: Chatto and Windus, 1984). An understanding of its place within the Greek tradition is usefully provided by Martha Nussbaum's *The Fragility of Goodness: Luck and Ethics in Greek Tragedy and Philosophy* (Cambridge: Cambridge University Press, 1986).

14   A useful collection of Walter Benjamin's writings is given in *Illuminations*, Hannah Arendt, ed., Harry Zohn, trans. (London: Fontana, 1973). There

are significant resonances with themes in Weil's work. Paradoxically some of these insights are not drawn from Greece but from a Jewish tradition.

15 It has been a strength of black, feminist, and gay writing to illuminate this crucial issue of *invisibility* in the 1960s and 1970s. Forced to accept terms that are not of their own making, people's experience is often devalued and rendered invisible within the dominant discourses. Powerful writings such as Franz Fanon's *Black Skin, White Mask* (London: Palladin, 1972) have often been marginalized in dominant modes of thinking and feeling. During the 1970s structuralism was often invoked to express the insights of these new social movements, which at another level subverted and challenged some of its central ideas.

16 Ludwig Wittgenstein, *Culture and Value*, G. H. Von Wright, ed., with Heikki Nyman, Peter Winch, trans. (Oxford: Basil Blackwell, 1980), p. 31.

17 Attention to some striking similarities between Weil and Wittgenstein has been drawn by Peter Winch in his introduction to Weil's *Lectures on Philosophy*. There is a particular resonance in the relation of language to our practice or deeds that has often been missed in interpretations of Wittgenstein made within the "philosophy of language." This is an issue Norman Malcolm helps with in *Nothing is Hidden* (Oxford: Blackwells, 1986).

18 Some of these themes are usefully illustrated in Nussbaum (*op. cit.*).

19 Useful accounts which help challenge this dominant vision of Weil's development appear in Richard Rees's *Simone Weil: A Sketch for a Portrait* (Carbondale, Il.: Southern Illinois University Press, 1966) and McFarland (*op. cit.*).

20 Recognizing its significance for the restructuring of the organization of work, Weil wrote a sort history of Taylor and Taylorism. This appears in her essay "La Rationalisation."

21 This has had important implications within a jurisprudence that conceives laws as commands. John Austin said that the notion of a command is "the key to the science of jurisprudence and morals" (*The Province of Jurisprudence Determined* [Library of Ideas, 1954], p. 13). See H. L. A. Hart, "Positivism and the Separation of Law and Morals" and "Is Law a System or Ruler?" in *The Philosophy of Law*, ed. R. M. Dworkin, ed. (Oxford: Oxford University Press, 1977).

22 Georg Lukács' *History and Class Consciousness*, Rodney Livingstone, trans. (London: The Merlin Press, 1971) attempts to show that the proletariat can achieve an objective understanding of capitalist society. This is the least convincing part of his writing. Weil breaks with relativism by refusing to conceive issues in terms of consciousness. If people are violated by their treatment at the hands of others an injustice is being done to them. Weil looks to the relationship between truth and justice to question relativist modes of thought.

23 Weil's movement towards Christianity gave her a way of taking the suffering of an inner life more seriously. It was also part of an involvement with

Eastern modes of thought that at some level might have made her more sympathetic to Jung than to Freud. She at least might have agreed with Jung's sense that with psychoanalysis the rationalizing mind of the West has been brought up to some kind of limit by the uncritical assumption that everything psychological is subjective and personal. Weil instead valued the impersonal as the source of her spirituality.

24 From Weil's translation in *La Source grecque*, which can be found in the English translation *Intimations of Christianity Among the Ancient Greeks*.

25 It is quite shocking to read her letter to the authorities pleading that she be given a teaching job and denying any reality to her connection with Judaism (November 1940, *Simone Weil Reader*, 79). Earlier she had unsuccessfully requested a teaching position. A racist statute instituted by the Vichy Government had denied the rights of Jews and persons of Jewish descent to such positions. She wants "to know to whom this statute applies so that I might be enlightened as to my own standing." And she says "Mine is the Christian, French, Greek tradition. The Hebrew tradition is alien to me, and no statute can make it otherwise" (80). She did not seem to identify herself with what was happening to Jews in Germany. She distanced herself also from the Old Testament, as she explains in a letter to Deodat Roche (January 23, 1940), agreeing with his notion that "the worship of power caused the Hebrews to love the idea of good and evil". She seemed to blame these Old Testament stories for whatever evils exist within Christian thought, as well as her own relationship to Christianity. "I have always been kept away from Christianity by its ranking these stories, so full of pitiless cruelty, as sacred texts; and the more so because for twenty centuries these stories have never ceased to influence all the currents of Christian thought" (*Seventy Letters*, 129). She did not seek to explore the responsibility of Christianity for the treatment of the Jews in Germany, nor did she explain the deafening silence in so many from whom we might have expected protest.

8 *Morality, truth, and politics*

1 Plato, *The Republic*, ed. and trans. F. M. Cornford (Oxford: Oxford University Press, 1941), Book VI, 493 c.

2 Simone Pétrement, *Simone Weil: A Life*, Raymond Rosenthal, trans. (New York: Pantheon, 1976), p. 495.

3 Part of the difficulty in reading Weil involves accepting that, like Wittgenstein, she goes against the current of our times. She reminds us of ways of thinking and feeling that we have almost lost relationship with. It demands *attention*, as Weil knew for herself, to recognize the light these notions can bring to our contemporary world.

4 This is a problem with much discourse theory and work within the sociology of language. It leaves us bereft of moral criteria. Worse still, it often takes itself to be an inheritance of Wittgenstein's work, thereby assimilating a

particular relativist reading of Wittgenstein with the very relativism he was struggling to break with in his *Philosophical Investigations*.

5   See John Rawls, *A Theory of Justice* (Cambridge: Harvard University Press, 1971) and R. M. Dworkin, *Taking Rights Seriously* (London: Duckworths, 1977).

6   Some difficulties with the language of rights' drawing on Weil's work are discussed in the concluding chapter of Victor Seidler's *Kant, Respect and Injustice: The Limits of Liberal Moral Theory* (London: Routledge and Kegan Paul, 1986). H. L. A. Hart, in his paper "Between Utility and Rights," in *The Idea of Freedom*, Alan Ryan, ed. (Oxford: Oxford University Press, 1979), expresses important reservations about this revitalized concern with rights, but he would have us settle for a form of utilitarianism. Recent work by Charles Taylor ("The Nature and Source of Distributive Justice," in *Philosphy and the Human Sciences*, Philosophical Papers 2 [Cambridge: Cambridge University Press, 1985]), Michael Sandel (*Liberalism and the Limits of Justice* [Cambridge: Cambridge University Press, 1982]), and Michael Walzer (*Spheres of Justice* [New York: Basic Books, 1983]) moves us in a different direction. Onora O'Neil, working within a more Kantian framework, would give priority to obligations over rights, as she feels Kant does, so challenging interpretations of Kant which have supported this shift towards rights in political theory. See, for instance, O'Neil's "Between Consenting Adults," *Philosophy and Public Affiars* 14:3 (September 1985): 252–77.

7   This is very much the framework adopted by J. Goldthorpe and D. Lockwood in their influential work on *The Affluent Worker in the Class Structure* (Cambridge: Cambridge University Press, 1969), which has guided so much sociological study into the nature of work.

8   Lukács, particularly in his relationship to the Frankfurt School, helped define the character of "Western Marxism" as a tradition existing in rough opposition to Marxism within the Soviet Union. Weil defines a position which is her own, particularly because "Western Marxism" is more sympathetic to Hegel's influence over Marx. She was thinking against a more orthodox tradition in ascendency in France, which makes her writings particularly relevant in the 1980s, when an orthodox position has seemed defensible again within an analytical tradition in Anglo-American philosophy. See, for instance, G. A. Cohen, *Marx's Theory of History: A Defense* (Princeton: Princeton University Press, 1978).

9   A useful discussion of this period is provided by Wilhelm Reich's *The Sexual Revolution* (Oxford: The Clarendon Press, 1972). Although his grasp of Marx's historical materialism is crudely sociological, he is able to illuminate difficulties within the previlaing notions of economic determinism. See also the fascinating autobiography of Emma Goldman entitled *Living My Life* (Salt Lake City: Gibbs M. Smith, 1o82).

10   One expression among many in recent feminist writing—particularly in its concern with non-violent forms of civil disobedience—is Joanna Macy's *Despair and Personal Power in the Nuclear Age* (Philadelphia: New Society

Publishing, 1983). This is also shown in feminist concern with the relationship of spirituality with politics. See, for instance, Jo Garcia and Sara Maitland, eds., *Walking on the Water: Women Talk About Spirituality* (London: Virago, 1983).

11 Iris Murdoch, *The Fire and the Sun* (Oxford: Oxford University Press, 1977), p. 13.

12 Ibid., p. 21.

13 Ibid.

14 Antonio Gramsci, *Prison Notebooks*, Quentin Hoare and Geoffrey Smith, eds. and trans. (London: Lawrence and Wishart, 1981), p. 323.

15 Ibid.

16 Ibid., p. 324.

17 In this sense Gramsci is critical of orthodox traditions, including the structuralist reading of Marx fostered by Althusser. These tend to see individualistic notions as essentially bourgeois and the development of class consciousness as a *replacement* of these notions by conceptions of class. Gramsci understood how a consciousness of class grows out of a sense of difference from others—as we reflect on this experience, we can grow into an awareness of class.

18 Gramsci's notion of hegemony is explained in his essay on "State and Civil Society," *Prison Notebooks* (*op. cit.*). Unfortunately, it has too often been interpreted within a structuralist framework. How far such an interpretation is from the spirit of Gramsci's work is made clear by a reading of the section on "Some Problems in the Study of the Philosophy of Praxis."

19 Gramsci (*op. cit.*), p. 327.

20 Ibid.

21 Ibid., p. 330.

22 Ibid., p. 327.

23 Ibid., p. 333.

24 Ibid., p. 355.

25 Ibid., p. 352.

26 Czeslaw Milosz' essay "The Importance of Simone Weil," in *Emperor of the Earth: Modes of Eccentric Vision* (Berkeley: University of California Press, 1977), pp. 85–98, can help us place a significant tendency in her thought.

27 Ibid., p. 96.

28 Ibid. p. 93.

29 Ibid., p. 93.

30 Ibid., p. 97.

31 Ibid., p. 97

32 Quoted in Józef Tischner, *The Spirit of Solidarity*, Marek B. Zaleski and Benjamin Fiore, trans. (New York: Harper and Row, 1984), p. 36. A feeling

for some of the ideas which motivated and nourished Solidarity can be found in this book. Tischner was the chaplain to the new union during the Solidarity Congress on Gdansk in 1981.

33 Ibid., p. 37.

34 Ibid.

35 Ibid., p. 17.

36 Ibid., p. 105.

37 Quoted in Tischner (ibid.), p. 106.

38 Ibid.

39 Ibid., p. 2

40 Ibid., p. 7

41 Ibid.

42 Ibid.

43 Ibid., p. 8.

44 Ibid.

45 Ibid., p. 9.

46 Ibid., p. 9.

47 Ibid., p. 3.

48 Ibid.

49 Ibid.

50 Ibid., p. 23.

51 Ibid.

52 Ibid., p. 24.

53 Quoted in Tischner (Ibid.), p. 106.

54 Ibid.

55 Ibid.

56 Ibid., p. 24.

57 Ibid., p. 24.

58 Ibid., p. 25.

59 Ibid., p. 43.

60 See J. S. Mill's "On Liberty," ch. 3. It is also useful to connect this to his revealing *Autobiography*, which shows how he was injured by the tensions and relations of his own upbringing. A useful discussion is also provided by Isaiah Berlin's "John Stuart Mill and The Ends of Life," in *Four Essays on Liberty* (Oxford: Oxford University Press, 1969).

61 "Interview with Jean Goss-Mayr," *The Catholic Worker* (September 1986), p. 4.

62 Quoted in ibid.

63 Ibid., p. 4.

64 Ibid.

65 Ibid., p. 5.

66 Milosz (op. cit.) p. 89.

67 Ibid., p. 89

68 Ibid., p. 89.

69 "Interview with Fernando Cardenal," in *Ministers of God, Ministers of the People* (London: Zed Press, 1984), p. 74.

70 Ibid.

71 Ibid., p. 75.

72 Ibid., p. 76.

73 Ibid., p. 77

74 Ibid., p. 76.

75 "Interview with Jean Goss-Mayr" (*op. cit.*), p. 1.

76 "Interivew with Fernando Cardenal" (*op. cit.*), p. 79.

77 Ibid.

78 Ibid., p. 80.

79 Ibid., p. 81.

80 Ibid.

81 This is a problem with recent attempts in political theory to give priority to a language of rights. Often we are left with an inadequate sense of how these particular rights are to be defended or justified. This is an issue that Ronald Dworkin is aware of in *Taking Rights Seriously* (London: Duckworths, 1977), but not one that he really comes to terms with.

82 "Interview with Fernando Cardenal" (*op. cit.*), p. 70.

83 Ibid., p. 80.

84 Ibid., p. 70.

85 Ibid., p. 57.

86 Ibid., p. 58.

87 Quoted in (*op. cit.*), p. .

88 Ibid.

89 Ibid., p. 31.

90 Ibid., p. 25.

Bibliography

Selected Works of Simone Weil

"Classical Science and After" ("La Science et nous"). In *On Science, Necessity, and the Love of God.*

"Cold War Policy in 1939" ("Réflexions en vue d'un bilan"). In *Selected Essays, 1934–1943.*

La Condition ouvrière. Paris: Gillimard, 1951.

"Critical Examination of the Ideas of Revolution and Progress" ("Examen critique des idées de revolution et de progrès"). In *Oppression and Liberty.*

Ecrits de Londres et dernières lettres. Paris: Gallimard, 1957.

Ecrits historique et politiques. Paris: Gallimard, 1951.

"Factory Work" ("Réflexions sur la vie d'usine"). In *The Simone Weil Reader.*

Formative Writings, 1929–1941. Dorothy Tuck McFarland and Wilhelmina Van Ness, ed. and trans. Amherst: University of Massachusetts Press, 1987.

"Forms of the Implicit Love of God" ("Formes de l'amour implicite de Dieu"). In *Waiting on God.*

"Fragments, London 1943" ("Fragments, Londres, 1943"). In *Oppression and Liberty.*

Gateway to God. David Raper, ed., with Malcolm Muggeridge and Vernon Sproxton. London: Fontana, 1974.

"The Great Beast: Reflections on the Origins of Hitlerism" ("Quelques réflexions sur les origines de l'Hitlérisme"). In *Selected Essays, 1934–1943.*

"Human Personality" ("La Personnalité humaine, le juste et l'injuste," or "La Personne et le sacré"). In *Selected Essays, 1934–1943.*

"The *Iliad*, Poem of Might" ("L'*Iliade* ou le poème de la force"). In *The Simone Weil Reader*. (Also translated as "*Iliad*, or the Poem of Force.")

"Is There a Marxist Doctrine?" ("Y a-t-il une doctrine marxiste?". In *Oppression and Liberty.*

"Journal d'Espagne." In *Ecrits historique et politiques.*

"Journal d'usine." In *La Condition ouvrière.*

Intimations of Christianity Among the Ancient Greeks (from *La Source grecque* and *Les intuitions pré-chrétiennes*). Elizabeth Chase Geissbuhler, ed. and trans. London: Routledge and Kegan Paul, 1957, 1987.

Lectures on Philosophy (*Leçons de philosophie*). Hugh Price, trans. Cambridge: Cambridge University Press, 1978.

"Lettre ouverte à un syndiqué." In *La Condition ouvrière.*

"The Love of God and Affliction" ("L'Amour de Dieu et le malheur"). In *Waiting on God.*

"Meditation on Obedience and Liberty" ("Méditation sur l'obéisance et la liberté"). In *Oppression and Liberty.*

The Need For Roots (*L'Encracinement*). A. F. Wills, trans. London: Routledge and Kegan Paul, 1952, 1988.

"A Note on Social Democracy" ("Méditations sur un cadavre"). In *Selected Essays, 1934–1943.*

"On the Contradictions of Marxism" ("Sur les contradictions du marxisme"). In *Oppression and Liberty.*

"On Lenin's Book *Materialism and Empiriocriticism*" ("Sur le livre de Lénine: *Matérialisme et empiriocriticisme*"). In *Oppression and Liberty.*

On Science, Necessity, and the Love of God. Richard Rees, ed. and trans. London: Oxford University Press, 1968.

Oppression and Liberty (*Oppression et liberté*). Arthur Wills and John Petrie, trans., F. C. Ellert, intro. Amherst: University of Massachusetts Press, 1973; London: Routledge and Kegan Paul, 1958.

"The Power of Words" ("Ne recommençons pas la guerre de Troie"). In *Selected Essays, 1934–1943.*

"Pre-War Notebook". In *First and Last Notebooks.* Richard Rees, trans. London: Oxford University Press, 1970.

"Profession of faith" ("Profession de foi," from "Etude pour une déclaration des obligations envers l'être humain"). In *Selected Essays, 1934–1943.*

"Prospects: Are We Heading for the Proletarian Revolution?" ("Perspectives. Allons-nous vers la révolution prolétarienne?"). In *Oppression and Liberty.*

"La Rationalisation." In *La Condition ouvrière.* (Unpublished English translation by Larry Schmidt).

Reflections Concerning the Causes of Liberty and Social Oppression (*Réflexions sur les causes de la liberté and de l'oppression sociale*). In *Oppression and Liberty.*

"Reflections on Quantum Physics." In *On Science, Necessity, and the Love of God.*

"The Responsibility of Writers" ("Lettres aux *Cahiers du Sud* sur les responsibilités de la litterateur"). In *On Science, Necessity and the Love of God*.

"Science and Perception in Descartes" ("Science et perception dans Descartes"). In *Formative Writings, 1929–1941*.

Selected Essays, 1934–1943. Richard Rees, ed. and trans. London: Oxford University Press, 1962.

Seventy Letters. Richard Rees, ed. and arr. London: Oxford University Press, 1965.

The Simone Weil Reader. George Panichas, ed. New York: David MacKay, 1977.

"The Situation in Germany" ("La situation en Allemagne"). In *Formative Writings, 1929–1941*.

"Spiritual Autobiography" ("Autobiographie spirituelle"). In *The Simone Weil Reader*.

Sur la science. Paris: Gallimard, 1966.

"Three Letters on History." In *Selected Essays, 1934–143*.

"La Vie et la grève des ouvrières metallos." In *La Condition ouvrière*.

Waiting on God (*Attente de dieu*). Emma Craufurd, trans. London: Fontana, 1959.

Other works

Anderson, Perry, *Considerations on Western Marxism*, New Left Books, London, 1975

De Beauvoir, Simone, *Memoirs of a Dutiful Daughter*, Penguin Books, Harmondsworth, 1963

———— *The Prime of Life*, Penguin Books, Harmondsworth, 1965

Benjamin, Walter, *Illuminations*, Fontana, London, 1973

Berger, John, *Pig Earth*, Writers and Readers, London, 1979

Berlin, Isaiah, *Four Essays on Liberty*, Oxford University Press, Oxford, 1969

———— *Against the Current: Essays in the History of Ideas*, Oxford University Press, Oxford, 1981

Braverman, Harry, *Labor and Monopoly Capital: The Degradation of Work in the Twentieth Century*, Monthly Review Press, New York, 1974

Breines, Paul, "Praxis and Its Theorists: The Impact of Lukàcs and Korsch in the 1920s", *Telos*, #11, Spring 1972

Buber, Martin, *Paths to Utopia*, Beacon Press, Boston, 1962

Buchanan, A. E., *Marx and Justice: The Radical Critique of Liberalism*, Methuen, London, 1982

Buck-Morss, Susan, *The Origin of Negative Dialectics*, The Harvester Press, Brighton, 1977

Caplan, Pat (ed.), *The Cultural Construction of Sexuality*, Tavistock, London, 1987

Caute, David, *Communism and the French Intellectuals, 1914–1960*, André Deutsch, London, 1964

Clark, S., Lovell, T., Robins, K., and Seidler, V. J., *One-Dimensional Marxism*, Allison and Busby, London, 1980

Claudin-Urondo, Carmen, *Lenin and the Cultural Revolution*, Harvester Press, Brighton, 1977

Cohen, G. A., *Karl Marx's Theory of History: A Defense*, Princeton University Press, Princeton, 1978

Cohen, M., Nagel, T. and Scanlon, T., *Marx, Justice and History*, Princeton University Press, Princeton, 1980

Coles, Robert, *Simone Weil: A Modern Pilgrimage*, Addison-Wesley, Reading, Mass., 1987

Day, Dorothy, *The Long Loneliness*, Harper and Row, New York, 1952

Debidour, V.-H., *Simone Weil, ou le transparence*, Plon, Paris, 1952

Dietz, Mary, *Between the Human and the Divine: The Social and Political Thought of Simone Weil*, Rowman and Littlefield, New Jersey, 1989

Douglas, Mary, *Implicit Meanings*, Routledge and Kegan Paul, London, 1979

Dunayevskaya, Raya, *Philosophy and Revolution: From Hegel to Sartre and From Marx to Mao*, Dell, New York, 1973

Durkheim, Emile, *The Elementary Forms of Religious Life*, Allen and Unwin, London, 1915

Dworkin, R. M., *The Philosophy of Law*, Oxford University Press, Oxford, 1977
——— *Taking Rights Seriously*, Duckworth, London, 1977

Easlea, Brian, *Science and Sexual Oppression*, Weidenfeld and Nicolson, London, 1981

Edwards, *Contested Terrain: The Transformation of the Workplace in the Twentieth Century*, Basic Books, New York, 1979

Elster, Jon, *Making Sense of Marx*, Cambridge University Press, Cambridge, 1985

Fanon, Franz, *Black Sign, White Mask*, Palladin, London, 1972

Farringdon, *The Philosophy of Francis Bacon*, Liverpool University Press, Liverpool, 1964

Freeman, M. and Robertson, D. (eds.), *The Frontiers of Political Theory*, Harvester Press, Brighton, 1980

Garcia, Jo and Maitland, Sara, *Walking on the Water: Women Talk About Spirituality*, Virago, London

Giddens, Anthony, *A Contemporary Critique of Historical Materialism*, Macmillan, London, 1981
——— *Profiles and Critiques in Social Theory*, University of California, Berkeley, 1981

Goldman, Emma, *Living My Life*, Gibbs M. Smith, Salt Lake City, Utah, 1982

Goldthorpe, J. and Lockwood, D., *The Affluent Worker in the Class Structure*, Cambridge University Press, Cambridge, 1969

Gouldner, Alvin, *The Two Marxisms*, Oxford University Press, New York, 1980

Gramsci, Antonio, *Prison Notebooks*, Lawrence and Wishart, London, 1981

Griffin, Susan, *Pornography and Silence*, The Women's Press, London, 1981

—————— *Women and Nature*, Harper and Row, New York, 1978

Heilbroner, Robert, *Marxism: For and Against*, Norton & Co., New York, 1980

Hellman, John, *Emmanuel Mounier and the New Catholic Left, 1930–1950*, Toronto University Press, Toronto, 1981

—————— *Simone Weil: An Introduction to Her Thought*, Wilfrid Laurier University Press, Waterloo, Ontario, 1982

Hillel-Rubin, D. and Mepham, J., *Marxism and Philosophy*, Harvester Press, Brighton, 1974

Horkheimer, M. and Adorno, T., *Dialectic of Enlightenment*, Herder and Herder, New York, 1972

Horkheimer, M., *Critical Theory: Selected Essays*, Herder and Herder, New York, 1972

Howe, Irving, *Leon Trotsky*, Penguin Books, Harmondsworth, 1979

Ignatieff, Michael, *The Needs of Strangers*, Chatto and Windus, London, 1984

Jacoby, Russell, *Dialectic of Defeat: Contours of Western Marxism*, Cambridge, Cambridge University Press, 1981

—————— "Toward a Critique of Automatic Marxism: The Politics of Philosophy from Lukàcs to the Frankfurt School", *Telos*, #10, winter 1971

Jay, Martin, *The Dialectical Imagination: A History of the Frankfurt School and the Institute of Social Research 1923–50*, Heinemann, London, 1973

King, Paul Edmond, *The Social and Political Thought of Simone Weil*, PhD dissertation, University of California at Los Angeles, 1975

Kolakowski, Leszek, *Main Currents of Marxism*, volumes 1, 2 and 3, Oxford University Press, Oxford, 1978

Lenin, V. I., "The Taylor System—Man's Enslavement by the Machine", in *Collected Works*, vol. XX, p. 153.

Leroy, Geraldi, "Simone Weil et le Parti Communiste", *Cahiers Simone Weil*, septembre, 1980, p. 208

Levidow, L. and Young, R., *Science, Technology and the Labour Process*, vol. 1 and 2, Free Association Books, London, 1981 and 1984

Levine, Andrew, *Arguing for Socialism: Theoretical Considerations*, Routledge and Kegan Paul, London, 1984

Lichtheim, George, *Marxism: An Historical and Critical Study*, second edition (revised), Praeger, New York, 1965

—————— *Marxism in Modern France*, Columbia University Press, New York, 1966

Lindemann, Albert S., *A History of European Socialism*, Yale University Press, New Haven, 1983

Littler, Craig, and Salaman, Graeme, "The Design of Jobs", in C. Littler (ed.), *The Experience of Work*, Gower Publishing, Aldershot, 1985

Lukàcs, Georg, *History and Class Consciousness*, The Merlin Press, London, 1971

Lukes, Steven, *Individualism*, Basil Blackwell, Oxford, 1973

Lukes, Steven, *Marxism and Morality*, Oxford University Press, Oxford, 1985

Macy, Joanna, *Despair and Personal Power in the Nuclear Age*, New Society Publishers, Philadelphia, 1983

Malcolm, Norman, *Nothing is Hidden*, Blackwell, Oxford, 1986

———— *Thought and Knowledge*, Cornell University Press, Ithica and London, 1977

Marx, Karl, *Kapital*, vol. 1, Penguin Books, Harmondsworth, 1976

McFarland, Dorothy Tuck, *Simone Weil*, Frederick Ungar, New York, 1983

McMurtry, John, *The Structure of Marx's World-View*, Princeton University Press, Princeton, 1978

Merchant, Caroline, *The Death of Nature*, Harper and Row, New York, 1980

Meyer, Alfred, "The Idea of Progress in Communist Ideology", in G. Almond, M. Chodorow, R. H. Pearce, *Progress and Its Discontents*, University of California Press, Berkeley, 1982

Mill, J. S., *Autobiography*, ed. J. Stillinger, Clarendon Press, Oxford, 1978

Miller, Richard, *Analyzing Marx: Morality, Power, and History*, Princeton University Press, Princeton, 1984

Miller, William, *Dorothy Day*, Harper and Row, New York, 1982

Milosz, Czeslaw, "The Importance of Simone Weil" in *Emperor of the Earth: Modes of Eccentric Vision*, University of California, Berkeley, 1981

Mouzelis, Nicos, *Organization and Bureaucracy: An Analysis of Modern Theories*, Revised edition, Routledge and Kegan Paul, London, 1975

Murdoch, Iris, *The Sovereignty of Good*, Routledge and Kegan Paul, London, 1970

Nussbaum, Martha C., *The Fragility of Goodness*, Cambridge University Press, Cambridge, 1986

Perrin, J. B. and Thibon, G., *Simone Weil As We Knew Her*, Routledge and Kegan Paul, London, 1953

Pétrement, Simone, *Simone Weil: A Life* (trans. Raymond Rosenthal), Pantheon, New York, 1976

Plato, *The Republic*, or Cornford, F. M., *The Republic of Plato*, Oxford University Press, Oxford, 1941

Rader, Melvin, *Marx's Interpretation of History*, Oxford University Press, New York, 1979

Rawls, John, *A Theory of Justice*, Harvard University Press, Cambridge, 1971

Rees, Richard, *Simone Weil: A Sketch for a Portrait*, Southern Illinois University Press, Carbondale, Illinois, 1967

Reich, Wilhelm, *The Sexual Revolution*, Clarendon Press, Oxford, 1972, Farrar, Strauss, Giroux, New York, 1977

Ridley, F. F., *Revolutionary Syndicalism in France*, Cambridge University Press, Cambridge, 1970

Rorty, Richard, *Philosophy and the Mirror of Nature*, Princeton University Press, Princeton, 1979

Rowbotham, Sheila, *Dreams and Dilemmas*, Virago, London, 1983

Ryan, Alan, *J. S. Mill*, Routledge and Kegan Paul, London, 1974

―――― (ed.), *The Idea of Freedom*, Oxford University Press, Oxford, 1979

Sabel, Charles, *Work and Politics: The Division of Labor in Industry*, Cambridge University Press, Cambridge, 1982

Sandel, Michael, *Liberalism and the Limits of Justice*, Cambridge University Press, Cambridge, 1982

Seidler, Victor J., *Kant, Respect and Injustice: The Limits of Liberal Moral Theory*, Routledge and Kegan Paul, London, 1986

Sennett, R. and Cobb, J., *The Hidden Injuries of Class*, Vintage Books, New York, 1973

Shaw, William H., *Marx's Theory of History*, Stanford University Press, Stanford, California, 1978

Skillen, Anthony, *Ruling Illusions: Philosophy and the Social Order*, Harvester, Sussex, 1974

Sohn-Rethe, Alfred, *Intellectual and Manual Labor*, Macmillan, London, 1976

Stearns, Peter, *Revolutionary Syndicalism and French Labor*, Rutgers University Press, New Brunswick, NJ, 1971

Taylor, Barbara, *Eve and the New Jerusalem*, Virago, London, 1983

Taylor, Charles, *Hegel and Modern Society*, Cambridge University Press, Cambridge, 1979

Thompson, E. P., *William Morris: Romantic to Revolutionary*, Merlin Press, London, 1977

―――― *The Poverty of Theory & Other Essays*, Merlin Press, London, 1978

Tischner, Josef, *The Spirit of Solidarity*, Harper and Row, New York, 1984

Traub, R., "Lenin and Taylor: The Fate of 'Scientific Management' in the (Early) Soviet Union", *Telos*, 37 (Fall, 1978), p. 84

Waldron, Jeremy (ed.), *Theories of Rights*, Oxford University Press,, Oxford, 1984

Waltzer, Michael, *Spheres of Justice*, Basic Books, New York, 1983

Weil, André, "Appendix" to Malcolm Muggeridge (ed.), *Simone Weil: Gateway to God*, Fontana Books, Glasgow, 1974

White, George Abbott (ed.), *Simone Weil: Interpretations of a Life*, University of Massachusetts Press, Amherst, 1981

Williams, Bernard, *Ethics and the Limits of Philosophy*, Harvard, 1985, Fontana, London, 1985

Williams, Raymond, *The Country and the City*, Chatto and Windus, London, 1973

——— *Problems in Materialism and Culture*, New Left Books, London, 1980

Winch, Peter *Just Balance: Reflections on the Philosophy of Simone Weil*, Cambridge University Press, Cambridge, 1989

Wittgenstein, Ludwig, *Philosophical Investigations*, Blackwell, Oxford, 1963

Wood, Allen, *Karl Marx*, Routledge and Kegan Paul, London, 1981

Index

Index

Index